COMMON PEOPLE

COMMON PEOPLE

A FOLK HISTORY OF LAND RIGHTS, ENCLOSURE AND RESISTANCE

Leah Gordon & Stephen Ellcock

With additional writing by Annabel Edwards

WATKINS
Sharing Wisdom
Since 1893

DEDICATED TO ALL REVOLTING PEASANTS – PAST, PRESENT AND FUTURE

COMMON PEOPLE

Leah Gordon & Stephen Ellcock

First published in the UK and USA in 2025 by Watkins, an imprint of Watkins Media Limited Unit 11, Shepperton House, 83–93 Shepperton Road, London N1 3DF

enquiries@watkinspublishing.com

Commissioning Editor: Fiona Robertson
Editorial Director: Ella Chappell
Editorial Assistant: Caitlin Nolan
Designer: Elizabeth Woodroffe
Copy Editor: Sue Lascelles
Proofreader: Andrew Chapman
Indexer: Charmian Parkin
Production: Uzma Taj

A CIP record for this book is available from the British Library

ISBN: 978-1-78678-999-0 (Hardback)

10 9 8 7 6 5 4 3 2 1

Typeset in Brandon
Colour reproduction by Rival Colour
Printed in China

www.watkinspublishing.com

CONTENTS

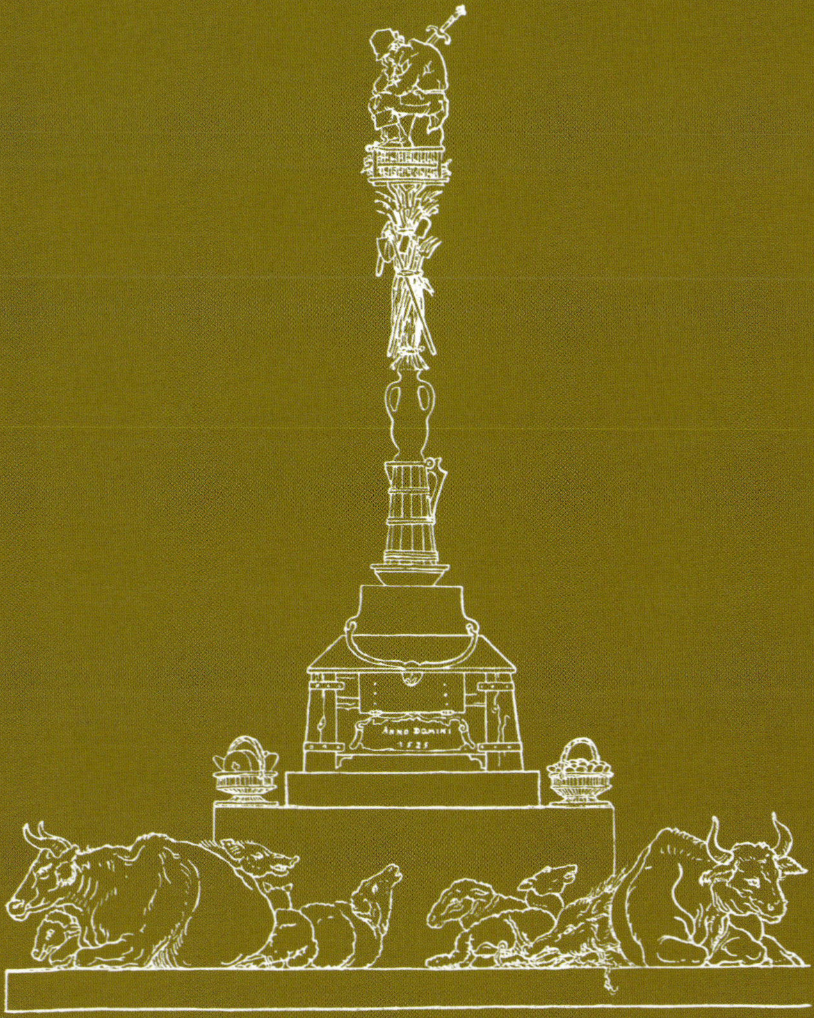

INTRODUCTION

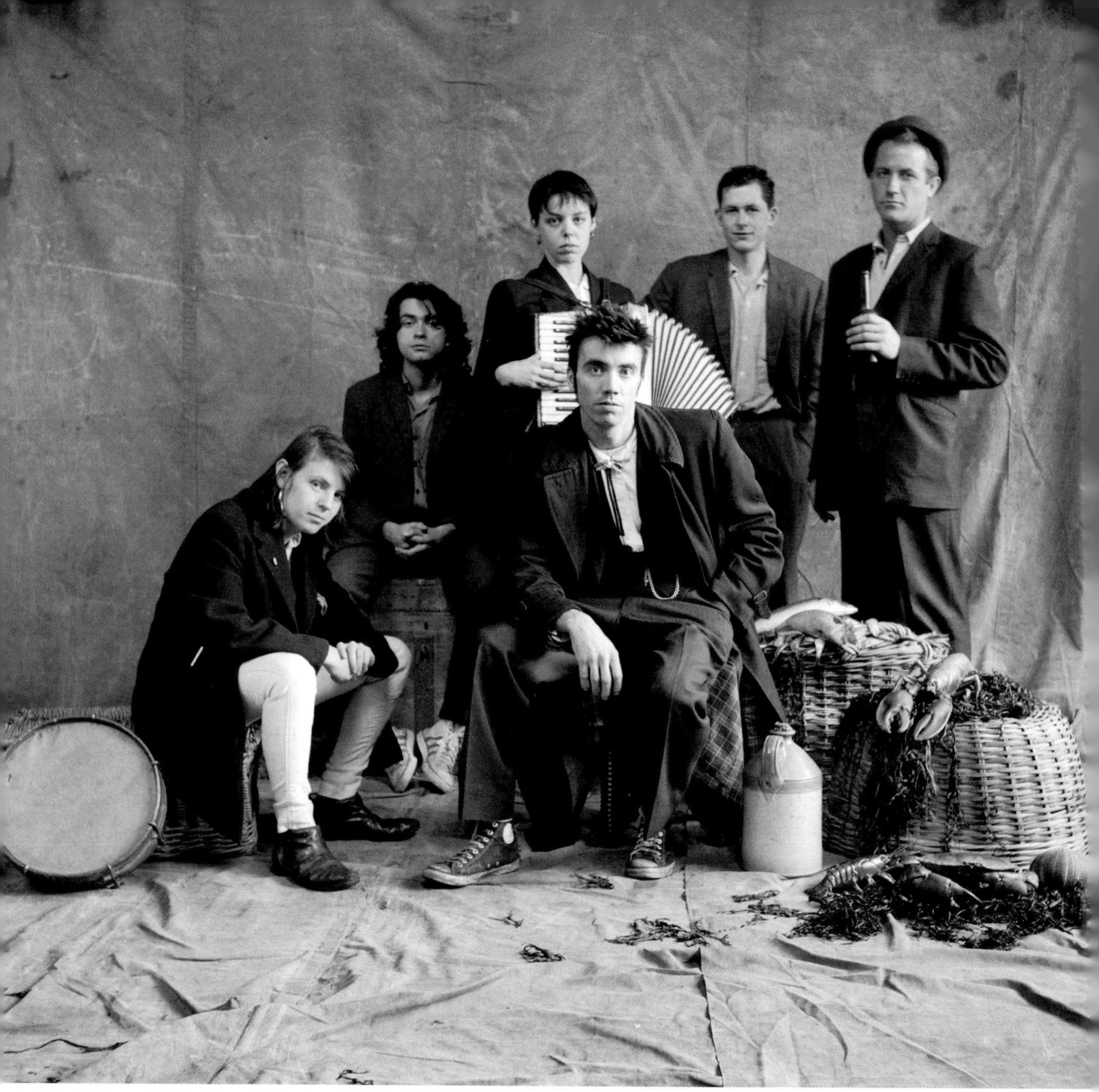

THE DOONICANS, from left to right Leah Gordon, James Pyott, Emily Dunbar, Duncan MacDonald, Mark Jackson, Johnny Sayer. *The Doonicans were active from 1983 to 1989, had an EP out with Probe Plus and played at Glastonbury in 1987. As the lyricist, I was interested in rewriting folk history from a woman's point of view with songs such as "Fisherwoman's Way" and "The Beggarwoman's Song". The original Doonicans aren't to be confused with later bands such as the Bar-Steward Sons of Val Doonican.* **Leah Gordon (1987)**

MONUMENT TO THE VANQUISHED PEASANT

LEAH GORDON

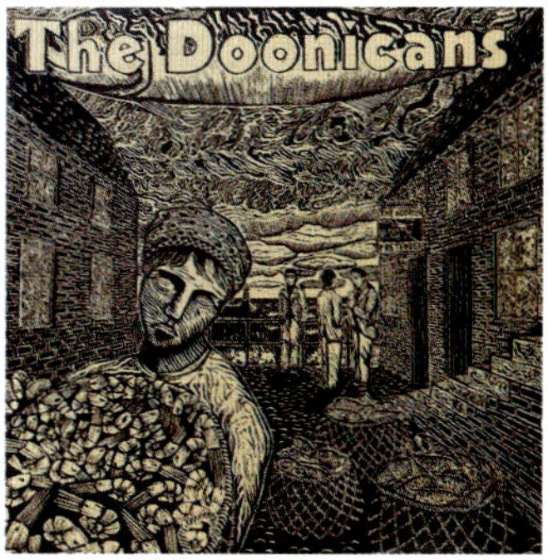

THE DOONICANS EP released on Probe Plus Records in 1987

This project is the culmination of ideas that have preoccupied me for almost 35 years. It marks a point on a trajectory from the folk punk band that I wrote lyrics and sang for in the mid-eighties; to my film, book and exhibitions on Haitian carnival; to my enduring regard for British folk traditions and my own image-making of these, and my respect for people's history, also known as history told from below, as celebrated by the historian E P Thompson, recorded by broadcaster Studs Terkel and told by historians Peter Linebaugh and Marcus Rediker. It's also an expression of my class politics. Along the way, Annabel Edwards, with whom I've collaborated on various projects over the years, and Stephen Ellcock, a maestro of visual imaginary, have become fellow travellers and have contributed excellent texts and visuals.

When I spoke at a conference in 2014 organized by the International Slavery Museum and called "History and Public Memorialization of Slavery and the Slave Trade", the event raised some questions for me. If we were to create a state monument in memory of the enclosures in England – the gradual but relentless loss by the peasantry of access and rights to common land through the enforcement of laws, extreme brutality and suffering that benefited English landowners – what might that possibly look like? There is only one statue that memorializes the Highland Clearances in Scotland, but nothing in England for the enclosures. Why is this? And why have we memorialized our nation's role in the slave trade but not the enclosures? Could it be that it's more politically expedient to memorialize our nation's brutality to other races and nations than to admit what has been done to our own people by the ruling class of Britain? There are always inherent dangers if a nation only monumentalizes one component of a far more complicated historical epoch, as it then renders other equally valid narratives invisible and can skew the direction of reproachment. My original photography project and this book, which grew out of it, are an attempt to be a small part of the remedy for that invisibility, for enclosure has often been one of the less visible elements of English historiography.

Over the course of several centuries, acts of law gradually prohibited forms of subsistence hunting by labelling this illegal poaching, made small-scale farming economically unviable, re-designated former peasants as wage-enslaved industrial workers and created a tribe of society's outriders, labelled vagabonds, who were condemned as soon as they existed. In essence, the rich and powerful took away nearly all forms of livelihood from the majority class of peasants, and then immediately criminalized them for their ensuing poverty.

Enclosure describes the legal process through which common rights over land were terminated and converted to the exclusive property and use of a landowner. While parliamentary enclosure (enforced through acts of Parliament) could be said to have started in 1709, the loss of rights by the common people began with the Norman Conquest. The enclosures, although often recalled by historians from below, have featured less in the mainstream discourse of history. This is also of contemporary relevance when considering attacks upon public lands today, which are being sold off by neoliberal governments, while our rights to roam are being eroded, and when from an environmental perspective control of land at a more grassroots level could not be more paramount.

At the heart of this book is the belief that an understanding of the process and history of enclosure is essential to a critical understanding of the systems and politics that we inhabit now. Early forms of enclosure were a prequel to, and enabler of, both the slave trade and the Industrial Revolution, while later forms of enclosure were funded and accelerated by the proceeds of colonialism. These formed a triumvirate of momentous epochal mechanisms of capital accumulation. A deeper knowledge of this history should help us to refigure the ruling class as oppressors, as opposed to being the paternalistic enablers they prefer to epitomize.

This book also hopes to bring to light a long and noble history of non-industrial struggle, including of radical groups such as the Levellers, the Diggers and the Luddites, which has so often been outshone by the more muscular industrial struggles of the last two centuries. The roots of capitalism are often portrayed as an inevitability, as if the inexorable march

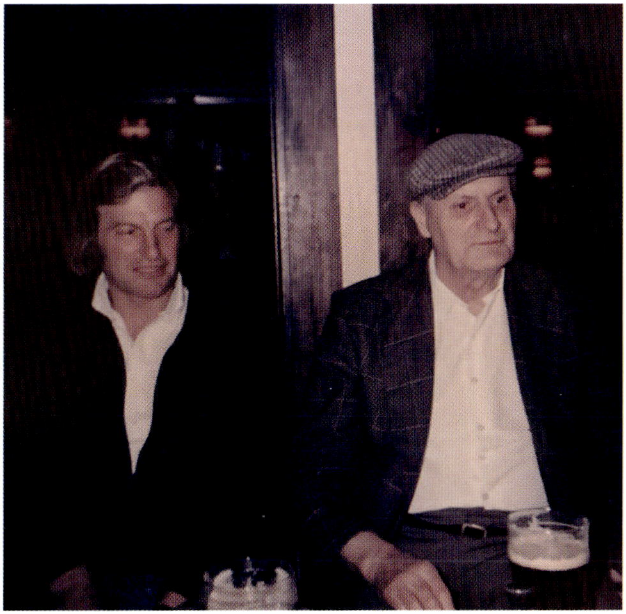

MY GRANDAD JESSE WALKER (RIGHT) AND HIS SON AND MY UNCLE, ALSO NAMED JESSE WALKER (LEFT)

Uncle Jesse shared Grandad's love of the countryside, went poaching with him and worked outdoors most of his life.

of progress is common sense, but the primary roots of capital are brutality, coercion, deceit and swindle. Enclosure was devised and enacted by our own ruling classes, and they continue to benefit from it. This is not only suffered in Britain, as the lessons learned from enclosure in England and Wales were swiftly re-enacted in the colonies, in order to create and sustain the British Empire.

More profoundly, this story has greater meaning for me because my grandfather, Jesse Walker, was a farm labourer who was divorced from the land surrounding Ellesmere Port in Cheshire when it was compulsorily purchased in 1948 to build the oil refinery Shell Stanlow, where he and many others from my extended family, including my father, were finally employed.

My grandfather was born in 1915, one of 14 children, and was a member of the Walker family, who had long farmed or worked as farm labourers in the Stoak and Stanney region, east of Ellesmere Port. Even when he was a plant operator at Shell, he continued rabbiting with the ferrets he kept in the back garden of the council house he lived in on Wolverham Road. Grandad was 6ft 7in, an impressive fellow, and when he went poaching, he tied string around both the top and bottom of his trouser legs. This way he could keep his ferrets hidden on the way to the surrounding woods but, at the same time, they couldn't do him any serious damage with their sharp teeth. So, for me, this history is not just an arcane historical event but an ongoing process that has even affected my close family, who have been forcibly driven from the rural to the industrial in the name of progress.

I quit studying history at the age of 14 as some instinct told me that those fetid ranks of kings and queens were not my history. Consequently, for many years I was unaware of the abject beauty and profound insights that can be garnered from the many forms of knowledge of the past. I'm unsure when I first learned of the enclosures, probably not soon enough, but once I knew about them, it became a thorn in my soul that festered.

Much of my work has tried to amplify histories from below and recognize the role of carnival, folk traditions and grassroots religion in both performing and sustaining radical histories. As part of this, I've found it's important to look at a history of non-industrial struggle alongside the traditions and rituals that nourish and preserve marginal histories. Ancient folk rituals in Britain often trace and embody our relationship to the land. These traditions are both corporeal expressions of the reverberations of history and kinetic forms of peoples' protection of the rights and benefits that come with a closer relationship with the land. While it's important to understand these histories through the lens of radical politics and ritual, it is also vital to consider the importance of noting the role of the enclosure outliers, a history of peoples who have attempted to "opt out" of a society which was and is inherently skewed to the benefit of the few, as opposed to the many. The state, long troubled by these outsiders, has created legions of legislation to ban and criminalize free movement and untethered living on land which was and should be common.

Common People opens with a timeline that maps out the dates of significant acts of law, anti-enclosure rebellions, broader historical contexts, notable personalities and major players, and seminal publications. In "Commoners", my own hand-tinted photographs of contemporary commoners are used to invoke a mystical and less mercantile connection to the land. Alongside these sit descriptions by Annabel Edwards, integrating oral histories, information about the commoners' status and local myths, and providing a kind of kaleidoscope all the way back into the 17th century to help us understand the historic legacy of enclosure and loss of commons.

Annabel Edwards' insightful essay "Enclosed Land and Vanquished Peasants" provides a succinct background, charting the history of enclosure from the Norman Conquest to the ways in which it still affects people today in England and Wales.

"Rural Rebels and Traditions" looks at the history of protest against enclosure and the loss of land rights. These selected short histories are illustrated by my stylized photomontages, which depict artefacts of peasant life and myth alongside images of rural traditions and objects relating both to land struggles and the violence of landowners and the state. These sit alongside photographic portraits of folk traditions that I have been documenting since the 1990s, showing how these often ancient rituals have performed the boundaries, histories and customs that mark our relationship to the land.

"Cosmology of the Rural" is a collaboration between Stephen Ellcock and me; we explore histories of representing the rural – from traditional crafts to landscape paintings

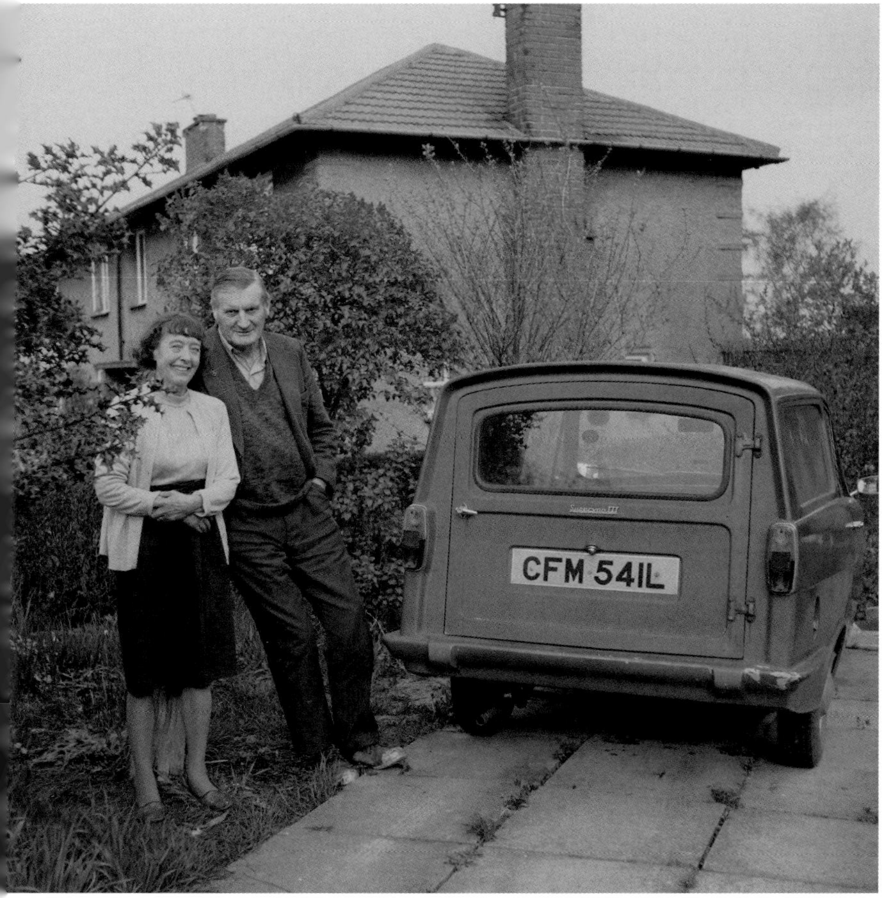

DOROTHY AND JESSE WALKER IN ELLESMERE PORT

My nan and grandad at their house in Wolverham Road with their Reliant Robin car, Grandad's pride and joy, which he resolutely drove with a motorbike licence... possibly illegally.

Leah Gordon (1982)

MONUMENT TO THE VANQUISHED PEASANTS
Albrecht Dürer (1525)

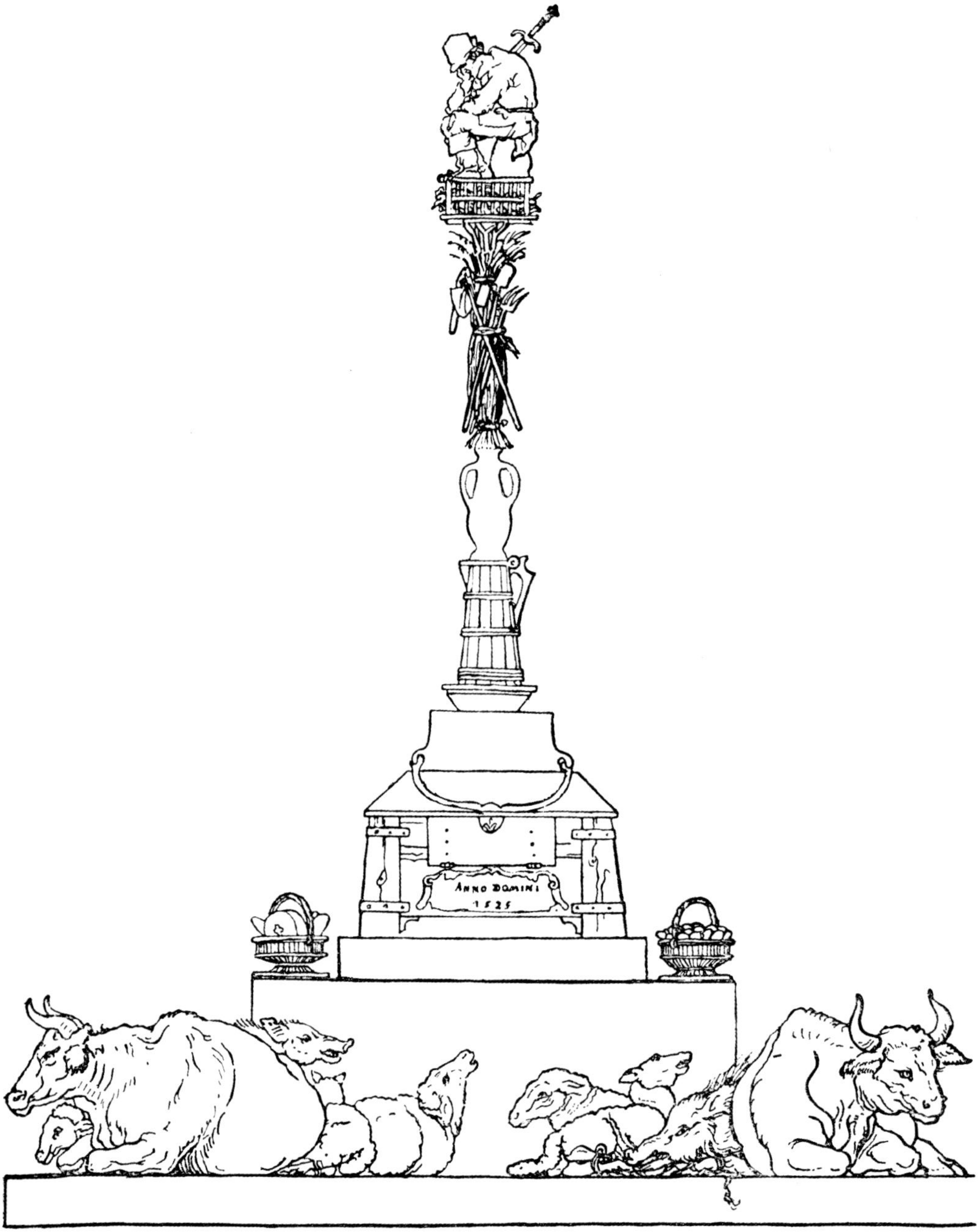

portraying rural losses and gains, and the tropes of folk-horror. My "Cosmology of the Rural" essay explores the gaps and omissions in the visual portrayal of the landscape, while an enlightening conversation with Stephen acts as an informed and thought-provoking counterbalance, illustrated with a radical, poetic and psychogeographical exploration of the English landscape in images from the past and the present that have been sourced by him.

"Vagabonds" acknowledges the social outcomes of the enclosures, which as well as creating a new class of industrial factory workers, created a disenfranchised vagabond class divorced from the land and any means of subsistence. The constructed images, inspired in part by an 18th-century book of illustrations by John Thomas Smith called *Vagabondiana, or Anecdotes of Mendicant Wanderers through the Streets of London*, portray the reality for disenfranchised peasants after the loss of the commons. Alongside these are images from my own extensive archive of photographic portraits taken in the 1990s of New Age travellers and anti-road protesters, drawing parallels between the outcomes of the enclosure acts, modes of collective resistance to Thatcher's Britain in the techno-trance rave culture, and the contemporary actions to protect public rights to roam. The chapter looks at the concept of "vagabondage" as being a radical mechanism for stepping outside of capitalist societal expectations. This is symbolized by photographs shot on large format analogue colour slide film of isolated ruins of caravans in rural settings, as exemplified by the stage set for the character of Rooster Byron in the renowned play *Jerusalem* by Jez Butterworth.

The essay "Arise Albion!" by Annabel Edwards is a round-up of these contemporary land struggles – from New Age travellers via the rave scene, the anti-road campaigns, and the Right to Roam campaigns. Finally, "Allotments" looks at reclaiming a connection with the land in a tradition first introduced by the Diggers in the 17th century.

My hope in these pages is to enable you to re-read histories, traditions and struggles "from below", to bring visibility to the marginalized, and to bring class politics to a wider audience. Finally, while this book, mirroring the title of Albrecht Dürer's unfulfilled "Monument to the Vanquished Peasants", is an attempt to memorialize the enclosure acts that took place on English soil and to remember the vanquished peasants, it is of paramount importance to be aware that struggles over the commons exist to this day. Land grabs are taking place worldwide and we must use this chance to build unity and comradeship with dispossessed Indigenous people suffering on the front line of global enclosures now. Finally and importantly, I would like to thank both GRAIN projects and Meadow Arts for their belief and support in this project.

TIMELINE OF LAND ENCLOSURE FROM 1066

1066

Norman Conquest

William I (the Conqueror) ascends the English throne

William I asserts the authority of the Crown as the ultimate owner of all land in England. He also designates at least 25 per cent of England as royal hunting grounds under forest law. Anyone guilty of killing a deer could be punished by blinding.

1079

The New Forest commons come under forest law.

1086

Creation of the Domesday Book, a manuscript that lists the findings of the Great Survey of much of England and parts of Wales, ordered by William the Conqueror.

1215

Magna Carta signed at Runnymede.

1217

Charter of the Forest redresses and re-establishes the rights of free men to access the royal forests, which had previously been denied to them by William the Conqueror.

1235

Statute of Merton passed by the Parliament of England, which allows enclosure as long as "sufficient" land is left for the tenants – but sufficient undefined.

1342

Disputed year of birth of Wat Tyler, who is to become one of the leaders of the Peasants' Revolt in England.

1348–50

Spread of Black Death, a bubonic plague spread by flea-infested rats that killed 40 to 60 per cent of the population.

c.1377

Piers Plowman written, an allegorical narrative poem attributed to William Langland, which criticizes the corruption of religious, political and social life, and was later quoted by leaders in the Peasants' Revolt.

1381

The Peasants' Revolt, also known as the Great Rising, was sparked by a poll tax and was the largest uprising in English history.

1389

Game qualification law stated that anyone without lands was forbidden from keeping hunting dogs and any other hunting equipment.

1452

First Doctrine of Discovery, which is a set of legal and religious principles that gave European nations rights to colonize lands outside of Europe. Papal bulls (edicts issued by the Vatican) in 1452, 1455 and 1493 state that non-Christians should not be recognized as legitimate land owners. The one of 1493 makes clear that the duty of Christian explorers was to seize the lands of non-Christians and convert the inhabitants to Christianity.

1455

Johannes Gutenberg prints an edition of the Bible in Germany – the first complete extant book in the West, and one of the earliest books printed from movable type, marking the start of the Printing Revolution. Print starts to enable free thinkers to disseminate their ideas.

1458

Oldest known Cockaigne text, with the mythical country of Cockaigne referring to a land of plenty in opposition to the strictures and hardships of peasant life.

1485

End of War of the Roses.

Henry VII ascends the throne (House of Tudor).

1489

Act Against Pulling Down of Towns, the first of many anti-enclosure acts, passed in an attempt to control enclosing.

1494

The Vagabonds and Beggars Act states that "vagabonds, idle and suspected persons shall be set in the stocks for three days and three nights and have none other sustenance but bread and water and then shall be put out of Town".

1509

Henry VIII ascends the throne.

1515–97

Fourteen more anti-enclosure laws passed.

Monarchs and heads of state

Rebellions

Important texts

Legal acts

Historical context (domestic and colonial)

Personalities

1516

Publication of *Utopia* by Thomas More, a philosophical work that includes a critique of enclosure.

1524–25

German Peasants' War.

1525

Albrecht Dürer sketches "Monument to the Vanquished Peasants".

1530

The Vagabonds Act, under which vagabonds are subject to the harsher punishment of whipping, rather than the stocks.

1536–41

Dissolution of the Monasteries, a legal process enabling Henry VIII to seize the wealth, assets and buildings owned in England by the Catholic Church. This eventually put land into the hands of the burgeoning merchant classes, which is believed to have ultimately led to the English Civil War.

1536

The Lincolnshire Rebellion takes place, a major uprising against Henry VIII's religious reforms which started in Yorkshire and led to the occupation of Lincoln Cathedral.

1541

The Witchcraft Act defines witchcraft as a felony, a crime punishable by death and the forfeiture of goods and chattels.

1547

Edward VI ascends throne)

The Vagabonds Act states that vagabonds could be enslaved for two years and continued weekly parish collections for the poor. The enslaved vagabonds were to be fed bread and water or a mug of beer and were allowed to be worked by beating, chaining or other methods chosen by the master. Vagabond slaves were allowed to be bought and sold just like other enslaved peoples.

1549

Kett's Rebellion, Norfolk is the first uprising directly in response to enclosure.

1551

The Act for the Provision and Relief of the Poor designates a new position, "collector of alms", in each parish to request, record and distribute charitable donations for poor relief.

1553

Lady Jane Grey is queen of England for nine days.

Mary I of England ascends throne (known as "Bloody Mary" by Protestant opponents).

Publication of *Book of Private Prayer* by Archbishop Cranmer (included a prayer beseeching landlords to have sympathy for their tenants).

1558

Elizabeth I ascends throne.

1562

Act Against Conjurations, Enchantments and Witchcrafts is passed, which is more merciful towards those found guilty of witchcraft than its predecessor, demanding the death penalty only where harm has been caused; lesser offences are to be punishable by a term of imprisonment.

1563

Statute of Artificers allows the imposition of forced labour on the unemployed.

1566

Publication of *A Caveat or Warning for Common Cursitors* by Thomas Harman, an early work in the popular genre of "rogue literature", instrumental in further vilifying idleness.

1572

The Vagabonds Act calls for offenders to be burned through the ear for a first offence, and that persistent beggars should be hanged; however, the act also made the first clear distinction between the "professional beggar" and those unemployed through no fault of their own.

1582

Publication of *Divers Voyages* by Richard Hakluyt, a proponent of the migration of the poor to the colonies in the New World.

1596

Oxfordshire Rebellion, Enslow Hill, an attempted peasant uprising in response to increasing rural poverty, in part due to the loss of common lands.

TIMELINE OF LAND ENCLOSURE FROM 1597

1597

The last act *against* enclosure.

Harvest failure and widespread famine.

The Vagabonds Act aims to address concerns of increased vagrancy, due to harvest failure and enclosures, by introducing penal transportation for the first time as a punishment and alternative to execution.

1599

William Shakespeare writes the play *As You Like It*, a pastoral comedy set in the Forest of Arden and a subtle satire on the artificial life of city dwellers in comparison to a more free and natural existence in the woods.

1601

Poor Relief Act formalizes earlier practices of poor relief distribution and moves away from forms of punishing the poor toward systems of correction.

The start of equipping and building houses of correction, in which over two-thirds of the prisoners were female.

1603

James I ascends the throne (House of Stuart).

Charter of the Forest Court of Grovely established for the collection of wood in the royal forest.

English Witchcraft Act makes it a capital offence to invoke evil spirits or commune with familiar spirits. This statute was enforced by Matthew Hopkins, the self-styled Witch-Finder General.

Game Act prohibits the sale of pheasants, partridges and hares to stem poaching.

1606

The Virginia Company grants charters by James I to colonize the east coast of North America, from present-day Maine to North Carolina.

1607

Midland Revolt takes place – an uprising against enclosure led by "Captain Pouch", the pseudonym of John Reynolds, and starting in Northamptonshire but spreading to Leicestershire and Warwickshire.

1608

The first limited pro-enclosure bill.

1609

The *Sea Venture*, a ship belonging to the Virginia Company and taking colonists to North America, is wrecked off Bermuda. The survivors try to claim common rights to live off the land but are suppressed by the company's agents. The event inspires Shakespeare's *The Tempest* (c.1610/1611).

Birth of Gerrard Winstanley, one of the founders of the True Levellers (also known as the Diggers).

1616

Horton Wood riots, Shropshire against loss of pannage rights.

1620–1780

Fenland Resistance takes place, the longest continuing struggle against enclosure in an attempt to resist the drainage of the wetlands in Lincolnshire, which had sustained the local population for umpteen centuries.

1621

The first general pro-enclosure bill.

1623

The first English colonies are established in Caribbean, thus beginning the growth of plantations worked by enslaved Africans.

1624

Nearly all the anti-enclosure statutes are repealed.

1625

Charles I ascends the throne.

1626–32

The Western Rising or Prayer Book Rebellion takes place in Devon and Cornwall, instigated by religious laws but also protesting against draconian taxes on sheep farming.

1628

Publication of poem "The Country Life" by Robert Herrick, exulting rural life in comparison to urban living.

1642–51

English Civil War.

Monarchs and heads of state

Rebellions

Important texts

Legal acts

Historical context (domestic and colonial)

Personalities

1647

Putney Debates, in which members of the New Model Army debate the form of political landscape that should follow the First English Civil War. Some participants, such as senior officers, favour a constitutional monarchy, whereas radicals such as the Levellers propose more radical changes, including one man, one vote, and greater religious freedoms.

One of the main sticking points is the demand for universal male suffrage in opposition to Cromwell's wishes that only landowners should be free to vote.

1649

Trial and execution of Charles I.

Commonwealth (republic) declared.

Leveller movement defeated at the Battle of Burford.

Creation of the True Levellers.

The True Levellers Standard Advanced manifesto published.

1649–50

Establishment of Digger communities on St George's Hill, Surrey.

1649

Publication of the Digger pamphlet *A Light Shining in Buckinghamshire*.

1650

Publication of tract *A Single Eye* by Laurence Clarkson (based on ideas of the radical religious sect the Ranters).

1652

Publication of *The Law of Freedom* by Gerrard Winstanley, arguing that private property should be abolished.

1653

Oliver Cromwell accepts role as Lord Protector.

1658

Richard Cromwell succeeds his father as Lord Protector.

1660

Charles II becomes king in restoration of the monarchy.

Royal African Company granted a monopoly on the Atlantic slave trade.

1671

Game Act prohibits all people from hunting game if they don't derive their income from the ownership of land.

1685

Catholic James II of England ascends the throne.

1688–89

The "Glorious Revolution" overthrows James II, which strengthens parliamentary power over the monarchy.

1688

Slave trade is opened to all merchants, which rapidly expands the business and traffic.

1689

Protestant William III of Orange and Mary II (daughter of James II) rule as joint monarchs until Mary's death in 1694, when William rules in his own right.

1702

Anne ascends the throne.

1709

The Ropely Inclosure Act to enclose Ropely Commons in the (then) county of Southampton becomes the first parliamentary enclosure act.

1714

George I ascends the throne (House of Hanover).

1723

The Black Act is passed in response to a series of raids against landowners carried out by two groups of poachers, known as the Blacks from their habit of blacking their faces when undertaking the raids. It is considered the most severe single statute to be passed in the 18th century and established the death penalty for economic criminality.

1724

Galloway Levellers' uprising takes place, an armed resistance to enclosure of land and eviction of tenant farmers in Galloway, Scotland.

1727

George II ascends the throne.

TIMELINE OF LAND ENCLOSURE FROM 1735

1735

The Witchcraft Act 1735 marks a reversal in attitudes. Penalties for the practice of witchcraft are replaced by penalties for the pretence of witchcraft. A person who claims to have the power to call up spirits, or foretell the future, or cast spells, is now to be punished as a vagrant and a con artist, subject to fines and imprisonment.

1745

The last rising of the Jacobite Rebellion defeated in Scotland and feudal rights are abolished.

1750s

Parliamentary enclosures become the norm and take place with increasing regularity.

1750

Lowland Clearances begin in Scotland, making thousands of tenant farmers homeless in the southern counties as a result of agricultural modernization.

Birth of Thomas Spence, English radical and advocate of the common ownership of land and a democratic equality of the sexes. He is born in poverty and dies the same way in 1814, after long periods of imprisonment.

1751

Birth of Edward Marcus Despard, who is critically vociferous against enclosure. He is executed in 1803 for conspiracy against the Crown.

1757

East India Company invades and takes Bengal.

1760

George III ascends the throne.

1770

Publication of poem *The Deserted Village* by Oliver Goldsmith, a condemnation of the ruination of rural communities due to enclosure.

1776

Publication of *The Wealth of Nations* by economist Adam Smith, which advocates for enclosure and a loss of the commons to facilitate the progress of a market economy and capitalist system.

1780s

Highland Clearances begin, which evict a significant number of tenants in the Scottish Highlands and islands in order to repurpose the land for large-scale sheep farming.

1783

Publication of *The Village*, a narrative poem by George Crabbe which is a direct riposte to Goldsmith's poem and depicts rural life in a more negative light.

1791

Publication of *The Rights of Man* by Thomas Paine, which defends the French Revolution and argues for universal suffrage and civil rights.

1792

The Year of the Sheep, in which Highland farmers in Scotland drive as many as 10,000 sheep off the land where they are being grazed as a protest against clearances.

The London Corresponding Society formed, a federation of reading and debating clubs that agitate for the democratic reform of the British Parliament, and which draws largely upon working men and is itself organized on a formal democratic basis.

1793

Publication of *Visions of the Daughters of Albion* by William Blake, criticizing slavery, women's oppression and organized religion.

Poem "An Evening Walk" by William Wordsworth reflects on the deep importance of contact with nature for human spirituality and wellbeing.

Publication of *The Real Rights of Man*, lecture by Thomas Spence, which along with universal suffrage, advocates for common ownership of land and the obsolescence of the land-owning aristocracy.

1793–1815

England at war with France.

1798

Publication of *An Essay on the Principle of Population* by Thomas Robert Malthus, criticizing the Poor Laws for leading to inflation rather than improving the wellbeing of the poor.

Monarchs and heads of state | Important texts | Historical context (domestic and colonial)
Rebellions | Legal acts | Personalities

1807

Publication of poem "The Parish Register" by George Crabbe, which is considered a compassionate but realistic depiction of rural life.

1808

Parliament outlaws the slave trade but not slavery.

1811–16

Luddite protests by English textile workers who oppose the use of certain types of cost-saving machinery.

1813

Publication of utopian poem *Queen Mab* by Percy Bysshe Shelley, calling for an end to oppression.

1814–55

The second phase of the Highland clearances, whereby landlords move to the draconian policy of expelling people from their estates, linking this with "assisted emigration".

1815

Corn Laws place tariffs on cereal grain imported from other countries such as wheat and maize to favour domestic agriculture.

1816

The Night Poaching Act, forbidding poaching at night, introduces the sentence of transportation for seven years for poachers caught with a net or stick with intent to take game. (This act makes headlines in 2007, when two rabbit poachers are convicted and fined under it before magistrates at Hereford.)

1817

The Pentrich Rising, an armed protest by stockingers, quarrymen and iron workers in Derbyshire, demanding better conditions.

1819

Publication of *The Mask of Anarchy* by Percy Bysshe Shelly (political poem responding to the Peterloo Massacre in Manchester, in which cavalry charged the crowd, who were demanding the reform of parliamentary representation).

1820

George IV ascends the throne.

Publication of poem "The Mores" by John Clare, a lament for the loss of natural beauty and community due to enclosure.

1822

Publication of travelogue and social commentary *Rural Rides* by William Cobbett, highlighting plight of the poor.

1824

Publication of *The Horrors of Slavery* by Robert Wedderburn.

1827

The Man Trap and Spring Guns Bill makes it illegal to set these devices.

1828

Night Poaching Act makes the "intention" of poaching an offence punishable by transportation.

1830

William IV ascends the throne.

Otmoor Riots against enclosure on wetlands in Oxfordshire.

The Swing Riots take place, a widespread uprising by agricultural workers in southern and eastern England in protest against agricultural mechanization and harsh working conditions.

Publication of poem "The Fallen Elm" by John Clare, which uses the loss of a beloved elm tree as an analogy for the destruction of village and community life after the enclosures.

1832

Reform Act abolishes rotten boroughs and extends voting rights to owners of smaller properties.

Publication of poem "Remembrances" by John Clare, which again expresses the human losses and suffering due to the enclosures.

TIMELINE OF LAND ENCLOSURE FROM 1834

1834

Parliament abolishes slavery but also financially recompenses the slave owners. (This debt is only finally paid off by British tax payers in 2015.)

The Poor Law Amendment Act, known as the New Poor Law, denying the right of the poor to subsistence and allowing the imposition of forced labour on the unemployed.

Trial of the Tolpuddle Martyrs, six agricultural labourers from the village of Tolpuddle in Dorset who are convicted and sentenced to be transported for swearing a secret oath as members of the Friendly Society of Agricultural Labourers.

1836

The Tolpuddle Martyrs are pardoned after mass protests.

1837–48

Chartist Movement which aimed to gain political rights and influence for the working classes.

1837

Victoria ascends the throne.

1839–43

The Rebecca Riots of West Wales against high tolls charged for driving livestock along the roads.

1845

General Enclosure Act appoints commissioners authorized to issue "enclosure awards" without submitting them to parliament for approval, which speeds up the process of enclosure. It also promises provision of "small field gardens" for the landless poor, the precursors to allotments.

1845–46

Andover workhouse scandal, in which inmates are found to be starving.

1846

Corn Laws repealed, eliminating tariffs on all imported cereal grains because the industrialists and urban dwellers are unhappy with high food prices.

1846–50

Irish famine kills over a million people and forces over a million more to emigrate.

1848

Publication of *The Communist Manifesto* by Karl Marx and Friedrich Engels.

1851

Publication of *London Labour and London Poor* by journalist Henry Mayhew, documenting lives of working people in London in the 1840s.

1862

The Poaching Prevention Act gives police unprecedented powers to stop and search people and carts suspected of poaching.

1865

Commons Preservation Society (now the Open Spaces Society) is founded.

1866

Metropolitan Act to protect common lands in metropolitan areas.

1867

Publication of *Capital*, Volume 1, by Karl Marx.

1870

Fakenham riots in Norfolk. Local resistance to the planned enclosure of Fakenham Commons includes arson and affray, and the townspeople turn to the newly formed Commons Preservation Society (now the Open Spaces Society) to help them save the common land.

1873

The Ascott Martyrs: 16 women from Oxfordshire imprisoned for supporting two labourers' membership of the new National Union of Agricultural Workers.

1896

Winter Hill mass trespass on the moors near Bolton.

1901

Edward VII ascends the throne

1903

Publication of *Inclosures in England in the Sixteenth Century* by E F Gay, a report denying any suffering created by the enclosures and subsequently instrumentalized by the right-wing.

Publication of *The People of the Abyss* by Jack London, describing lives of the poor in the East End of London.

1908

Small Holdings and Allotments Act required local authorities to maintain an "adequate provision" of land, usually a large allotment field, which can be subdivided into allotment gardens at low rents.

Monarchs and heads of state

Rebellions

Important texts

Legal acts

Historical context (domestic and colonial)

Personalities

1910

George V ascends the throne.

1911

Publication of *The Village Labourer* by John and Barbara Hammond, historical account describing life of rural labourers before and after enclosure.

Publication of pamphlet "Smash Up the Workhouse!" by Labour politician George Lansbury, advocating the abolition of the workhouse system.

1912

Publication of *The Agrarian Problem in the Sixteenth Century* by R H Tawney, a left-wing response to E F Gay's previous study.

1926

Publication of *Religion and the Rise of Capitalism* by R H Tawney, an account of connections between social and religious criticisms of Tudor England.

1932

Kinder Scout mass trespass, seeking to highlight how walkers were being denied access to areas of open countryside that had been fenced off by landowners.

1936

Edward VIII ascends the throne.

George VI ascends the throne.

1952

Elizabeth II ascends the throne.

1965

Commons Registration Act is passed, requiring all common land to be registered, which ultimately leads to the loss of more common land.

1968

Publication of "The Tragedy of the Commons" by the ecologist Garrett Hardin, which is an influential, but controversial, article arguing that common land would always lead to degradation. This speculative and unproven text is enthusiastically adopted by capitalist agricultural modernizers.

1971

Charter of the Forest replaced by the Wild Creatures and Forest Laws Act.

1972

First Windsor Free Festival.

1973

Publication of *The Country and the City* by Raymond Williams, surveying changing attitudes to city and countryside.

1974

First Stonehenge Free Festival.

1981

Greenham Common Peace Camp set up.

1985

Eviction of Molesworth Peace Camp.

Battle of the Beanfield clash between police and festivalgoers at Stonehenge.

1987

Publication of *This Land is Our Land* by Marion Shoard, examining patterns of land ownership in the UK.

1992

Twyford Down Protest.

Castlemorton Common Festival.

1993-4

M11 link road protest.

1994

Criminal Justice and Public Order Act to curb illegal raves and free parties, especially in the traveller festival circuit.

1995

The Land is Ours land rights campaign group set up by George Monbiot and others.

First Reclaim the Streets street party.

Newbury Bypass Protest

2018

Stop the Arc formed to fight the proposed Oxford to Cambridge expressway.

2020

Right to Roam founded by Nick Hayes and Guy Shrubsole.

Publication of *Green Unpleasant Land* by Corinne Fowler and *Book of Trespass* by Nick Hayes.

2022

Charles III ascends the throne.

The Stars are for Everyone campaign group set up to protect the right to wild camp on Dartmoor.

2025

Open Spaces Society criticised the government's "Land-Use Framework" for failing to address public access.

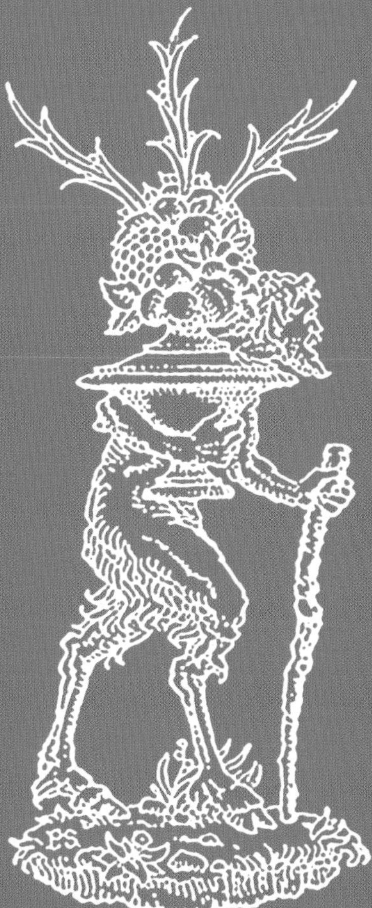

COMMONERS

Introduction to Commoners

The existence of common land and the common rights held on them stretches back to before the Anglo-Saxon period. In the past, almost half of the land in England and Wales was common, but now only about 3 per cent of land remains so.

A person who holds common rights, jointly with another or others, is known as a commoner. In the 17th century, most peasant farmers had some level of access to common land, which enabled them to subsist and survive. The gradual loss of common rights through enclosure often made the lives of the rural majority classes untenable.

It's frequently believed that all people have rights to all common land but, in reality, it was and is far more exclusive and particular than that. While the general public now have foot access rights to nearly all common land, they don't have rights to graze animals or gather resources such as firewood, for example. Currently in England and Wales, six different types of common rights remain: pasturage, estovers, turbary, pannage, common in the soil and piscary.

- **Pasturage:** the right to graze and pasture domesticated animals on common land, usually sheep, cattle and horses and sometimes goats and donkeys.
- **Estovers:** the right to collect fallen wood for repairs or fires and bracken or heather.
- **Turbary:** the right to cut turf for fuel.
- **Pannage:** the right to turn out your pigs in the woods to scavenge for acorns and beech nuts.
- **Common in the soil:** the right to extract minerals from the land, including sand, gravel, stone and lime.
- **Piscary:** the right to take fish from stretches of rivers.

A YOUNG BOY SITTING ON A FENCE, SCARING AWAY CROWS WITH A PAIR OF CLAPPERS
Coloured process print after W Bromley (1835–88)

Young boys were often employed on farms for jobs such as bird scaring, as this was more effective than a scarecrow and cheaper than employing an adult. Young girls were rarely employed on farms, because they were usually at home child-minding their siblings so their mothers could go out to work for a higher wage. Early football rattles were usually repurposed bird-scarers, often painted in the team's colours.

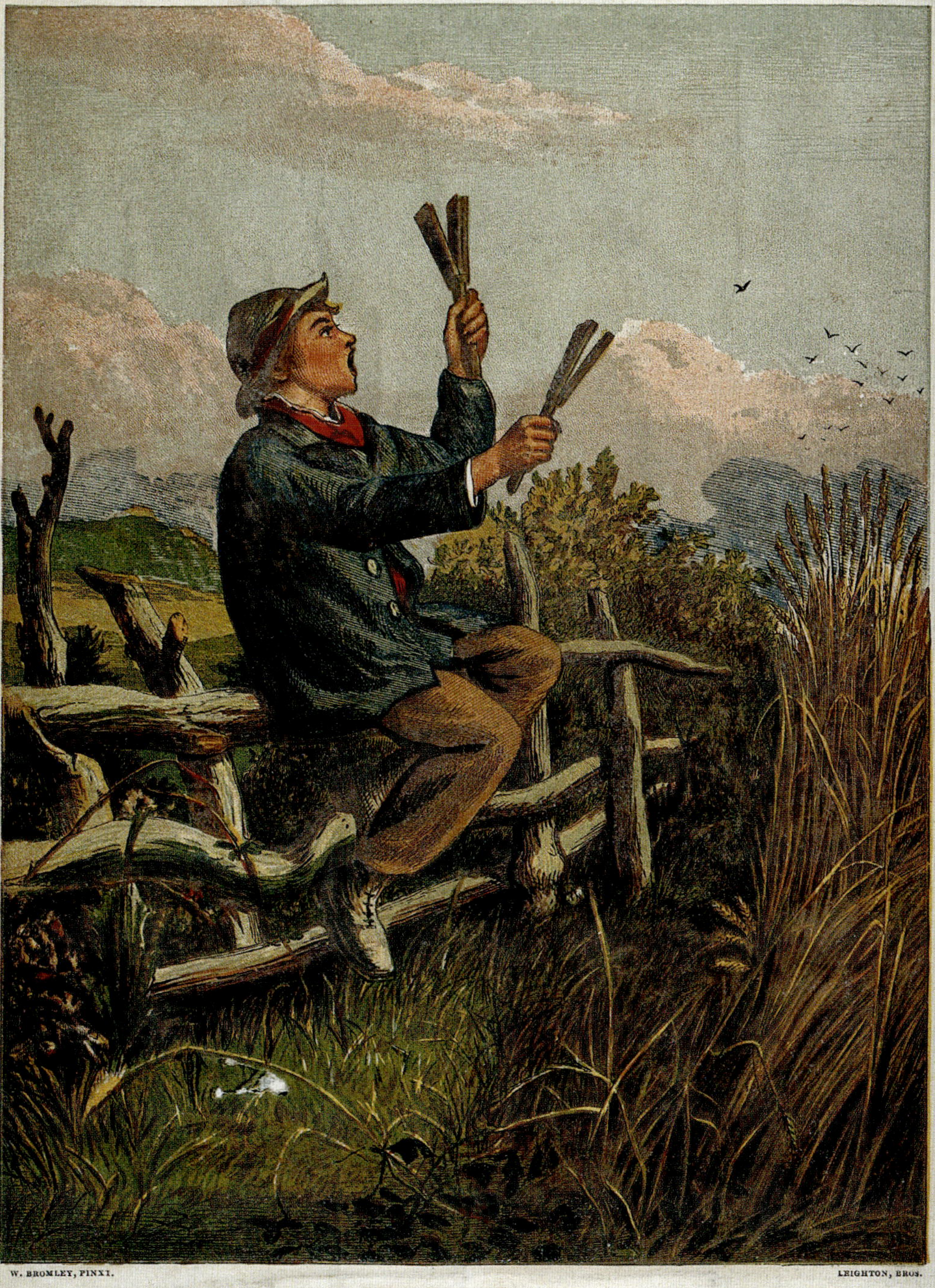

W. BROMLEY, PINXT. LEIGHTON, BROS.

CROW-SCARING.

GATHERING TWIGS

Simon Bening (c.1550)

Peasants often had the common right to take wood from the forest to use as fuel and for fencing, making furniture and repairs to buildings, carts, tools, etc. The word "estovers" is derived from a French word meaning "that which is necessary" – demonstrating how vital access to wood was. When fires and stoves provided all means of household heating and cooking, and coal was not readily available or too expensive, it was an onerous task to gather enough wood (or sometimes peat or turf) to "keep the home fires burning". People trying to live a simple life close to nature in contemporary times are often dismayed at quite how much time and energy it takes to gather suitable dry wood, cut it up and get the stove to light.

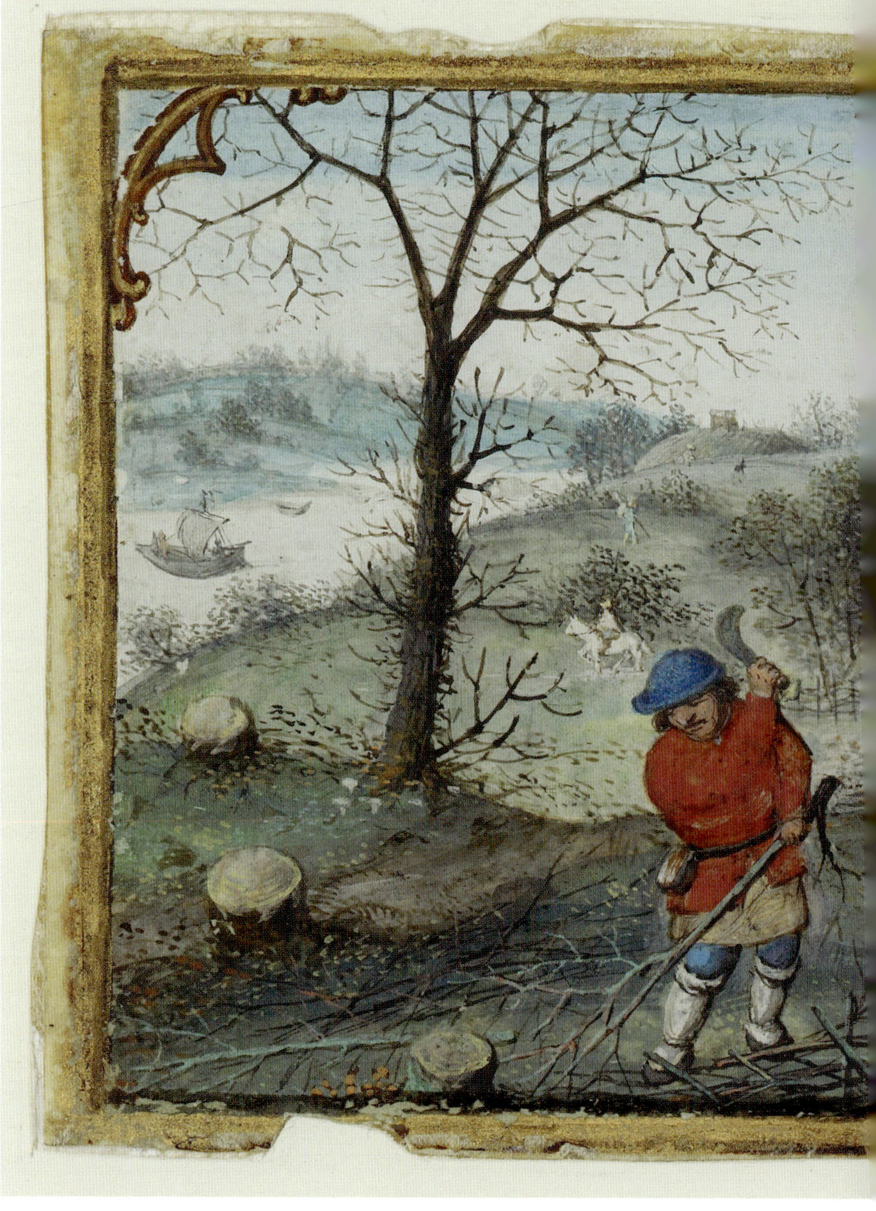

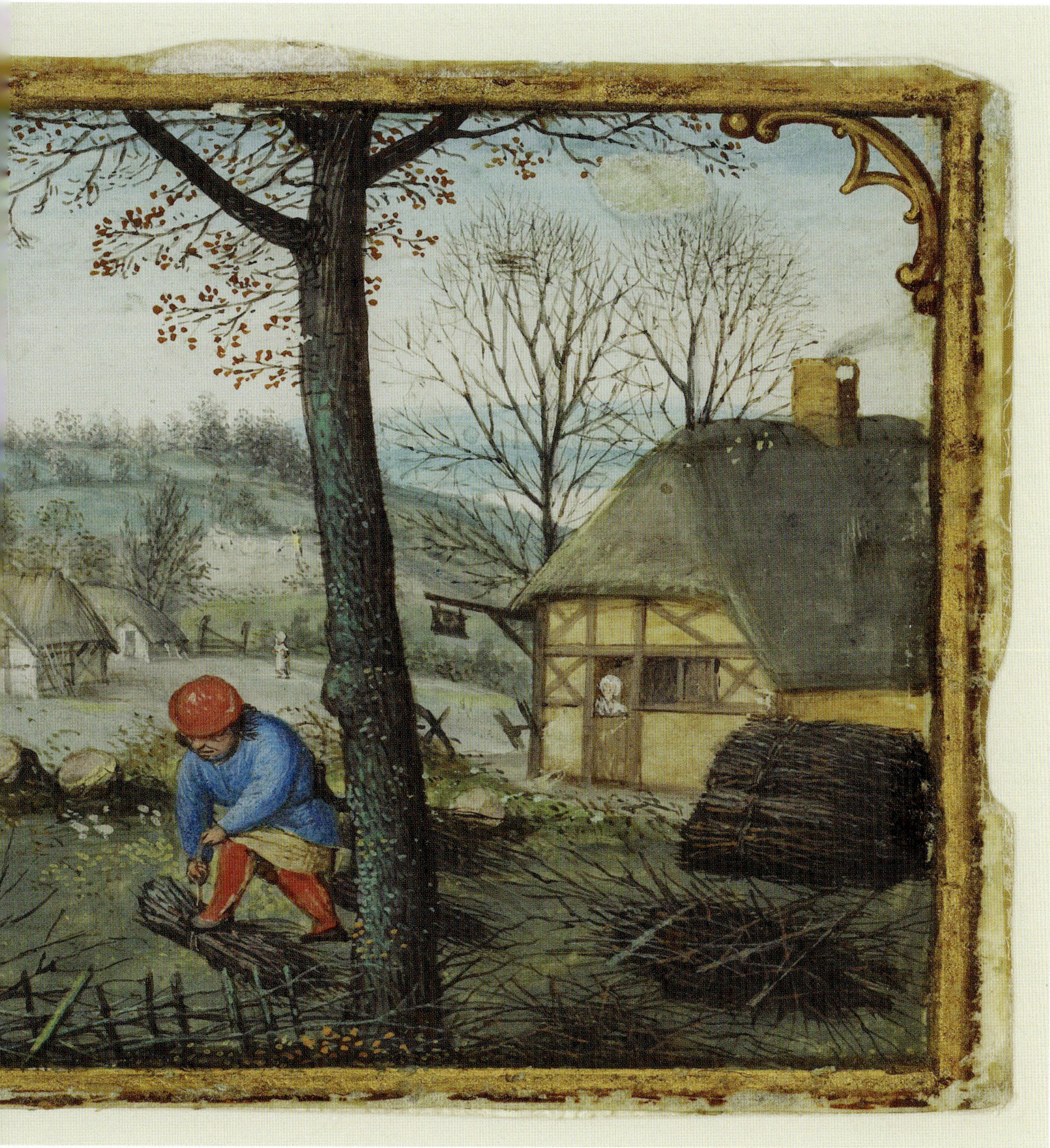

GLEANERS IN THE WHEAT FIELD

John Martin (1847)

Since biblical times it has been customary for the poor to be allowed into the fields after harvest to gather or "glean" the remaining corn or other crop lying in the field. In some villages a bell would be rung to announce the gleaning time. In the USA today, food banks and other charities are sometimes allowed to glean left-over vegetables and fruit from the fields. The modern ideology of freeganism, whereby people avoid participation in the conventional economy by means such as taking waste food from supermarkets, has been compared to gleaning.

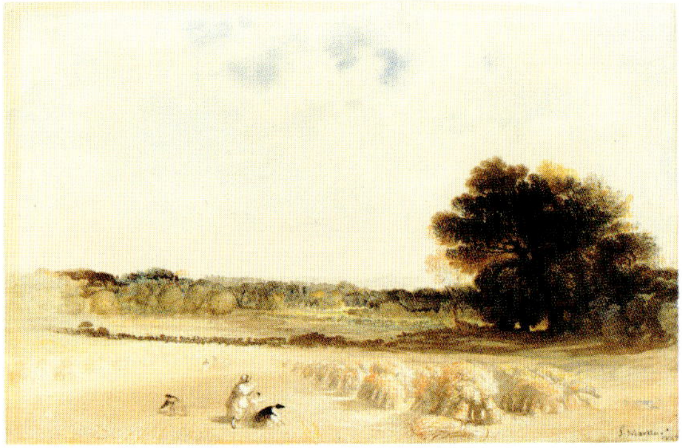

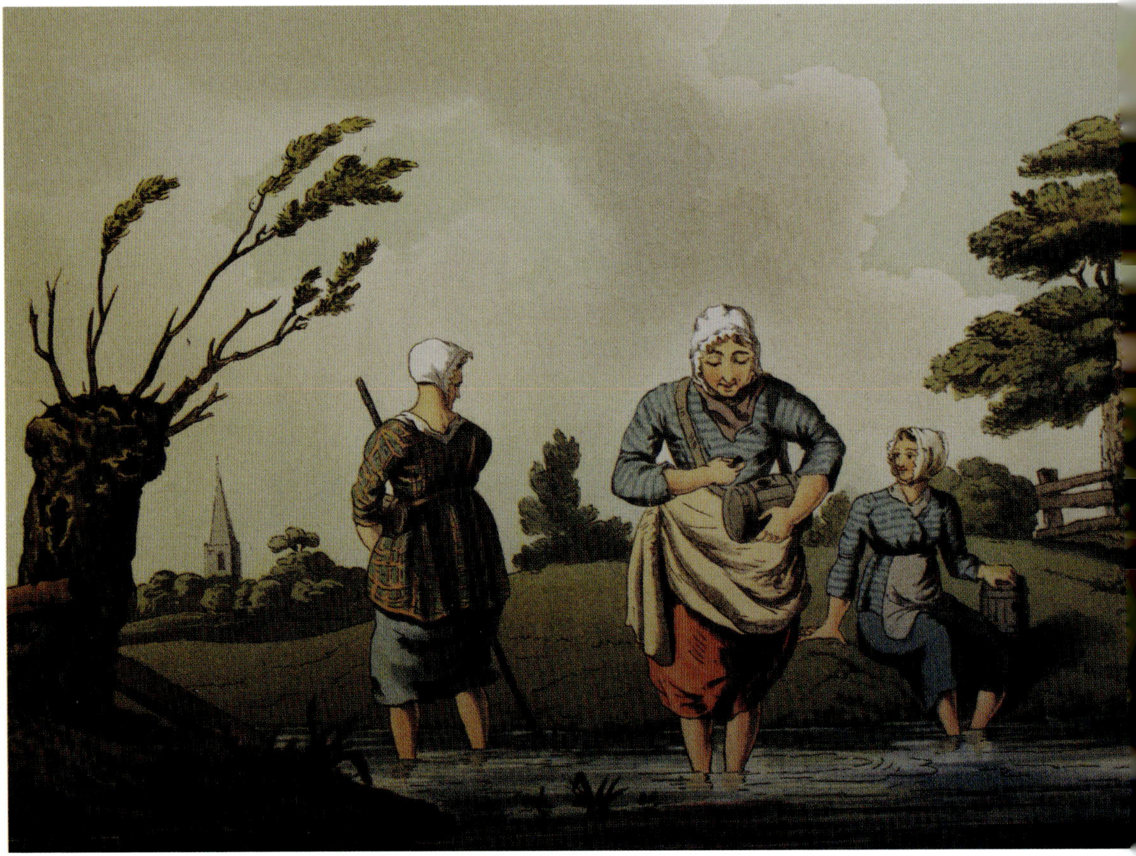

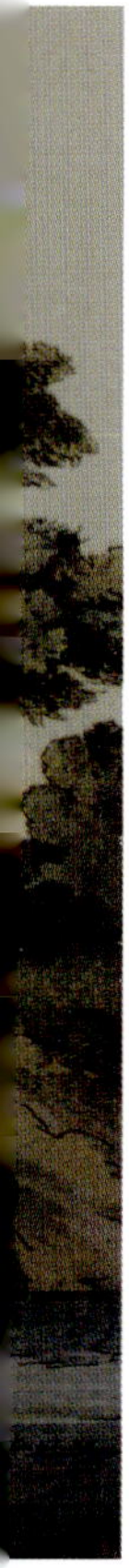

LEECH FINDERS FROM *THE COSTUMES OF YORKSHIRE*

George Walker (1814)

The women wade through the water bare-legged – not just to keep their clothes dry but so that the blood-sucking leeches will attach themselves to their legs and they can then pick them off and put them in their basket. Leeches have been used in medicine for thousands of years and were in great demand in the 18th and 19th centuries, as they were believed to remove excessive blood and restore internal balance. Modern medicine is now finding new uses for these vampiric black worms for promoting blood flow in plastic surgery and other procedures.

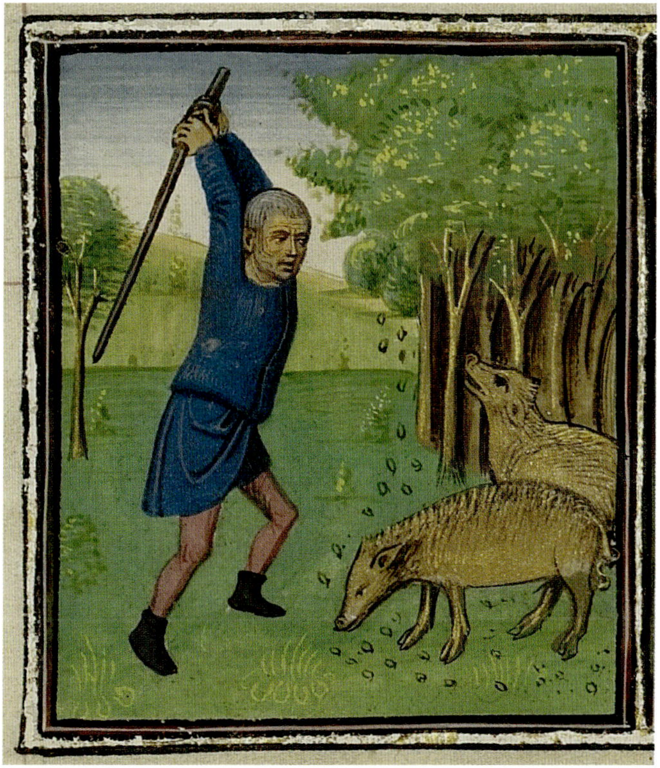

A MAN KNOCKING ACORNS FROM A TREE; ZODIACAL SIGN OF SAGITTARIUS

Workshop of Willem Vrelant (1454–1481)

Although it may look as if the man is about to attack an animal resembling a giant hedgehog, he is actually knocking acorns down for his pigs to eat. "Mast" is the word for all acorns and nuts and every few years trees will produce a bumper crop, known as a "mast year". The evolutionary reason for this is unclear; however, it may be that there are too many nuts for the animals to eat, so some are sure to grow into new trees.

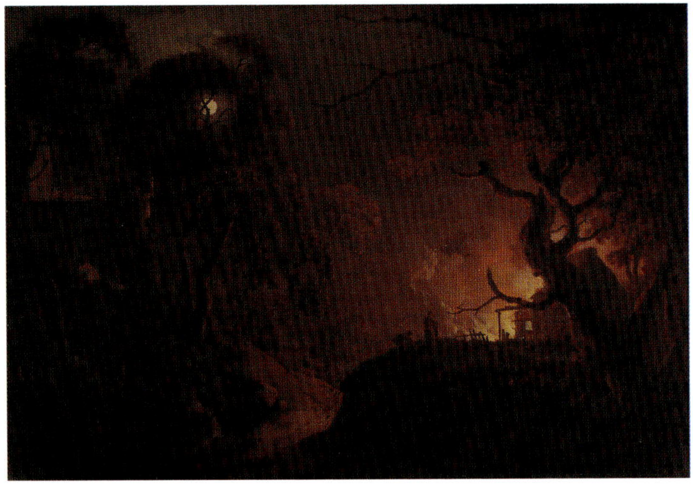

COTTAGE ON FIRE AT NIGHT

Joseph Wright of Derby (1785-93)

Many cottages were lost and destroyed during the enclosures as poorer tenant farmers were no longer able to sustain their families. During the Highland Clearances in Scotland it became normal practice to destroy the roof timbers of vacated cottages to ensure that other families couldn't squat in them after the evictions.

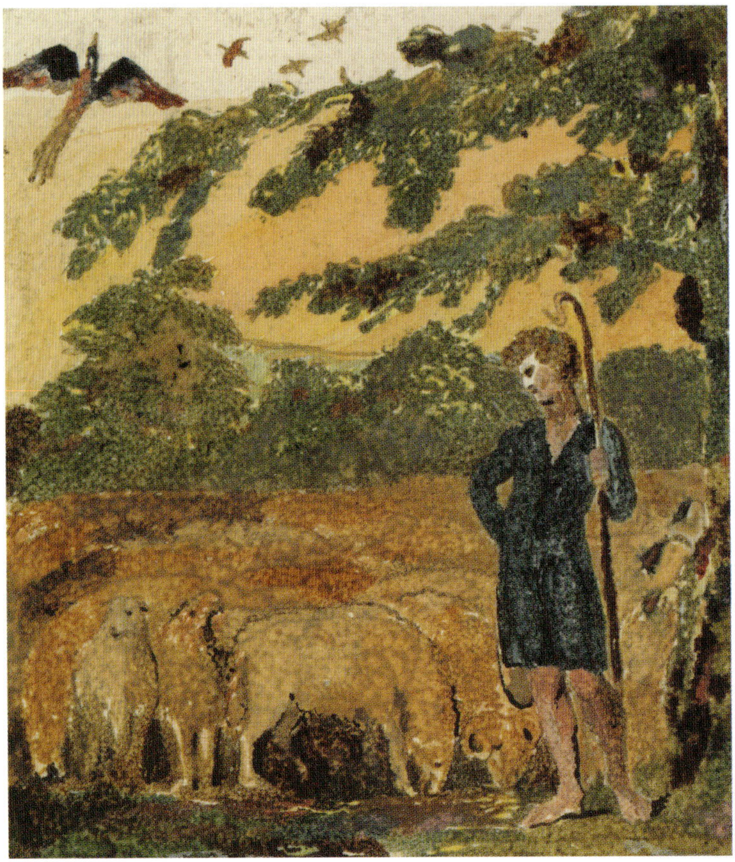

THE SHEPHERD

from *Songs of Innocence*, William Blake (c.1795)

After making etchings of his illustrations to his poems Songs of Innocence, *Blake would print and hand-colour different versions of them over the years, so each one was unique. The poem "The Shepherd" likens the shepherd to Christ tending his flock, which feels peaceful in the knowledge that he is with them, and references Psalm 23. Although Blake was forgotten for a generation after his death, his importance has grown exponentially in the last century or so. He has influenced artists, musicians and writers such as Paul Nash, Bob Dylan and Philip Pullman. The lead singer of Iron Maiden Bruce Dickinson recently published a graphic novel where earth from Blake's grave was mixed with the printing ink in recognition of Blake's importance as an inspiration.*

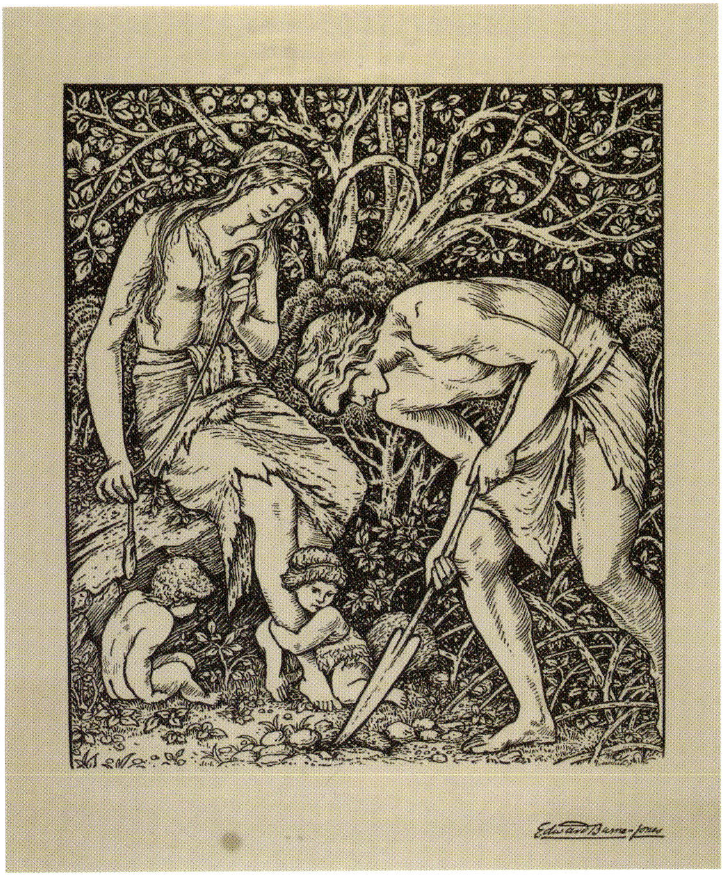

ADAM AND EVE (LABOUR: WHEN ADAM DELVED AND EVE SPAN, WHO WAS THEN THE GENTLEMAN)

By Carl Hentschel after Sir Edward Burne-Jones (1895)

This medieval saying was quoted by John Ball at the time of the Peasants' Revolt in 1381. Burne-Jones contributed this frontispiece to a novel by his friend William Morris, set at the time of the Peasants' Revolt and called A Dream of John Ball. Although they were long-standing friends, their friendship was often tested by their political differences as Burne-Jones didn't share Morris's socialism. When Burne-Jones accepted a baronetcy, they found it safer in their later years to limit conversation to the subjects of "art, stained glass and tapestry".

A SHEPHERD AND HIS FLOCK UNDER THE MOON AND STARS

Samuel Palmer (c.1827)

Samuel Palmer's enigmatic paintings, in which nature is infused with spirituality and mysticism, were made early in his career. He was only about 22 years old when he painted this. He was a great admirer of William Blake, whose influence can be seen in Palmer's work. Before enclosure, which enabled livestock to be shut up in fields, flocks of sheep would need a shepherd to guide and protect them as they ranged over extensive commons.

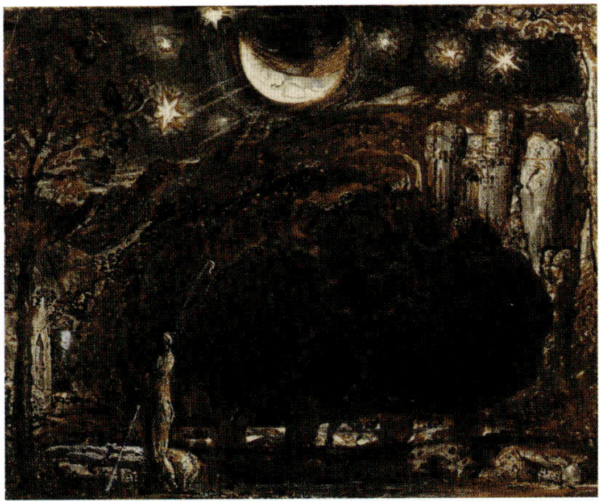

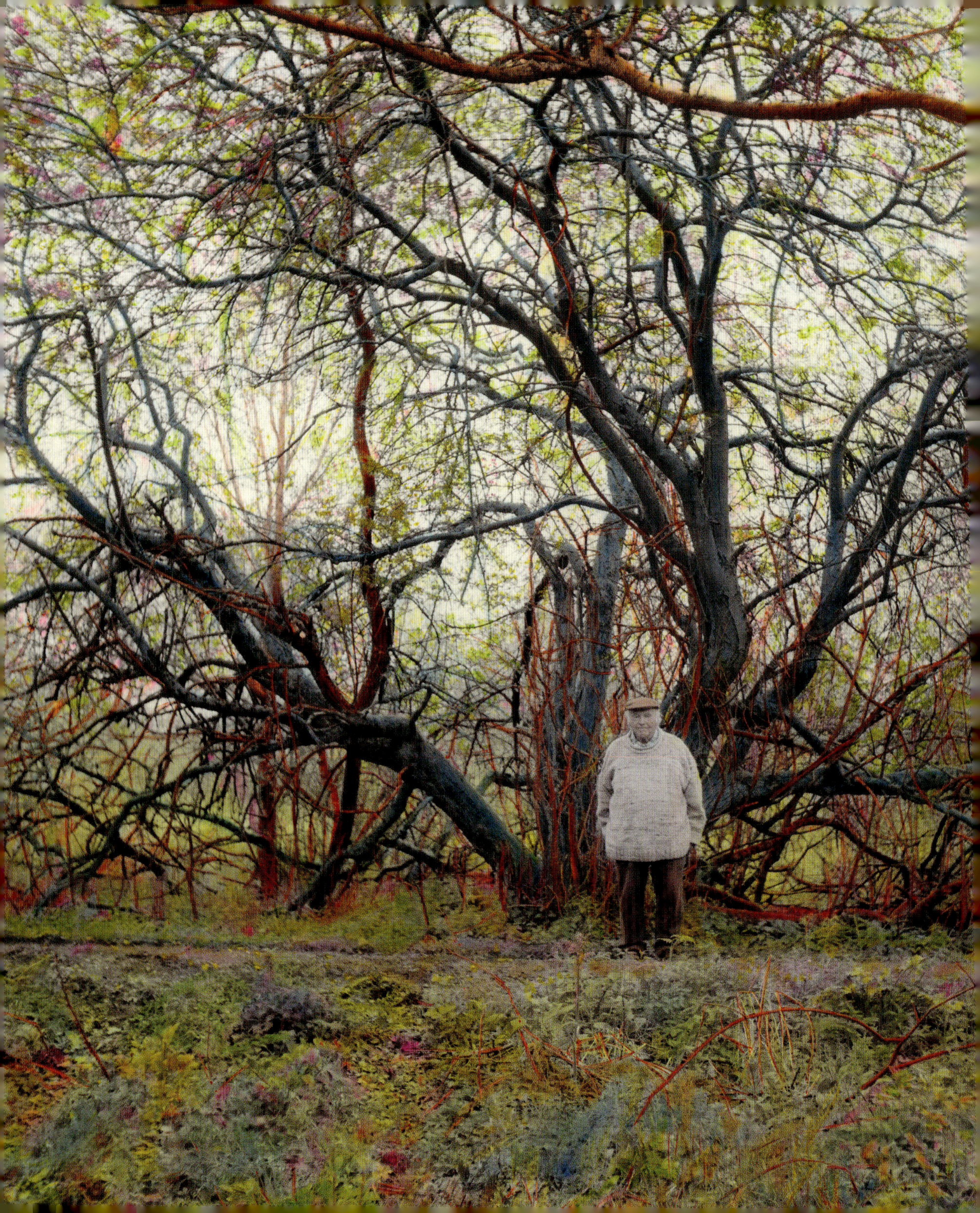

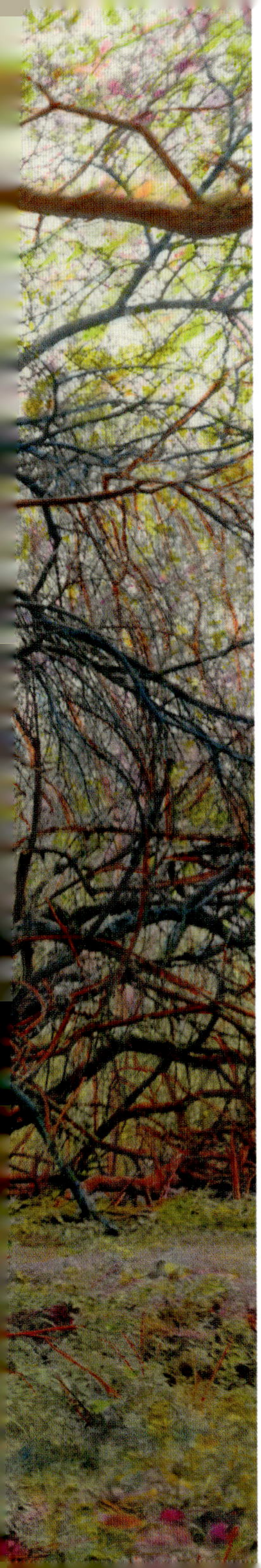

Commoners by Leah Gordon

There are still small pockets of common land in existence in Shropshire, and the portraits that follow are of some of the people who continue to have common rights there, documenting the present while providing a glimpse back to the 17th century. The people in these photographs share their family stories, which help explain the commoners' status, and explore the history and local myths of the land. Today, these stories can help us understand the historic legacy of the enclosure acts. For many of the upland farming commoners, their common rights are still central to their farming practice. However, in the case of commoners who've acquired these rights through the purchase of property, the rights can often seem quite random in the 21st century and are rarely exercised.

The photographs that follow were taken on an analogue medium format camera with black and white film, and the subsequent prints were hand-tinted using traditional photographic dyes. This process was used to invoke both the uncanny and magical nature of the land – to convey a more spiritual relationship with it, the breaking of which the Italian feminist historian Silvia Federici argues in her ground-breaking text *Caliban and the Witch* was central to capitalist expansion and the loss of the commons.

HENRY HAND, HENLEY COMMON

Rights: grazing sheep and cattle (2021) Hand-tinting by Marg Duston. A GRAIN Projects commission

Henry Hand's father had the right to graze livestock on the common when he owned a nearby farm. One of Henry's jobs when he was a boy was to ensure that the ponies they grazed there didn't wander away. During World War II, armaments were stored in huts on the common. Common land was often requisitioned in wartime because, as it wasn't prime agricultural land, it wasn't as important to the war effort. The family farm was sold in 1968 and, as usual, the rights to graze the common went with it. Henry still keeps sheep, but his cottage doesn't have grazing rights. Henry's jumper was a gift from a friend who arranged for it to be spun and knitted using wool from Henry's Badger Face Welsh Mountain sheep. Over the centuries, more and more of the original common was enclosed and commoners stopped grazing their animals there. Nature is reasserting itself and barn owls are often spotted swooping over the rough grassland, searching for voles and mice.

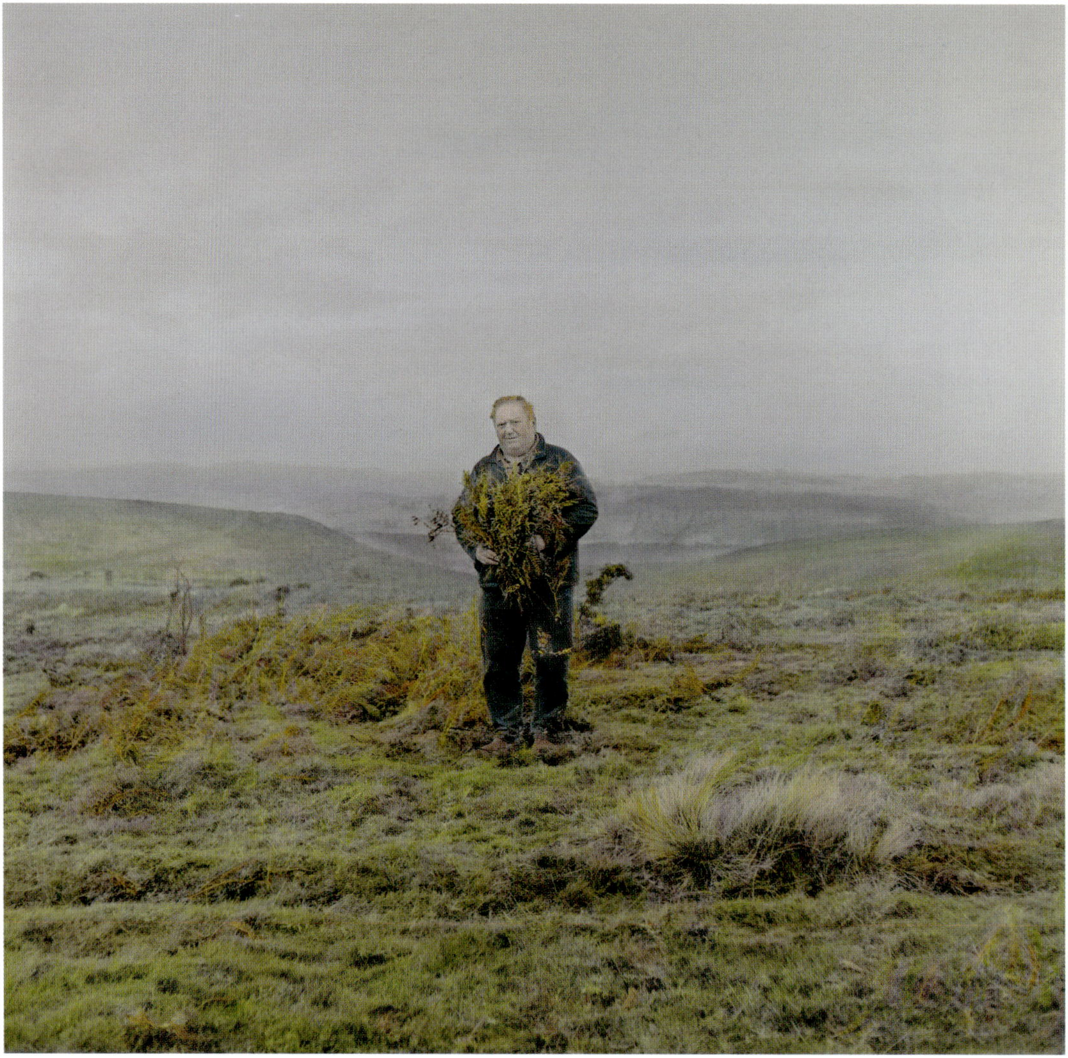

ROY GRIFFITHS, STAPELEY COMMON

Rights: grazing cattle, sheep and horses; estovers (bracken) (2020) Hand-tinting by Marg Duston. A GRAIN Projects commission

The legend of Mitchell's Fold, a Bronze Age stone circle on Stapeley, is a parable for overexploitation of the land. Many years ago, during a famine, a magic cow appeared on the hillside and would fill a bucket of milk for anyone who came. One day, an evil witch milked the cow into a sieve. The cow could never fill the sieve, the witch milked her dry, and the cow was never seen again. The witch was turned into stone and the stone circle erected to keep her in. The small farm called Giant's Cave, where Roy Griffiths grew up, lies on the edge of Stapeley Common. Roy's father grazed sheep on the hill and cut bracken as bedding for livestock as, according to Roy, "back then no one grew barley or wheat for straw round here and it cost too much to buy". Roy carried on keeping sheep on Stapeley, though he no longer needed to cut bracken. Sadly, Roy died in 2022 – a great character missed by all who knew him.

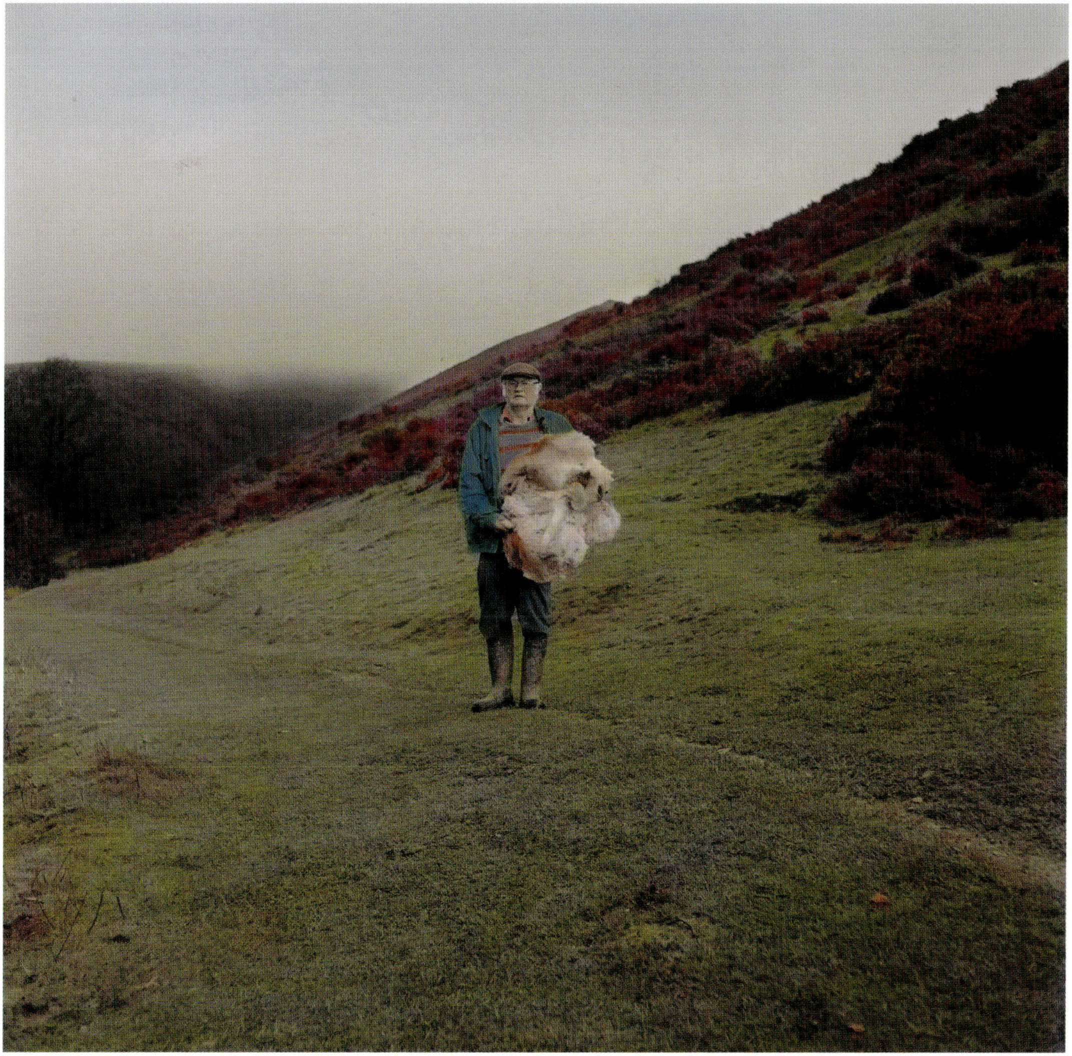

DAVID DAVIES, COMMON LANDS OF MANOR OF STRETTON EN LE DALE AND THE LONG MYND

Rights: grazing sheep, cattle and horses; fern and whinberries (2020) Hand-tinting by Marg Duston. A GRAIN Projects commission

David Davies can graze 600 sheep, 35 ponies and 25 cattle on the upland Long Mynd, but grazes considerably fewer sheep, and no cattle or ponies. A stewardship scheme compensates the commoners for putting fewer animals on the hill to avoid overgrazing. About 16 commoners actively keep sheep; they work together to bring the sheep down in July for shearing and again in November for dipping and tupping. After the "gather" in November, most of the sheep stay down on the farms for the winter until they've lambed. It's one of the few places in England where communal farming traditions survive. The Long Mynd's popularity with walkers, cyclists and other visitors can sometimes conflict with the fact that it's a working landscape for farmers. Excessive footfall can cause environmental depredation, and people's dogs can harm sheep and wildlife. There's a delicate balance to achieve in this important area with respect to people accessing nature and open spaces.

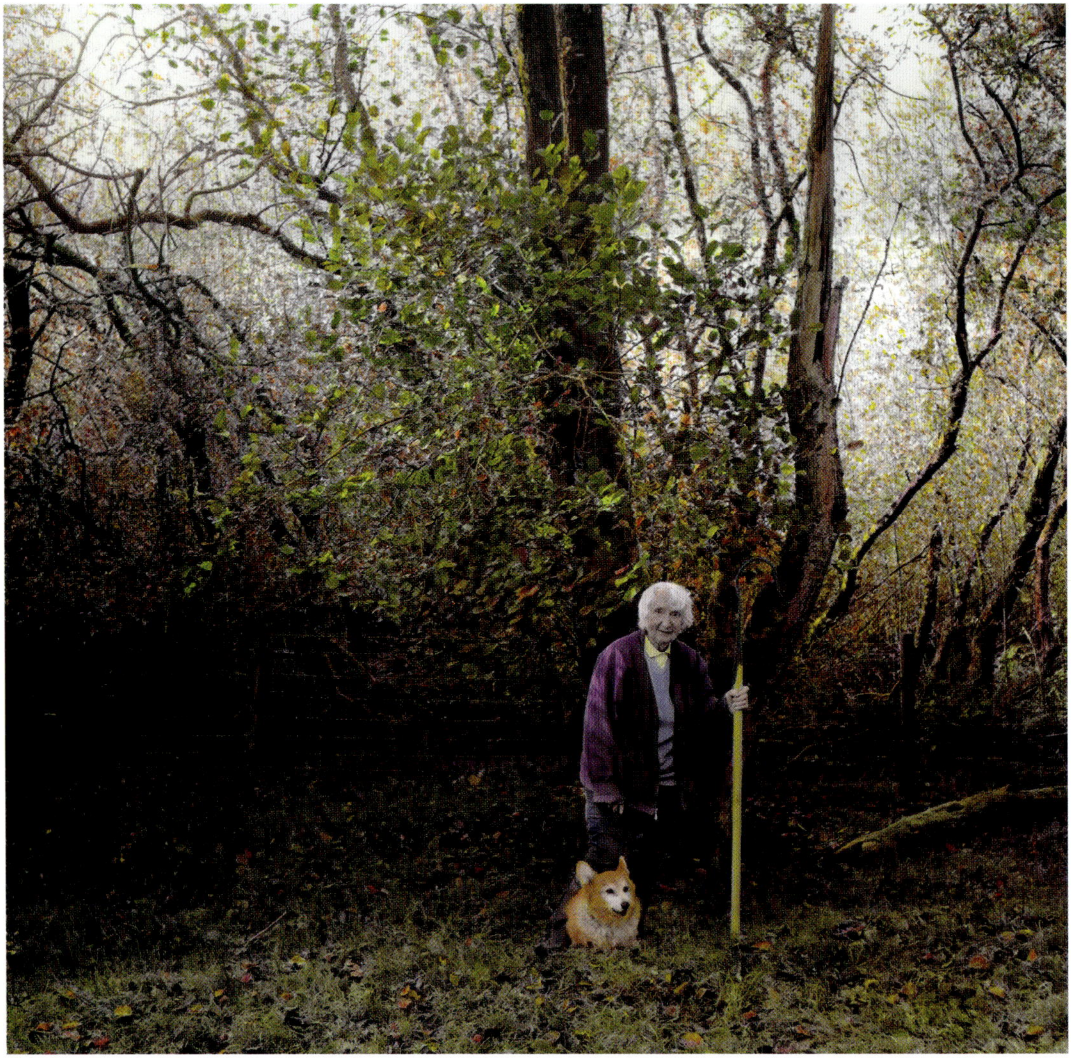

ANNE BEESLEY, BETTWS POOL

Rights: water in gross (2020) Hand-tinting by Marg Duston. A GRAIN Projects commission

Anne Beesley owns the land where Bettws Pool lies. It's an overgrown, mossy green and swampy wood with small pools of dark water. In the past, it was an important watering place for drovers from Wales. Anne has a small flock of sheep and a corgi, traditionally a Welsh livestock dog, tough enough to herd cattle, but low enough to be safe when the cattle kick out. The nearby ancient church is one of the highest and most remote in England. In the graveyard lies an unknown pedlar whose corpse was found one winter on the ridgeway, a victim of thieves or hypothermia. He was buried as "William Cantrell", probably a compound of "can't" and "tell", a 17th-century version of John Doe, which over time became Cantlin. The eponymous Cantlin Stone marks the remote spot where he was found. Throughout the 1980s, New Age travellers held a free festival there. A small rebellion against land enclosure and celebration of alternative ways of life, the festival continued until 1991, when access was blocked.

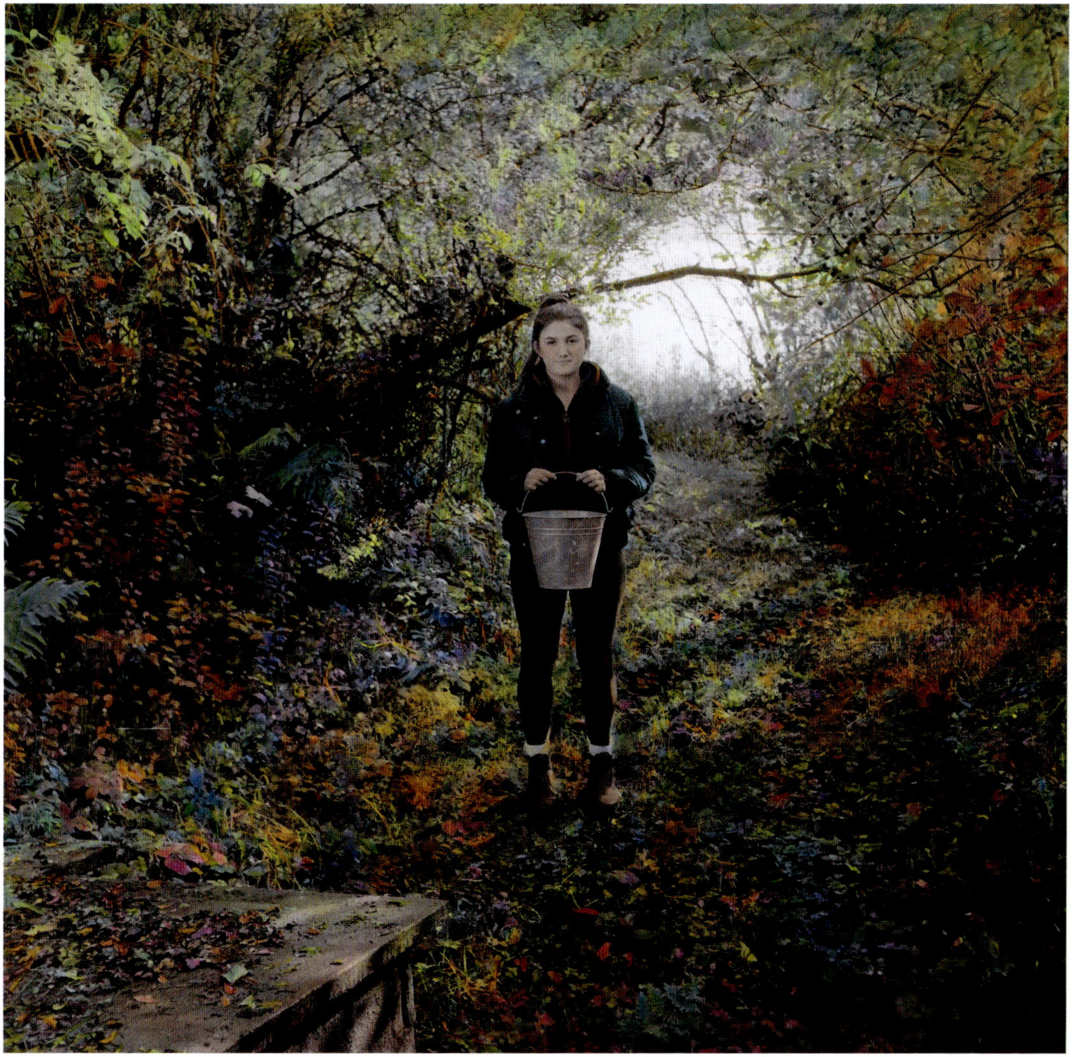

GRACE LAYTON, TRAVELLY WELL

Rights: to water livestock at the well with a right of access to the watering place, in gross (2020)
Hand-tinting by Marg Duston. A GRAIN Projects and Meadow Arts commission

Travelly Well lies near the Kerry Ridgeway, an ancient route over the hills that has been used by travellers for thousands of years. In the days before railways, the ridgeway was used by Welsh drovers to bring animals to markets in England and it could take months to walk their sheep, cattle, pigs and even geese there. They needed to keep the animals healthy to get a good price when they finally sold them, and it was challenging at times to find fodder and water. "Rights in gross" means that anyone can use the right, so any traveller, or drover with their livestock, could draw water from Travelly Well. It must have been a welcome landmark. Grace Layton is studying agriculture. She also works at a farm and plays football for Shrewsbury Town Women's team, but still finds time to keep her own flock of six sheep. However, she doesn't walk them to market – modern disease legislation would forbid that.

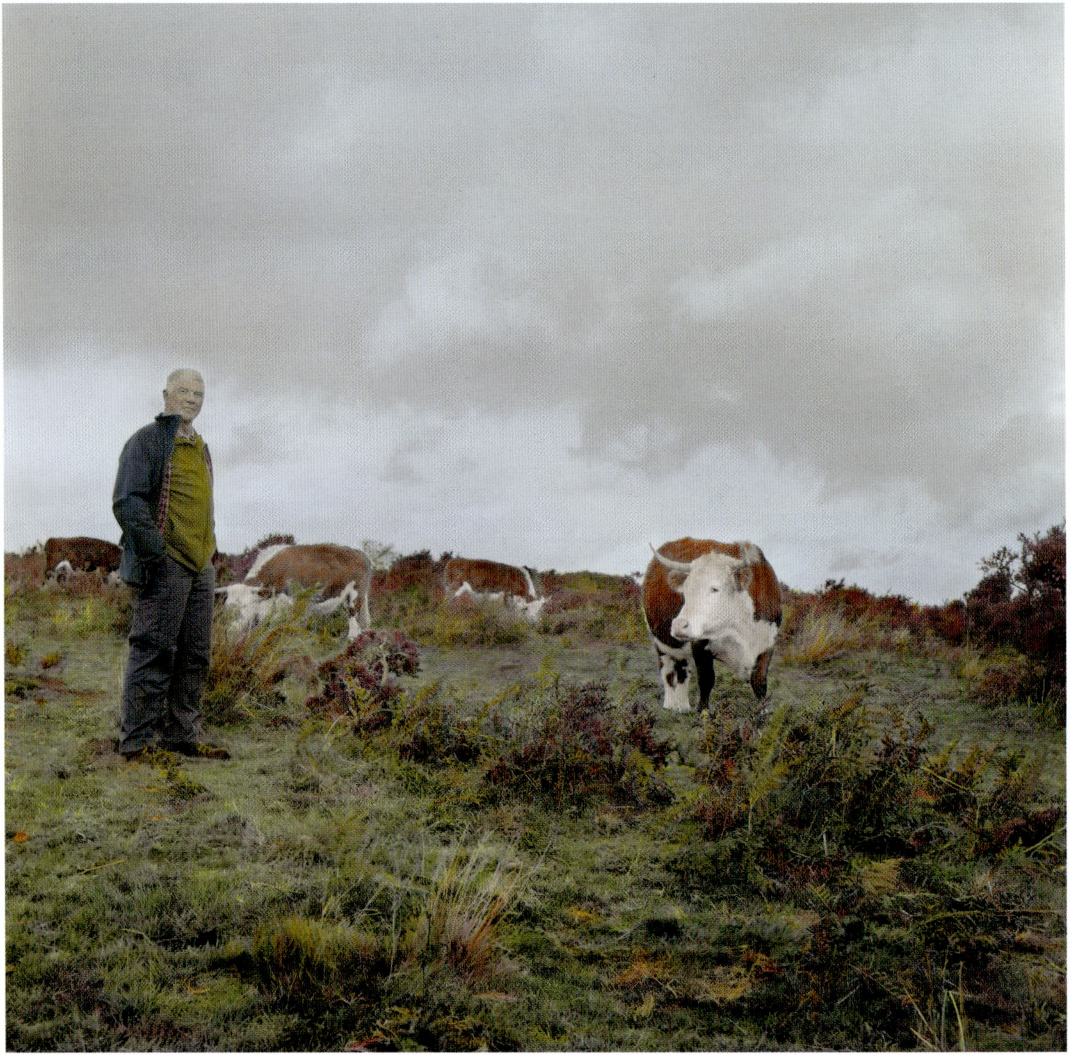

JOHN LYDEN, RHOS FIDDLE

Rights: turbary (2020) Hand-tinting by Marg Duston. A GRAIN Projects commission

John Lyden is the warden for the nature reserve at Rhos Fiddle, where grazing Highland cattle help keep the gorse and bracken under control. Many pools have formed from local villagers exercising their turbary rights, digging peat for fuel. These attract curlew and snipe, as well as rare insects such as the UK's smallest dragonfly, the black darter. From May to July, thousands of yellow mountain pansies bloom across the grassland. Eadric the Wild, the Anglo-Saxon resistance fighter, was said to have found his faerie bride in this remote place. Returning late from a hunting trip, he saw a group of beautiful women dancing in a mysterious house. He fell in love with one and stole her from her sisters, and they were happily married for many years. Then, one day, he forgot the warning she had given him never to criticize her sisters: "On that very day, your happiness will forsake you. I shall be taken away, and you will suffer misfortune, and long for your own death."

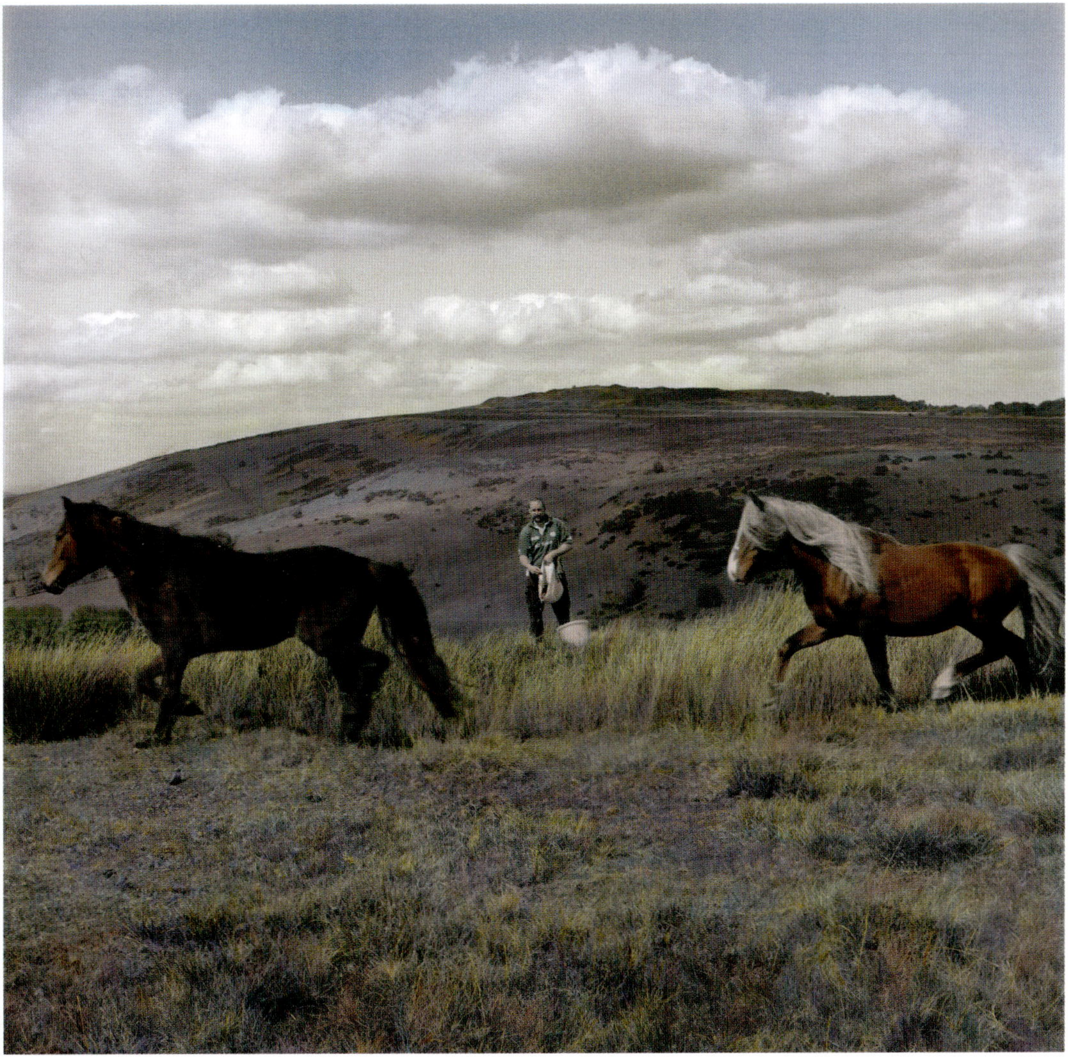

JOHN HEIGHWAY, CLEE LIBERTY

Rights: grazing sheep, cattle and horses (2022) Hand-tinting by Marg Duston. A Meadow Arts Commission

Brown Clee Hill is the highest point in Shropshire. In Norman times it was a royal forest and this led to the unusual right of intercommoning. People who lived in the outlying villages could graze there, but they could only take their animals along special routes, known as "outracks" or "driftways", which can still be seen today. John Heighway's family has been farming here for at least seven generations. Although he admits it's "not the easiest way of keeping sheep", he wouldn't have it any other way. They bring the sheep down in the autumn, although the hardy Welsh Mountain sheep would be quite happy to lamb on the hillside. "It's purely because of the predators – fox, crow and badger," he explains. Nowadays, John is the only commoner to graze horses. John says, "There's no profit, but they're an old line that goes back to my great-grandfather's horses. It's said that ponies 'keep the ground sweet', but mainly it's just lovely to see wild ponies up there."

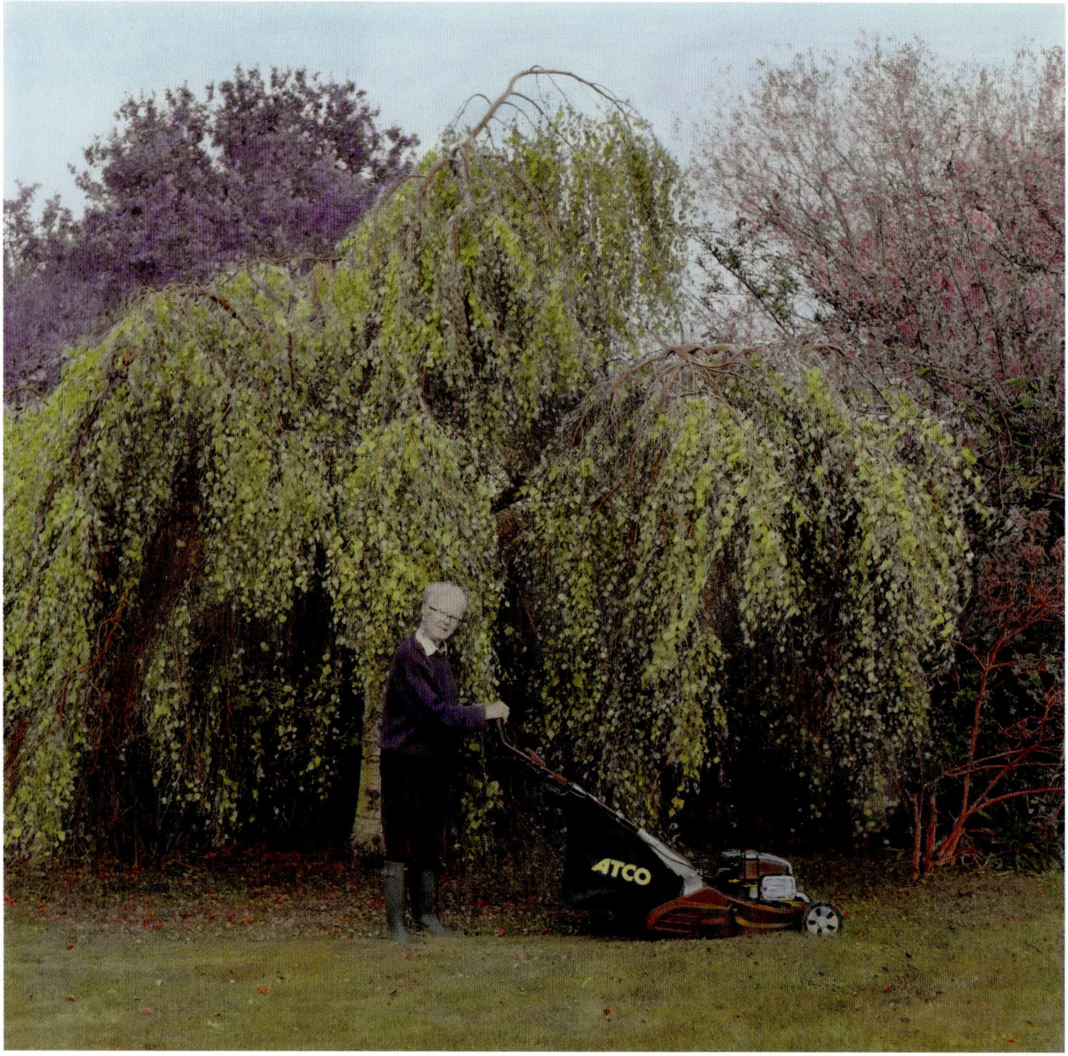

REVEREND PAUL ROBSON, HENLEY COMMON

Rights: grazing sheep and cattle (2020) Hand-tinting by Marg Duston. A GRAIN Projects commission

Common rights are attached to a property, so even if there's no livestock or the house is sold, the rights continue. The Reverend Paul Robson retired to Henley after working in Tanzania and as a prison chaplain in Shropshire. In 1821, one local freeholder accused the commoners of overexploiting the resources. He was robustly challenged by another landowner who wrote, "Your mentioning my cottage tenant turning out more stock than he has a right to do made me smile seeing when I was at his place only a solitary cow and four geese… they can scarcely be said to be an engrossing stock…" The letter demanded "that you will not allow any further encroachment", for "if any single Freeholder has a right to enclose a rood [quarter of an acre] of land without the consent of the rest, he may upon the same ground take in an acre and so on ad infinitum…" The remaining small triangle provides a pocket of wildness in an intensively farmed landscape. The Reverend keeps the part outside his front gate neat and tidy.

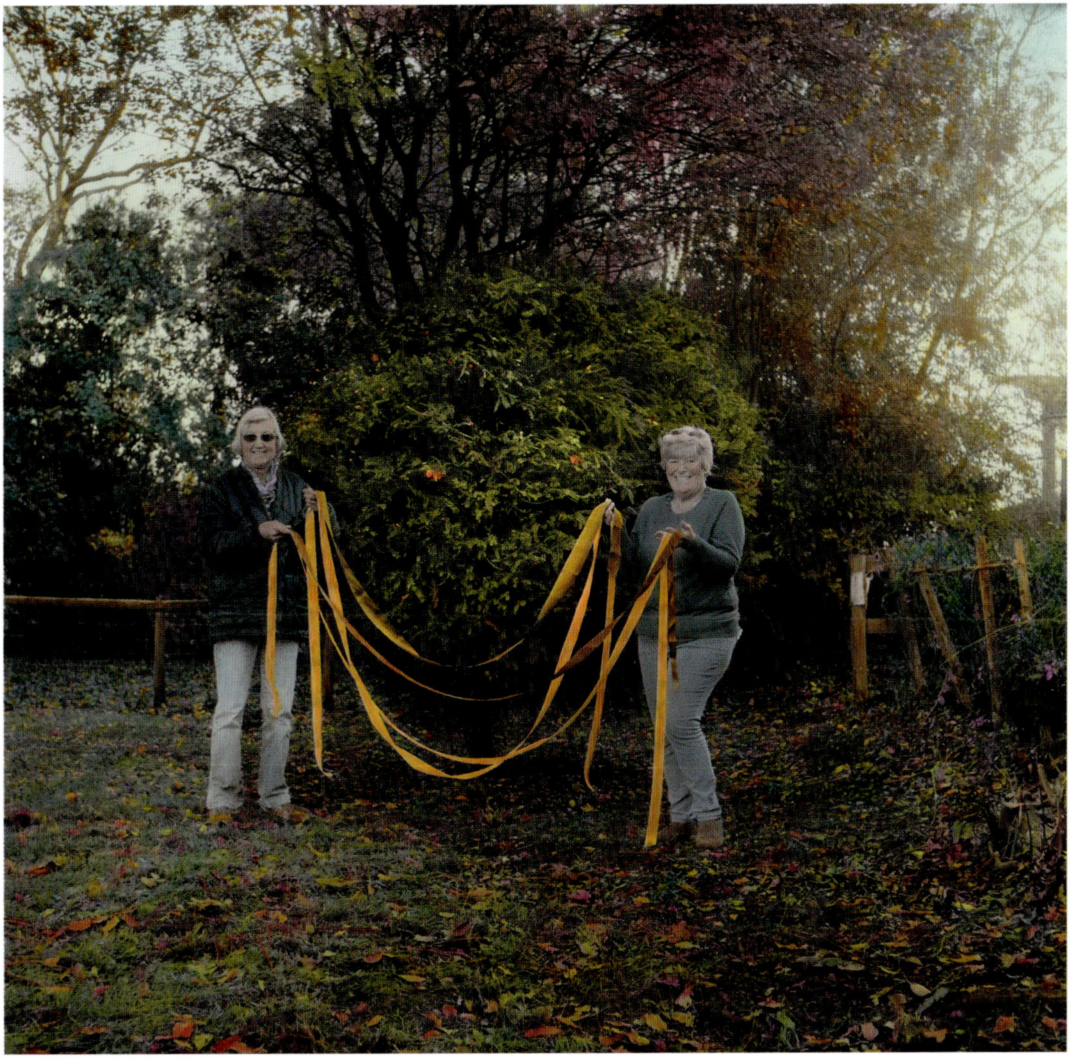

JACKIE BRUNDRETT AND MARILYN HEATH, THE MAYPOLE PIECE, ASHFORD CARBONELL

Rights: village green (2020) Hand-tinting by Marg Duston. A GRAIN Projects and Meadow Arts commission

The Maypole Piece is a patch of land that had become completely overgrown, but Jackie Brundrett and Marilyn Heath led a campaign to restore it to a state worthy of its history. Traditionally, village children could play there for two days a year, though in fact the whole village regularly used it. In 1874, hostilities broke out after the landowner, Mary Ann Hall, closed the only pub in a bid to curb drunkenness. As her workers harvested the field, three villagers threw the hay out of the cart and trampled it. They were accused of causing damage "to hay or grass... to the amount of sixpence". Their lawyer argued that it wasn't a case of damage but of disputed title. Witnesses described how generations of villagers had used the Maypole Piece. Miss Hall lost the case, her subsequent appeal in the Court of Exchequer was dismissed and she had to pay all the costs. The villagers' victory was celebrated in the national press as a stand against "the incursion of landlords' fences and trespass boards".

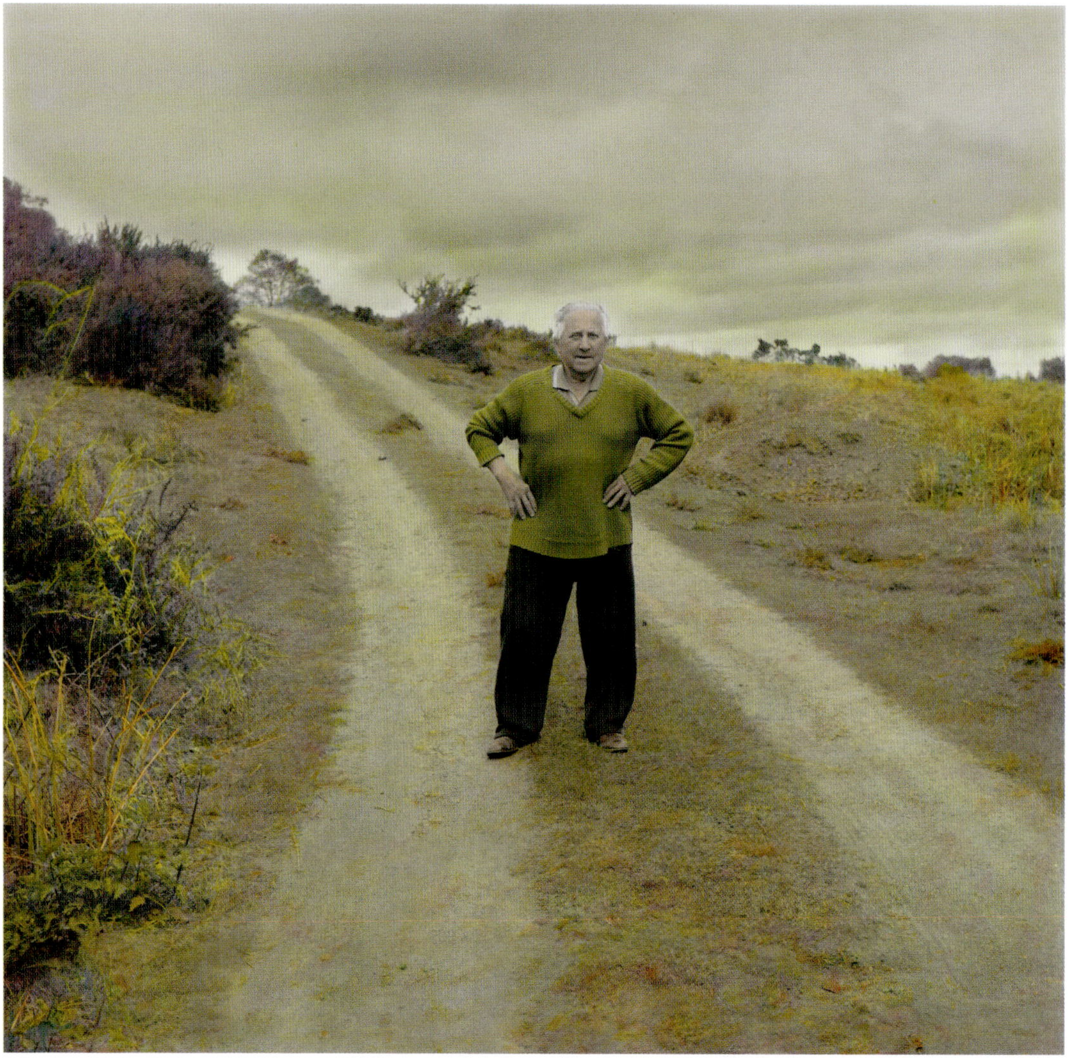

DONALD DOLPHIN, CATHERTON COMMON

Rights: grazing sheep (2022) Hand-tinting by Marg Duston. A Meadow Arts Commission

Catherton Common lies near Titterstone Clee, a prominent hill in south Shropshire. Coal was mined on Catherton from the 13th to the 20th century. The people who came to work there built squatter dwellings and these cottages, with their irregular enclosures, remain today. Donald Dolphin lives in one of them, surrounded by the common, which is now a wildlife haven. Donald grew up here and his parents made ends meet by doing other work in addition to running their smallholding. "They had a haulage business and delivered coal, and transported livestock to market in Shrewsbury, and then came home and milked nine or ten cows. I did a milk round on my pony every day before school," he remembers. When Donald was a child there was no road to the house; everyone had to come over the heath for half a mile or so. He helped his parents build the road he's standing on. He still keeps nine ewes on the common although he stopped lambing a couple of years ago, when he turned 86.

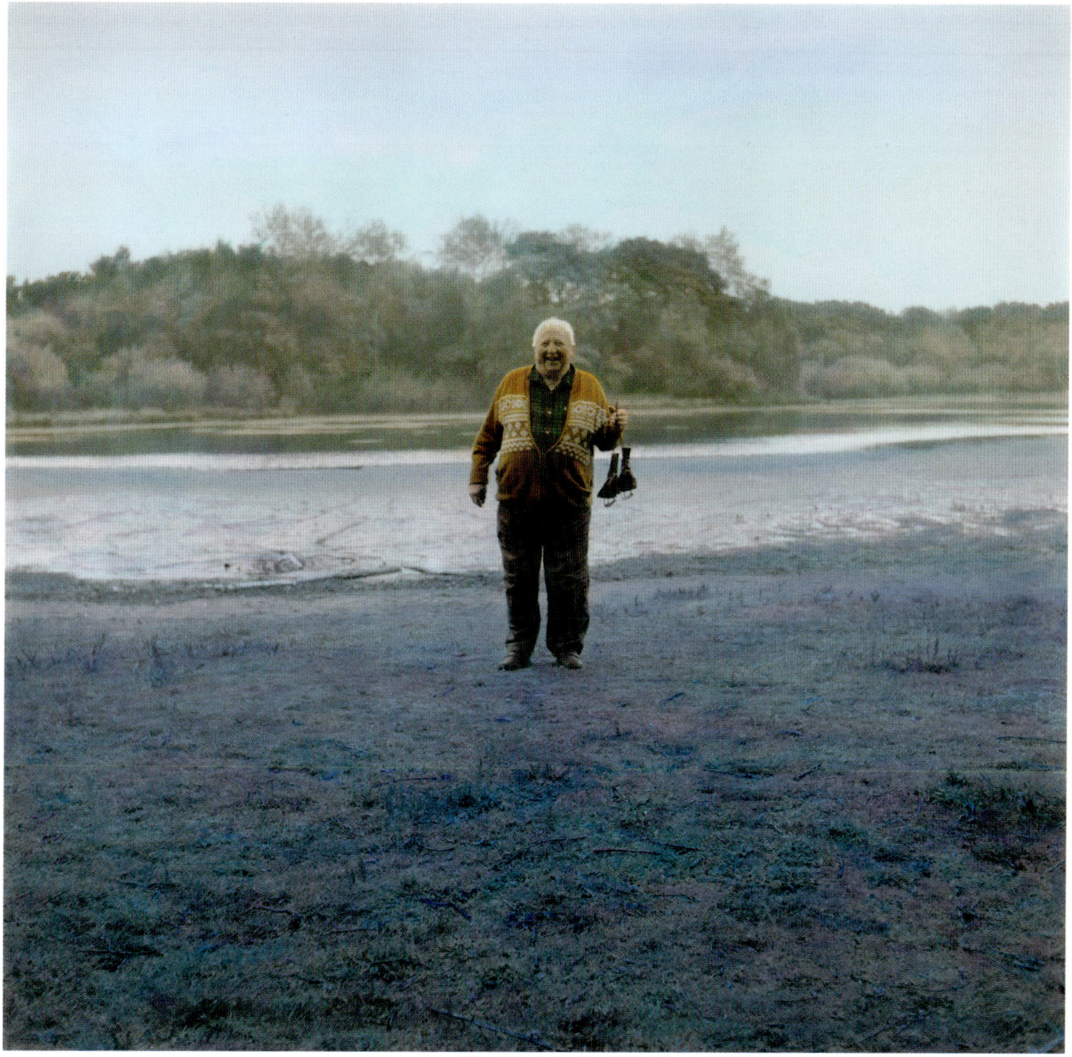

NORMAN WELCH, BROWN MOSS, HOLLINWOOD COMMON AND STEEL HEATH

Rights: grazing cattle, sheep, pigs, horses, goats, geese, fowls; estovers; sand and gravel; air, exercise, games, swimming and skating (2022) Hand-tinting by Marg Duston. A Meadow Arts Commission

Norman Welch's cottage, where he has lived for 54 years, has an impressive list of rights. While the other commoners of Steel Heath can graze a few animals over the 13-acre common, Norman can graze 100 cattle, 200 sheep, 50 pigs and 7 horses, and his other rights include swimming and ice-skating. A previous owner of his cottage, a solicitor, spotted a loophole in the registration process: provided no other commoners objected, those rights would stand, no matter how absurd they were. At least at Brown Moss, there's some water for Norman to skate on. He grew up nearby and remembers cycling back from work and seeing the other lads skating in the beam of a car's headlights. However, Norman wouldn't join them because, after an early start and a hard day milking cows and feeding pigs, he admits, "I wanted to get home to the fireside."

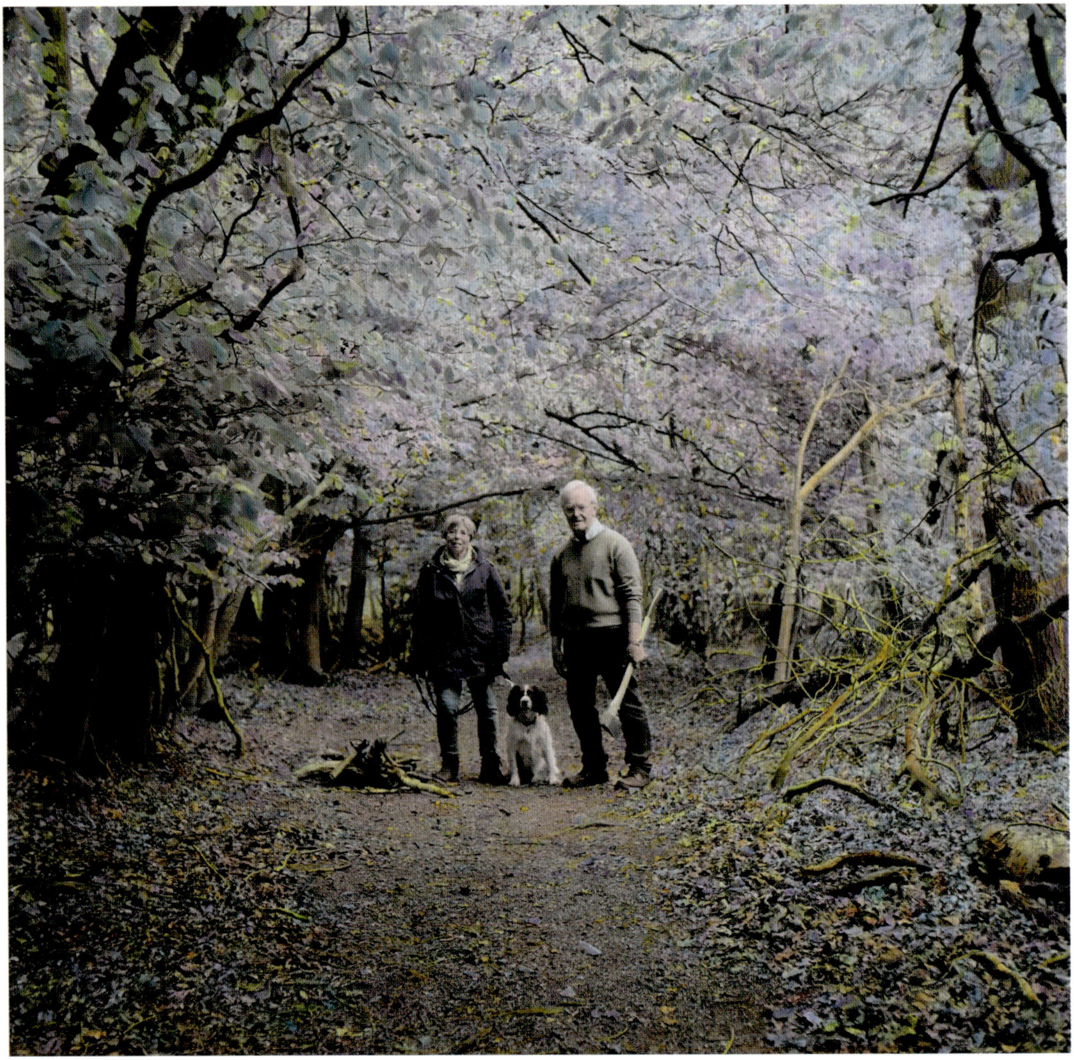

DAVID AND SANDRA WEBB, SILVINGTON COMMON

Rights: grazing four beasts of each sort; estovers; turbary; pannage; piscary (2022) Hand-tinting by Marg Duston. A Meadow Arts commission

David and Sandra Webb's property originally had these rights over two other commons as well. However, the rights were reduced when the Commons Registration took place in the 1970s. The rights on Silvington were uncontested, presumably because it's steep and north-facing and doesn't provide very desirable grazing. The right of pannage allows them to put pigs (if they had any) to feed in the woods; estovers enables them to take wood for fuel and fencing; turbary to dig turf and peat for fuel; and piscary to take fish (which they're unlikely to find there). The Clee Hill area has a wild, bleak beauty, although some people find it a forbidding landscape and may find it easy to believe the local legend about a witch called Becky Smout. Writer Catherine Gaskell describes how: "Some folks say she came to Shropshire on a broomstick… 'Tis a land of witches that Clee Hill, and allus have been a stronghold of the Devil."

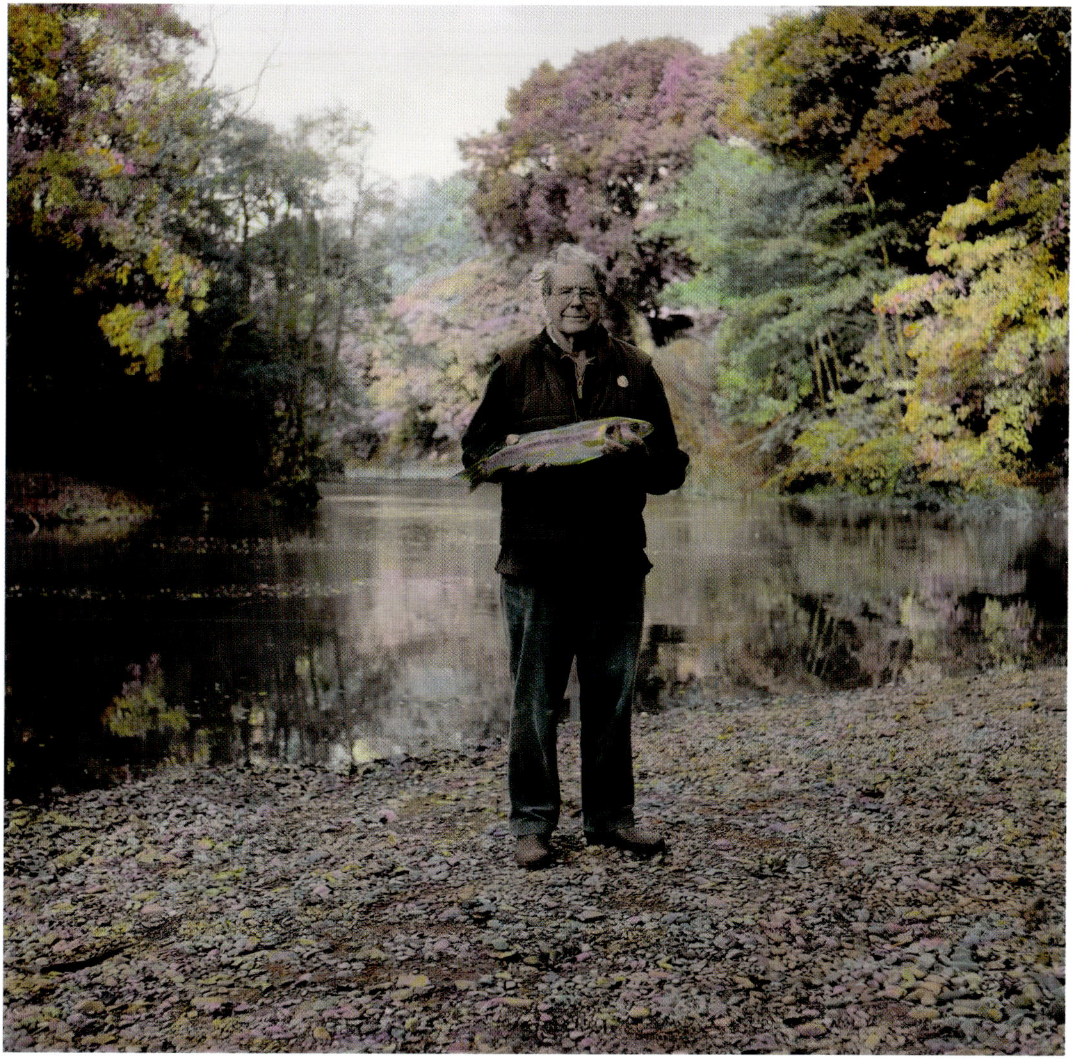

JOHN COBB, TEME'S GREEN, ASHFORD CARBONELL

Rights: piscary; common in soil (gravel) (2020) Hand-tinting by Marg Duston. A GRAIN Projects and Meadow Arts commission

John Cobb's cottage, like many in the village, has fishing rights on the River Teme, and he enjoys "coming home with three grayling for supper". This right enabled villagers to supplement their diet legally. However, people's right to catch wild game such as fish, rabbits, pheasants and deer has been severely restricted ever since the Norman Conquest; punishments for illegal poaching were very heavy. In Ironbridge, on the River Severn in Shropshire, the coal and iron workers often poached rabbits and pheasants from the countryside, and eels and salmon from the river. They used the typical local coracle (a small, round, lightweight boat) to fish and to transport any poached game. If a group went poaching upstream, one of them would carry his coracle on his back. Afterwards, the boatman would paddle the bounty back home and quickly hide everything. The other poachers could walk back to town, confident that if the local police or gamekeepers stopped them, they would find no incriminating evidence.

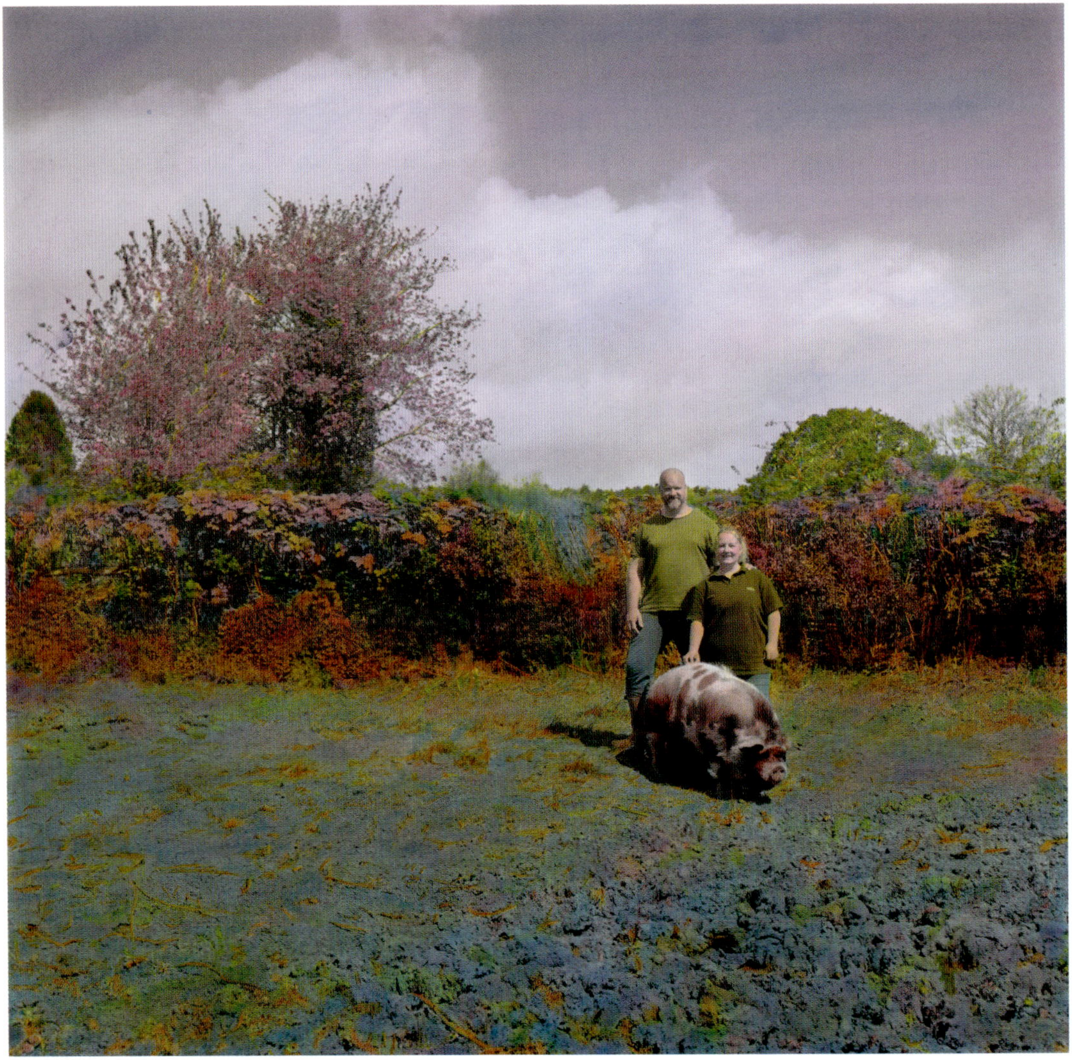

SIMON AND JENNY WILLIAMS, SILVINGTON COMMON

Rights: grazing sheep, cows and pigs; herbage; estovers; turbary; piscary; pannage (2022) Hand-tinting by Marg Duston. A Meadow Arts commission

Simon and Jenny Williams have rights of pannage: the right to release pigs into woodland to eat acorns and beech nuts. However, their pigs remain in the paddock by their cottage the whole year. The New Forest in southern England is one of the only places in England where commoners still exercise this right. About 600 pigs are released in autumn when the acorns fall. Acorns are poisonous to horses and cattle, so the pigs hoover them up and then the horses and cattle can safely graze. Pannage pork is sold as a delicacy by local butchers. In 1616, in Horton Wood in Shropshire, a "riotous assembly" of 50 people objected to their loss of pannage rights when the landowner fenced off part of the wood. However, as the rioters were backed by a neighbouring lord of the manor, it's possible that the real impetus was rival landowners competing for valuable mineral rights. Horton Wood was near Ironbridge, and coal and iron ore were already lucrative resources in the 17th century.

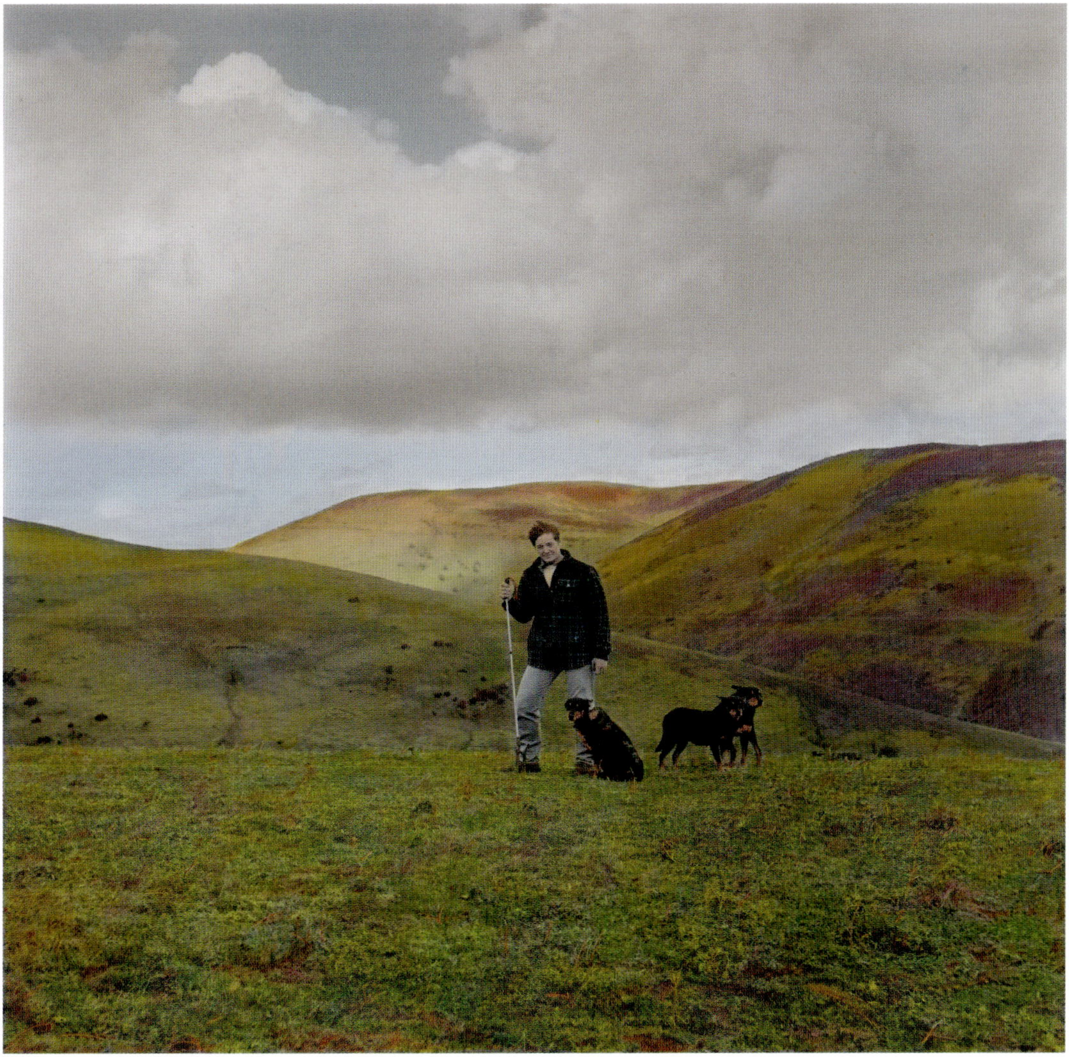

TOM LLOYD, COMMON LANDS OF MANOR OF STRETTON EN LE DALE AND THE LONG MYND

Rights: grazing sheep, cattle and horses (2021) Hand-tinting by Marg Duston. A Meadow Arts Commission

Tom Lloyd's family run about 400 sheep on the Long Mynd, only part of their large flock, and have farmed there for four generations. His dogs are Australian Kelpies, a breed he prefers: "They work differently from the traditional border collies, as they find the point of balance where they have control of the sheep mob – similar to a centre of gravity. Rounding up sheep off the Long Mynd is very different to a sheepdog trial, with three sheep on a flat field." Tom is secretary of the Longmynd Commoners' Association. The commoners have always worked hard to protect their traditional rights. In 1610, they rioted against enclosure. They were charged with "destruction of property, unlawful assembly and conspiracy" when they tore down the new fencing. Even today, there is controversy over plans to enclose a part of the Long Mynd that has traditionally been grazed unfenced, though the modern commoners are unlikely to take such direct action.

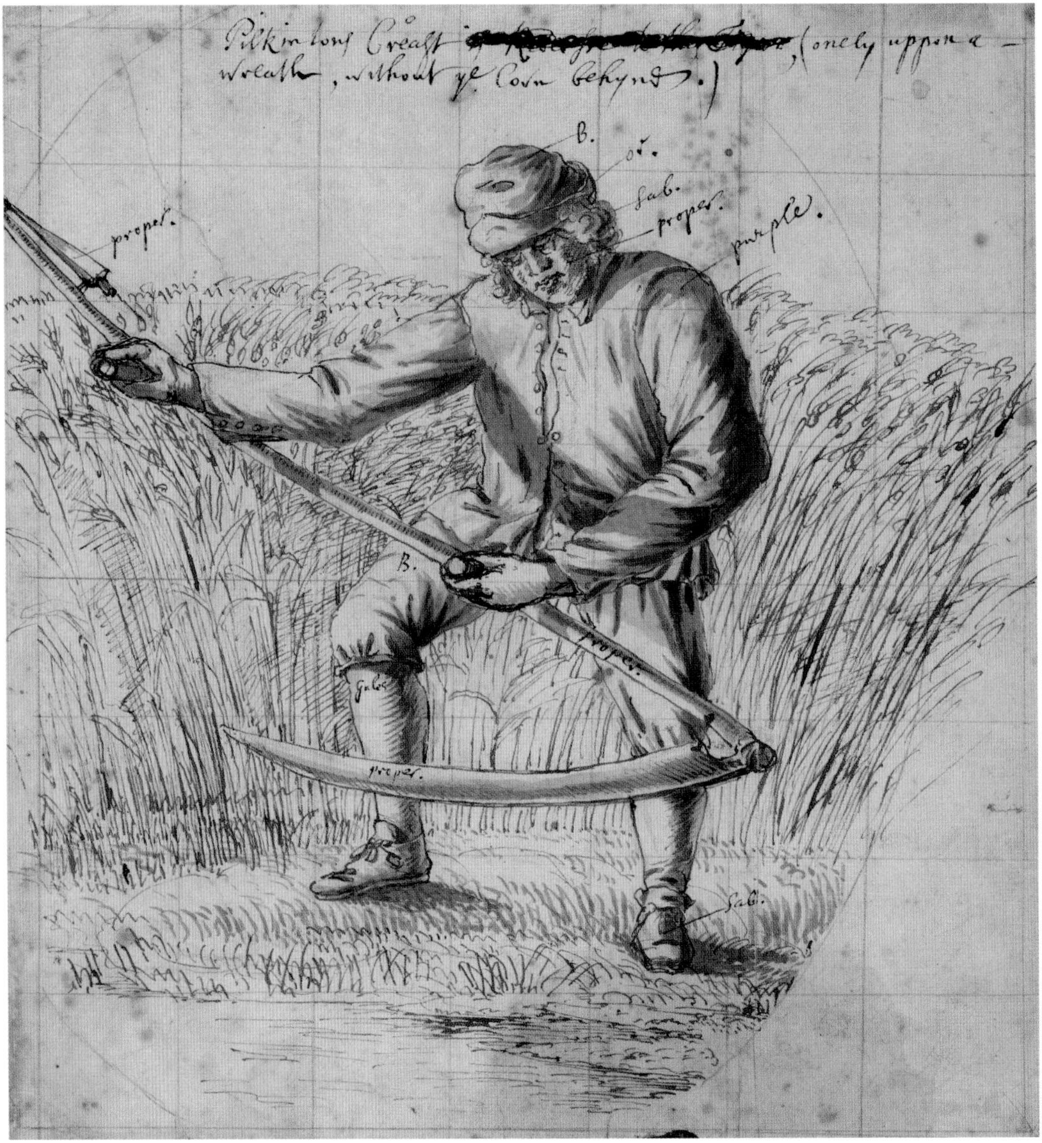

A STUDY FOR THE PILKINGTON CREST: A MOWER WITH A SCYTHE Francis Place (undated, 1647–1728)

ENCLOSED LAND AND VANQUISHED PEASANTS

ANNABEL EDWARDS

England is one of the most densely populated countries in the world, so it's hard to imagine the wild and unpeopled landscape that groups of Mesolithic hunter-gatherers encountered roughly 10,000 years ago after the end of the Ice Age as they made their way from what is now mainland Europe. Although we can only speculate about their attitude to the land that provided their sustenance, we can picture them following the river courses up into the forests around them, travelling down to the coast, hunting animals, fishing and finding seasonal harvests of plants and shellfish.

When archaeologists excavated Star Carr, a marshy site on the edge of a now-vanished post-glacial lake in Yorkshire, in the 1950s, they found antler headdresses with holes to allow them to be fixed in place. While these may have been used to disguise hunters as they crept up on their dinner, a ritual element is suggested by the fact that a number of them had been laid into the edge of the lake, possibly as some kind of offering.[1] Perhaps the early hunter-gatherers saw the land and the natural world as a communal treasury and didn't believe that they owned it – just that they were able to benefit from what it gave and that they belonged to the land as much as it belonged to them.

Certainly, when European colonizers arrived in North America, they found attitudes among the native North American peoples that might give a clue to how early hunter-gatherers understood the land. In 17th-century North America, although tribes or individuals might claim specific territories and fight to defend them and their resources, they didn't recognize the all-excluding ownership of land that the Europeans introduced. Tecumseh, the leader of the Shawnee in the early 19th century, is reported to have remonstrated in his famous speech of 1810, "Sell a country! Why not sell the air, the great sea, as well as the earth? Did not the Great Spirit make them all for the use of his children?"[2] Even if the Indigenous people recognized territories and boundaries, the idea that you could sell the land was an alien concept to them, one that had developed in Europe over centuries and which the colonizers brought with them. In the 15th century, a series of papal bulls were issued authorizing Europeans to claim any land they encountered in the "name of God", unless it was already under the control of another "Christian ruler". The right of Indigenous people to own the land wasn't recognized. The bulls were only formally revoked by the Vatican in 2023, and the influence of legislation based on the definition of "discovery" means that Indigenous people and nations around the world didn't and do not own the full title to their lands, and this is still the law in many countries today.[3, 4]

The history of land enclosure is the story of our relationship with the ground on which we stand and on which we carry out our lives. If you have ever wondered how land comes to be owned by some people and not by others – or even to be owned at all – you are wondering about the long history of enclosure. The concept of property and landownership developed by a lengthy and tortuous route, and different cultures took different approaches, but during the last 300 years, one system has achieved dominance globally: the idea of individual, exclusive ownership, not just of "what can be carried or occupied, but of the immovable, near-eternal earth".[5]

For all the benefits in innovation, development and wealth (for some) that are claimed by the defenders of enclosure and the private property revolution, a huge price has been paid. Until the 1800s, great expanses of the world's surface, including the North American prairies, the South American pampas, the Australian outback and the African savannah, were still communally owned by Indigenous people and the majority of the world's population saw landownership in relation to the needs of different types of peasant agriculture. The change from the more communal relationship with land that had existed in one form or another around the world throughout history "has eliminated ancient civilisations wherever it has encountered them, and displaced entire people from their homelands", according to the historian Andro Linklater.[6]

Enclosure is the process by which people's common rights to use the land's resources are transferred exclusively to a landowner. Historically in Britain, even if land was owned by a king or a feudal lord, people had extensive customary and, in theory, inalienable rights of usage – to graze animals, take wood or peat for fuel, to get water, to hunt wild animals, to grow certain crops at certain times of year. Agriculture in Britain developed differently in the different landscapes and consequently the method of enclosures also often differed. In areas where there was more uncultivated land available (known as "waste"), such as in the more upland counties in the west and north of England, people were able to enclose areas to enlarge their smallholdings and farms without affecting other people's ability to graze their animals, and enclosure seems to have taken place piecemeal, with minimal protest, as long as local commoners' needs could still be met. The term "waste" may be misleading to contemporary ears, as we tend to think of "waste land" as being of no use to anyone, but to a rural peasant it was a rich communal resource that could be heathland, useful for grazing and gathering berries; or gorse as fuel, or bracken (known as fern) for animal bedding; or woodland, where wood for building or fuel could be taken, and pigs released to feed on acorns. However, in areas such as the more densely populated lowland areas of the central and southeast England, enclosure tended to be much more contentious, as the effects of lords or landowners overgrazing the common or fencing off land for their exclusive use were more keenly felt. In the central and eastern Midlands, open-field farming (based on pre-Norman agriculture) was most prevalent and was still widespread in the 19th century. In fact, it is still practised in the village of Laxton in Nottinghamshire. In this system, the fields typically radiated out from a central village and were divided into strips, which were allotted to the villagers. The land was cultivated communally, and animals grazed on the uncultivated common land nearby and on the fields once the crops had been harvested.

As land became enclosed, the relationship of the rural population to the land underwent profound changes, too. The English peasants lost the independence that the commons provided – whether they remained as waged labourers in the countryside, migrated to the rapidly expanding urban industrial centres in search of work or joined the ranks of vagabonds and vagrants. A centuries-long process of enclosure was met by a centuries-long history of resistance and protest, whether that was through tearing down the fences and hedges that physically enclosed the land or rising up in armed revolt. In a way, you can only really understand the society in which we live today if you understand the long and contentious history of enclosure and its crucial role in the arrival of capitalism, the creation of the urban proletariat and the lost connection with nature and the countryside.

In England, the peasant majority lost their common rights and their access to common land in a process that unfolded gradually from the 11th century onward, starting with the forest law introduced by William I, which created the royal hunting forests. In 1235, the Statute of Merton formalized the feudal lords' right to enclose common land – "wastes, woods, and pastures" – as long as their neighbours and tenants had "sufficient" pasture. The process picked up speed in the 16th and 17th centuries, and culminated in the hyper-drive towards enclosure and capitalism brought about by the enclosure acts of the 18th and 19th centuries, when it is estimated 7.25 million acres of open field and common pasture (nearly a quarter of England) were enclosed.[7] Although subject to a complex web of feudal obligations, rental and taxation demands, the medieval peasants were often able to maintain a degree of independence, thanks to the equally complex web of customary rights over the land. They had a profound belief in the sanctity of their traditional rights, and were prepared to take action to protect them.

After the devastating depopulation caused by the Black Death in the middle of the 14th century (the overall mortality rate is estimated to stand as high as 50 per cent, but among the peasants, who lived in closer proximity to both rats and each other, the rate could be up to 70 per cent), much land was left unclaimed and unfarmed as all the potential heirs and tenants had died, and there was also a shortage of rural labour. The remaining peasants benefited from this, gaining access to more land and demanding higher wages. All these changes enabled the peasants to see the possibility of a freer and more equitable society, and a possibility of ending feudal serfdom. Around 1350, legislation was introduced to try to limit their wages to pre-plague levels, and to restrict their freedom to negotiate better wages and to travel in search of more favourable employment.[8] This was a direct assault on their income, when they were already burdened with the tithes and other payments they were obliged to pay to lords and the Church.

Then, in December 1380, a poll tax was levied to fund a military campaign against France. The tax proved very unpopular, but in June 1381 a second attempt was made to collect the money. This was the trigger for the Peasants' Revolt of 1381. The uprising began in southeast England, and the rebels made their way to London, burning taxation and land records and beheading some of the people they held responsible for the injustices, such as tax collectors and bailiffs. In his *Chronicles*, a 14th-century account of the Hundred Years' War, Jean Froissart quotes John Ball, one of the rebellion's leaders, as saying:

> My good friends, matters cannot go on well in England until all things shall be in common; when there shall be neither vassals nor lords; when the lords shall be no more masters than ourselves. How ill they behave to us! For what reason do they thus hold us in bondage? Are we not all descended from the same parents, Adam and Eve? And what can they show, or what reason can they give, why they should be more masters than ourselves?... They have handsome seats and manors, while we must brave the wind and rain in our labours in the field; and it is by our labour they have wherewith to support their pomp. We are called slaves, and if we do not perform our service we are beaten.[9]

In fact, Froissart included this example from one of John Ball's sermons to demonstrate how absurd and wicked Ball's ideas of justice and equality were – ironically thereby creating a clarion call that resounds through the centuries. Although enclosure was only a side issue in the Peasants' Revolt, it was certainly one of the injustices they were rebelling against. The actions of the peasants returning to St Albans demonstrate this, when a large mob destroyed enclosures erected in the woods by the Abbot of St Albans.[10] The revolt was unsuccessful, and initially did little to change the lot of the peasant, as Richard II's victorious words suggest:

> You wretched men, detestable on land and sea: you who seek equality with lords are not worthy to live... so give this message to your colleagues from the king. Rustics you were and rustics you are still; you will remain in bondage, not as before but incomparably harsher. For as long as we live and, by God's grace, rule over the realm, we will strive... to suppress you so that the rigour of your servitude will be an example to posterity.[11]

Despite Richard's threats, serfdom did gradually disappear during the following century and conditions improved. The Peasants' Revolt may have been quelled, but the seriousness of the threat they had posed and the violence they had directed at figures of authority lingered in the minds of the lords when the peasants negotiated with them. As the historian Christopher Dyer explains, "The revolts established a new balance, in which the authorities adjusted to the reality that the peasants, artisans and wage

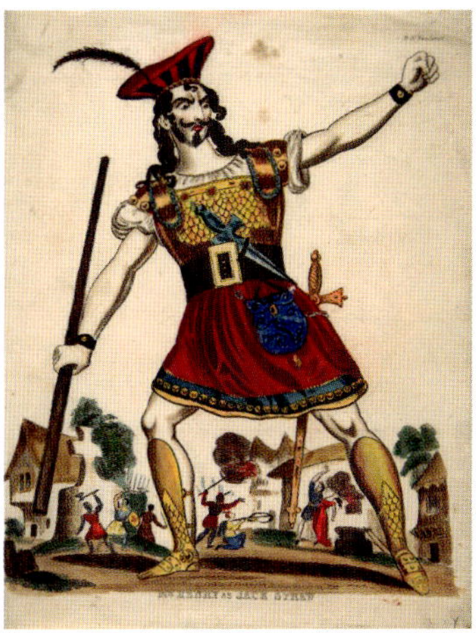

MR. HENRY AS JACK STRAW
by Anon, 1848

earners had improved their bargaining power."[12]

The Reformation under Henry VIII in the 16th century paved the way for the advance of capitalism, including the private ownership of land and other formerly communal assets. Despite their frequent corruption, the monasteries and their farms often acted as the social and economic heart of the local community. During the Dissolution of the Monasteries between 1536 and 1541, in which Henry VIII confiscated monastic property and sold it off to families who were sympathetic to his break from Rome, the land was snapped up by wealthy landowners and merchants. They often turned out to be absentee landlords who saw their new domains as a source of financial profit before all else, providing what the economic history Joan Thirsk has described as "a miserable substitute for the monastic brotherhood".[13]

In the 15th and 16th centuries, the sale of wool became so profitable that landowners and wealthy farmers started looking for places to graze their increasing numbers of sheep. To that end, they began to enclose not only common land, but also enclose arable land and convert it to pasture, thereby depriving the local people of their means of subsistence. In response, the government enacted several laws *against* enclosure because villages were becoming depopulated and there was a surge in numbers of vagrants. As Thomas More famously put it in his book *Utopia*, published in 1516, "Your sheep, that were wont to be so meek and tame and so small eaters, now, as I hear say, be become so great devourers and so wild that they eat up and swallow down the very men themselves. They consume, destroy, and devour whole fields, houses, and cities."[14]

Other changes brought by the lengthy process of changing from Catholicism to Protestantism also affected the rural peasant population profoundly. In a secular age it is hard to imagine the psychological effect of being expected to change your entire belief system and the rise in witch trials in the 16th and 17th centuries across northern Europe was a symptom of the spiritual uncertainty engendered by the Reformation.[15] Anxiety about heresy made it easy to identify an "enemy within". The changes also affected the peasants' working life as the Roman Catholic calendar contained many saints' days, which were a chance for a holiday. The switch to Protestantism meant radically fewer saints' days and fewer days off work. Holidays began to be seen by the ruling classes as an encouragement to licentious behaviour and a waste of good working hours. In 1536, rural uprisings such as the Lincolnshire Rebellion and the Pilgrimage of Grace protested at the changes to their fundamental belief system and way of life. Nevertheless, this change became progressively more complete until, by the 18th and 19th centuries, workers were expected to work every day (with time off for church on Sunday).

Unlike the rebellions earlier in the 16th century, enclosure of pasture and loss of common rights were major causes of Kett's Rebellion, which began in Norfolk in 1549. From their camp at Mousehold Heath outside Norwich, the rebels issued demands including, "no lord of no manor shall common upon the Commons... We pray that all bond men may be made free for God made all free with his precious blood shedding. We pray that Rivers may be free and common to all men for fishing and passage."[16]

Kett's Rebellion was one of several widespread protests that took place across England and Wales at the time, but it was the only one that turned into an armed insurrection, with a rebel army of about 16,000 men. There were so many encampments of protestors throughout the country that the summer of 1549 became known as the "Commotion Time" or the "Camping Time". Kett and his men were finally defeated when 1,400 mercenaries arrived to bolster the king's troops. In the final battle, about 3,000 rebels were killed and after their defeat up to 300 of the rebels were executed, including the leader, Robert Kett.[17]

After this, there was a great sense of fear among the governing classes that there might be another rebellion, so any hint of sedition was brutally suppressed. Three successive poor harvests in the 1590s resulted in near-starvation among the poor, exacerbated by corn hoarding by merchants in the hope of increased profits. There were fears "of suche as Kettes campe was, and ther men should fytt [fight] for corne".[18] Poor harvests and profiteering continued and, in 1607, hunger drove a series of rebellions known as the Midland Revolt or Rising. It began around the time of the May Day festivities, which were an occasion when the rural population gathered together, dissenting opinions could be shared and plans communicated. In various villages in Northamptonshire, Leicestershire and Warwickshire, large groups of people began to tear down the fences and hedges and fill in the ditches around the hated enclosures; in some cases, the riots were estimated to involve 3,000 to 5,000 people. The protestors were referred to as "diggers" and also "levellers" as a result of their actions in destroying the fences, hedges and banks of the enclosures.

They were led by a tinker called John Reynolds, who went by the name of Captain Pouch because he carried a small leather bag which he claimed contained "sufficient matter to defend them against all comers". When he was captured, it apparently contained nothing but a mouldy bit of cheese. He instructed his followers "not to swear, not to offer violence to any person". However, this show of restraint didn't protect them from the bloody ending of the uprising, when armed militiamen charged a large crowd who had refused to disperse. At first the crowd stood firm and fought back, but at the second charge they tried to retreat and about 50 of them were killed and many more injured. The leaders were executed, and parts of their dismembered corpses were displayed in towns throughout the area as a warning.[19]

In 1625, Charles I declared war on Spain. Parliament refused to fund the war sufficiently, leading to a conflict between king and Parliament that ultimately paved the way for the English Civil War. One of the ways in which Charles tried to raise money was by selling off the remaining royal forests in a legal process known as "disafforestation", which resulted in widespread enclosure and loss of common rights. The purchasers were encouraged to fell the timber and clear the land for farming. The war was not the only expense Charles had to pay: when he sold Braydon Forest to his jeweller for £21,000, £10,000 of that went toward writing off his jewellery bill (the equivalent of £2,267,000 now, a fair amount of bling by anyone's standards). There were a series of riots against disafforestation in Wiltshire, Dorset and the Forest of Dean in Gloucestershire, known as the Western Rising (1626–32). Even though the protests were largely separate actions, not part of a larger, organized insurrection, the prosecuting authorities were keen to portray them as such in order to justify harsher punishments. Large groups of local inhabitants destroyed enclosing fences; sometimes as many as a thousand people gathered. According to the official records, the various riotous assemblies could consist of anything from "a certain number of ignorant women" to hundreds of men with drums and musical instruments and "armed with gunnes, pykes, halberds and other weapons".[20,21] One tactic the various riots often shared was the use of the traditional Lady Skimmington figure, where a man was dressed as a woman. This was a means of disguise for the leaders, but also a symbolic recognition that customary rules had been breached with the loss of traditional rights in the forests.[22]

In *The World Turned Upside Down*, Christopher Hill describes a period roughly between 1645 to 1653 during the English Civil War when the old hierarchies, beliefs and values were suddenly questioned and re-evaluated. Radical ideas swirled round the country, and for a heady period of time "literally anything seemed possible" – whether widening democracy in political and legal institutions, ending the stranglehold that the established Church had on society or even introducing communal property ownership. In the end, Cromwell and his followers ensured that the old order was not overturned as completely as it might have been, and the "sacred rights

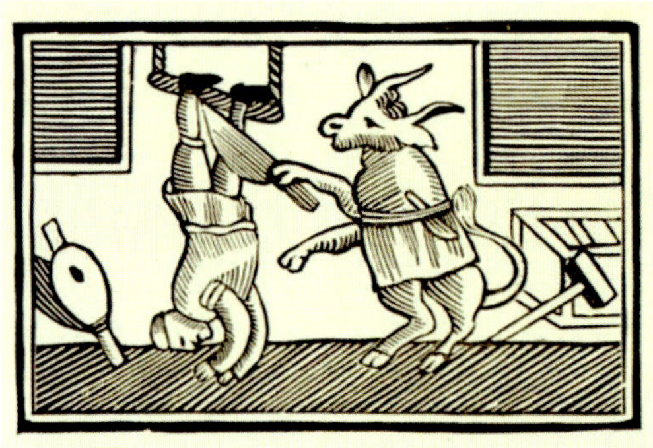

OX TURNED BUTCHER woodcut from *Chapbooks of the Eighteenth Century*, compiled by John Ashton (1882)

of property" were established and political power was given to the propertied, described by Hill as "the triumph of the ideology of the men of property – the protestant ethic".[23]

It was during this period that the political movement that came to be known as the Levellers appeared, named after the levellers of the hedges and fences in the rising of 1607. They hoped to secure the rights, freedom and wellbeing of every man, woman and child, and their demands included universal male suffrage (with some exceptions), greater religious tolerance and the removal of the recent enclosures of fens and other commons.[24] However, most Levellers stopped short of demanding the end of private property, unlike Gerrard Winstanley and the Diggers who, initially calling themselves the True Levellers, declared that no one had the right to rule over other people, and that the earth "with all her Fruits of Corn, Cattle, and such like, was made to be a common Store-house of Livelihood to all Mankinde".[25]

Winstanley is an extraordinary figure. When his cloth business collapsed amidst the upheavals of the Civil War, he was forced to move to Cobham in the Surrey countryside and work as a farmer. There he revealed himself to be a radical thinker and gifted writer, developing his philosophy of universal equality and Christian communism. As he believed that "action is the life of all, and if thou dost not act, thou dost nothing", he and a small group occupied some common land on nearby St George's Hill in April 1649 and started to cultivate the ground and sow root crops.[26] Winstanley believed that if "us that are called common people... manure and work upon the common lands", there would be enough food for everyone and they would "lay the Foundation of making the Earth a Common Treasury for All".[27,28] Their efforts inspired several other Digger colonies, and Winstanley's ideas spread, but by the end of 1650 the commune had been driven off the hill after violent attacks by local people and soldiers. Although Winstanley's vision of communally digging up and cultivating all the "waste" in England didn't succeed (which was probably just as well – however worthy this egalitarian and utopian goal, it would have been environmentally disastrous, nature conservation not being a 17th-century priority), the power of his writings and his ideas has remained inspirational to the current day.[28,29]

A less positive and idealistic result of the upheavals of the 17th century was the increase in witch trials, which peaked during the time of the Civil War. The febrile atmosphere enabled all kinds of suspicions and paranoia to ferment, and Silvia Federici has argued that the persecution of women as witches was a direct result of enclosure and the development of capitalism, as it destroyed social cohesion, particularly between men and women, and paved the way for the subjugation of women as machines for the production of the labour force: "Just as the Enclosures expropriated the peasantry from the communal land, so the witch hunt expropriated women from their bodies."[30] Certainly, from the maelstrom of the mid-16th century capitalism emerged triumphant.

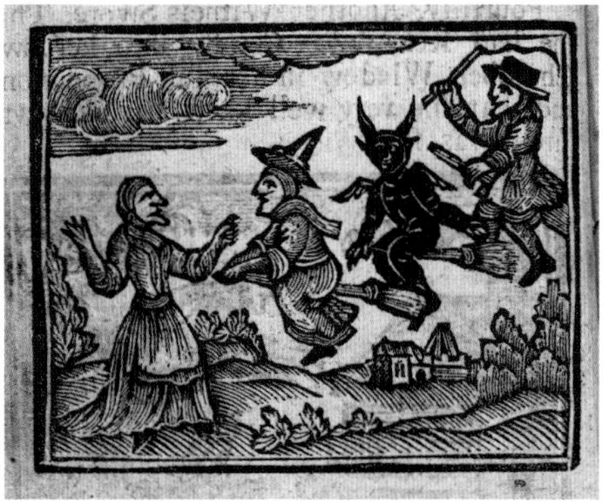

THE HISTORY OF WITCHES AND WIZARDS (1720)

The execution of Charles I in 1649 didn't bring an end to the disafforestation he had overseen as Parliament continued the policy. In 1657, Parliament enclosed a third of the Forest of Dean to preserve timber stocks. At that time, there were estimated to be about 400 cottages and cabins in the woods, whose inhabitants made a living from the woodland and pastures. Although the terms of the enclosure were quite generous with regard to rights in the remaining unenclosed area of the forest, there were widespread riots where the new fences were torn down and cattle were driven in. The local people not only objected to the enclosure, but feared that it was only the beginning of the rest of the forest being divided up and enclosed. Rural riots against enclosure during this time are less to be seen as partisan to Royalist or Parliamentarian causes, but rather as protecting the needs and rights of the poor and disenfranchised against the propertied and powerful of either side.[31]

After the restoration of the monarchy in 1660, Charles II didn't just carry on pursuing enclosure as a means of revenue; in the case of the townspeople of Coventry, he used it as a punishment for their enthusiastic support for the Parliamentary side during the Civil War. In 1661, Charles granted the lease of the manor of Cheylesmore to the south of the town to the Royalist Robert Townshend, on condition he stopped the townspeople's commoning rights in Cheylesmore Park. The people of Coventry had a proud history of defending their commoning rights with vigour. In 1374, a large group of "disturbers of the peace" accompanied by musicians had marched to the house of the mayor and forced him to join them in breaking down enclosures. In 1421, they rioted and in 1469, an armed crowd assembled and attacked the hedges and dykes when a local common was enclosed. Afterwards they marched back to the town piping and singing. They were especially incensed by this particular enclosure, because the land had previously been used for pastimes such as "shooting, running, dancing, bowling alleys, and other sports".[32] Another enclosure riot in 1525 saw 40 people imprisoned and, in 1628, "the poor people" broke open an enclosure that had customarily been used for holding pageants. Consequently, the people of Coventry didn't acquiesce in this instance either and they constantly rioted and attacked the enclosures and eventually, in 1666, Townshend had to grant them pasturage on some other land to keep them quiet. After the Revolution of 1688 when the

Stuarts lost the throne, the Townshend family lost their royal protection and the people of Coventry wasted no time in taking advantage of this. In January 1689, "a great rabble of dissolute people" broke down their fences and drove them from their home.[33]

Another community who vehemently opposed enclosure were the inhabitants of the fens in East Anglia. There had been plans to drain and enclose the wetlands for centuries. In 1630, Charles I had started a programme to drain the fens and the resistance was immediate and violent, as the fenmen, known as the Fen Tigers, smashed dykes and dams and attacked the workmen. The people of the fens were regarded as almost a separate race, described in one publication of 1635 as "halfe fish".[34] They made a living from fishing, wildfowling and pasturing livestock on the fertile water meadows, and had their own very distinctive culture. They have been described as representing the last surviving remnant of hunter-gatherers in England.[35] An anti-drainage pamphlet issued in 1646 made the accusation that the would-be enclosers "have alwaies vilified the fens, and have misinformed many Parliament men, that all the fens is a meer quagmire... and of little or no value: but those that live in the fens, and are neighbours to it, know the contrary."[36] The pamphlet then lists all the benefits the fens provide, including grazing and fodder for horses, cattle and sheep, and "osier, reed, and sedge", which had many uses. It points out "we have many thousand cottagers, which live on our fens, which otherwise must go a begging".[37]

Although Cromwell's family owned land in the fens and he initially opposed the draining, when he was in power he saw the financial advantages, and the project was continued. There were various schemes to drain the fens throughout the 17th and 18th centuries, always accompanied by violent protest and even several murders of supporters of the drainage.

Despite the brief glimmer of hope for a more communal future, with the interests of private property ownership having won the day in the upheavals of the Civil War, the process of "primitive accumulation" – whereby privatized capital is created by the enclosure of previously communal assets and by the divorcing of the producer from the means of production – continued to gather pace. In *The Invention of Capitalism*, Michael Perelman compares primitive accumulation to a pair of scissors cutting through traditional ways of life. One blade slices away people's ability to provide for themselves and the second blade, consisting of newly imposed social and economic measures, cuts people off from any chance of finding a way of surviving outside the system of wage labour.[38] When common assets were enclosed, people had fewer alternatives to wage labour as a means of surviving, but numerous commentators have observed that even then most people in Britain didn't enthusiastically engage in the new economic reality if they could help it.

As capitalism developed in the 18th and 19th centuries, parliamentary enclosure legislation enabled the would-be encloser to petition Parliament to enclose whichever bit of common land took their fancy. It was very hard for the poor commoners to understand the legal procedure or find the time or money to journey to London and oppose a bill. It wasn't until 1774 that a landowner who wanted to enclose his neighbours' land was even obliged to inform them that he was petitioning Parliament to do so.[39] The odds were stacked against the poor, such as the smallholder who was observed "in great distress" in the House of Commons, having come to London on foot because he couldn't afford to travel any other way or afford legal representation, only to learn that he would lose everything because of one clause in a bill.[40]

Although there were politicians who were concerned about the disastrous effects of the passage of the enclosure bills on the rural poor, the majority exhibited a callous disregard, with the biased system often crossing the line into corruption. One example is the attempt to enclose Sedgemoor in Somerset by Lord Bolingbroke (known as "Bully") to pay off his gambling debts: "Bully has a scheme of enclosure, which, I am told, if it succeeds will free him of all his difficulties."[41] In this case, the attempted enclosure failed because "Bully" had also fraudulently submitted one version of the bill to the people affected in Somerset and another one to Parliament – with 20 different clauses. Even the very prejudiced land-owning politicians were unable to pass the bill in those circumstances.[42]

The injustices didn't end with the passing of the enclosure bills, because often the distribution of the land was made by commissioners, who were either the majority landowners or in their pay, or expecting to receive other benefits from them. In many cases, even if the commoners were granted some small parcel of land to enclose for themselves, they not only had to pay for their own fencing but contribute to the fencing of the rest of the common. In one instance, the commoners who were awarded fractions of an acre were forced to pay for the fencing of the landowner who had been awarded 500 acres. This, and the fact that commoners were often given plots that were inconveniently far from their dwellings and too small to graze an animal on, meant that it was no surprise that they were often forced to sell up to the enclosing landowner.[43]

The brutal large-scale enclosures that took place in areas such as the east Midlands were portrayed powerfully in the poetry of John Clare. In poems such as "To a Fallen Elm" and "Remembrances", he laments the destruction caused:

> Inclosure like a buonaparte let not a thing remain
> It levelled every bush and tree and levelled every hill
> And hung the moles for traitors – though the brook is running still
> It runs a naked stream cold and chill[44]

Clare spent his youth wandering the countryside around Helpston, where he was born, observing the natural world in radiant detail. Local agriculture was still based on the open-field farming system described earlier, where the fields radiated outward like a wheel around the village, and there was extensive common heathland nearby. But then, as Jonathan Bate describes in his biography of Clare, "Fences, gates and No Trespassing signs went up. Trees came down. Streams were stopped in their course so that the line of ditches could be made straight."[45] A sense of freedom, so crucial to Clare's wellbeing, was destroyed by the harsh linear nature of enclosure's rectangular fields:

> Fence now meets fence in owners little bounds
> Of field and meadow large as garden grounds
> In little parcels little minds to please
> With men and flocks imprisoned ill at ease[46]

The effects of enclosure on the way of life with which Clare was familiar were numerous. He had liked to spend time with the Gypsies, who camped on the common and had nowhere to go once it was enclosed. A family he knew well were evicted from their small farm by their landlord with no compensation. The nearby spring, where all the youth of Helpston would traditionally gather on Whit Sunday to drink the water as a good luck charm, was made private property and the custom abolished. This destruction of the world he loved had a profound effect on Clare, who spent many of his adult years suffering from mental illness and was committed to an asylum.[47]

As such large areas were changed to pasture for cattle and sheep, and later for intensive arable farming, the previously self-sufficient smallholders and cottagers were forced to rely on earning low and uncertain wages as farm labourers, and may well have ended up in the poor house or had to move to the urban areas to find work in the generally terrible labour conditions of the new factories of the Industrial Revolution.

The independence and protection from starvation that the right to graze a few animals gave people was seen as a threat by the governing classes – and by the 18th and 19th centuries, it was seen as a moral issue, giving the rural peasant a chance to be "idle", i.e. not totally dependent on wages. John Billingsley, the writer of the "Uselessness of Commons to the Poor", described the "moral effects of an injurious tendency" that the cottager risked by his "reliance on the imaginary benefits of stocking a common... In sauntering after his cattle, he acquires a habit of indolence."[48]

Another 18th-century commentator noted that the commons were detrimental to the poor, "by being made a plea for their idleness; for some few excepted, if you offer them

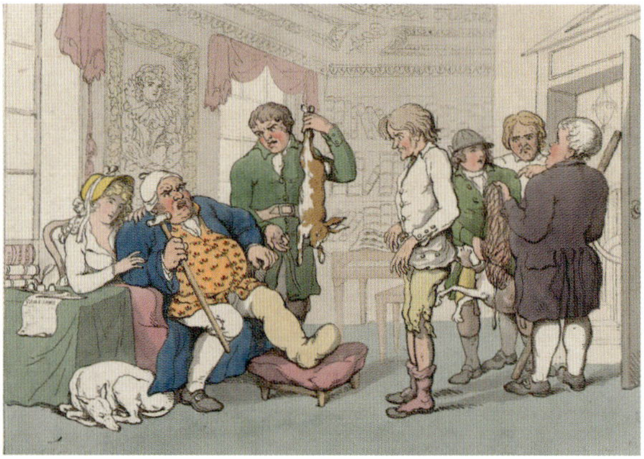

THE POACHER Thomas Rowlandson (1790-1795)

work, they will tell you, that they must go to look up their sheep, cut furzes, get their cow out of the pound..."[49] The overarching intention was encapsulated in a report made in 1794, in which the writer looked forward to the successful enclosing of the commons as bringing nearer the day when the loss of any remaining scrap of independence meant that "the labourers will work every day in the year, their children will be put out to labour early... [and] that subordination of the lower ranks of society which in the present times is so much wanted, would be thereby considerably secured."[50]

One benefit and aim of enclosure was agricultural improvement. Larger, more centralized farms enabled new agricultural technologies to be introduced, and fences meant that breeds of livestock could be refined and specialized. Eighteenth-century landowners commissioned portraits of their prize animals, emphasizing their desired traits – the bigger and fatter the better. In 1800, the celebrated Durham Ox, weighing nearly 3,000 pounds, toured round Britain, and people paid to see it and buy an engraving of it.

Enclosed land was seen as more efficient, enabling the rapidly growing urban populations to be fed. However, the changes it caused in the countryside were far reaching and often devastating to the rural poor. A letter written to the Marquis of Anglesey expresses the suffering and the sense of injustice felt, "Should a poor man take one of your sheep from the common, his life would be forfeited by law. But should you take the common from a hundred poor men's sheep, the law gives no redress." The writer goes on to delineate the inequality in society, "The poor man is liable to be hung from taking from you what would not supply you with a meal and you would do nothing illegal by depriving him of his subsistence; nor is your family supplied for a day by the subtraction which distresses his for life."[51]

Even enthusiastic advocates of enclosure such as Arthur Young, a celebrated agricultural economist, later realized that the cost had been very great when he wrote that in 19 out of 20 enclosure bills, the poor were "injured, in some grossly injured... The poor in these parishes may say, and with truth, 'Parliament may be tender of property; all I know is, I had a cow, and an act of Parliament has taken it from me.'"[52]

These profound changes to our relationship with the ground that we live on, and the inequalities around access to what were once communal resources, did not go

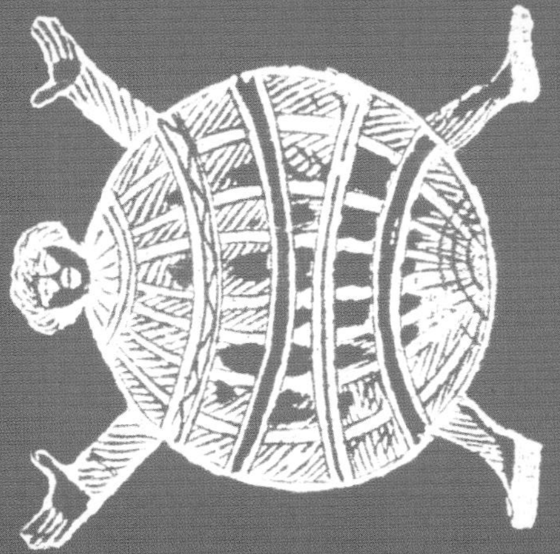

RURAL REBELS & TRADITIONS

Introduction to Rural Rebels and Traditions

Capitalism emerged from the systematic erosion of rural communal rights, practices and lifestyles. These rights weren't relinquished without many struggles and battles. As the enclosures were enacted in a progressive but piecemeal fashion from county to county over several centuries, there was no broad national anti-enclosure movement as such, just smaller localized clashes which were often extremely harshly punished by local courts.

Over the centuries, there were many rural rebellions spurred by reactions to enclosure. These gained momentum from the 14th century onward, with famous uprisings including Kett's Rebellion (1549), which started at the market town of Wymondham in Norfolk when a group of rebels destroyed fences that had been put up by wealthy landowners; the Midland Revolt (1607), which started in Northamptonshire and spread to Leicestershire and Warwickshire; the Western Rising (1626), a series of riots in the south west of England caused by the disafforestation and sale of royal forests, and enclosure by the new owners; the defiant agrarian socialism of the Digger communities on St George's Hill, Surrey (1649–50); and the Otmoor Riots (1830), which was a reaction to the enclosure, hedging, ditching, dredging and drainage of Otmoor wetland, which deprived locals of their rights to thousands of acres of common.

PORTRAIT OF CAPTAIN SWING Anon (1830)
Captain Swing was the fictional alias that signed off threatening letters sent during the Swing Riots in 1830. Since then, the figure of Captain Swing has inspired many writers and artists. He appears as a character in the novel The Difference Engine *by William Gibson and Bruce Sterling, which helped establish the steam punk genre, as Findthee Swing in* Night Watch *by Terry Pratchett, and in Warren Ellis's graphic novel* Captain Swing and the Electrical Pirates of Cindery Island. *An album by folk funk singer Michelle Shocked is named after him, too.*

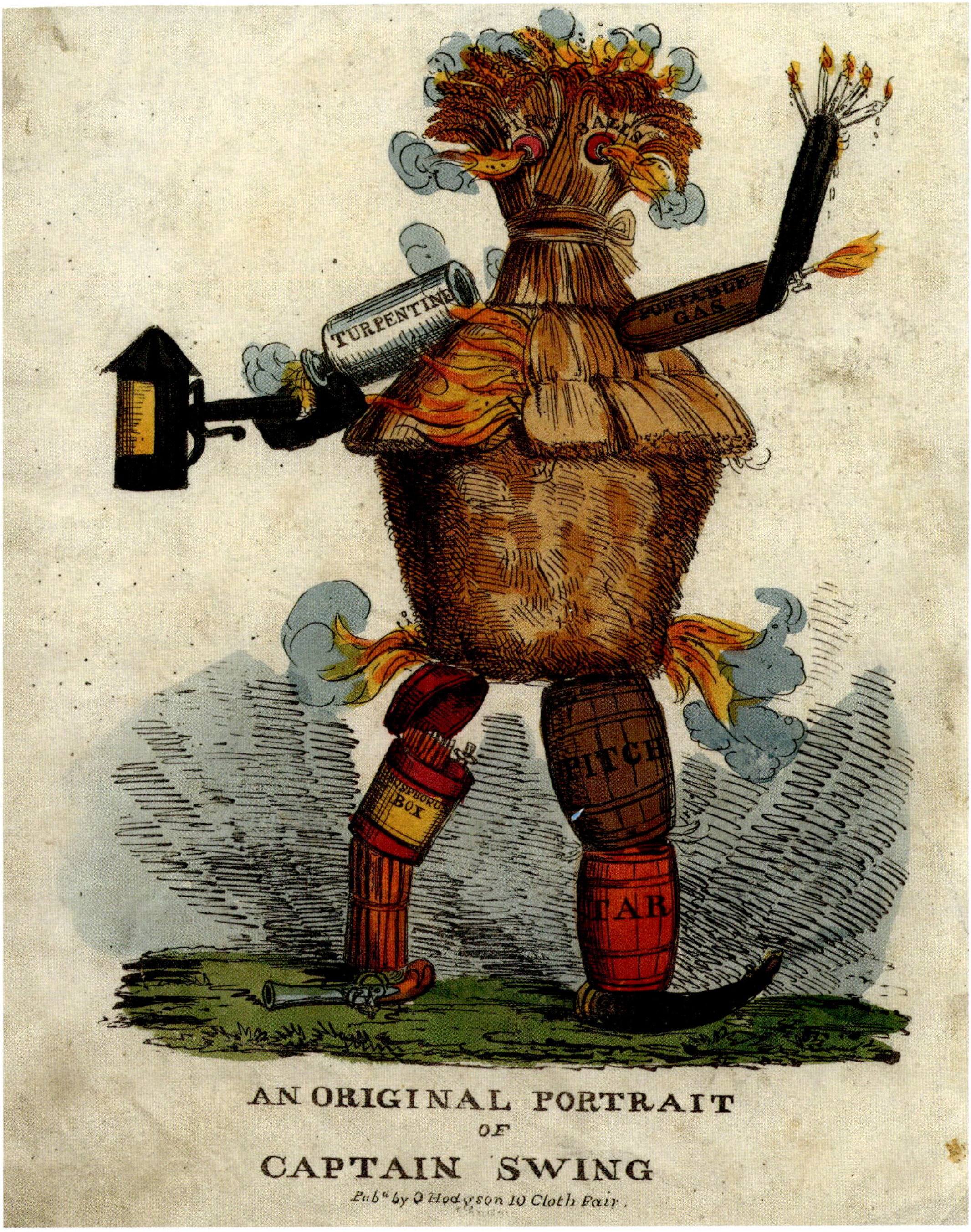

AN ORIGINAL PORTRAIT
OF
CAPTAIN SWING

Pub^d by O Hodgson 10 Cloth Fair.

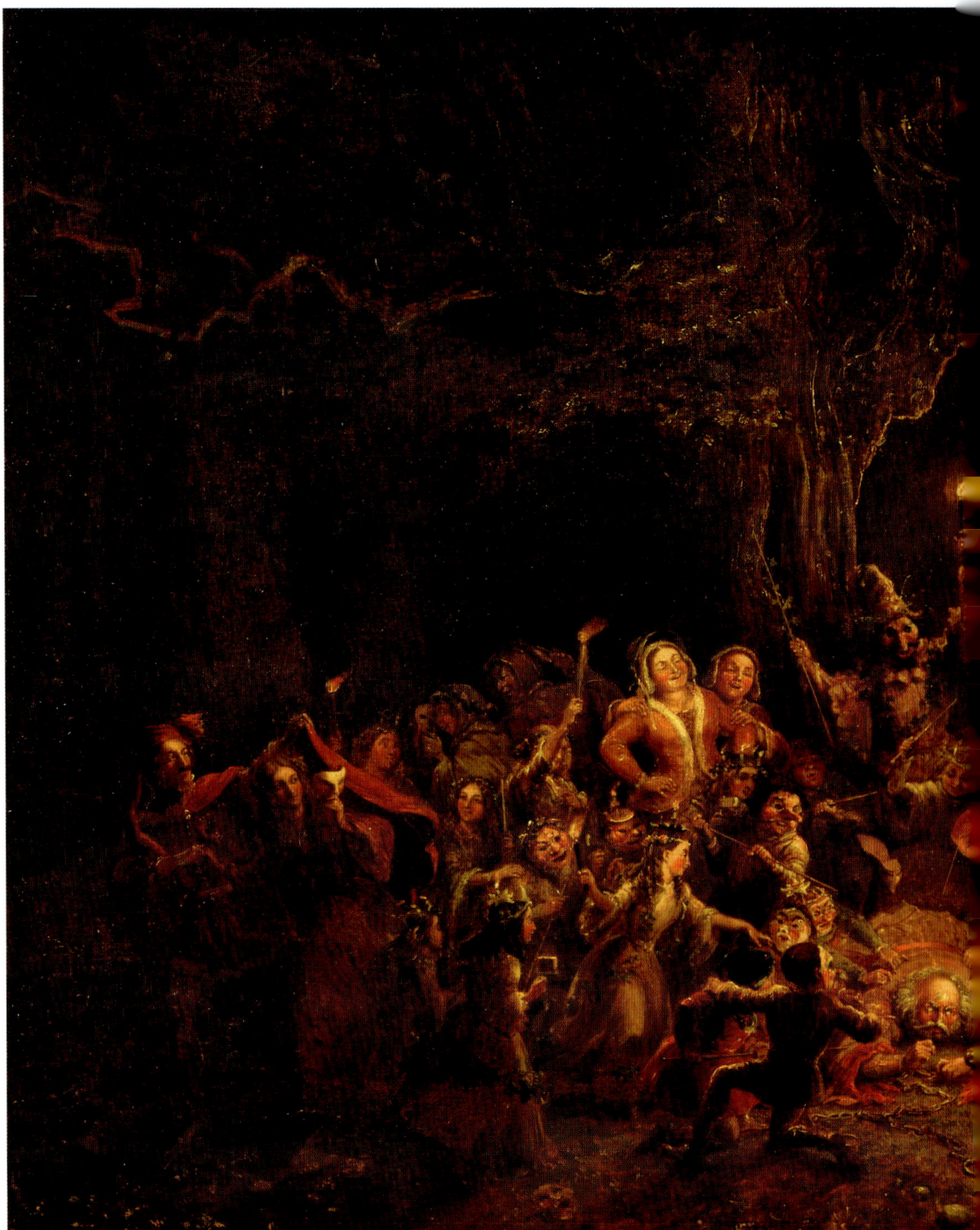

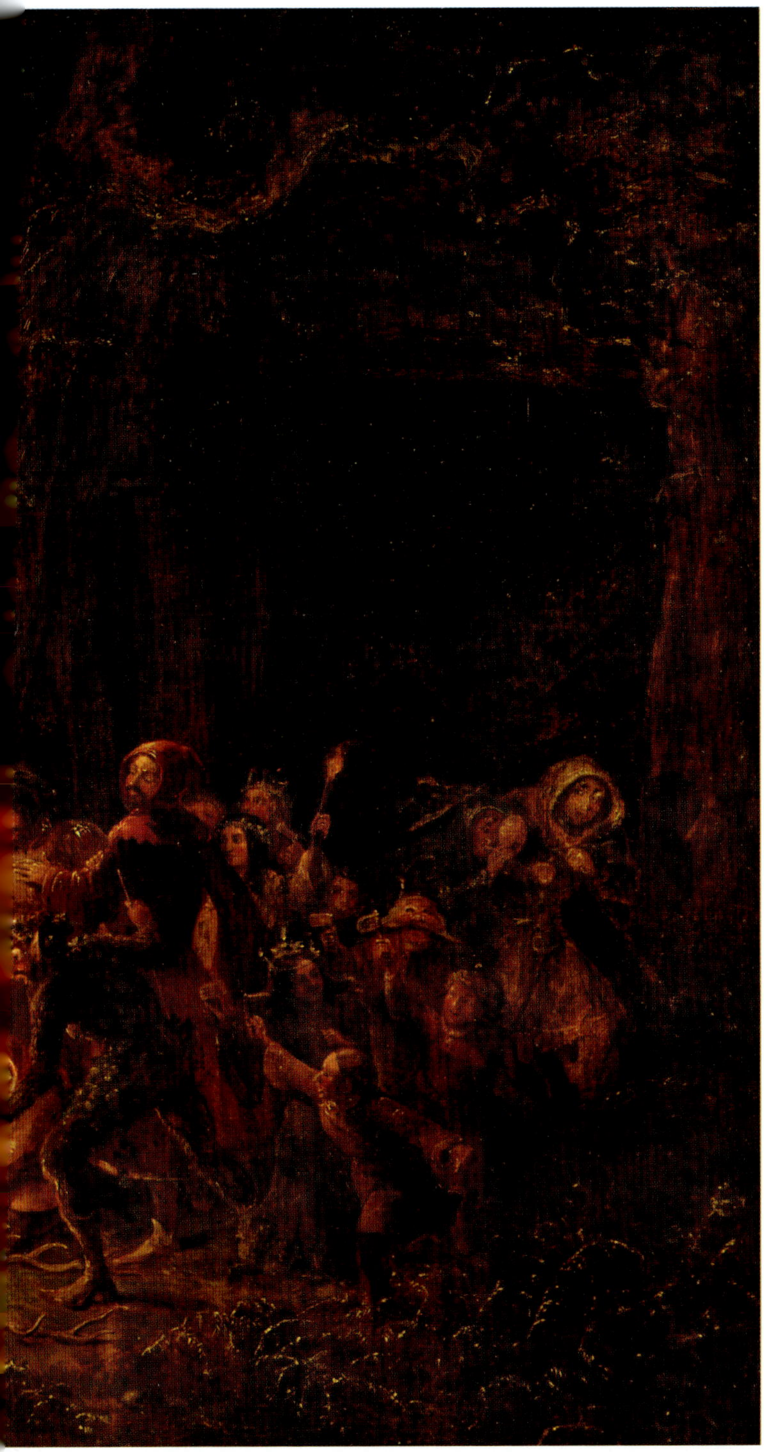

HERNE'S OAK FROM "THE MERRY WIVES OF WINDSOR"

George Cruikshank (1857)

Herne the Hunter is a mythical antlered figure who rides at night, tormenting cattle and people. He is associated with Herne's Oak, the legendary tree in Windsor Woods. Shakespeare mentions him in The Merry Wives of Windsor, *a scene that George Cruikshank depicts in this painting. Herne also appears as a character in novels such as Susan Cooper's* The Dark is Rising *and Terry Pratchett's* Discworld, *and features in an unproduced* Doctor Who *script, as well as in the TV adaptation of John Masefield's* The Box of Delights *aired in the 1980s.*

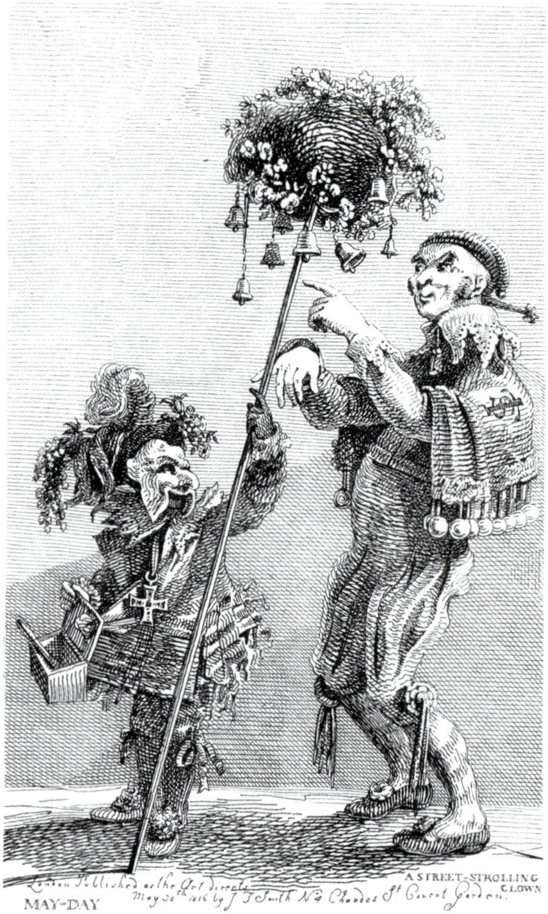

MAY DAY

John Thomas Smith (1817)

This illustration is taken from Vagabondiana; or, anecdotes of mendicant wanderers through the streets of London. With portraits of the most remarkable, drawn from the life *by John Thomas Smith. These men are taking part in the May Day festivities on the streets in London, but Smith bemoans in the accompanying text that these reprehensible fellows have replaced any "innocent scene of May Day gaiety".*

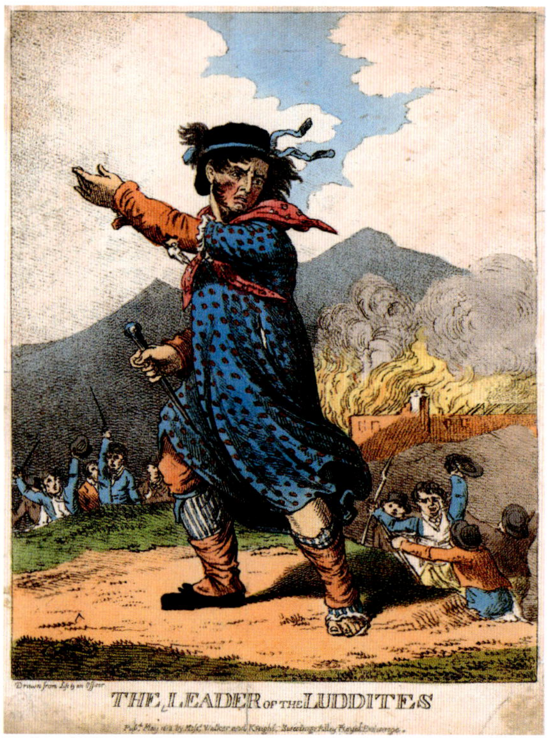

THE LEADER OF THE LUDDITES

Anon (1812)

The Romantic poets Shelley and Byron were both deeply influenced by the Luddite movement. Shelley wrote the poem Queen Mab *in 1812 to critique the alienating forces of industrialization, admiring the Luddites' resistance to the new machinery. Besides appearing in Edmund Cooper's novel* The Cloud Walker, *the mythical figure of Ned Ludd has been celebrated in songs such as "The Triumph of Ned Ludd", a folk ballad recorded by Chumbawamba, in the song "Ludd Gang" by the Fall, on Steeleye Span's album* Bloody Men *and by the Divine Comedy in the song "You'll Never Work in this Town Again".*

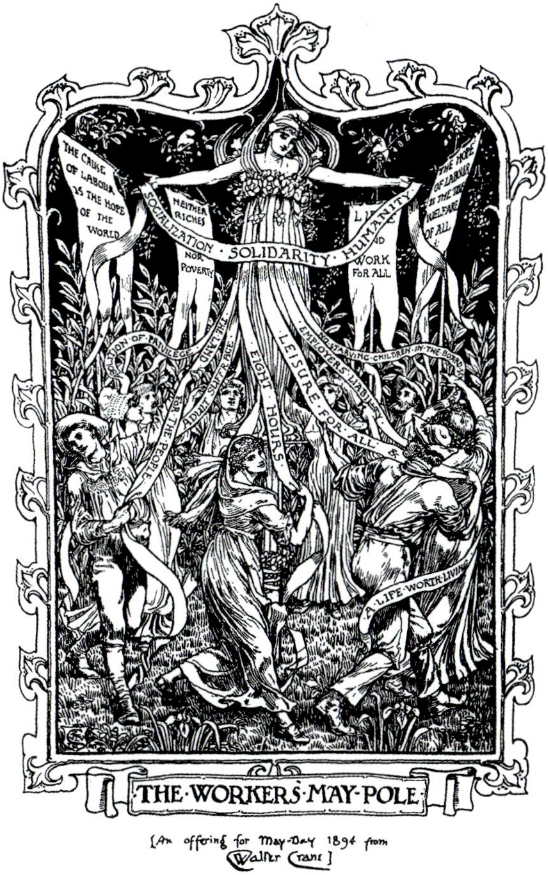

THE WORKERS' MAY-POLE

Walter Crane (1894)

Walter Crane, born in Liverpool, was part of the Arts and Crafts and British socialist movements in the late 1800s. Here, the May Queen watches over the workers who surround the maypole. Her maypole ribbons are banners asking for solidarity, employers' liability, an eight-hour day and the end to starving children. The illustration is a perfect fusion of the political and mythical aspects of May Day.

FOOLS, OR JESTERS

John Augustus Atkinson (1813)

The fool or jester was often the only member of the court in England who could, however obliquely, speak truth to power. In many cultures, such as those of the ancient Norse, Native Americans and West Africans, the jester or trickster is an important figure who embodies the sacred and the divine, challenges social boundaries and questions conventional authority.

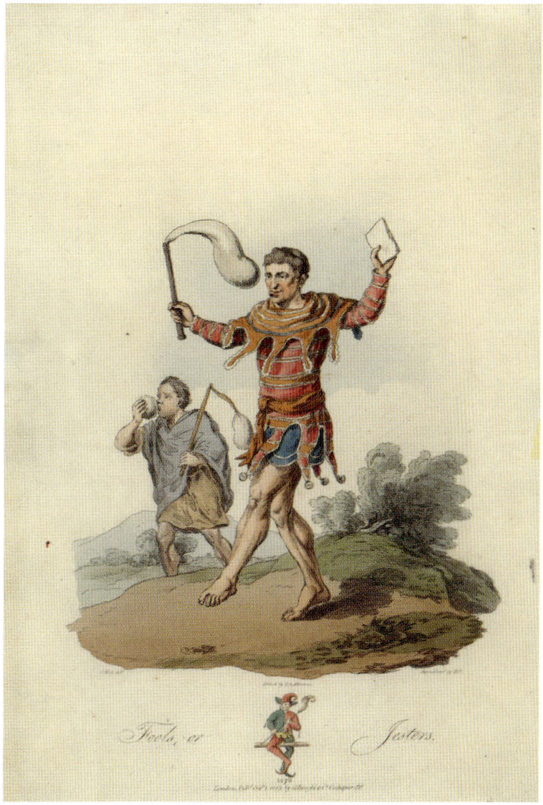

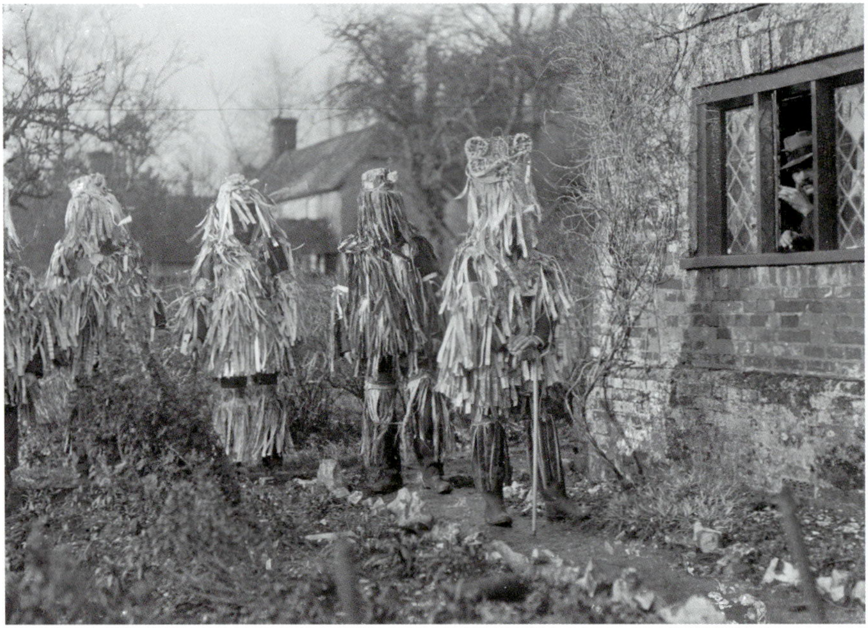

OVERTON MUMMERS, HAMPSHIRE

George Long (c.1930)

When the Overton Mummers come knocking at your door, you must guess their true identity before offering them food and drink. The mummers go to great lengths to conceal who they are, including their seemingly impossible ingressive speech, speaking while inhaling.

PLOUGH MONDAY FROM *THE COSTUME OF YORKSHIRE*

George Walker (1814)

Plough Monday is held on the first Monday after Twelfth Night. This was a tough time as there was little work around. The farm labourers would don disguise and drag a decorated plough from door to door, appealing for money, ale and victuals. Walker published The Costume of Yorkshire, *including this illustration of Plough Monday. You can see the precursor of the tatters now worn by most Border Morris groups, cross-dressing by men and women, and the fool with a pig's bladder.*

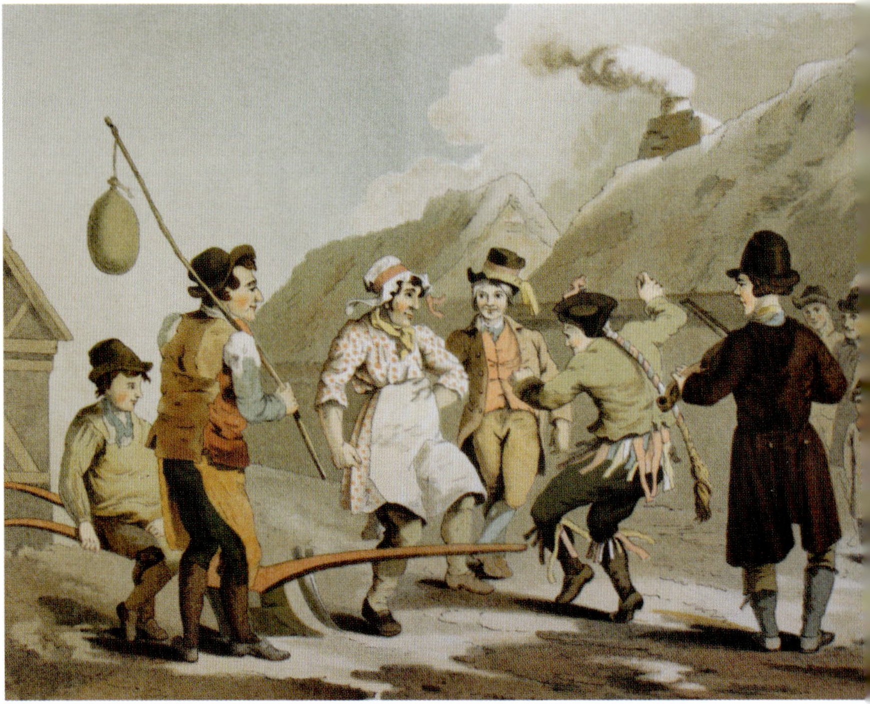

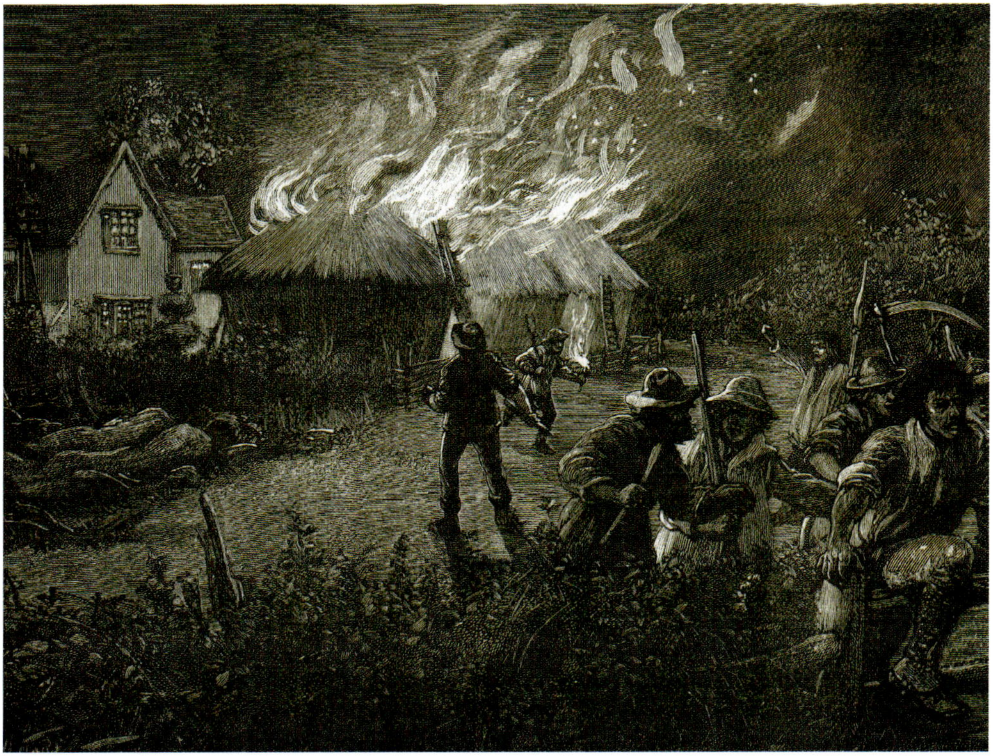

SWING RIOTS IN KENT MOB BURNING A FARM IN 1830 Anon (c.1900)

In Britain in the 1800s, setting fire to buildings, including barns and stacks of hay or grain was punishable by death. This meant the stakes were high for the rebels in the Swing Riots. While the Swing Riots themselves never appeared explicitly in literature or popular culture, Charlotte Brontë sets her novel Shirley *around Luddite activity in the early 1800s. This illustration was first published in Cassell's nine-volume* History of England.

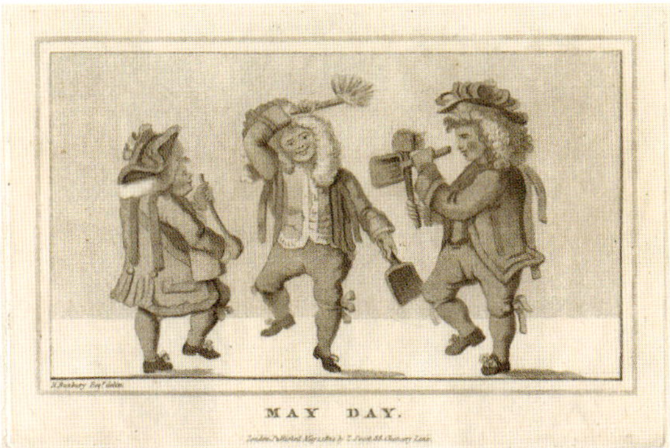

MAY DAY Henry William Bunbury (1824)

These three characters are possibly road sweepers celebrating May Day in London. Road sweepers would clear horse manure from the streets, so the middle and upper classes could cross without dirtying their expensive shoes and dresses. They worked at busy intersections close to theatres, bars and restaurants. The character of Jo, a poor lad who sweeps the streets around the Chancery court, appears in Charles Dickens' novel Bleak House *and foregrounds the issues of poverty and homelessness.*

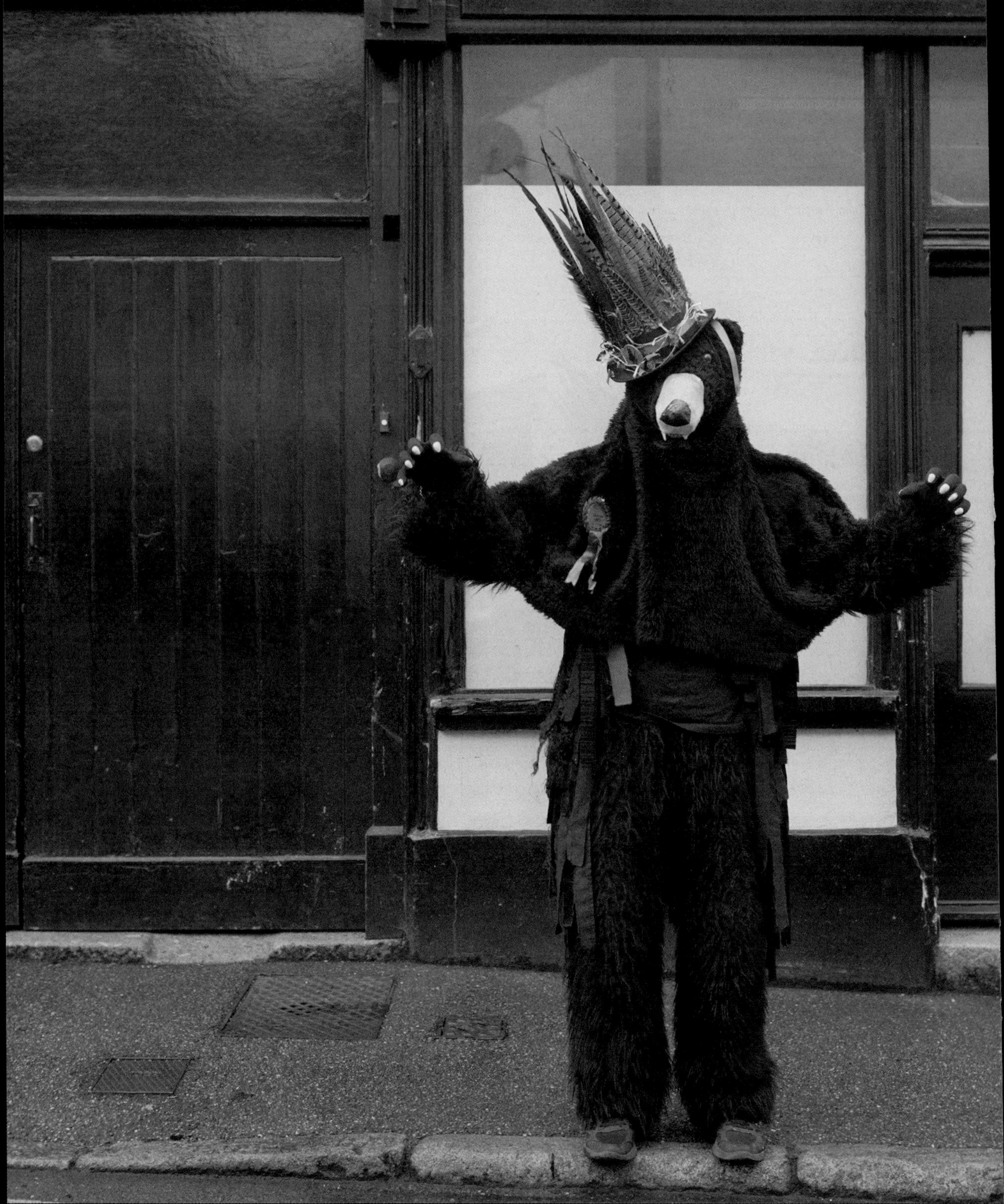

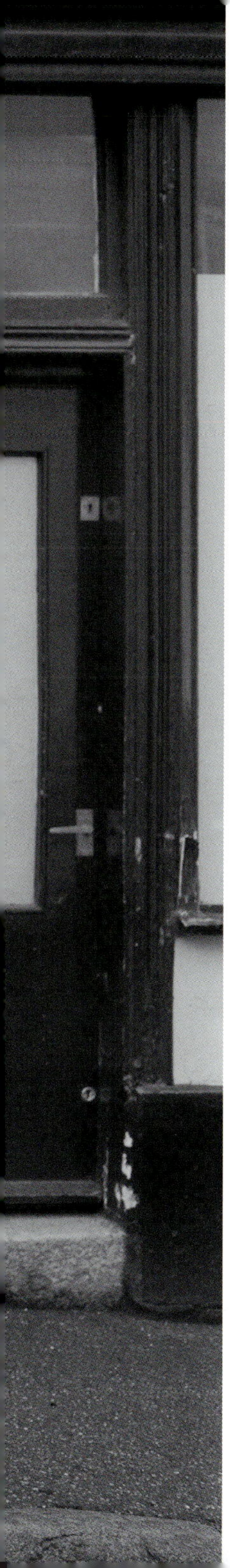

Rural Rebels and Traditions by Leah Gordon

The images in this section are stylized photomontages depicting artefacts of peasant life, shown alongside representations of rural traditions and objects relating to contemporary land struggles to question the nature of land ownership and people's access to the land. The montages sit alongside photographic portraits of UK folk traditions to show how these often ancient rituals have performed the boundaries, histories and customs that mark our relationship to the land.

Oak Apple Day is a celebration in Great Wishford, Wiltshire, which annually commemorates and proclaims the villagers' ancient rights to collect firewood from adjacent Grovely Wood. In this fascinating tradition, the link between commoners' rights and ritual performance is direct, but in many other traditions the parallels are less literal, although they are still mapping out majority-class relationships to land boundaries, rural rebellions and the seasonal calendar. For example, enclosure is obliquely referenced in the masks of morris dancers and the tatters of their garb, in the routes of the Abbots Bromley Horn Dancers and the Burryman of South Queensferry, and in many boundary beating traditions.

GRIMBEAR, GRIMSPOUND BORDER MORRIS, NEWTON ABBOT, DEVON (2024) **A Meadow Arts commission**

Grimspound Border Morris is named after a prehistoric settlement where the remains of 24 roundhouses surrounded by a massive boundary wall survive in the heart of Dartmoor. Grimbear is their mascot – a character invented in 2023 but who cemented his place in the Grimspound team by winning the Sidmouth Folk Festival Horse Trials, a competition for all the animal mascots of the different morris teams or sides. Grimbear's rivals included unicorns, horses, goats, sheep and dragons; it was probably the somersaults and breakdancing that nailed it for him. Border morris teams often blackened their faces as a way of disguising themselves, particularly if they were trying to obtain money from spectators. Although it's unlikely that this has anything to do with "blackface" (as poachers often disguised themselves in the same way to avoid identification), many morris teams such as Grimspound have adopted different coloured face paints or now wear masks so that there can be no confusion among onlookers who are unfamiliar with the tradition of "blacking" as a disguise.

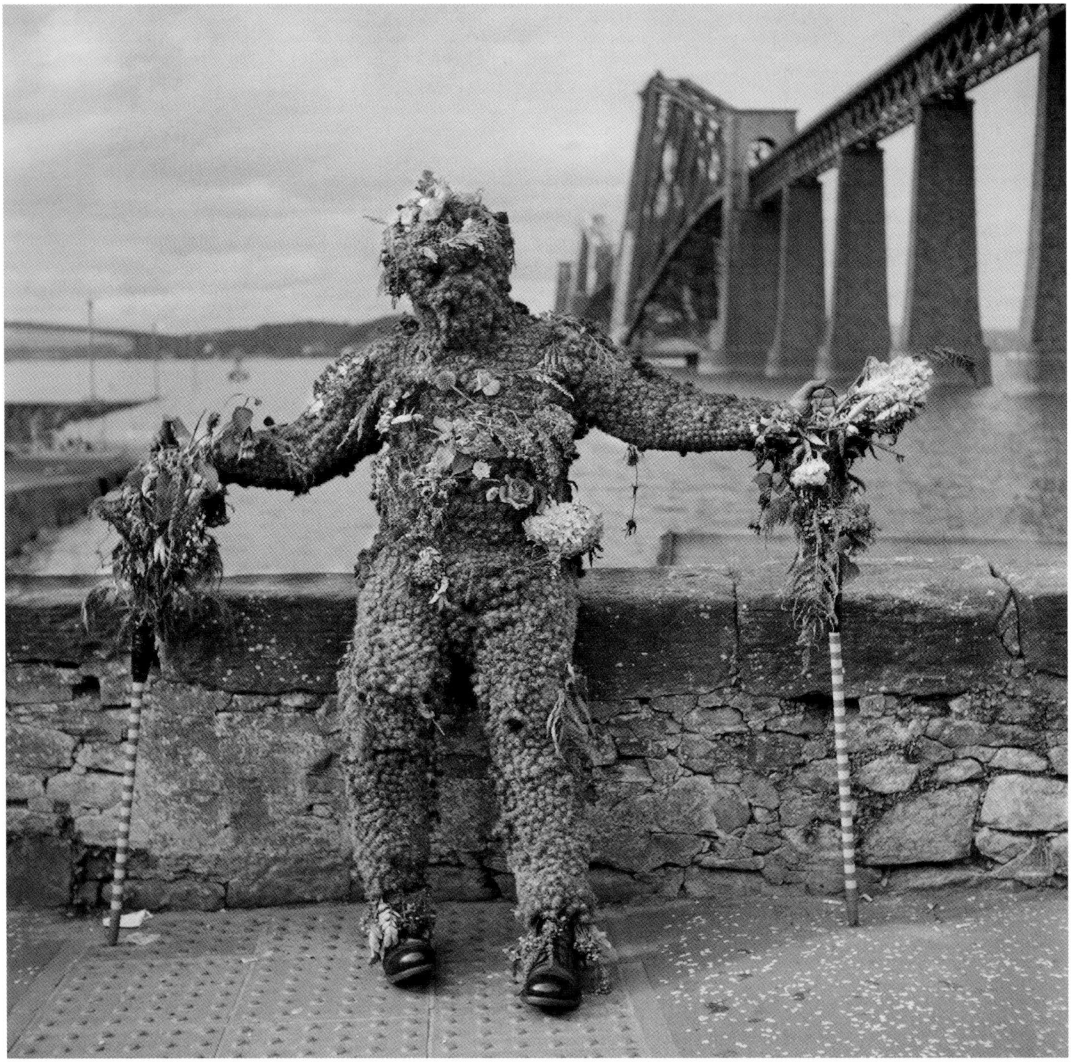

THE BURRYMAN, SOUTH QUEENSFERRY, WEST LOTHIAN (2010)

The Burryman tradition in South Queensferry is over a thousand years old; it maps boundaries, links humankind and nature, and binds a community. The role is open only to a man born there and requires deep commitment. On the second Friday in August, about 11,000 burrs (the scratchy, multi-hooked seed head of the burdock plant) are attached to an undergarment encasing the Burryman's body, leaving holes for his eyes, nose and mouth. The cumbersome get-up forces him to walk with legs apart and arms outstretched, grasping a flower-covered rake in each hand as supports. He is accompanied by two attendants as he makes his way round a nine-mile route. While he can imbibe liquids via a straw, he can't relieve himself for nearly ten hours. The origins of the ceremony may have been to bring good luck to local fishermen or to commemorate the Scottish king Malcolm III, hiding from the English covered in burrs. Nowadays, people give him a sip of whisky through his straw in return for a lucky burr.

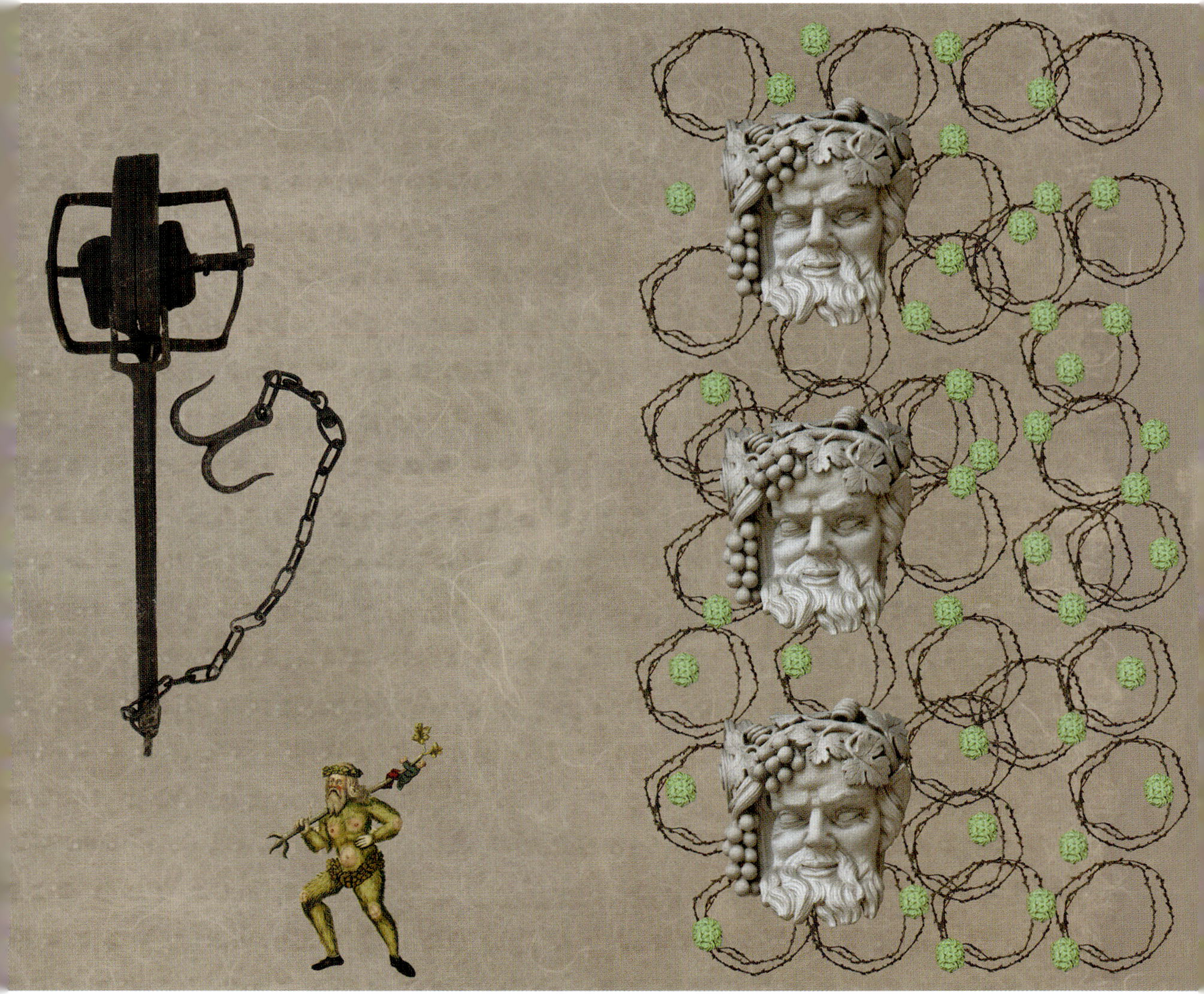

RURAL REBELS UNTITLED MONTAGE (2023) A Meadow Arts commission

Although most folk traditions in Britain are of uncertain origin, some apparently preserving pagan rituals or celebrating an ancient local legend, some clearly recent revivals or even inventions, they all demonstrate people's timeless urge to create meaningful rituals and preserve traditions that reinforce their community identity. The enthusiasm and determination involved often confirms this, although not all are as dangerous as the Ottery St Mary blazing tar barrels and the precipitous downhill dash of the Gloucestershire cheese rollers.

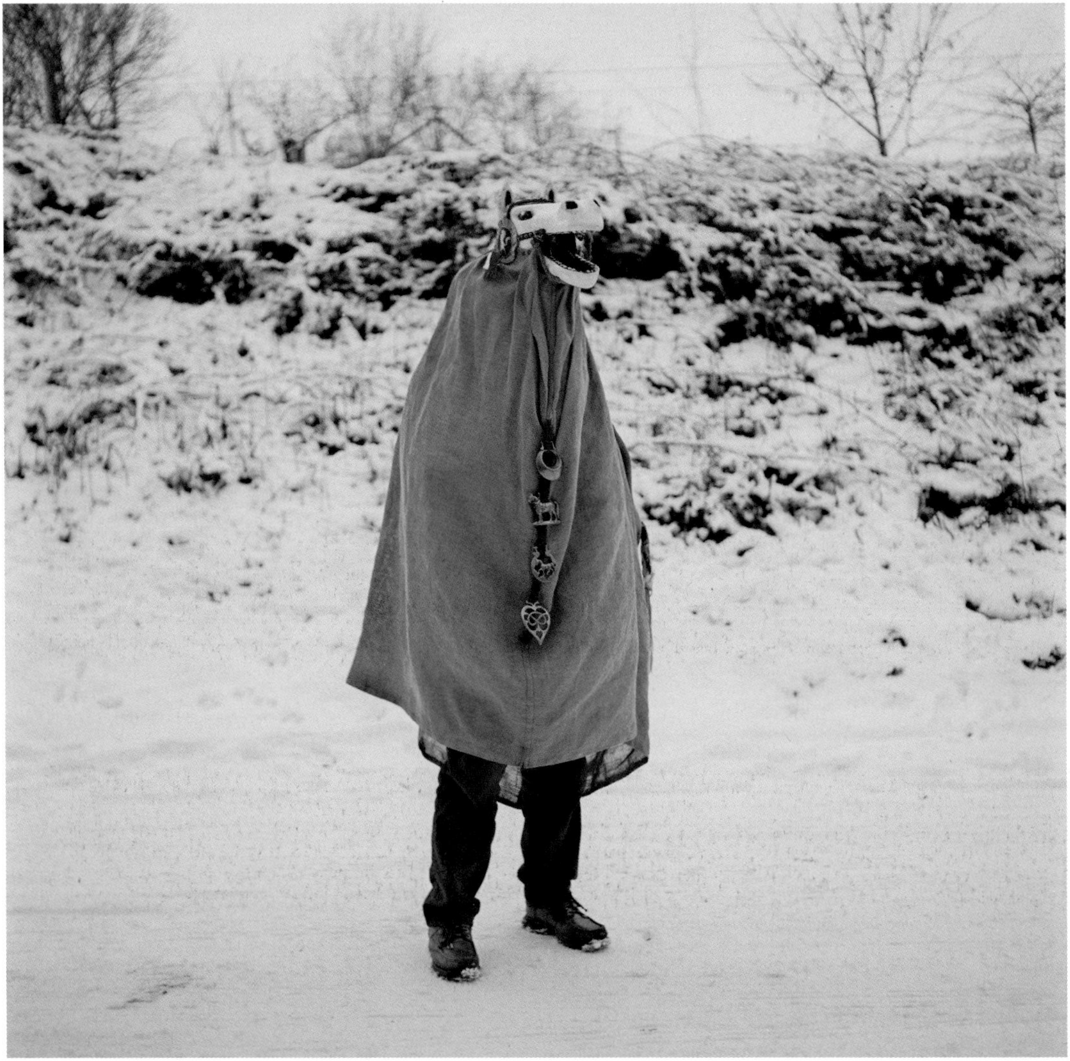

INVICTA OF HYTHE – HOODEN HORSE, KENT (2010)

Hoodening is a folk custom found in the county of Kent. The tradition entails the use of a wooden horse's head mounted on a pole, known as a hooden horse, and carried by a person hidden under a sackcloth. The person can clap the horse's jaw by pulling a string attached to it. The hooden horse is usually accompanied by a groom or ostler, who leads the horse, and a Maid Marian figure (a man dressed in women's clothing) known as Molly. They would go round at Christmas time to collect donations, performing a rough mummers' play which often involved people trying to sit on the horse's back and ride it. The story goes that in former times, a real horse's skull was used, but this was banned in the early 19th century when a woman died of shock upon opening her door to such a ghoulish sight. Most of the heads are black but this one, owned by East Kent Morris, is based on a prancing white horse called Invicta, a symbol of Kent.

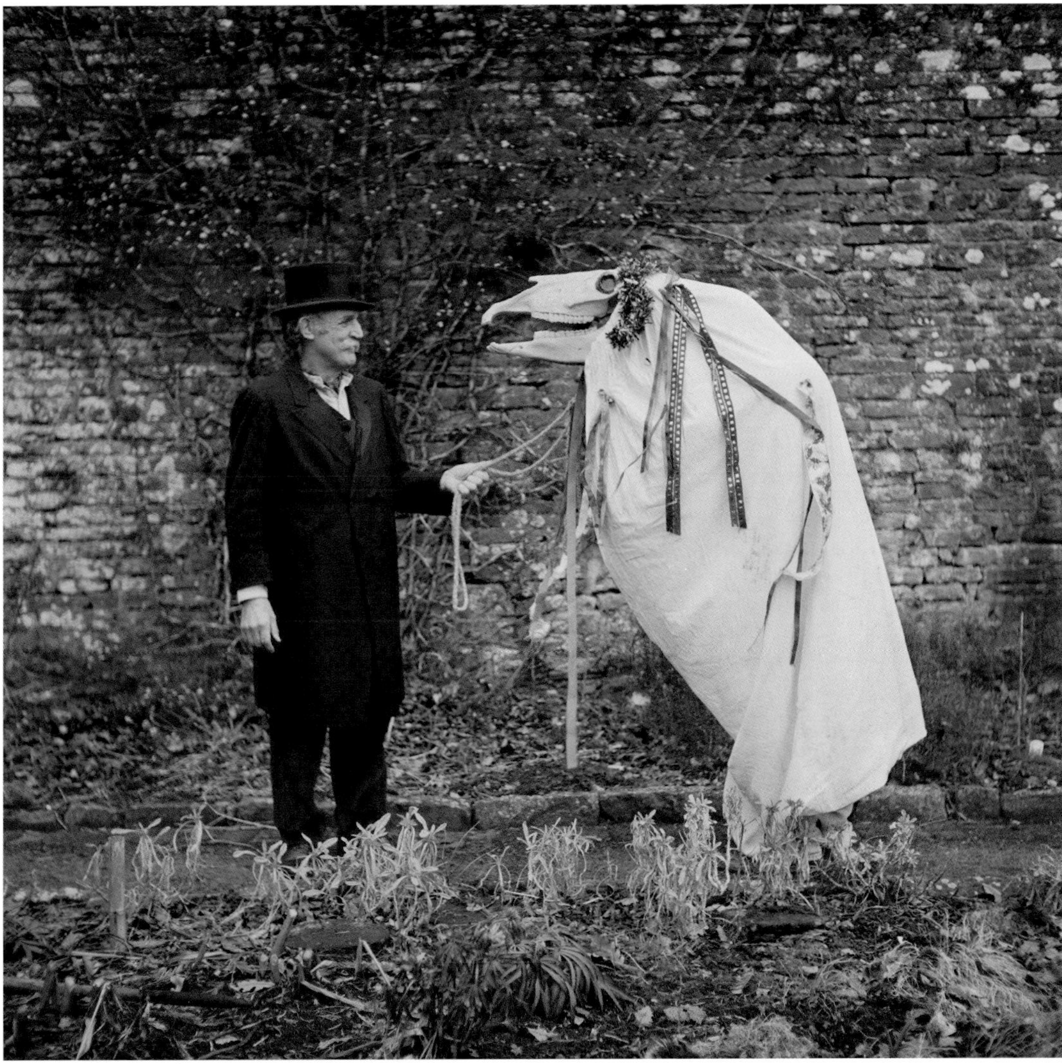

THE MARI LWYD, BRIDGEND, GLAMORGAN (2011)

The Mari Lwyd is part of a wassailing folk custom found in South Wales. Wassailing is an ancient tradition, with the word "wassail" coming from the Old Norse for "good health". It usually involves a celebratory drinking of spiced cider, ale or wine, often from a communal bowl and in the depths of winter, bringing good luck and harvest for the coming year. The Mari Lwyd, Welsh for "Grey Mare", entails the use of an eponymous hobby horse, which is made from a horse's skull mounted on a pole and carried by an individual hidden under a sheet. Around the time of Christmas and New Year, these ghostly figures wander from house to house, and there is an exchange of traditional verses whereby the Mari Lwyd demands entry and victuals, and the occupants of the house sing back their refusal. Eventually, the Mari Lwyd and its entourage win this rhyming battle and are let into the house to be given festive food and drink.

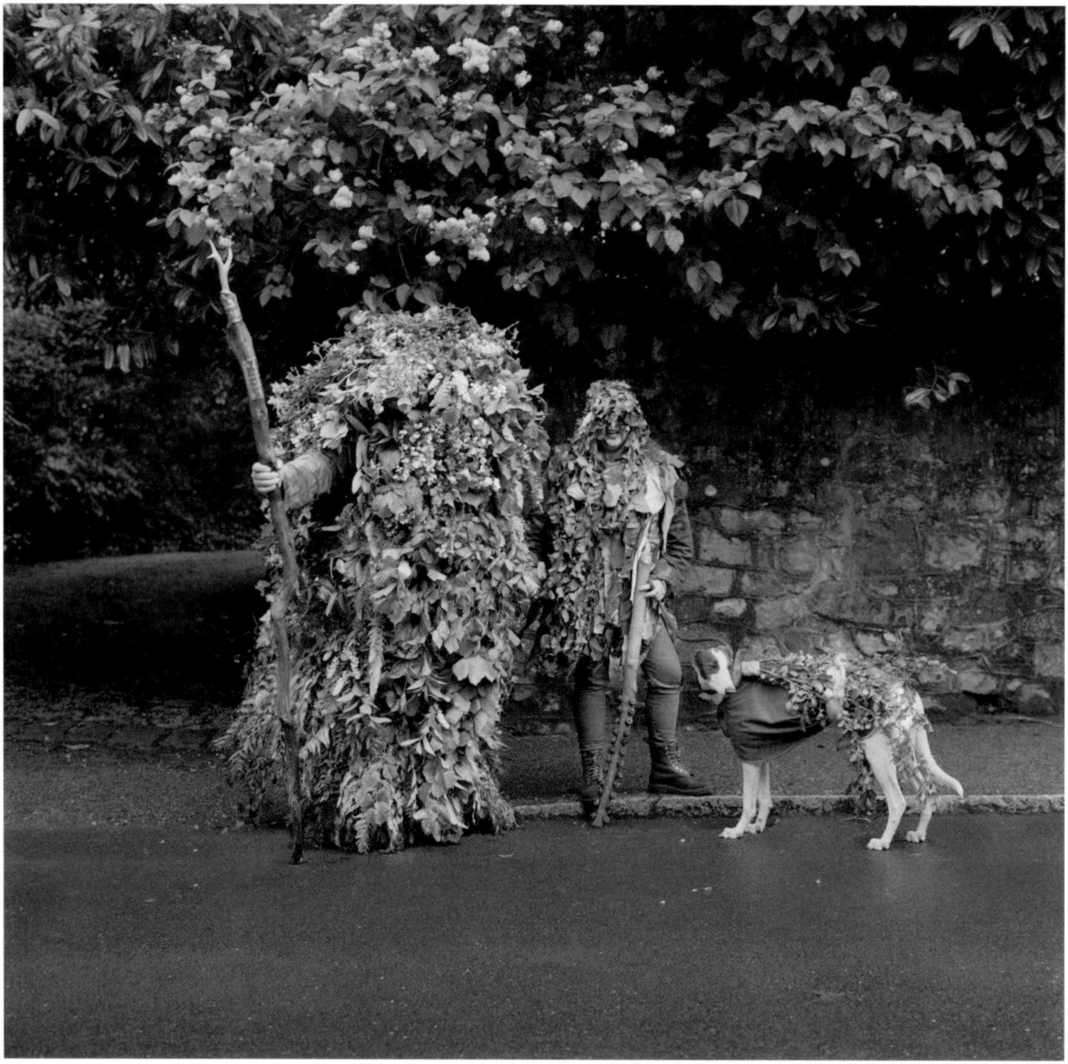

GREEN MAN FESTIVAL, BOVEY TRACEY (2024) A Meadow Arts commission

The Green Man festival takes place in April in Bovey Tracey, Devon. Teams of morris dancers, multiple Jack in the Greens and Green Men parade through the streets in this celebration of spring. The Green Man is believed to symbolize the power of nature and renewed life after the dark, dormant winter. His importance has grown during the current revival of folk traditions, and he's often associated with our pagan past. However, there isn't much historical evidence to support the idea of a vestigial shamanistic presence in Christianity: academic research has suggested that carvings of Green Men in medieval churches, with leaves and branches twirling out of their mouths, may represent demons or even human mortality (as the original paintwork was often not green but brown, suggesting autumn, and many were carved during the time of the Black Death). Yet none of this detracts from the Green Man's contemporary inspirational role as a symbol of nature and renewal in a world threatened by environmental devastation from many sides.

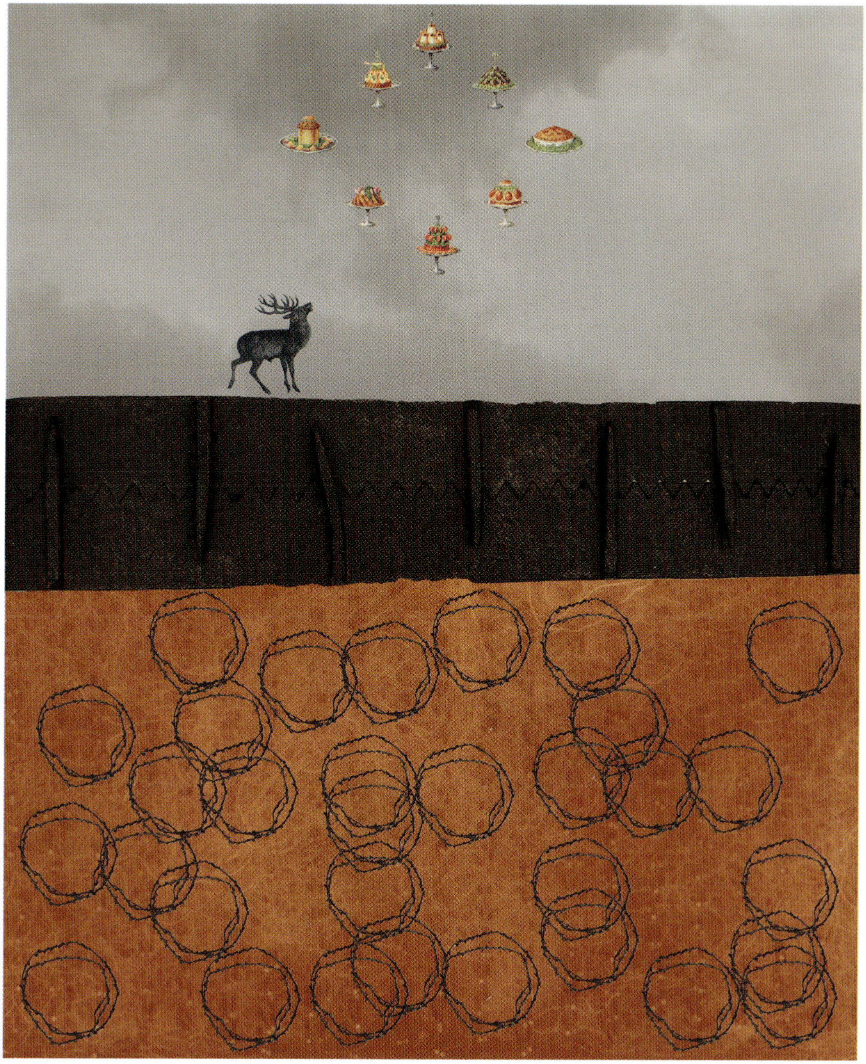

RURAL REBELS UNTITLED MONTAGE (2023) A Meadow Arts commission

The attempts of landowners to keep poachers from their land in the 18th century began to be seen more and more as a "war". They used a brutal armoury – not only were the gamekeepers and the poachers armed, but spring guns, where a hidden gun was triggered by a trip wire, or man traps where flesh-cutting teeth sprang shut on a man's legs, were introduced. Professional poachers learnt how to avoid the traps, and it was pointed out at the time that victims were often unsuspecting flower-picking children, mushroom-foraging women and butterfly-pursuing vicars.

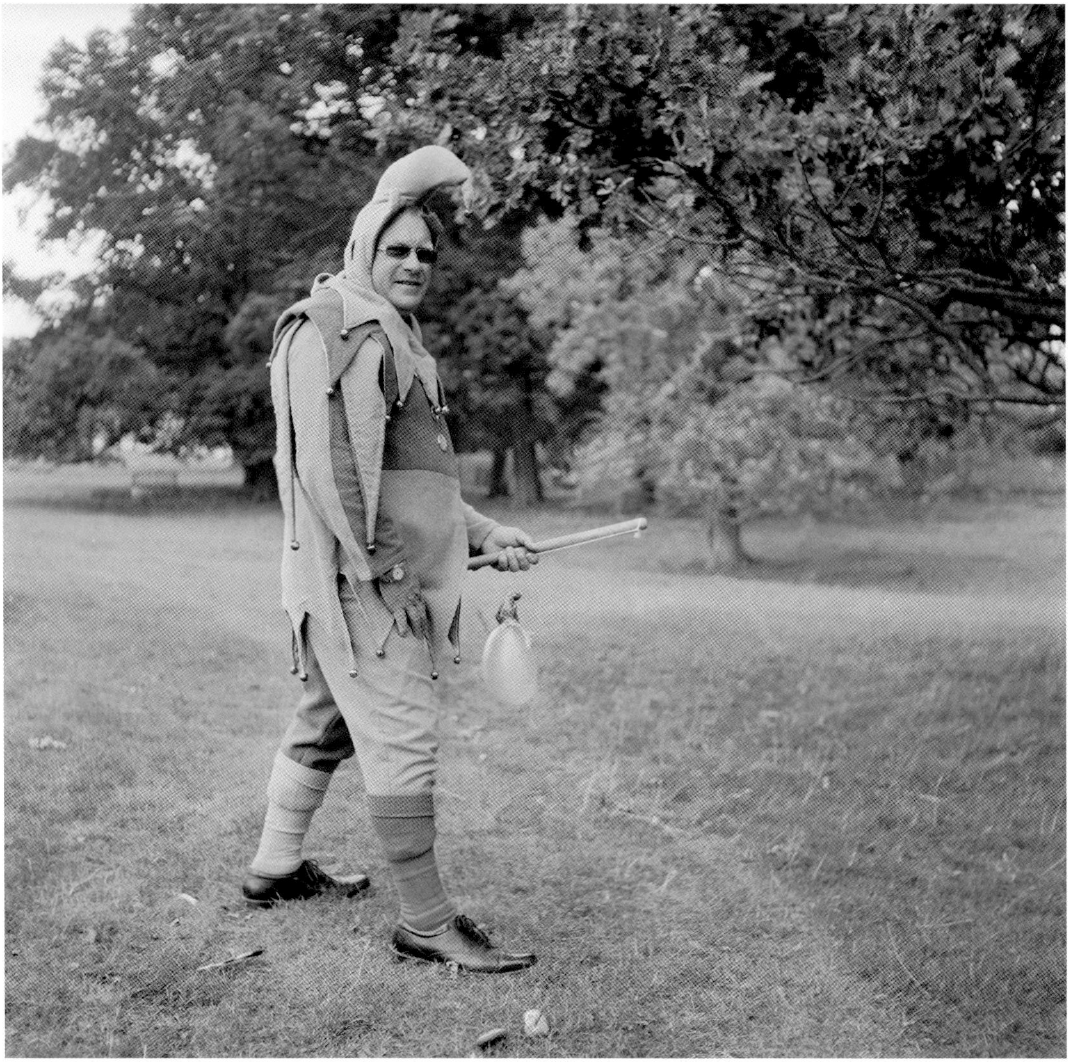

ABBOTS BROMLEY FOOL, STAFFORDSHIRE (2010)

This is the fool that leads the Abbots Bromley Horn Dancers. He is holding a pig's bladder on a stick, a customary piece of equipment for a fool or jester, with which he can hit the dancers or passers-by without hurting them. The bladder will have been picked up from a local butcher's first thing in the morning and is inflated nowadays using a bicycle pump. The fool or jester was traditionally seen in a carnival role, when the traditional hierarchies were mocked, and has the privilege of being able to ridicule figures of authority with impunity – of speaking truth to power.

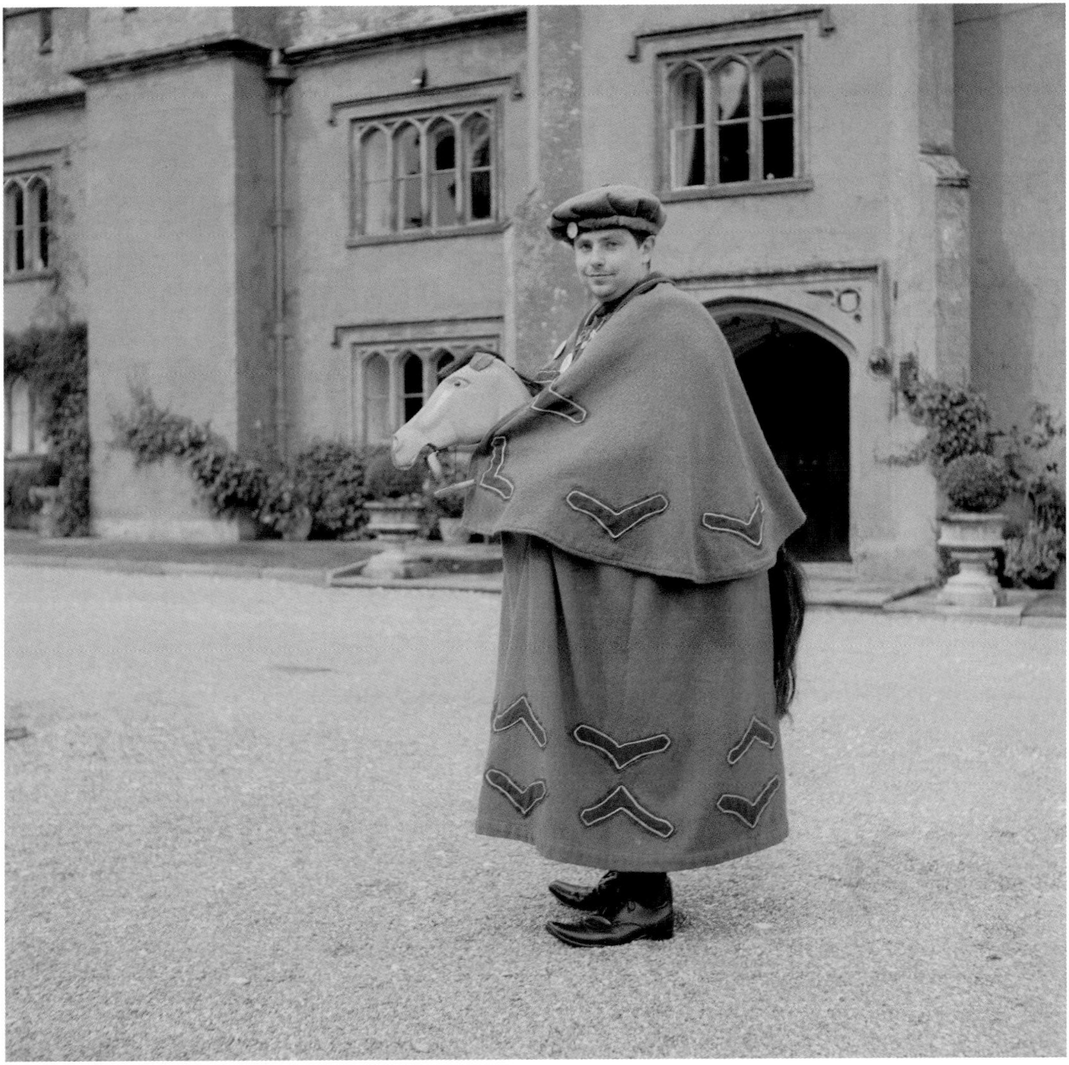

ABBOTS BROMLEY HOBBY HORSE, STAFFORDSHIRE (2010)

This is the traditional hobby horse that follows the Abbots Bromley Horn Dancers. The day begins at the church of St Nicholas in the village, where the antlers hang on the wall during the rest of the year, and after a blessing, the group makes its way around the parish, covering about 20 miles. They usually stop for lunch at Blithfield Hall, where this photograph was taken. The Bagot family has lived at Blithfield Hall more or less continuously since the 13th century, and the eponymous Bagot Forest is one of the last remaining parts of Needwood Forest, which was enclosed by the Crown in 1803 despite widespread opposition. Most of the trees were felled, including about 150,000 hollies to make bobbins for the cotton mills of Lancashire, and only 490 acres of woodland survive of the original 9,000 acres. The dance originally took place around Christmas time, so it may have been connected to wassailing or raising money at a lean time of year for agricultural workers. For the current participants, it's a celebration of their community and an important symbol of continuity.

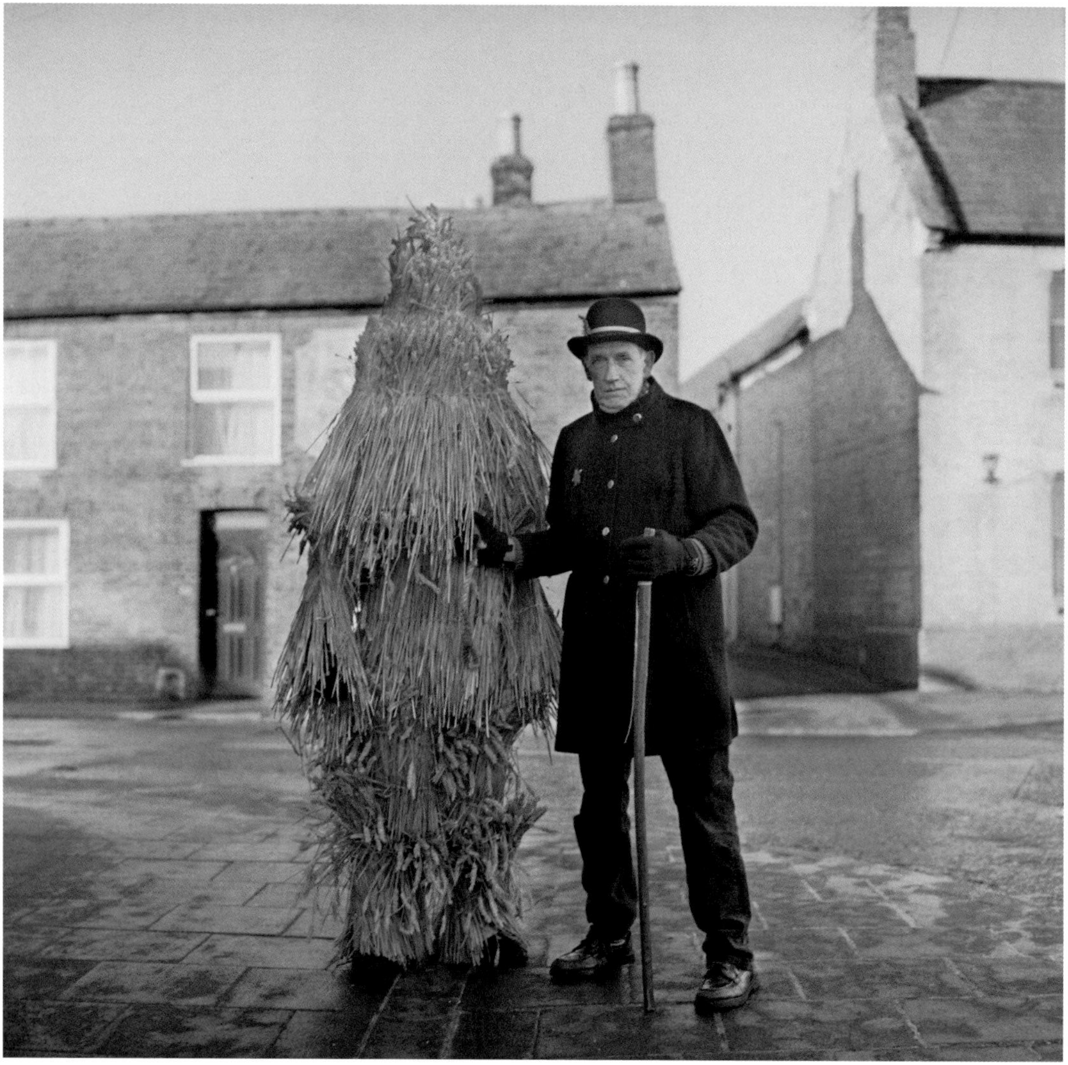

WHITTLESEA STRAW BEAR, WHITTLESEA, FENLAND DISTRICT OF CAMBRIDGESHIRE (2025) A Meadow Arts commission

In Whittlesea, it was the custom on the Tuesday following Plough Monday to parade a man covered in straw around the town, cavorting and dancing. This resembled other plough traditions in January, when there was little agricultural work. Labourers went round begging, and might plough up your garden if you didn't give them money. The Whittlesea Straw Bear may be named after the chained dancing bears that were once a familiar sight as street entertainment until the 19th century. However, several other European countries have customs involving similar straw figures, possibly representing winter or a type of wild man. The tradition died out in Whittlesea (or Whittlesey – both spellings are correct) in the early 20th century, reputedly because an over-officious policeman believed the bear contravened anti-begging laws, but was revived in the 80s. Nowadays, the bear is accompanied through the streets by musicians and morris dancers on a Saturday in January. The following day the straw bear is ritually burned (with no man inside).

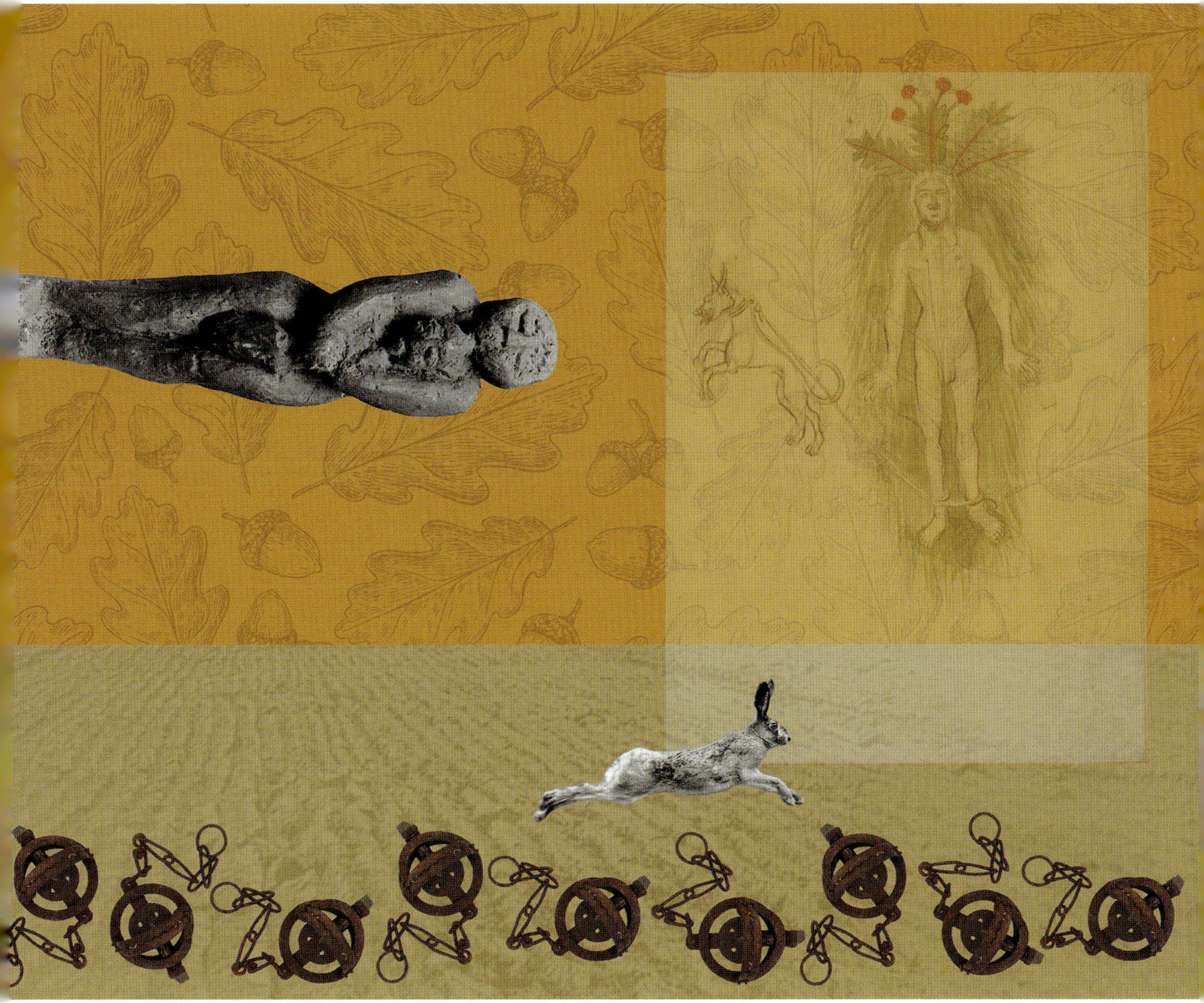

RURAL REBELS UNTITLED MONTAGE (2023) A Meadow Arts commission

On Otmoor in Oxfordshire there is a legend that all the land encircled as a mysterious woman rode round the moor carrying a magically burning oat sheaf was given forever to the people of Otmoor (Oatmoor). They fought back hard when enclosure was threatened in 1830. A thousand people gathered to destroy enclosing fences and when 41 of them were arrested and sent to Oxford for trial, the crowds attending St Giles' Fair attacked the soldiers accompanying them and set them free.

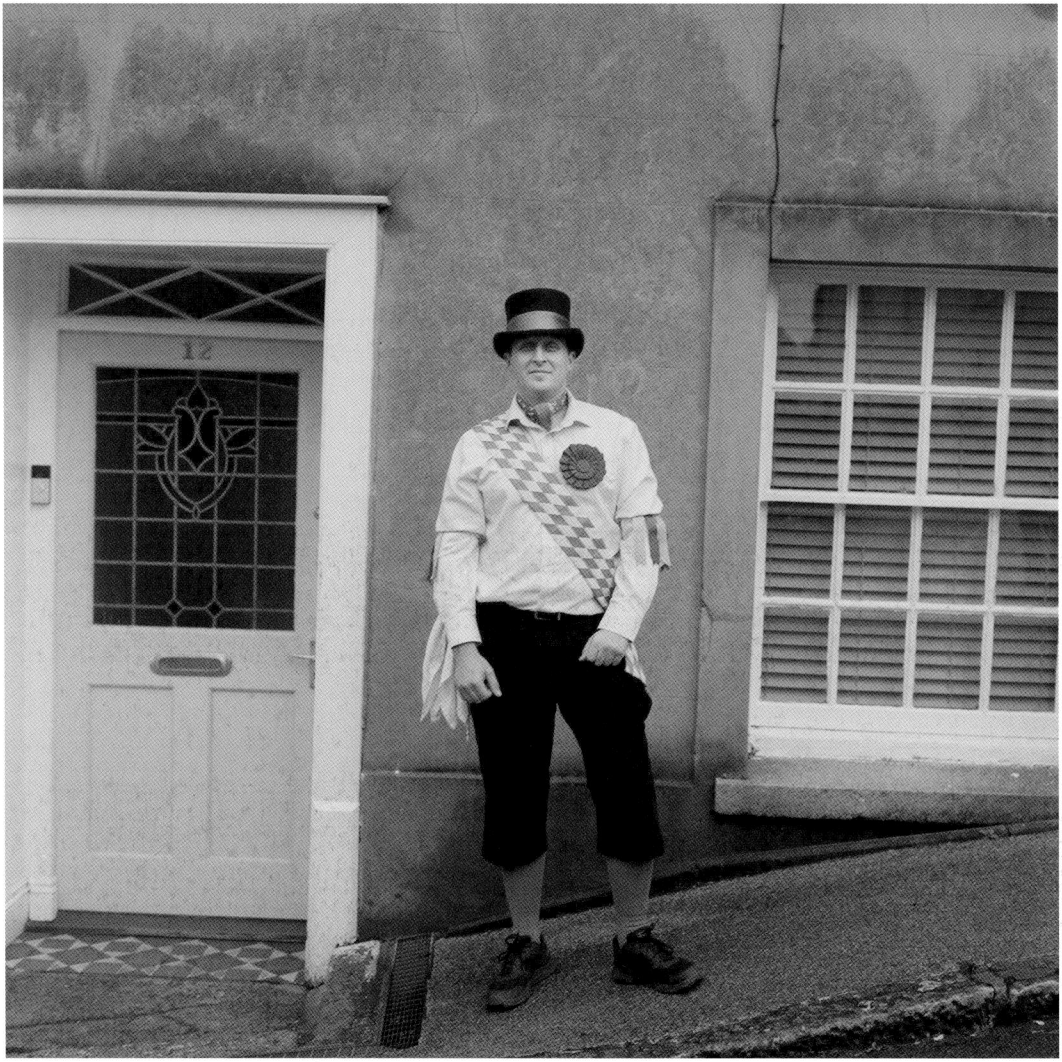

GREAT WESTERN MORRIS, EXETER, DEVON (2024) A Meadow Arts commission

The costumes of Great Western Morris, a more traditional morris side from Exeter, are based on 19th-century clothing and their dances are rooted in the Cotswold tradition of morris dancing. They were formed in the 1960s as part of the great folk revival that took place then. Cotswold is the typical morris style of dancing associated with nostalgic visions of village greens and country pubs, involving men with bells and ribbons on their legs, who skip around and wave handkerchiefs, and are frequently mocked in comedy sketches – and who were excluded from the representation of everything British in the opening ceremony of the 2012 Olympics in London. Some morris dancers threatened to invade the ceremony when they heard they'd been left out, although they did make it into the closing ceremony, performing while Eric Idle of Monty Python fame sang "Always Look on the Bright Side of Life". However, they would claim they're misunderstood, and that their dances are more skilled and elaborate than the more (in their eyes) rough and ready Border Morris.

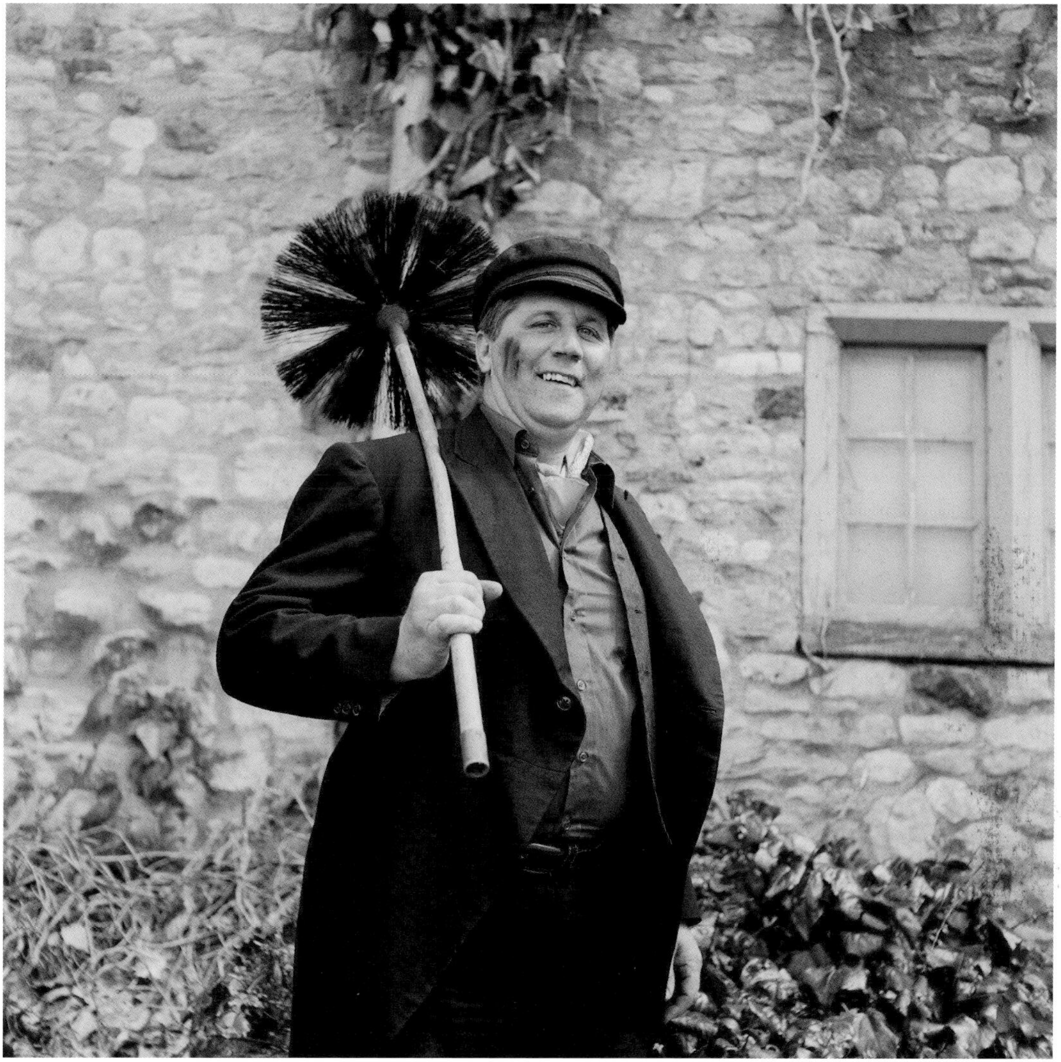

ROCHESTER SWEEP DAY (2005)

This May Day festival in Rochester, an ancient city on the Medway in Kent, was started in 1981. It revives a 300-year-old tradition of chimney sweeps celebrating May Day, often the only day that they had off in the year. In the past, boys were sent up the narrow chimneys to clean them, as the build-up of soot and tar was a fire risk. They often died after getting stuck in the chimney, or later, developed a fatal cancer from the carcinogenic soot. Eventually, the mechanical chimney brush was developed, and the practice of sending small children to risk their lives up chimneys was banned. May Day was traditionally seen as a celebration of fecundity and sex, which encouraged young people to get together – and which is certainly how the Puritans interpreted it when they banned May Day celebrations in the 17th century. However, it has a further important significance as a workers' holiday, which the Labour government recognized when they introduced the May Day bank holiday in the 1970s.

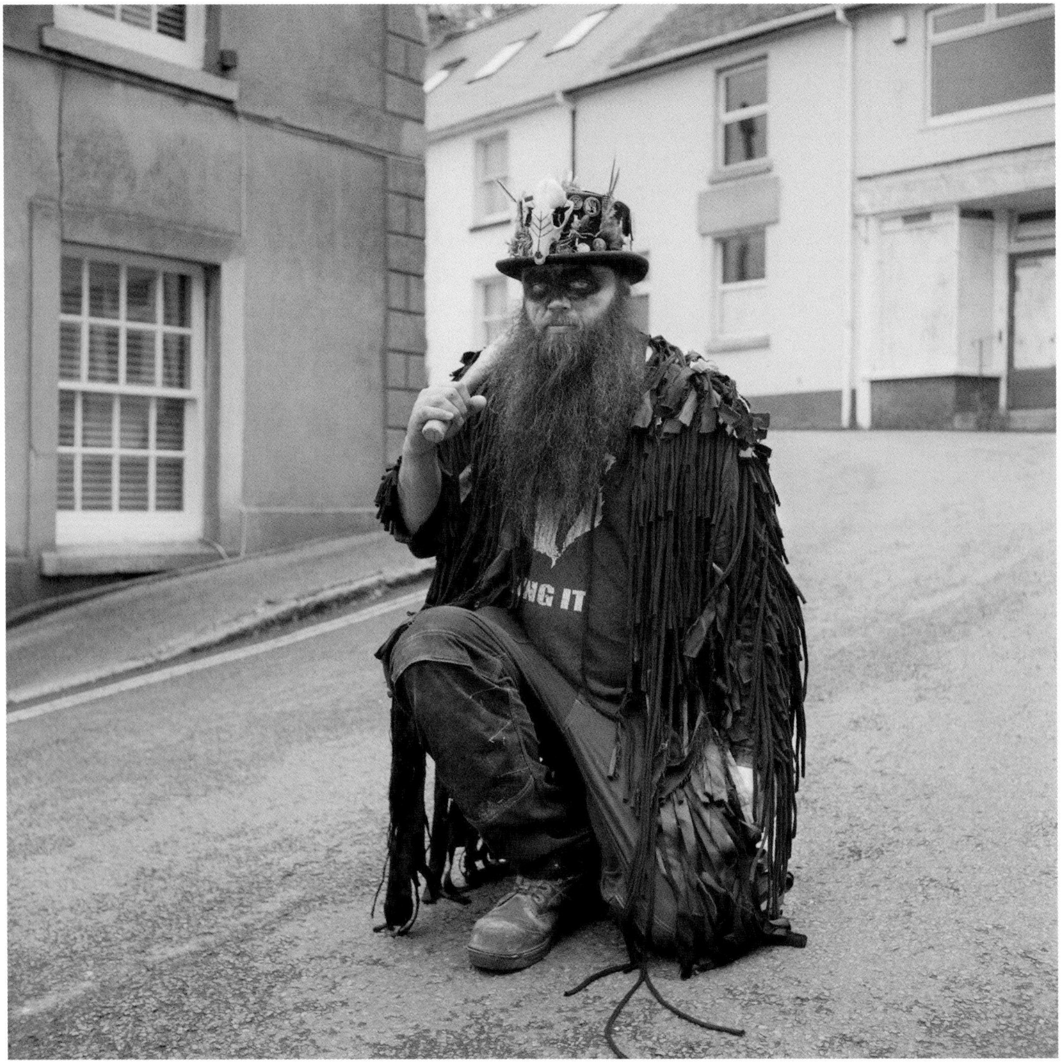

BELTANE BORDER MORRIS, BOVEY TRACEY, DEVON (2024) A Meadow Arts commission

Beltane Border Morris are a new generation of dancers who see themselves as channelling the wild, mysterious energy of Dartmoor, where they are based. They are environmentalists and bring a steampunk aesthetic to morris dancing, with their black tatters, top hats and disguised faces. Beltane is the ancient Celtic ceremony marking the beginning of summer and involving the lighting of ritual bonfires. At dawn on 1 May, the morris dancers perform at the isolated rocky outcrop known as Haytor, on the wild open common land of Dartmoor. Several of the Beltane Border side are involved in the campaign to protect the right to camp on Dartmoor. The attempt by local landowners to prevent people from sleeping under the stars on Dartmoor is a modern version of enclosure, depriving people of customary rights to the land.

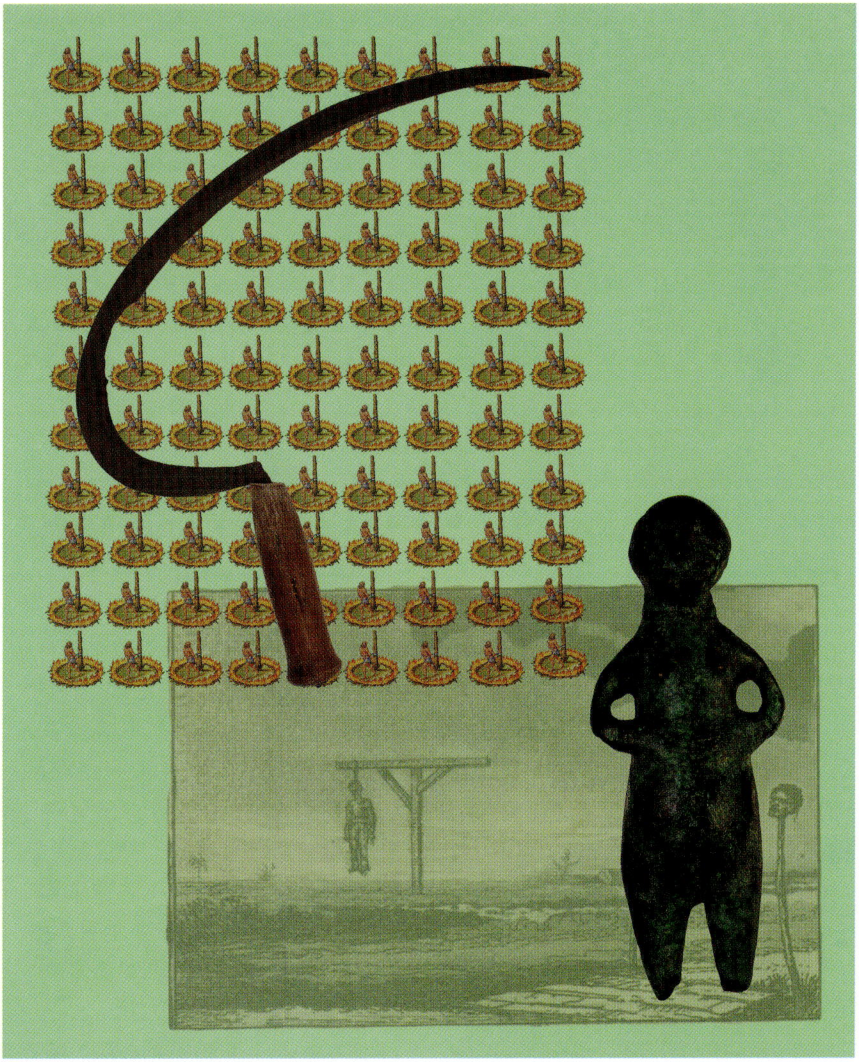

RURAL REBELS UNTITLED MONTAGE (2023) A Meadow Arts commission

As society moved from a communal to a capitalist model, many rights that had previously been taken for granted became crimes against property and the punishments very harsh, as the laws against poaching demonstrate. Certain types of theft became a capital offence as a deterrent rather than a punishment fitting the crime: "Men are not hanged for stealing horses, but that horses may not be stolen." Charges of riot were often made in order to portray the protests as sedition not just vandalism.

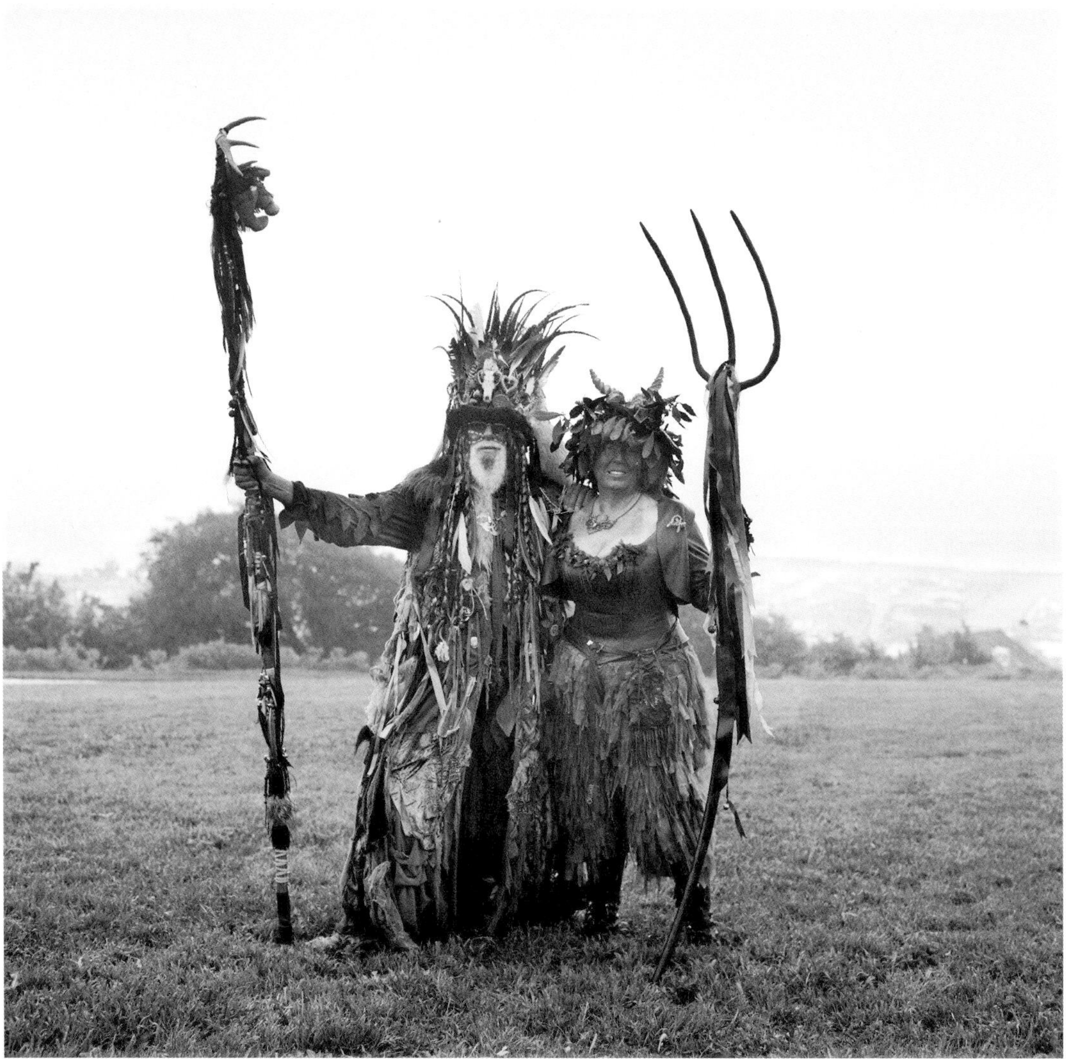

JACK IN THE GREEN FESTIVAL, HASTINGS, EAST SUSSEX (2024) A Meadow Arts commission

The Jack in the Green festival in Hastings has been resurrected in recent decades. New costumes symbolize our connection with nature, May Day being the time to celebrate the returning green after winter. Jack in the Green has its origins in the mid-17th century, when London milkmaids celebrated the coming summer and the growth of fresh grass for their cows by wearing elaborate garlands on their heads and collecting money as they went through the streets. By the 18th century, chimney sweeps were copying the milkmaids in the hope of raising funds at a time of year when there was less work for them as households lit fewer fires. By the late 19th century, Jack in the Greens could be seen throughout England – wooden frames supported on their shoulders, and completely covered in greenery and flowers. The Jack in the Green has been described as a man dressed as a hedge and, like the Green Man, celebrates nature's fecundity.

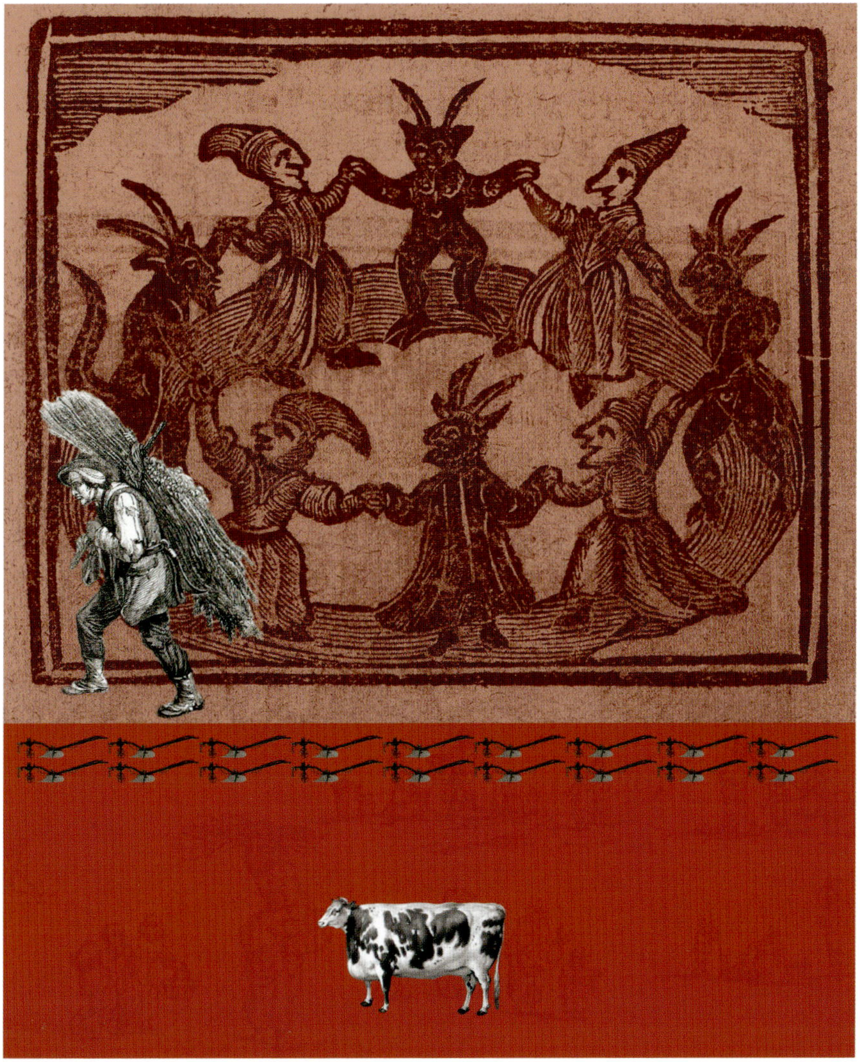

RURAL REBELS UNTITLED MONTAGE (2023) A Meadow Arts commission

The historian Silvia Federici argues that witch trials were a symptom of the subjugation and demonization of women that accompanied the arrival of capitalism. As independent peasants were turned into waged labourers, women and their bodies became unwaged workers in the home, and mere breeders of workers. Although infrequently, some women were accused of witchcraft in order to get their land. The witch hunts that continued in some parts of the world in the 20th and 21st centuries, often triggered by evangelical Christian ideas and economic upheaval, were frequently used as a means of achieving land privatization.

COSMOLOGY OF THE RURAL

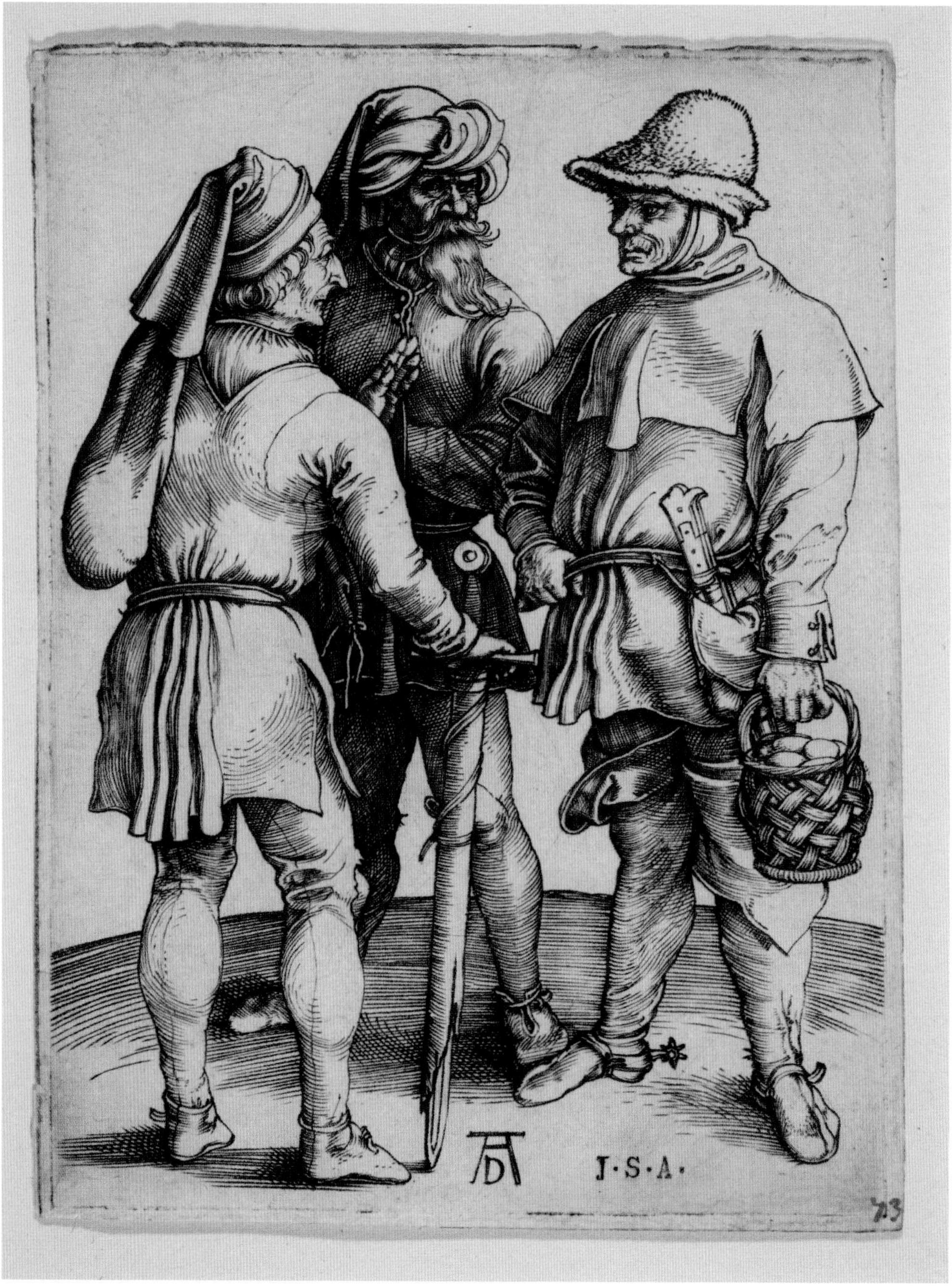

THREE PEASANTS IN CONVERSATION Albrecht Dürer (1497)

COSMOLOGY OF THE RURAL

LEAH GORDON

They say history is written by the victorious, and it might equally be said that the landscape is depicted and interpreted by those who have appropriated it. When we consider the merciless treatment of the English peasant in the name of agrarian progress, especially in the 18th and 19th centuries, it can be confusing to view landscape painting of the same epoch and find little sign of this traumatic social upheaval. The viewer needs to probe beyond the surface symbolism of English landscape painting to detect the disjuncture between the subject matter and the codes of representation and the inherent class structures and political ideologies behind them.

In this context, the word cosmology applies to the depiction of constellations of interconnected symbols, images and artworks. If we think about these in relation to images of the land and its people, we might wonder whether there exists a rural cosmology "from below" that can act as a counterpoint to mainstream rural representations. What symbolism and imaginaries, if any, did peasants create and hold for their own? And we might also question why folk art is often considered lesser than art created, or at least commissioned, by the land-owning elites of fair Albion.

As a young student, I was enthralled by the social aspects of figurative art and blind to the lessons that landscape art could deliver. I always bent toward portraits, as both a creator and a viewer, because they could tell both social and cultural stories. And I've been uncertain about how to explore human existence without representing the people. Working on this book has made me revisit the rural landscape as scarred territory – and to re-read landscapes as revealing the subtle traces and scars of dispossession, extraction and profit. I'm more aware now that the representation of the rural and its folk has never been a nonpartisan territory, and also more aware of how to deconstruct that apparent neutrality. Recently I have, through my own work in representing rural people, started questioning the history of the visibility, or rather invisibility, of the English peasantry. This re-reading of the rural requires us to dismiss our city-centric and often either patronizing or unrealistic nostalgic positions, and to reappraise rural imagery as being of a vital importance, rather than a backwater of contemporary debate.

When reflecting on the portrayal of the land and its people, I've found the artist Albrecht Dürer's unrealized plans for his "Monument to the Vanquished Peasants" in 1525 to be a source of enduring inspiration. It's a sketch for what appears at first glance to be a conventional civic monument, but which depicts a peasant who has been stabbed in the back with a large sword, and who sits atop a pillar made of objects and livestock that represent peasant life, including oxen, hoes, picks and bales of hay. The monument, which appears to portray great sympathy for the peasant, would have been politically difficult to create and install in any German town.

Dürer was born in Nuremberg in 1471 and died there at the age of 56 in 1528. During his lifetime society underwent rapid changes, and as trade, guilds and industry were increasing there was a strengthening of the middle classes. He lived at a time when the priest and theologian Martin Luther was challenging the orthodoxy of the Catholic Church and unwittingly unleashed the revolutionary imaginations of the peasant classes, who started to believe that they could also challenge social hierarchies. This led to the German Peasants' War, a far-reaching uprising in some of the German-speaking regions in Central Europe from 1524 to 1525. Ironically, this deeply threatened Luther, as his theological reform was never rooted in class antagonism or struggle.

Dürer is considered to be one of the first artists to depict the burgeoning confidence of the peasant classes and his images of peasants are said to have been used on the rebels' own political pamphlets. The engraving *Three Peasants in Conversation* (1497) is a great example of the poise and status that Dürer affords his subjects. The men look full of self-respect and are engaged in attentive conversation with each other. Moreover, they are carrying swords and daggers, which could suggest they're members of the armed rebellion.

The encyclopaedic works of Pieter Bruegel the Elder, such as the panel painting *Netherlandish Proverbs* (1559), similarly depict village life as being full of vitality and character. Bruegel is the paramount portrayer of Netherlandish peasantry, which he does by endowing the rural majority class with a rumbustious energy, panache and surreal creativity. *The Fight Between Carnival and Lent* (1559), while showing a scene of wild abandon and community exuberance, also depicts the granular minutiae of quotidian peasant activities, such as cooking bread, selling fresh fish and frequenting the tavern. And in the right-hand side of the painting we can see the inauspicious arrival

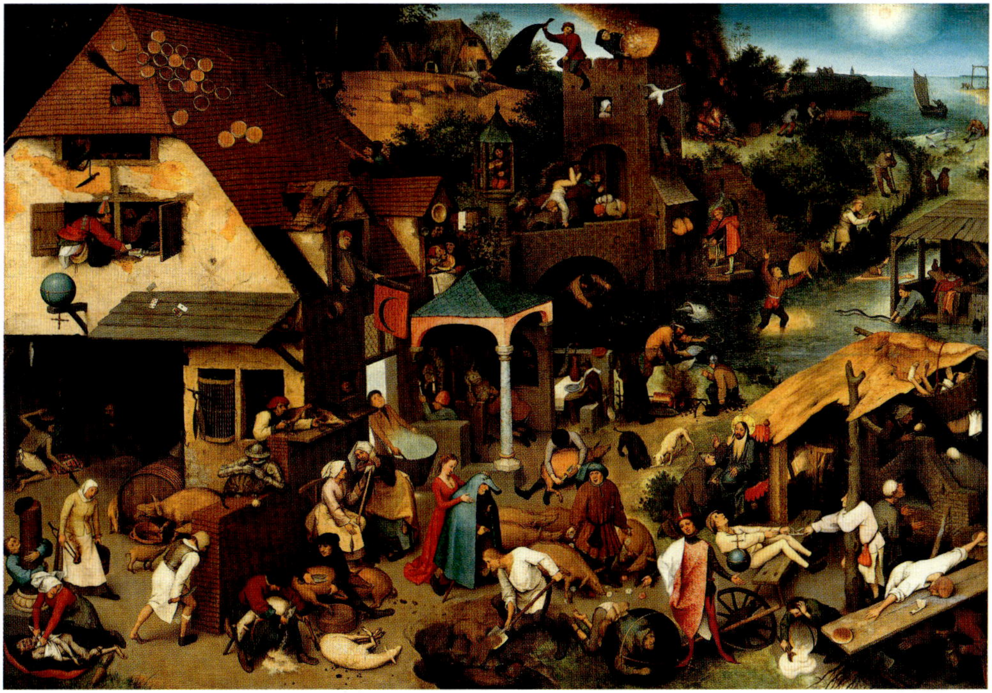

THE NETHERLANDISH PROVERBS (THE BLUE CLOAK) Pieter Bruegel the Elder (1559)

of the miserabilist church folk, cloaked in black. It's difficult to imagine a more inclusive depiction of life – from the literally legless, to the drunkenly legless, to the spiritually legless – from the workaday to the carnivalesque, with the religious orders sidelined as toothless and ineffective.

Art historians today can only speculate as to why the peasant was such a significant subject for Bruegel and, in some ways more importantly, who the patrons were that were willing to support the creation of these paintings. Most of Bruegel's paintings were commissioned and owned by Antwerp's rich and influential merchant class. Perhaps they sought reassuring tableaus of traditional Flemish life during this epoch of advancing mercantile capitalism and insecurity in the face of Spanish continued aggression. The period also corresponds with the beginning of an epoch of classification in Europe, which saw the evolution of the first encyclopaedias, the emergence of collections of curiosities and the publication in Antwerp in 1570 of the *Theatrum Orbis Terrarum*, considered to be the first atlas. Perhaps this marks the beginning of the ethnographic turn in Western culture whereby the peasants became one of the subjects in the Low

Countries, especially as they were gaining notoriety through acts of rebellion?

More importantly, why does there appear to be nothing like these representations in English art, depicting the peasant with a radical and rumbustious strength? Why, for example, was there never an English Bruegel, representing the peasantry with humour and downright anarchy? The peasant is afforded no such visibility or agency in England. It's as if the ruling classes were trying to exile the peasant not just from the land but the imagination.

There appear to be many constraints to their portrayal, as John Barrell discusses in his influential study of the peasant paintings of Gainsborough, Stubbs and Constable in *The Dark Side of the Landscape* (1980). Barrell believes that English art representing rural life from 1730 to 1840, during the height of the parliamentary enclosures, was subservient to the political and economic needs of the country. By painting, on the one hand, a meek and passive cohort of agricultural workers, but on the other hand showing them as content and industrious, the artists were conveying important moral, and therefore economic, messages.

The mid-18th century to the mid-19th century was a period of great upheaval in England as the Industrial Revolution was in full flow alongside increased enclosure and the so-called "modernization" of the agricultural economy. Cities were booming and villages were emptying. The discourses around rural and urban oscillated between the virtues and the vices of both, swinging from praising cities as hubs of sophistication against the asininity of the rural classes, to decrying the depravity of urban life in comparison to the moral purity of the countryside.

In England, any representation of the peasant seemed to serve a greater purpose than simply entertaining the upper classes, as portrayals of rural life were also actively masking the actual brutality and suffering of the times. The narrow depiction of the peasant classes in art could be the result of aesthetic choices based on images fitting prettily into home interiors belonging to wealthy patrons, but aesthetics were secondary in some respects to the subtle imposition and advocacy of economic ideology. The rustic peasant classes had to be depicted as hard-working, which helped to conserve the political hegemony of the landed gentry. Two works by George Stubbs, *Haymakers* and *Reapers*, both painted in 1785, are prime examples of this, in which while obviously labouring hard, the agricultural workers are depicted as neatly dressed, their clothing unstained and untorn. These two paintings seem to fold the landed classes' aesthetic and ideological needs seamlessly together into scenes deemed acceptable by the upper classes.

In his seminal TV series *Ways of Seeing* (later made into a book), the art critic John Berger famously exposes the special relationship between landownership and painting through his penetrating analysis of *Mr and Mrs Andrews* by Gainsborough. In the painting, dating to about 1750, the couple are posed in front of their – as we can see by the fences and hedgerows – newly enclosed land. This isn't simply a depiction of a husband and wife sitting in the countryside, but of landowners and enclosers performing and displaying their status and propriety.

In his book *Common Land in English Painting 1700–1850*, Ian Waites re-reads notable landscape paintings for what they hide rather than disclose. A stark caption to *Lilford Hall, Northants. View from the North Across Water Meadows of the Nene* (c.1760) attributed to Anthony Devis, mentions that this peaceful landscape belies the brutal changes that took place over a 30-year period, including the demolition of Lilford village and the enclosure of the common land.[1] It remains imperative to re-read landscape art from the perspective of its objectives to uphold, while camouflaging, the neoliberal conditions that underpin English politics.

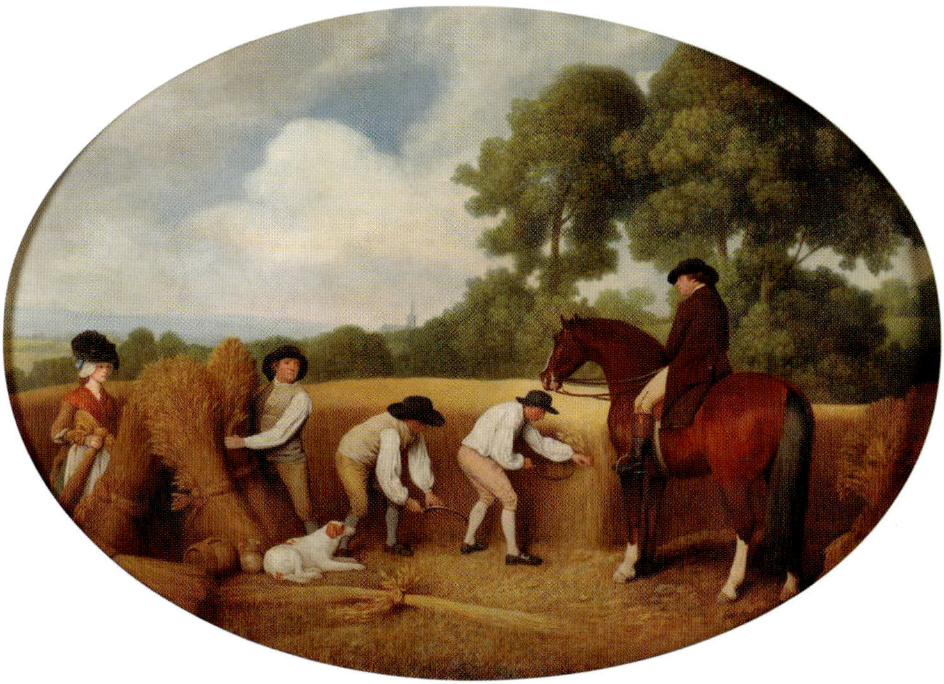

REAPERS, George Stubbs (1795)

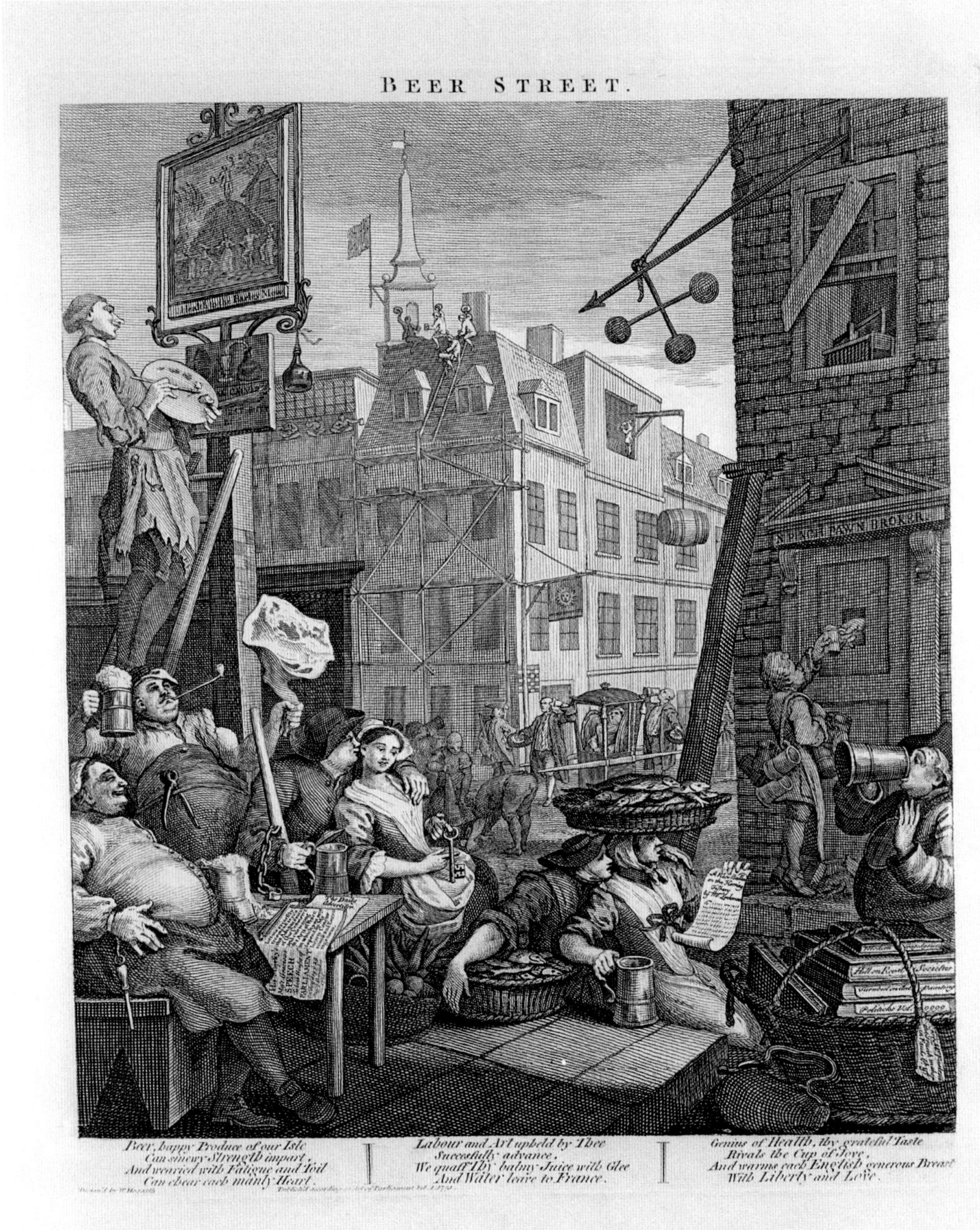

BEER STREET William Hogarth (1751)

The new urban lower classes, freshly exiled from the countryside, came under increasing scrutiny as a class to exploit but also fear. The artist William Hogarth started out satirizing the lower and the wealthy classes in works such as the series *A Harlot's Progress, A Rake's Progress and Marriage A-la-Mode*. But by the 1750s, his moralizing was also aimed at the urban poor in the series *Industry and Idleness* and the prints *Beer Street* and *Gin Lane*, and no doubt stoked debate as to how to handle the urban and rural "vagabond" question.

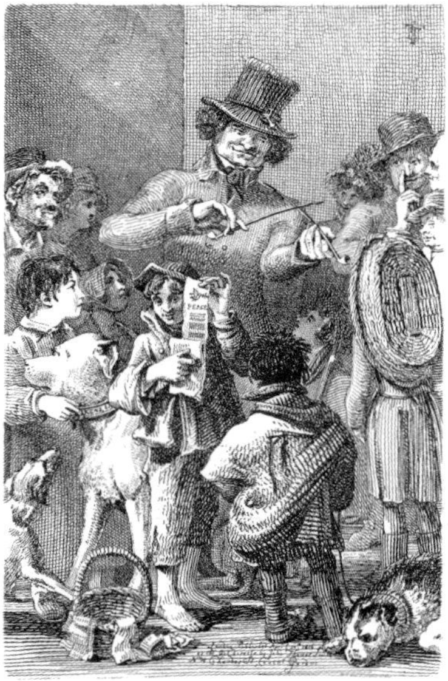

ILLUSTRATION FROM *VAGABONDIANA*
John Thomas Smith (1800s)

In the early 1800s, the illustrator John Thomas Smith, a friend of the artist and poet William Blake and informal artistic mentor to Constable, produced two books, *The Streets of London: Anecdotes of Their More Celebrated Residents* and *Vagabondiana, or Anecdotes of Mendicant Wanderers through the Streets of London*. These works were far less moralizing and there is a more egalitarian quality to the representations in them. Smith's work has more of a documentary and reportage approach to it, perhaps reflecting a growing sympathy for the fates and misfortunes of the dispossessed peoples.

While peasants were rarely literate enough to write about their own relationship to the land, they continued to celebrate this through their seasonal traditions. British folk traditions have long performed the boundaries, histories and rituals that mark our relationship to the land, as well as been a precursor to – and sometimes peasant camouflage for – riot and rebellion. But alongside the catastrophic effect of expropriation of the land and the ensuing destruction of the peasants' symbiotic relationship with common land, there have been massive losses of traditions, customs, local dialects and traditional skills.

Peasants and the majority class were generating their own artistic traditions from below that continued to flourish during the 18th and 19th centuries. This was art created by the English majority class to be consumed by the English majority class. However, because much of this art entailed the application of decoration to functional objects, it was deemed by the social elite to be "craft" rather than art. When the Royal Academy of Arts was established in 1768, a list of barred forms was published that included needlework, cut paper and shell work, in order to distinguish the fine arts from these crafts. This indicates how class prejudice is enacted through the elevation of certain art forms over others and, again, how the agency of the majority class is both eroded and rendered invisible. Folk

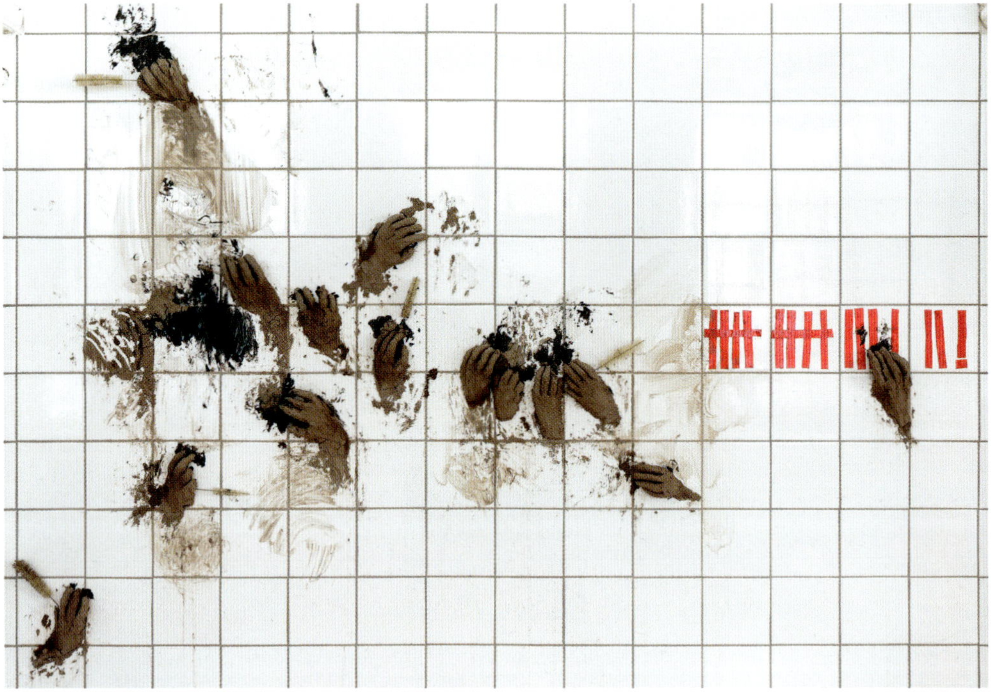

HOARDING, ENCLOSURES at Camden Arts Centre, Jesse Darling (2022)

art was profoundly rooted in the rural and working-class communities and often, along with customs and traditions, helped bind people together during brutal and taxing times. Unfortunately, eventually the new forms of cheap mass production heralded by the industrial era tolled the final death knell for folk art and while intellectuals attempted to promote new craft-based art movements, these were no longer economically sustainable means of making a living.

The stronghold that the elite establishment has had over cultural production ever since has often stifled imagery that preserves peasant philosophy, values and spirituality, and that keeps open connections with practical and traditional skills. What has been lost is a representation of the land revealing the evidence and traces of ancestral traditions, common access and spiritual relationships.

In the 20th and 21st century, folk reasserted itself into the public consciousness through the folk-horror film. Many films within the folk-horror genre tend to locate the menace in the audience's subconscious fears of the hidden vestiges of paganism and often show the local rural people being under the sway of an evil landowner. This renders invisible the fact that the real folk-horror could be seen through the lens of twin anxieties in the past: that of the abject terror of peasants ejected from their common lands, and also the trepidation of the elites, fearful of another, more successful, peasants' revolt. It seems that the film industry, as the landowning elites before them, has little interest in creating a cinematic, gothic hauntology of the rural that is based on an understanding of the economic and social conditions underpinning the anxieties in Arcadia.

Across the globe, brutal territorial wars are taking place, climatic and ecological collapse are becoming increasingly catastrophic and Indigenous peoples are suffering even more drastic extractivist invasions onto their ancestral lands. It's no surprise that the art world is now becoming more attentive to issues surrounding land ownership, access and land loss. Artists have been exploring the nefarious ways in which the past inhabits the present and have been creating numerous strategies to allow the silenced histories to slither through to our collective consciousness. Turner Prize winner Jesse Darling produced an installation called *Enclosures* for the Camden Arts Centre in 2022 and the same year the American artist Rachel Rose produced a show called *Enclosure* for the Pilar Corrias Gallery. [2,3] In 2024 and 2025 alone, many international contemporary group exhibitions tried to highlight our ongoing dislocation from the land. Alongside this, there has been an increase in the visibility of Indigenous arts and amplification of their voices.

In short, as we claw back the land through allotments, protect remaining common lands through the Open Spaces Society, and challenge access rights through the Ramblers and Right to Roam movements, we have also loosened the stronghold in some small ways that landowning patrons hold over both the representation of the landscape in art and the people who work on it and enjoy its benefits. We may not be able to return to an Arcadian pre-enclosure utopia, but we can begin to explore alternative relationships to the land other than what's currently on offer.

A CONVERSATION ABOUT THE COSMOLOGY OF THE RURAL

In June 2023, Annabel Edwards and I collaborated with the visual arts charity Meadow Arts on an event called "Cosmology of the Rural", in which we explored the historical significance of rural enclosure and its contemporary symbolism. As part of this, the image collector and author Stephen Ellcock and I engaged in a labyrinthine discussion, ranging from rural riots to morris mayhem. To a certain extent we were both wary and critical of how embracing folk traditions can be a toothless exercise without an understanding of the historical precedents and political struggles. One thing we both agreed on was that "you can't morris dance your way to a revolution". Inspired, I wrote the essay on page 105 afterwards and upon reading it, Stephen and I talked some more. This is a shortened version of that second conversation.

LEAH GORDON:

They say that history is written by the victorious, so could it be said that landscape is depicted and interpreted by those who have appropriated it?

STEPHEN ELLCOCK:

It makes sense, but I don't think it's 100 per cent accurate. From the late 19th and the early 20th century onward, there have been ways of looking at and depicting the landscape that aren't dictated by those who own it. There are alternative narratives: whether visionary interpretations and evocations of landscape, or more agitprop-sympathetic depictions of rural life that are often more subtle and understated.

Take John Constable (1776–1837), for example: my grandparents would probably have bought a reproduction of *The Hay Wain* (1821) from Woolworths or Boots, which they would have had in their living room.

Perhaps it could be considered sentimental, but there's an empathy there – a deep connection to people's lives. And many artists weren't from the gentry or the upper echelons of society.

When you said the more visionary artists, whom did you have in mind?

The obvious answers are Samuel Palmer and William Blake, but there are also deeply underappreciated artists who depicted the realities of rural life and rural life in transition, such as John Sell Cotman (1782–1842). If you look at Cotman's work, it's full of visual clues that are definitely political and subversive. But because he was dependent upon the patronage of rich people, these are deeply embedded within depictions of the landscape that the gentry would approve of. His painting *Ruined House* seems to me to embody the rottenness and sickness at the core of English rural life. My favourite painting by Cotman is a watercolour of a scarecrow (*The Ploughed Field*, c.1805). It feels timeless. However, it embodies folk-horror in a way that prefigures the genre. Somehow, he captures a sense of the uncanny, of unease beneath the surface.

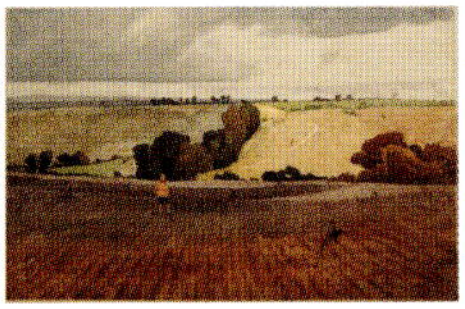

A PLOUGHED FIELD

John Sell Cotman (1923)

There are numerous works by British artists of the 18th and, in particular, 19th century, which are equally disconcerting and filled with that sense of foreboding. Consider the work of Joseph Wright of Derby (1734–1797) (see page 32), whose extraordinary painting *Cottage on Fire at Night* (1785–93) is like an amazing foreshadowing of the century to come, prefiguring the devastating fate in store for the working peasantry and the destruction of a whole way of life. The painting depicts a typical workers' cottage but it's ablaze; the traditional vision of Arcadia has become a vision of Hell on Earth. This is the new reality, ushered in by the nascent Industrial Revolution, where people are herded into cities and forced to become wage slaves.

Visitors to a typical British municipal art gallery might see works by these artists, and their immediate response might be, "How picturesque!" In a culture saturated with sentimental evocations of an idealized past, it's all too easy to fall prey to pre-programmed nostalgia. However, artists have always been well aware of the contradictions and the struggles of people who work the land.

You mentioned that you have a more nuanced reading of Thomas Gainsborough (1727–1788) – can you expand?

Gainsborough is a slippery customer, because he became extremely wealthy for flattering the gentry. There's an extraordinary John Berger essay about Gainsborough's famous portrait of *Mr and Mrs Andrews* (c.1748). Berger gives a political analysis of that work: that all is right with the world, and that these aristocrats have dominion over nature. There are no signs of any activity in the landscape – the people who work the land aren't visible.

Yet Berger discerns a subtle satirical intent in Gainsborough's work. He and his contemporaries were artists for hire, earning a fortune through what was essentially hack work, churning out vanity portraits with considerable skill and talent. He also produced extraordinary small-scale works of people working with livestock that aren't overly sentimental and cloying. There is grit and authenticity to these descriptions, and a degree of truth.

Of course, there are artists whose sentimental depictions of rural lives are nauseatingly twee and offensive. Take the work of George Morland (1763–1804), for example. His paintings of little orphans clustering around an idealized English squire, handing out alms to the poor, and of cherubic children working in the fields… now those are toxic. These works function as propaganda: they are visions of a hierarchical social order viewed through the prism of the landowning class.

With the birth of photography, there were also more nuanced depictions of rural life. For example, Peter Henry Emerson (1856–1936) took hundreds of photographs of life in the fens that are extraordinarily beautiful, but which don't stint on depicting those people's hard-scrabble existence, whether collecting reeds, fishing for eels or collecting peat. An interesting element of realism enters English visual culture with the early years of photography that acts as a counterbalance to Victorian sentimentality.

What would you consider to be a rural cosmology from below of the British Isles?

It's probably best encapsulated in the work of the visionary, of people like Palmer and Blake. But perhaps they leaned too much toward an idealistic, spiritual connection to the landscape and the earth; most rural people – for example, a stonebreaker working in the most godawful conditions – would never have felt that spiritual connection. Could a rural cosmology in Britain be expressed in rituals and ways to mark the seasons and the natural processes of nature or the seasons? I think people have tried to superimpose that kind of cosmological framework on English history, too, but most people who lived and worked in rural England probably didn't feel that sort of connection – other than at certain shared moments when they may have been involved in a collective response to prevailing material conditions.

Why is folk art treated as a lower art form?

I definitely think this is related to class – the hierarchy of taste and values that's a hangover from the Classical tradition, which dictates that the highest arts are painting, architecture and sculpture. An artificial barrier separating "high art" from "low art" has been erected by the self-appointed custodians of taste and propriety. If an unlettered *peasant* creates a work of great beauty, whether it be something carved, crafted with a practical purpose or purely decorative, then their achievements will automatically be considered inferior to those artworks created by those who belong to the predominant elite or who genuflect before it. This deep-rooted prejudice still permeates our culture today.

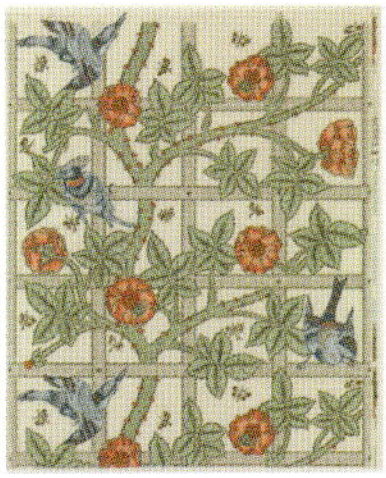

TRELLIS WALLPAPER DESIGN
William Morris (1862)

L S Lowry (1887–1976) is an interesting example. The more of his work I see, the more I appreciate it. His paintings are unsentimental depictions of ordinary people. Yet because of his background, the subjects that he was depicting and the commercialization of his work in cheap prints and that 1970s song "Matchstalk Men and

Matchstalk Cats and Dogs", people dismiss his art. A painting created by a rent collector from Salford will automatically not be granted the same consideration or value as a work by somebody who has spent God knows how long studying at the Royal Academy, Chelsea or the Slade.

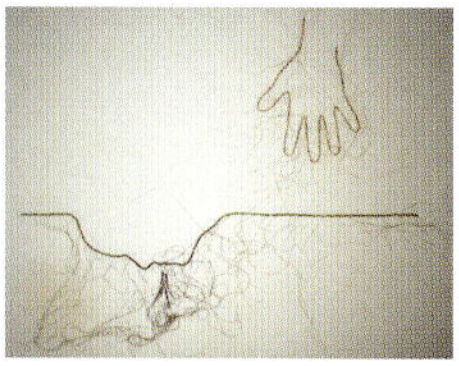

THIS ISLAND EARTH
Abigail Lane (2022)

Class is the original sin of English society, the inescapable trap that we all have to try to operate within as best we can. It affects every aspect of life, even today. The rich have re-established their dominance multiple times over the course of the centuries. There was a brief period lasting from the 1940s until the election of Thatcher in 1979 where social mobility was allowed and even encouraged, and previously suppressed working-class and diverse voices were heard and respected for the first time. But those opportunities have once again been shut down and brutally suppressed. We are becoming an atomized, fearful and semi-feudal society of landlords, robber barons, serfs and peasants.

It's no coincidence that, in a time of great social division, people are rediscovering an interest in folk customs, superstitions and vernacular art. Some of it undoubtedly is the novelty value and the sheer weirdness and hallucinatory "otherness" of much folk art and traditions, but I think there's also a visceral connection to folk art that fulfils a need that isn't met in other aspects of British culture.

What is your relationship to landscape art?

I was always drawn to landscape art before portraiture and other genres. I suppose I was brought up with a somewhat romantic idea of the landscape due to my grandparents' influence on my childhood. My maternal grandparents had worked in the fields, while my other grandparents lived on the outskirts of Chelmsford, surrounded by farms and extensive allotments, and they were also deeply connected to the land. Both of my grandfathers were expert gardeners. So I don't know whether it's something genetic or something drilled into me, but I've always had an abiding love for depictions of landscapes and the natural world.

I'm becoming more aware that the representation of the rural has never been nonpartisan territory, as well as the history of visibility or invisibility of the English peasantry. What do you feel?

You have to delve quite deeply to find depictions of the English peasantry, agricultural workers and ordinary rural people before the 18th century. There are very few and they are hard to find, but they're there. Sometimes it's as presences in the portraits of the great landowners, where they are spectres in the background.

And then there is the continued popularity of hunting and sporting prints. The landscape was shaped to a great extent by rural sport; in particular, by hunting, whether it be fox hunting, deer or hare coursing, or stag hunting – those sorts of barbaric activities. Ordinary people also feature in those artworks, but they're present as onlookers or tending to the horses or the hounds. There is still a lucrative market for art and literature devoted to hunting and those pursuits euphemistically described as "rural sports", but it's something of a dirty secret outside of certain circles.

The population's enduring obsession with hunting itself explains a lot about English politics and attitudes of the upper classes: the fact that the countryside, as well as being a source of food and raw materials, is also a playground for the rich and their pursuits. And even though the rural poor may have hunted and fished out of necessity, they also did so for pleasure, too.

This is root cause of my now increasingly ambivalent relationship with the countryside. I never feel completely at ease in a rural environment nowadays, my childhood connections having been well and truly severed, and my Arcadian reveries shattered beyond repair. Large tracts of the British landscape are bleak agri-deserts where ancient privilege and faceless multinational oligarchies hold sway. Lobbies for blood sports retain a pernicious and disproportionate influence in the corridors of power in this country. I can think of few things more likely to trigger widespread unrest and rebellion in the UK than the prospect of some putative future government threatening to ban horse racing or non-commercial fishing. I do, however, take some consolation in the fact that in the increasingly unlikely event that the human race manages to survive for another century or two, then such pursuits will inevitably regarded with the same revulsion we now reserve for bear-baiting and the ducking of suspected "witches".

Why do you think there was never an English Bruegel representing the peasantry with a sense of agency?

That is the key question! Though the peasantry has always been represented in English culture, this tends to be in literature, not the visual arts. Langland's *Piers Plowman*, Chaucer and Shakespeare all depict peasant life in all its rawness, ribaldry, rebellious nature and vivacity. So if I were to answer "Who's the English Bruegel?", it would be them or other Elizabethan and Jacobean playwrights. And that acts as a displacement, where these ideas are embodied in words rather than images.

Religion must have something to do with the primacy of the word in English culture over visual arts until fairly recently. I might be completely off the mark there, but why is there no English Caravaggio? Why is there no English Dürer or Bruegel? They weren't encouraged. If you can imagine going to the great Catholic cathedrals, it's basically theatre. The ritual imbued within Catholicism and other, more theatrical manifestations of Protestantism is largely absent within British culture. There is an element of it in Anglicanism, but it's pretty mundane compared to the extravagances of full-scale Catholic masses. That must be part of the reason why English visual culture differs.

What are your feelings about Hogarth's depictions of the lower classes – either rural or urban?

I slightly disagree with what you say about William Hogarth (1697–1764). While a bit of an English Bruegel figure, I believe he was a genuine anarchist. If you look closely at his work, he's prone to biting the hand that feeds him and satirizes everything.

Others who were also considered bastions of the establishment produced some surprising works. For example, in Dublin, there's an extraordinary painting in the National Gallery by Joshua Reynolds (1723–1792), *Parody of Raphael's School of Athens* (1750–51), in which he satirizes the government and skewers the aristocrats of the day in the most unforgiving, brutal way. It's quite shocking, as Reynolds was the Royal Academy's founder and traditionally regarded as the quintessential artist of the English establishment of his time – but he also produced cartoon-like works that really surprised me. It may be significant that I spotted this on display in Dublin and not in the Royal Academy or Tate Britain.

Do you have any opinion on the loss of traditions and artistic skills due to the loss of commons?

You mean the loss of traditional skills or creative outlets for people? I think those things have been displaced and diverted to other things. Today, people will find other outlets for their creativity, which won't necessarily involve working with their hands, creating functional and beautiful objects, or involving visual sophistication or sophisticated skill.

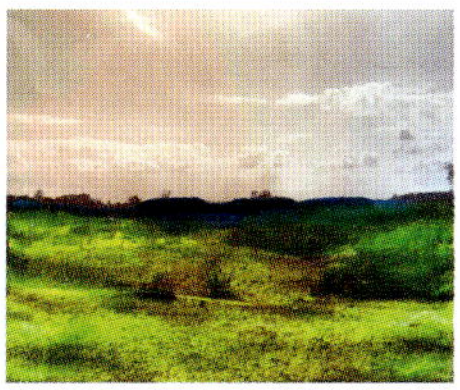

BLUE BUNKER, GREENHAM COMMON NATURE RESERVE

Alison McKenna (2021)

To bring up my grandparents again: they were all incredibly creative in so many ways, and that's not me over-sentimentalizing them. My grandfather would carefully arrange his flower garden and his rows of vegetables and fruits. And both of my grandmothers could sew and knit beautifully.

But people don't need to do that now (though they may need to in the future). It's terrible: the impact on the planet of losing those skills and that connection to making and doing. It's to the detriment of the planet, and probably to the spiritual wellbeing of most people. So yes, there is an element of regret and a sense of loss for the traditional skills, but it's not a lost paradise. No one should ever forget how shitty most people's lives were – just because they might have owned a beautiful hand-sewn smock doesn't mean that we should envy them and the lives that they undoubtedly would have led.

Many have suggested that by the time people like William Morris tried to reinstate folk crafts, mass production was already an inevitability.

People appreciate the Arts and Crafts movement and people such as William Morris, Walter Crane and Charles Rennie Mackintosh. Their art, creations and designs are extraordinarily beautiful and still speak to us, but that kind of art style and ideology was a dead-end response to the rampant advance of mass production and consumerism. It was an incredibly laudable and praiseworthy effort; I'm a huge admirer of Morris and Crane, but it had little relevance to ordinary working people's lives, whether in a rural or an urban environment, which is a terrible shame. Their kind of yearning – to go back to being an idealized, medieval peasant with a loom at home – though a utopian idea, was impractical and would never happen. It was never going to gain traction in late-Victorian Britain.

Here's a quote out of a Sherlock Holmes novel: "It is my belief, Watson, founded on my experience, that the lowest and vilest alleys in London do not present a more dreadful record of sin than does the smiling, beautiful countryside." What do you think he meant by that?

I agree with that completely, though I have lived through a different time and have had a different experience than Conan Doyle or his fictional alter ego. I used to love the countryside. Now, as I've said, it freaks me out completely.

But the issue surrounding English farmers' protests about inheritance tax is surprisingly interesting. My natural inclination is to feel no sympathy for these people, but it's more complicated than that. I've seen left-wing people, socialist writers and commentators that I admire pointing out the fact that this is an important battle. Never mind the Nigel Farages and Jeremy Clarksons of this world, there is actually an important principle here – in that this taxation on farmers could lead to the countryside being purchased by [the investment company] BlackRock and similar evil monopolies. Do we really want food production to be controlled by BlackRock and other evil bastards? No, we don't.

Finally, do you have any opinion on the meaning and subtext of folk-horror?

I think the folk-horror genre is a more general fear of uncontrollable forces underneath the surface – whether subconscious urges, dark forces, ghosts, monsters or demons. Things like ideas of possession and representations of witchcraft stand in for nature bursting through the veneer of civilization. So folk-horror is the terror of natural forces that we can't quite understand, and of things that we may have suppressed bursting through.

The popularity of the British ghost story, crime fiction and crime stories – whether "cosy" fiction or gruesome true crime recreations – is about much the same thing: that the veneer of civilization is fake, that these things are bubbling away under the surface, and could break through at any time. And woe betide if that should happen!

Folk-horror is interesting because often the outcome is extremely nihilistic and there's no resolution. I'm thinking of *The Wicker Man, Witchfinder General, The Blood on Satan's Claw* or M R James's writings. There are no happy endings; nobody is coming along to solve the mystery. At the end of *Witchfinder General*, Matthew Hopkins, the Vincent Price character, may get his comeuppance, but it's not in a satisfying form of justice in the way that an Agatha Christie novel is, where a bad guy is revealed and gets his just deserts. Folk-horror reveals our fear of the unknown, the uncanny – the fear that the natural world is impossible to control, read or decipher completely. Some things are seemingly inexplicable; for all our vaunted rationality and mastery over natural forces, we don't have any control over those things.

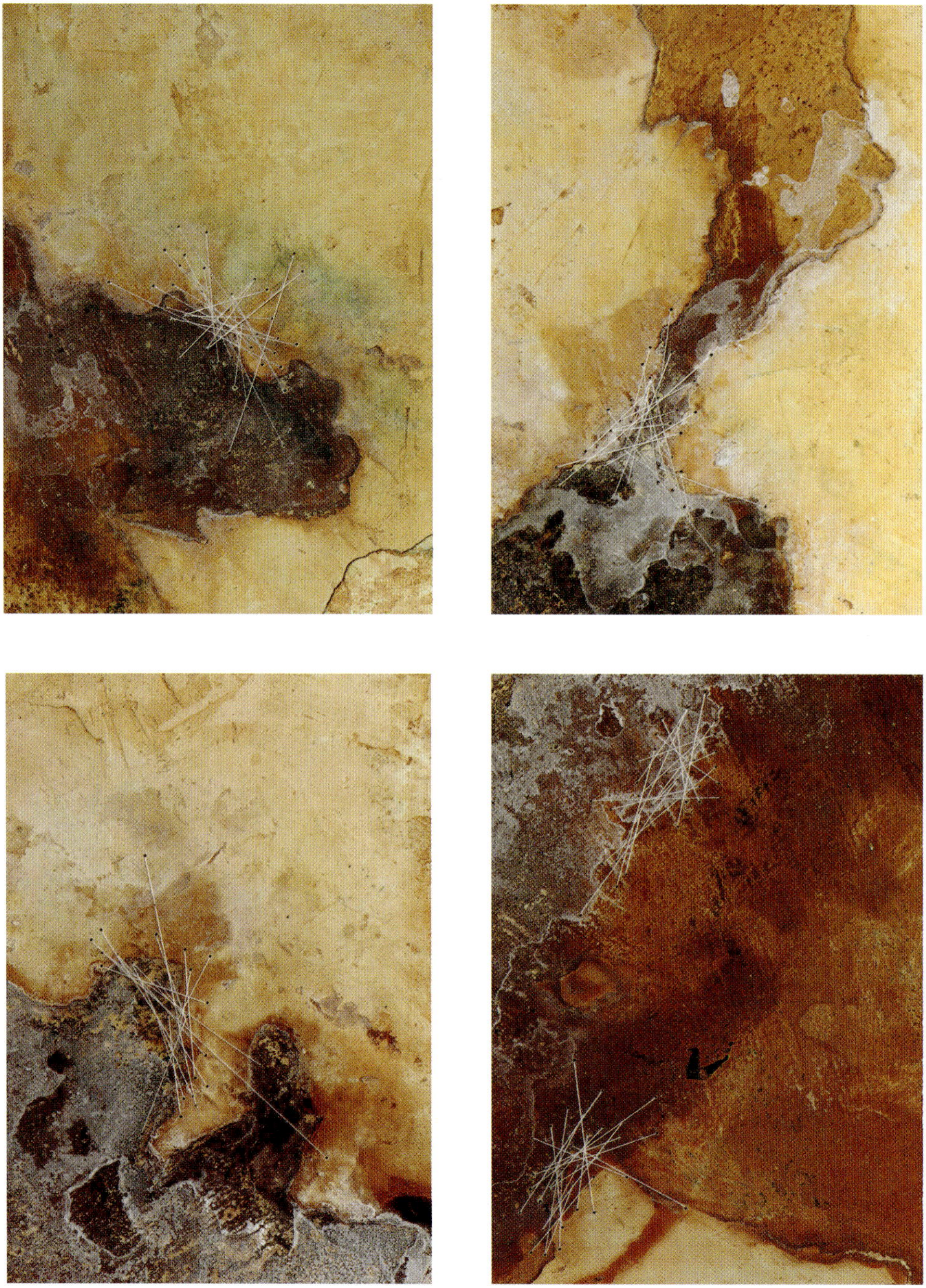

ECHOES OF THE LAND I, V, IX, XII Poppy Lennox (2024)

THE FRAGILE SHELL OF THE PRESENT COLLAPSES

Hugo Winder-Lind
(2025)

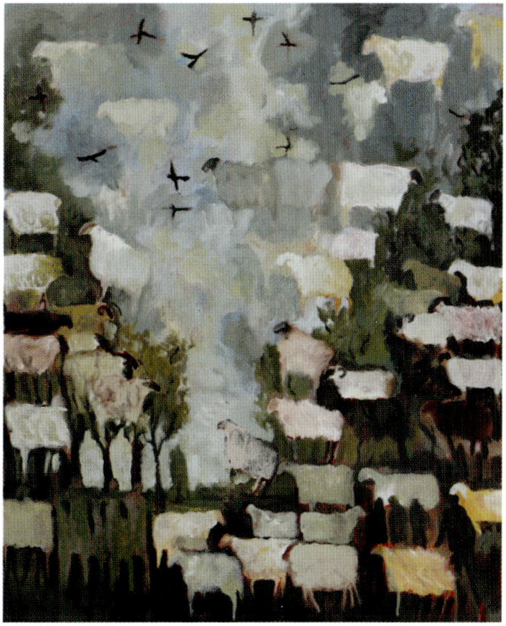

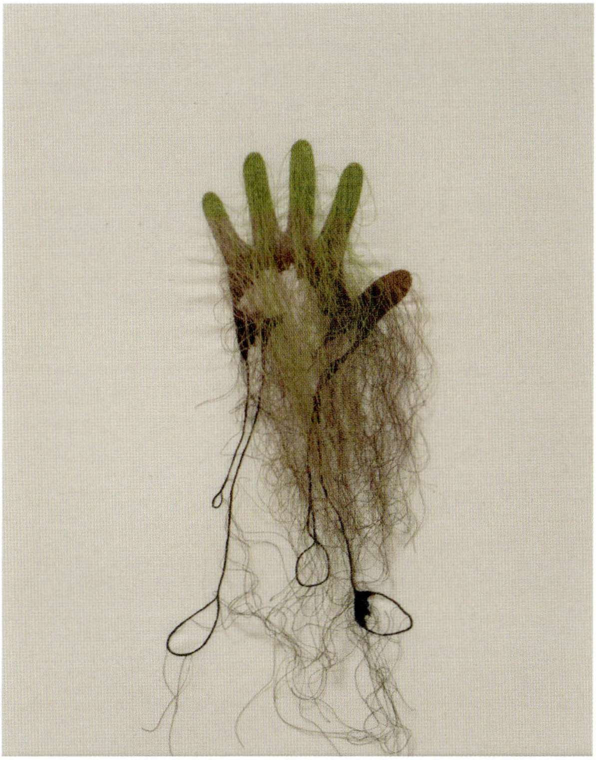

NEW SEASON

Abigail Lane
(2022)

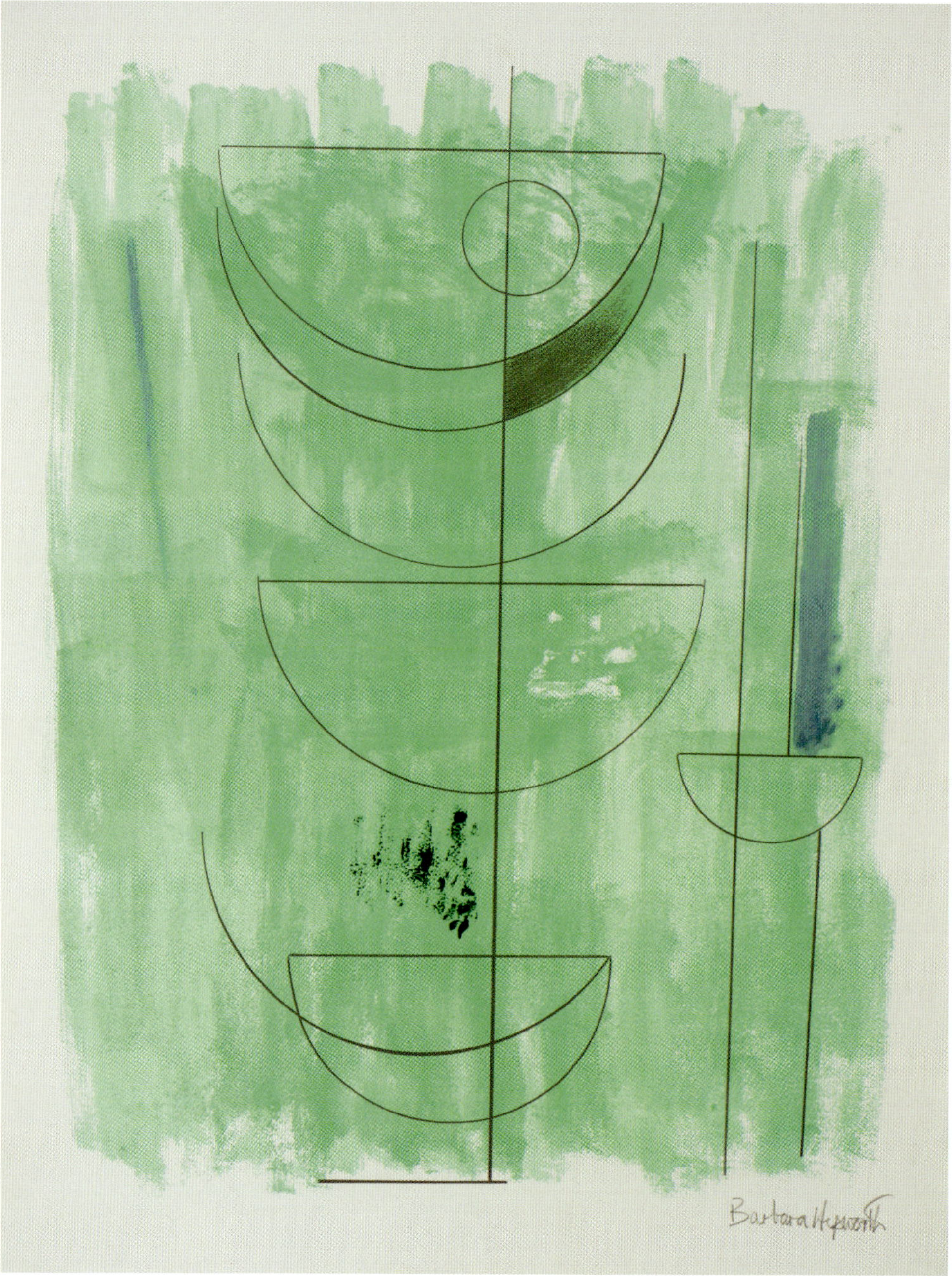

GREEN MAN Barbara Hepworth (1972)

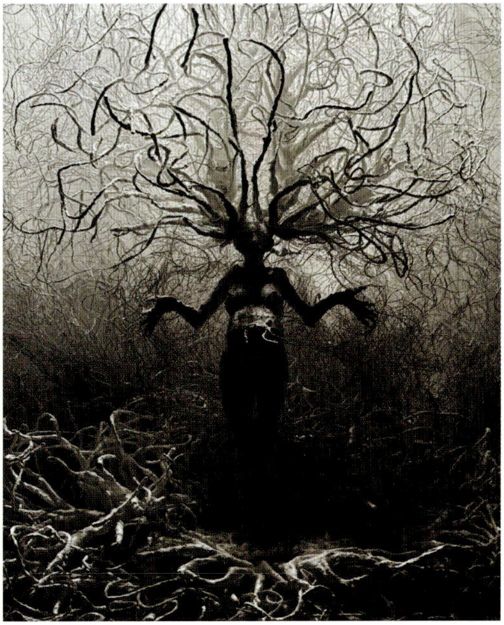

HEALER –
PORTRAIT OF LIZZIE

Cathy de Monchaux
(2024)

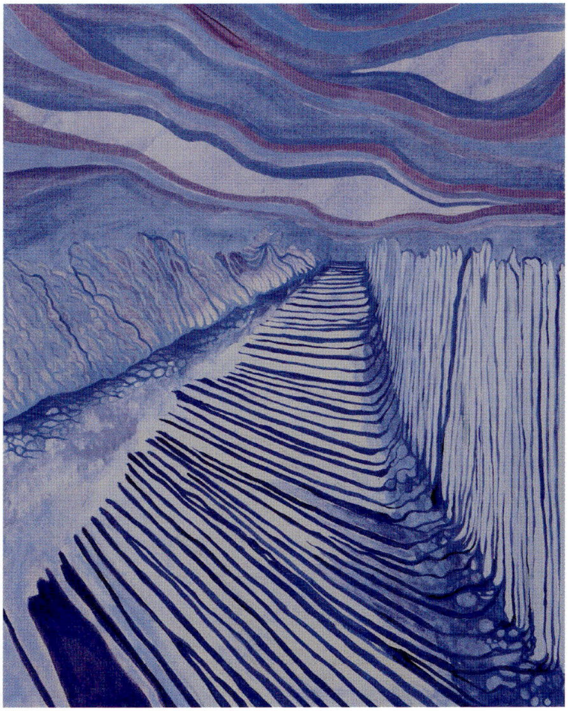

THE DARK GLOW

Laura Olohan
(2024)

FUTUROMA

Delaine Le Bas
(2018)

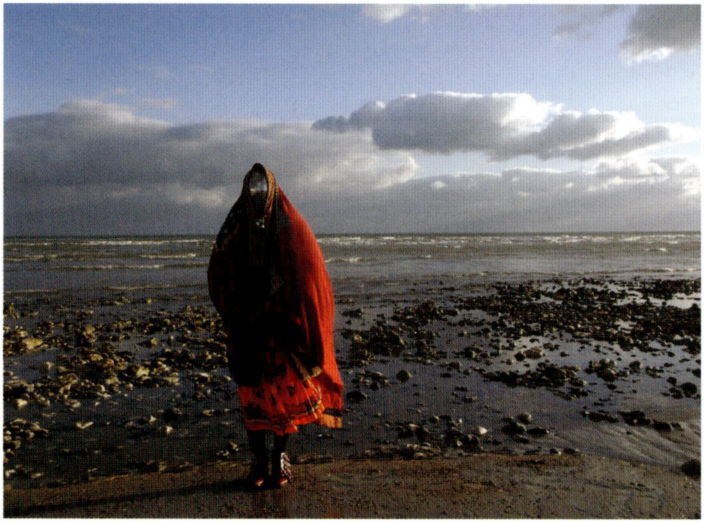

NEWS FROM GYPSYLAND LOVE IS ANARCHY

Delaine Le Bas
(2019)

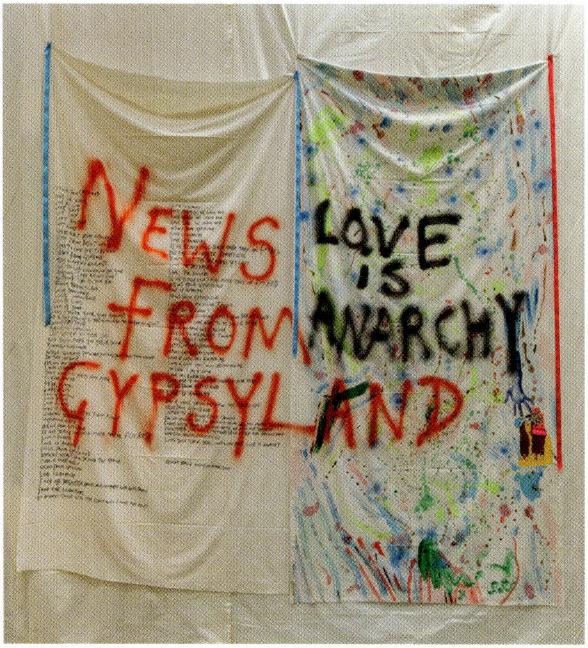

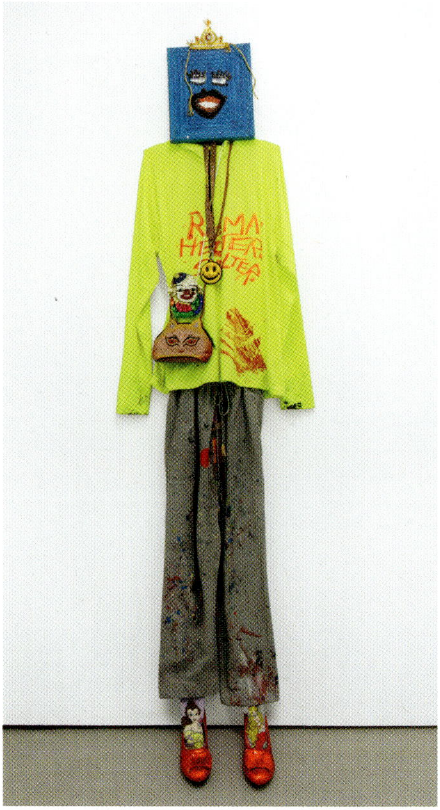

ROMA HELTER SKELTER (SELF PORTRAIT)

Delaine Le Bas
(2005)

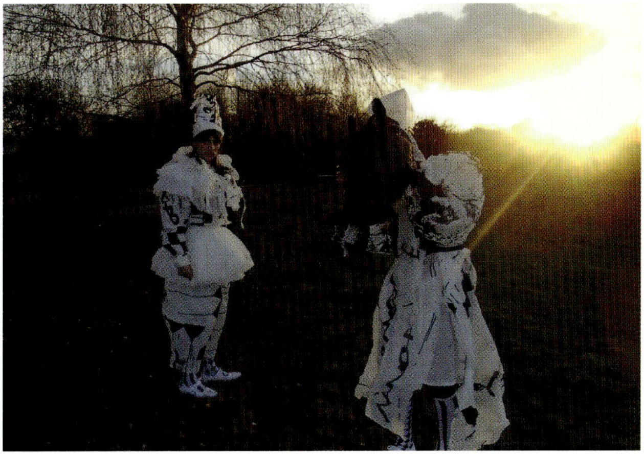

VIDEO WORK INCIPIT VITA NOVA

Delaine Le Bas and Hera Santos (2023)

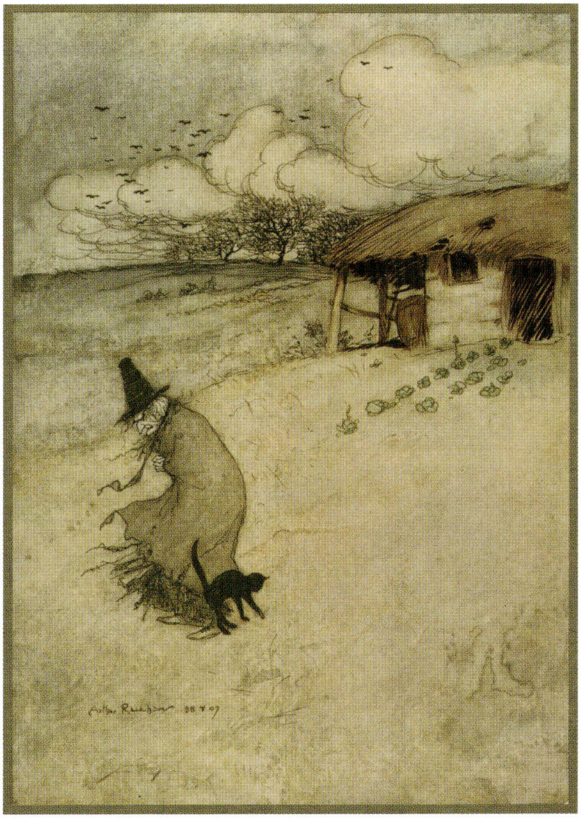

THERE'S AN OLD WOMAN DWELLS UPON TAPPINGTON MOOR

Arthur Rackham (1911)

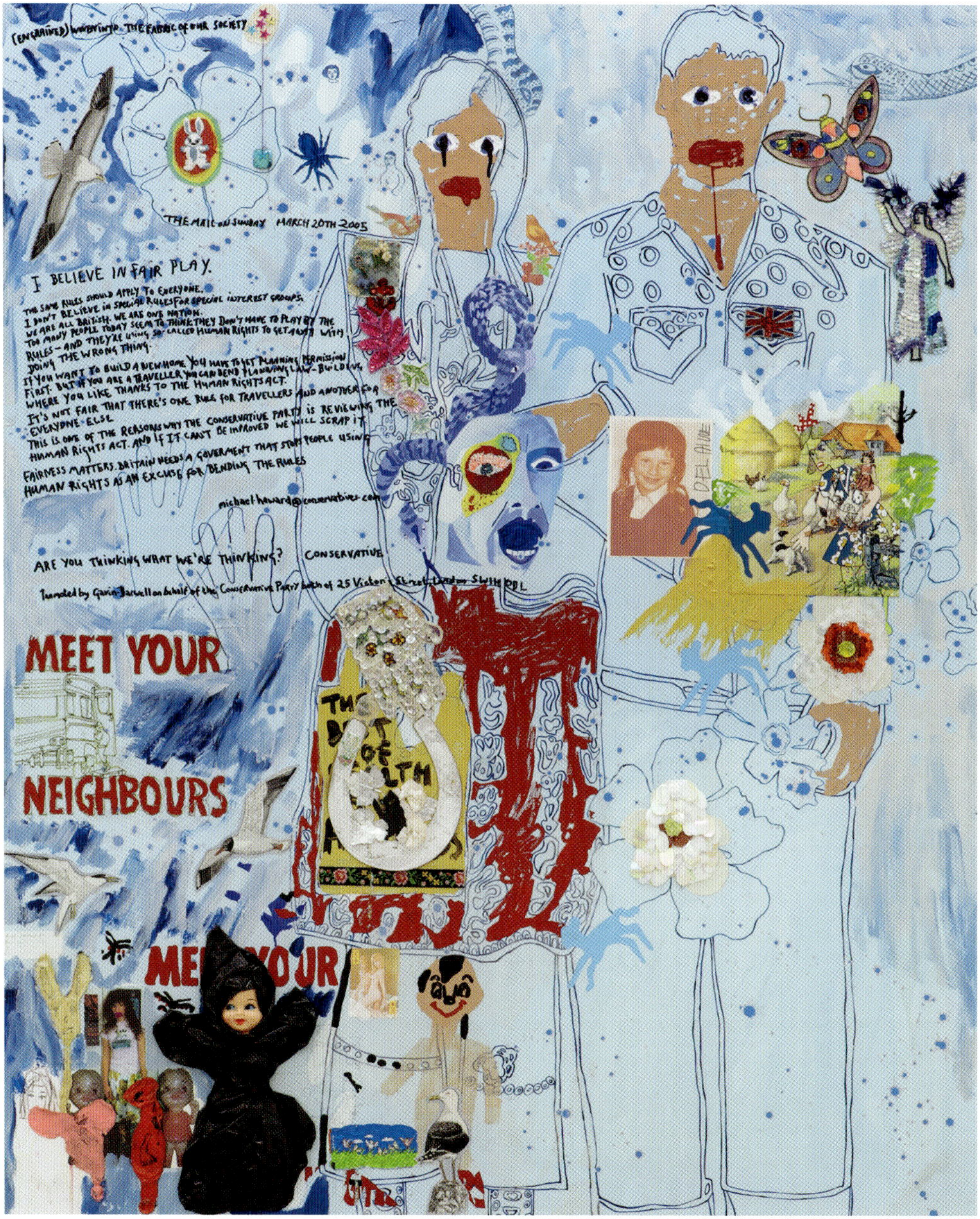

MEET YOUR NEIGHBOURS – (ENGRAINED) WOVEN INTO THE FABRIC OF OUR SOCIETY Delaine Le Bas (2005)

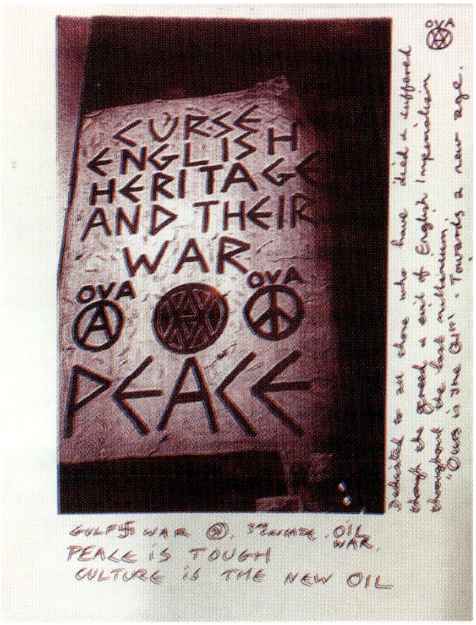

CURSE ENGLISH HERITAGE (XEROX)

Jamie Reid (1990)

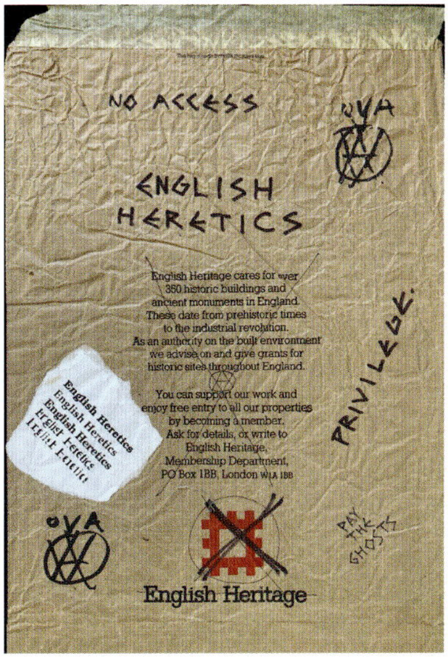

CURSE ENGLISH HERITAGE BAG

Jamie Reid (1990)

ACCESS TO STONES

Jamie Reid (1990)

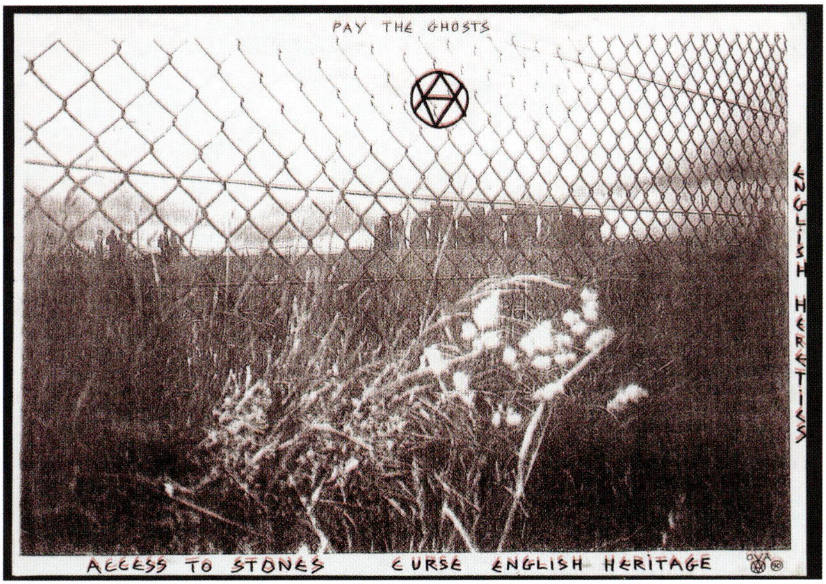

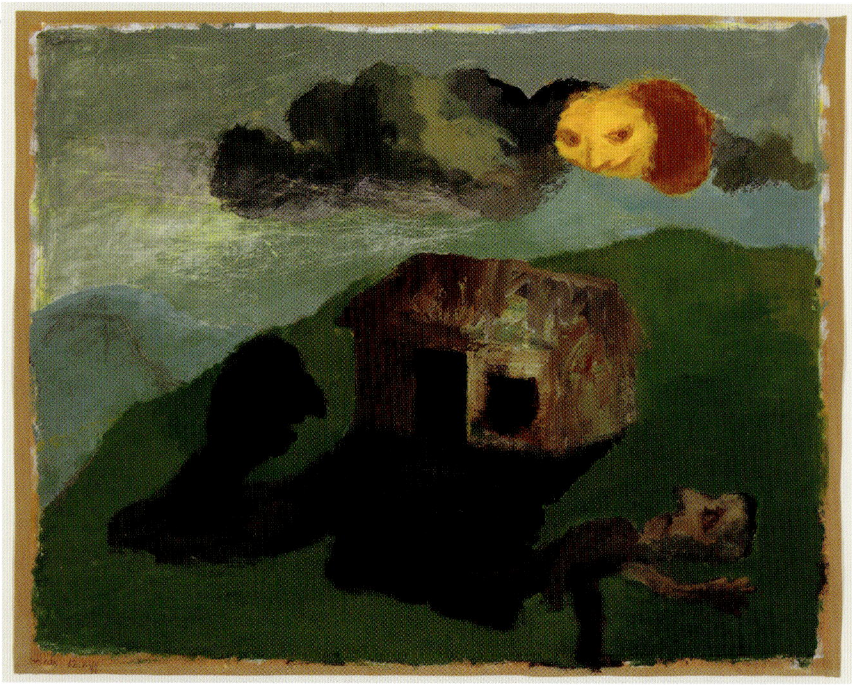

COTTAGE IN A FIELD

Ken Kiff (1979)

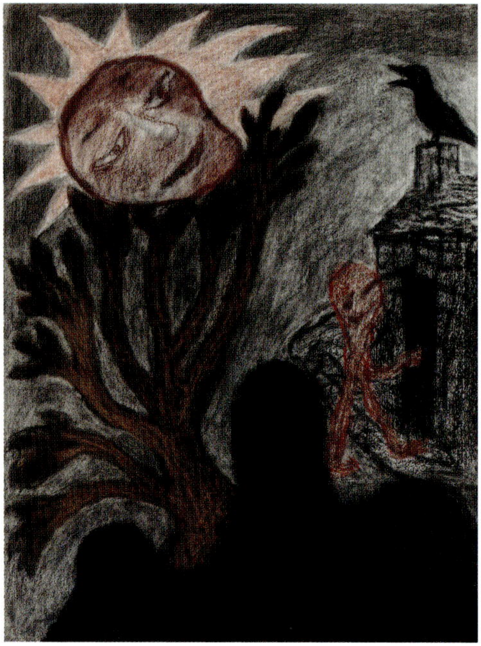

SUN AND SINGING BIRD

Ken Kiff (1985)

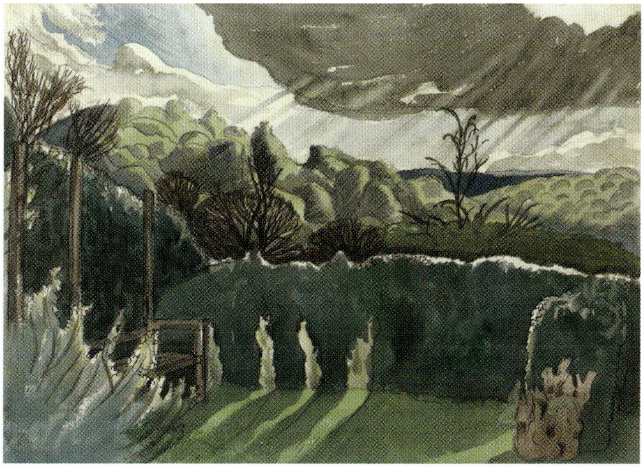

LANDSCAPE Paul Nash (undated)

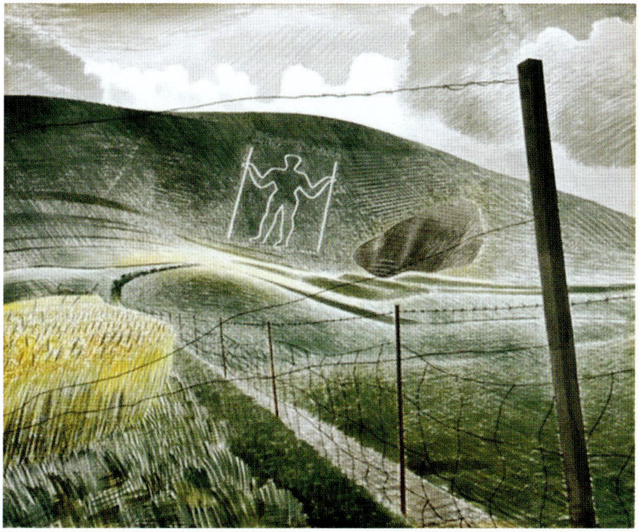

THE WILMINGTON GIANT Eric Ravilious, 1939

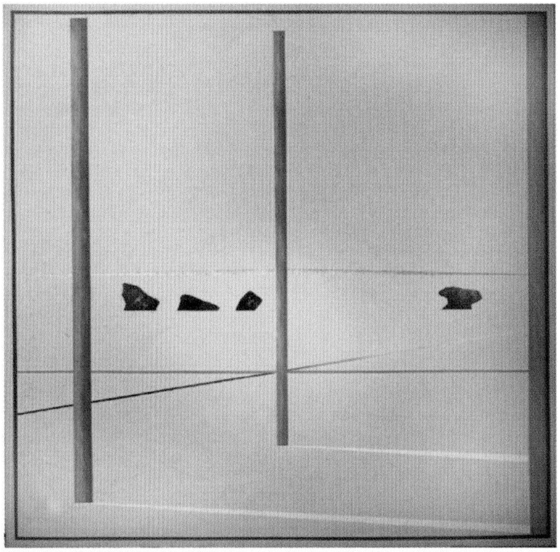

AVEBURY SERIES NO. 2 Derek Jarman (1973)

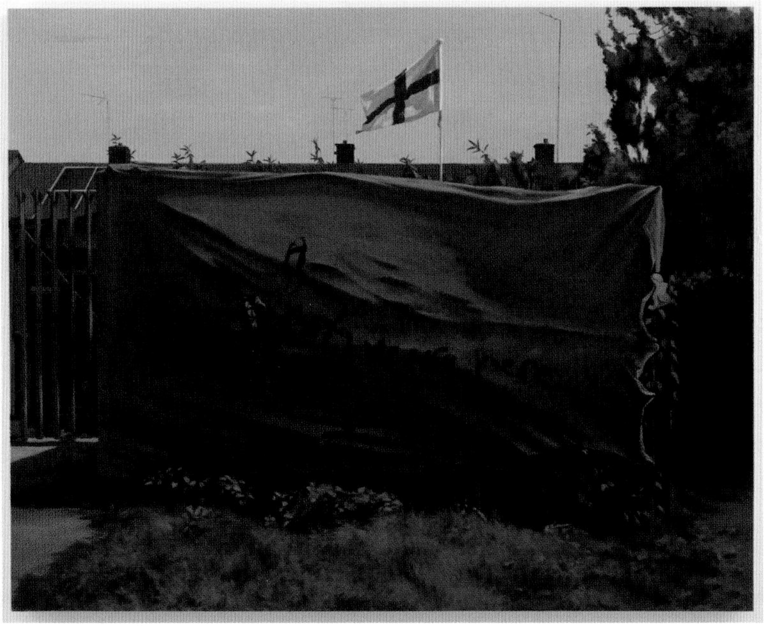

THE PASSING WIND George Shaw (2023-2024)

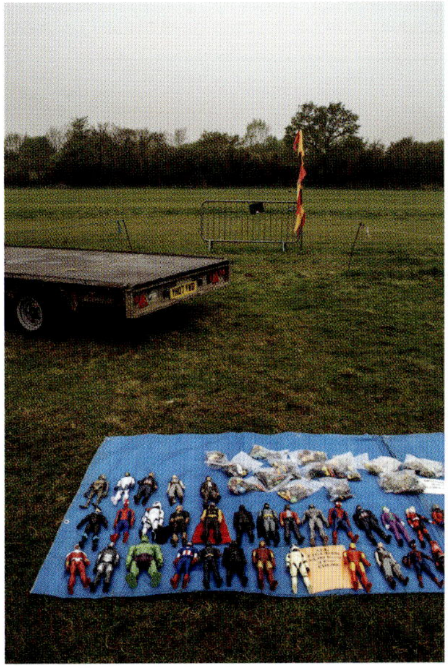

CAR BOOT SALE, SAYERS COMMON, SUSSEX

Jeff Pitcher
(2025)

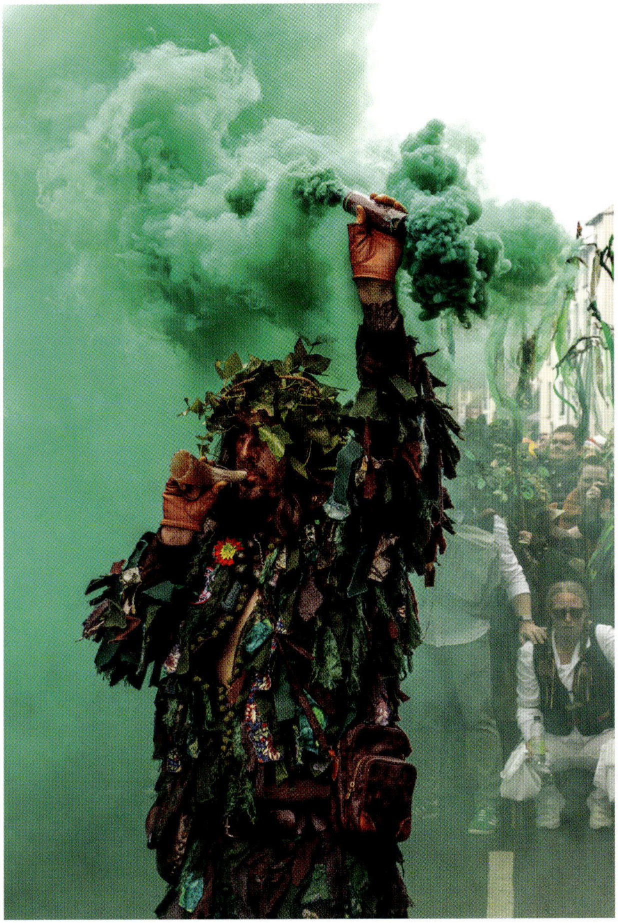

JACK IN THE GREEN, HASTINGS Jeff Pitcher (2024)

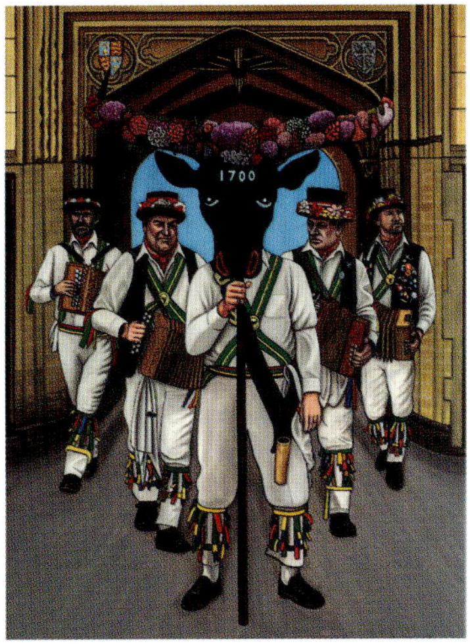

THE HORNS OF OCK STREET

Ben Edge
(2017)

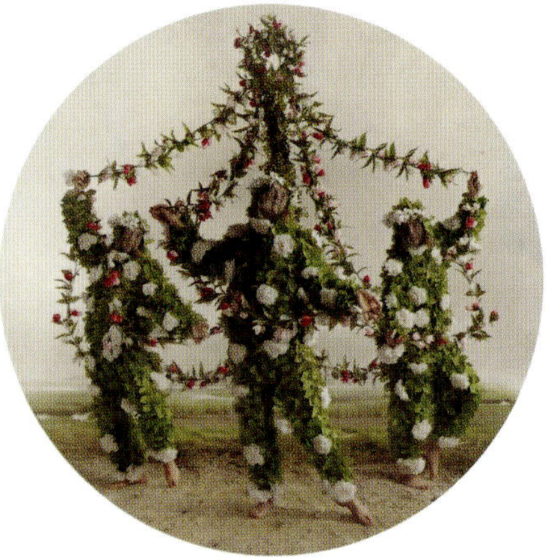

THE LESSON OF THE MAYPOLE
Kahn and Selesnick (2019)

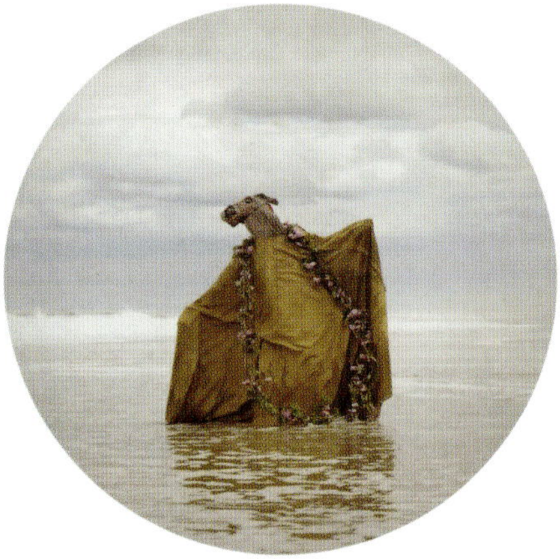

THE AUGURY OF THE COMPASS
Kahn and Selesnick (2019)

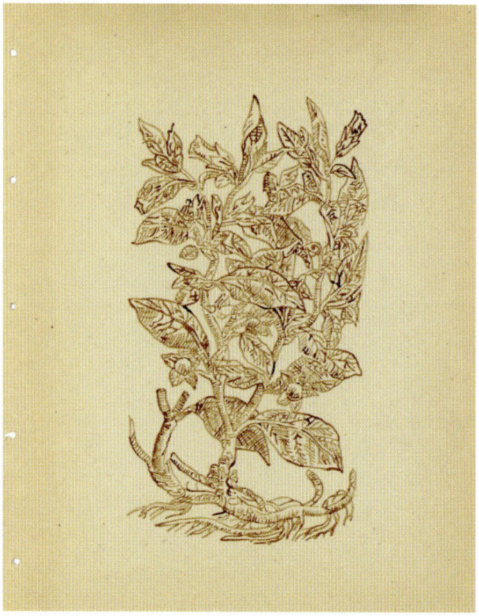

DEADLY NIGHTSHADE (BLOOD DRAWING)
Mathew Weir (2021)

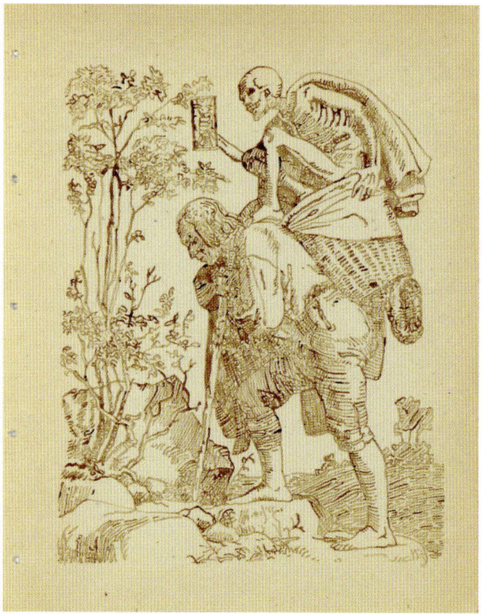

MAN WITH DEATH UPON HIS BACK (BLOOD DRAWING) Mathew Weir (2021)

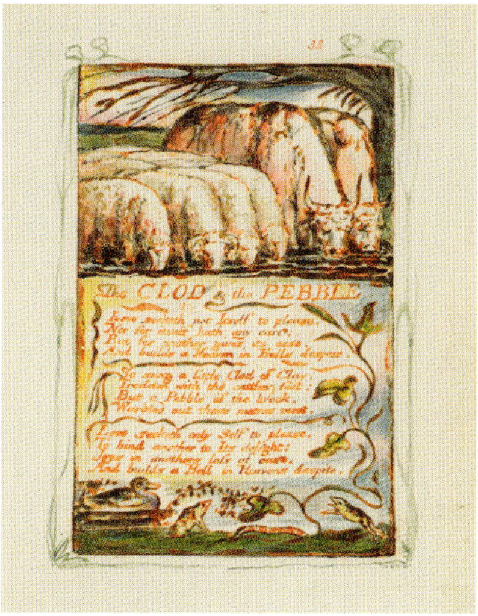

***SONGS OF EXPERIENCE,* THE CLOD AND THE PEBBLE**

William Blake (1794)

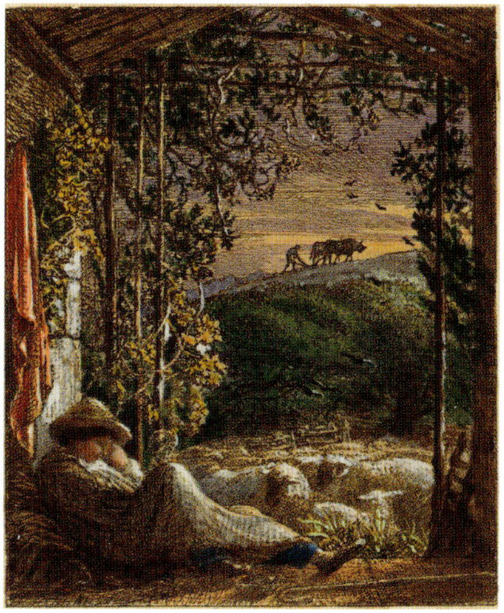

SLEEPING SHEPHERD Samuel Palmer (1833–34)

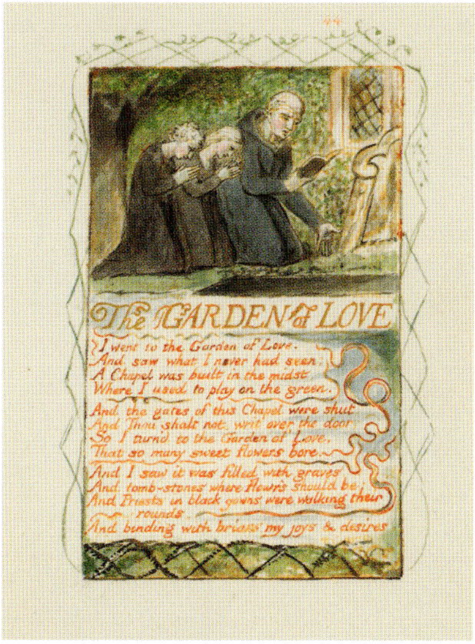

***SONGS OF EXPERIENCE,* THE GARDEN OF LOVE**

William Blake (1794)

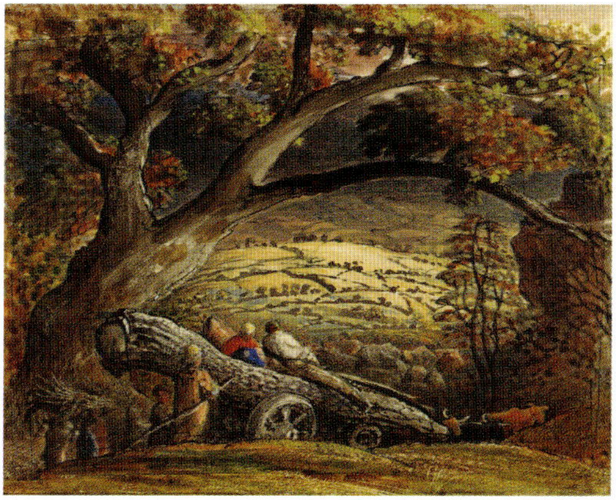

THE TIMBER WAIN Samuel Palmer (1833–34)

VAGABONDS

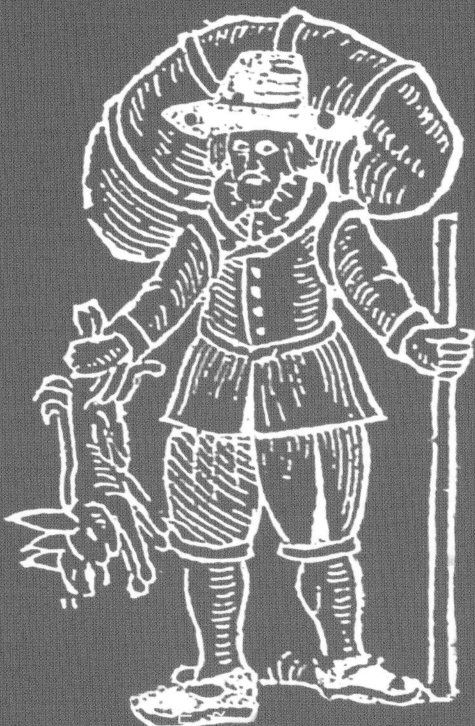

Introduction to Vagabonds

It's important to acknowledge the enduring social outcomes of the enclosures, which as well as creating a new class of industrial factory workers, created a disenfranchised vagabond class divorced from the land and any means of subsistence. Their lives were precarious and dangerous as the government created law after law to make survival almost impossible. The "Poor Laws" separated families in godawful conditions and led to the creation of workhouses. Friedrich Engels, writing in *The Condition of the Working Class in England*, saw enclosures as a process that displaced rural workers, transforming them into a class of landless wage labourers which enabled the growth of industrial capitalism.

But at the same time itinerancy was on the rise and led to a rural exodus to London where many of the urban poor contrived creative and imaginative means of surviving within self-supporting communities. So, we can also view the concept of "vagabondage" as being a radical mechanism for stepping outside of capitalist societal expectations and applaud anyone with the anarchistic spirit to challenge power with activism as well as withdrawal.

RABBITS

Thomas Lord Busby (1816)

This portrait of a rabbit seller is taken from the book Costume of the Lower Orders of the Metropolis. *Like John Thomas Smith in London and George Walker in the north of England, Thomas Lord Busby used illustration to document the changing social conditions of the early 1800s.*

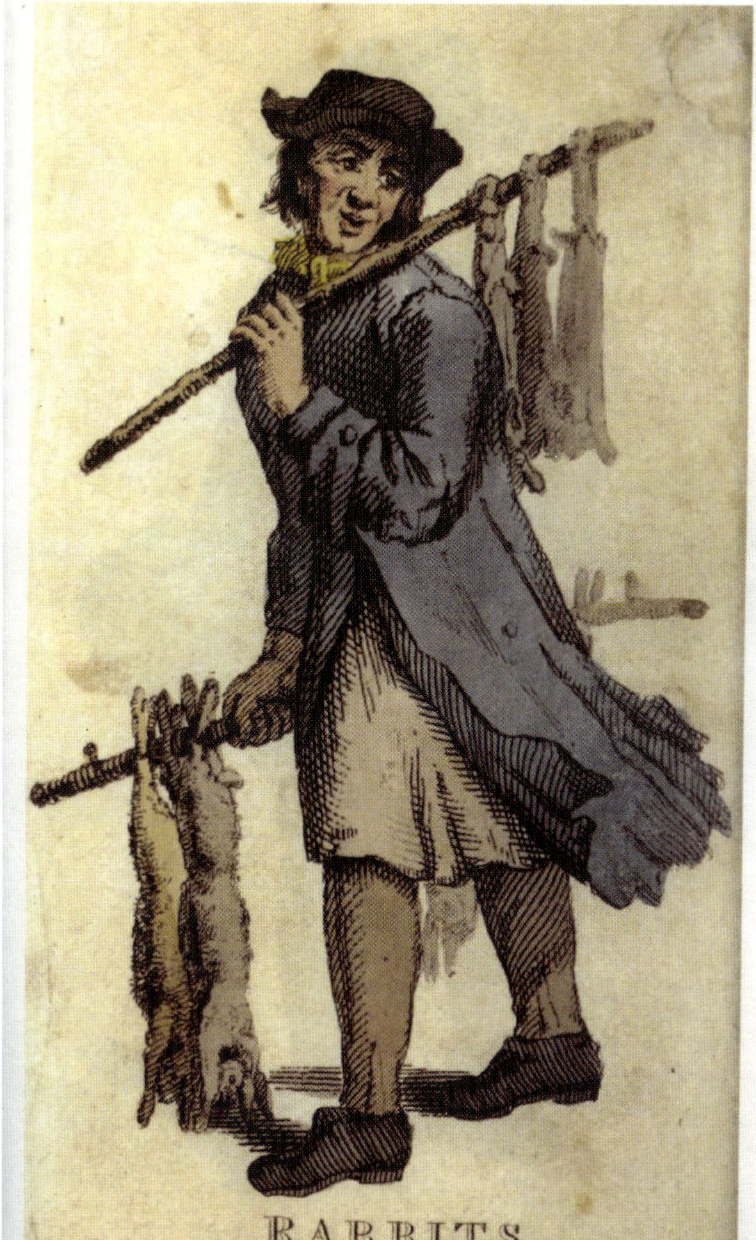
RABBITS

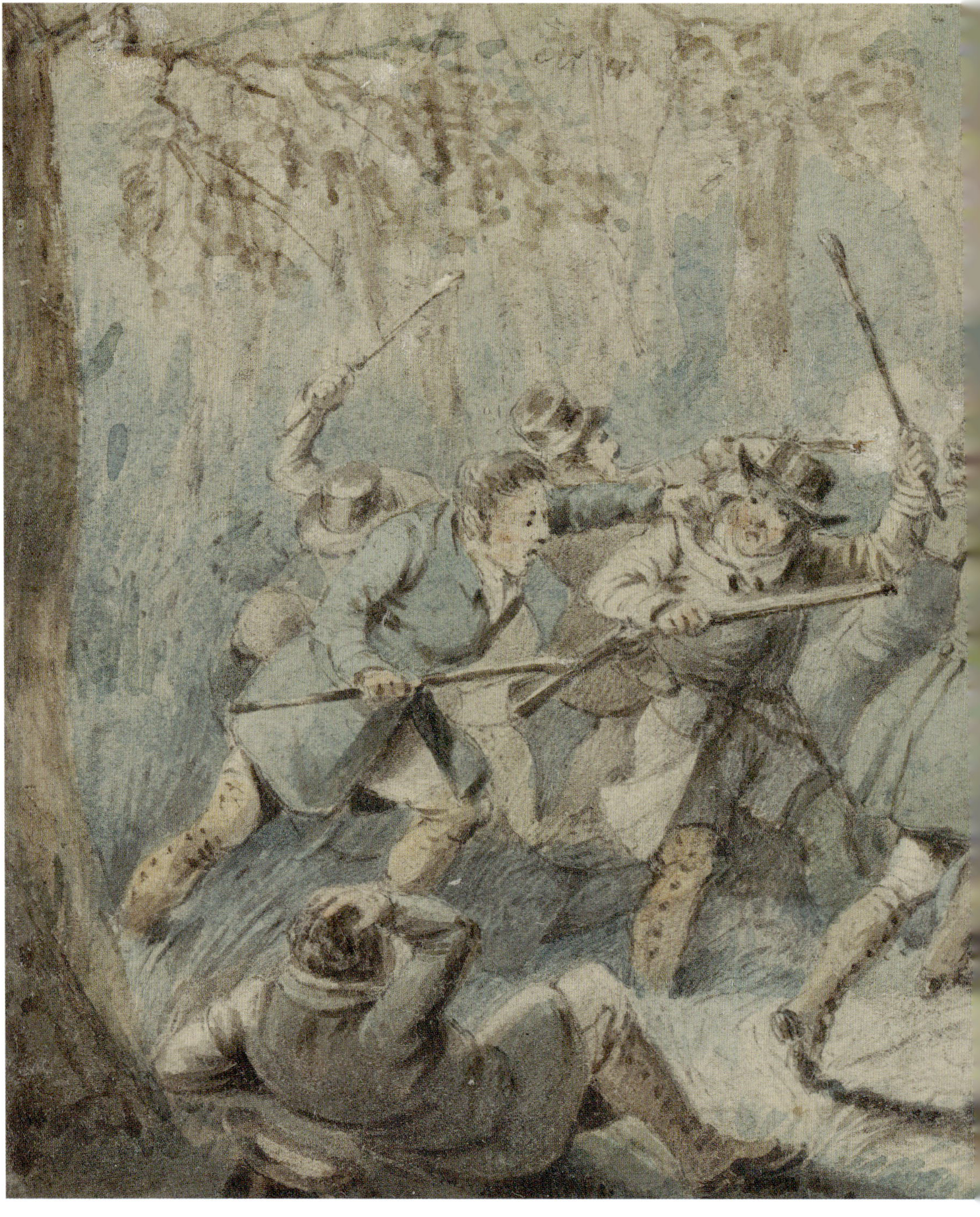

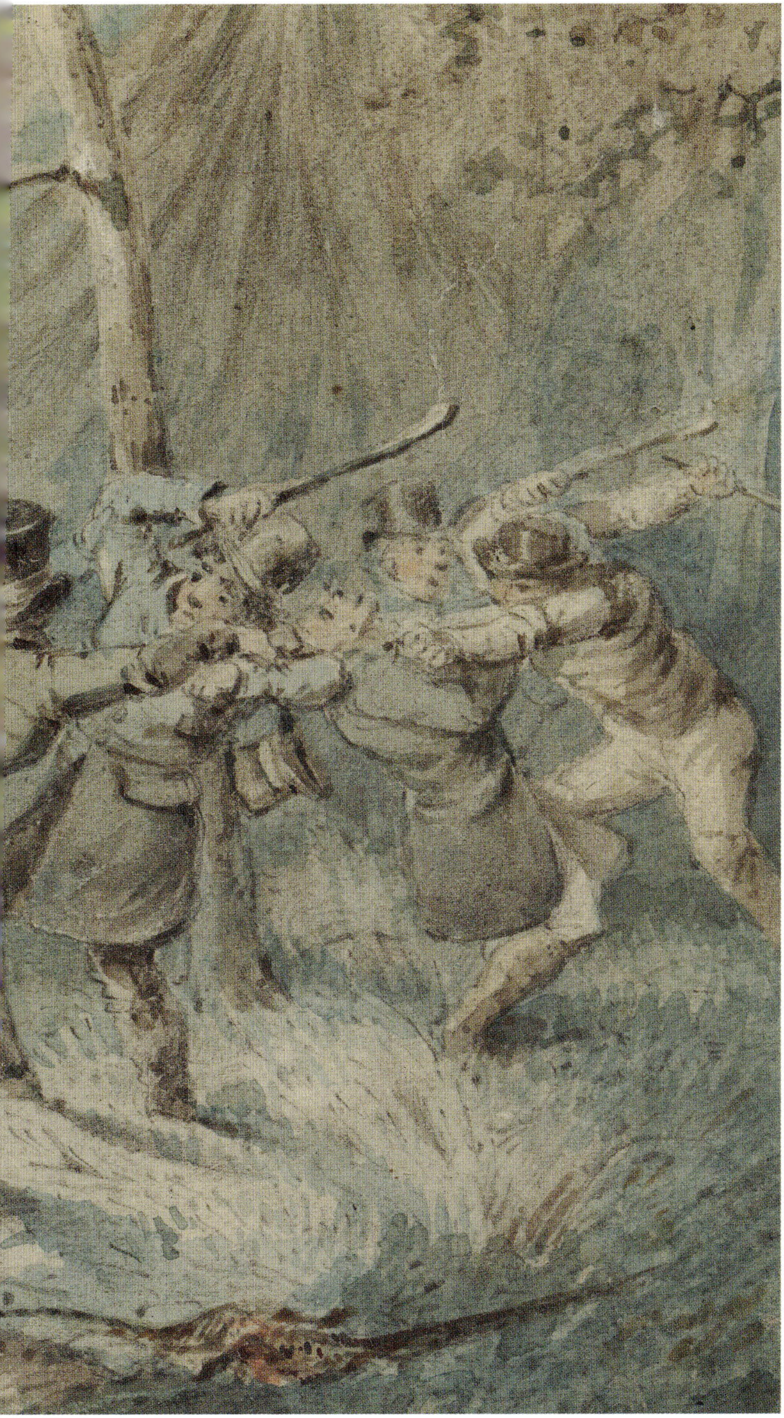

POACHERS SURPRISED

Henry Thomas Alken (c.1800)

The Robin Hood legend, passed down through ballads and oral history, fed into a sense of poaching as a heroic and radical act. In his poem "The Land", Rudyard Kipling describes a wise old poacher, Hobden, while Edward Thomas's search for the everyman sage poacher in his poem "Lob" alludes to a poacher's breadth of local knowledge.

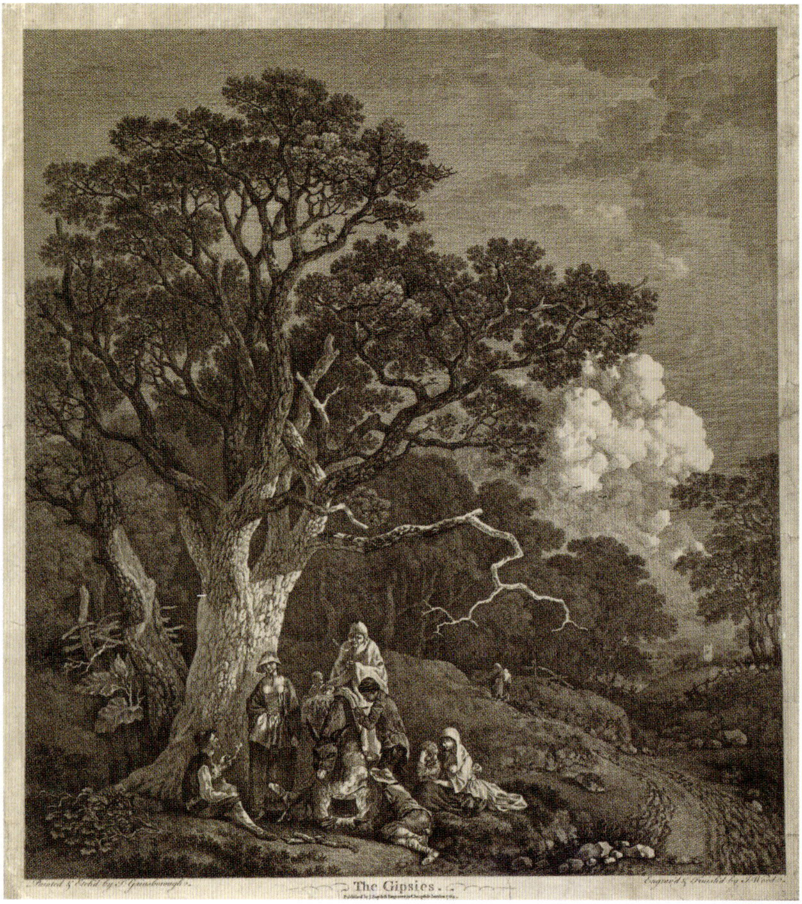

THE GIPSIES

Thomas Gainsborough (1764)

Gainsborough was supposedly the first English artist to portray the Roma people in paintings and etchings. The Roma are alluded to in Shakespeare's plays A Midsummer Night's Dream *and* As You Like It. *However, in most English literature they were portrayed as sinister, occult and other. Philip Pullman portrayed the bargee Roma in the* His Dark Materials *trilogy in a positive light as a group of people on the side of good.*

THE FRIAR AND THE BOY FROM *CHAP-BOOKS OF THE EIGHTEENTH CENTURY*

John Ashton (1882)

This tells the story of a young boy, Jack, who charms cattle and oxen with his pipe playing. Chap-books of the Eighteenth Century *was a compilation of the popular reading matter sold to rural communities by itinerant traders called chapmen.*

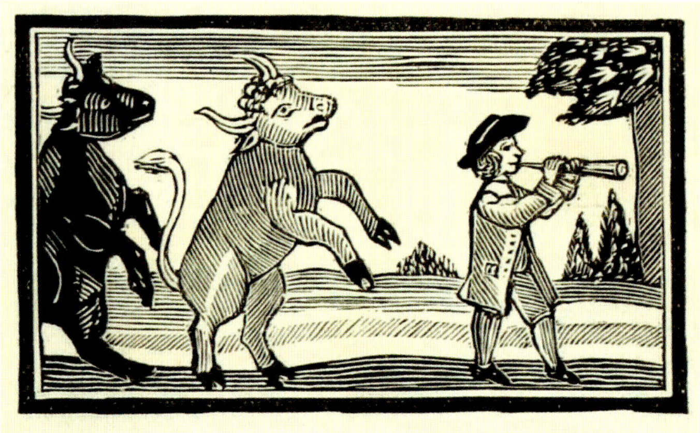

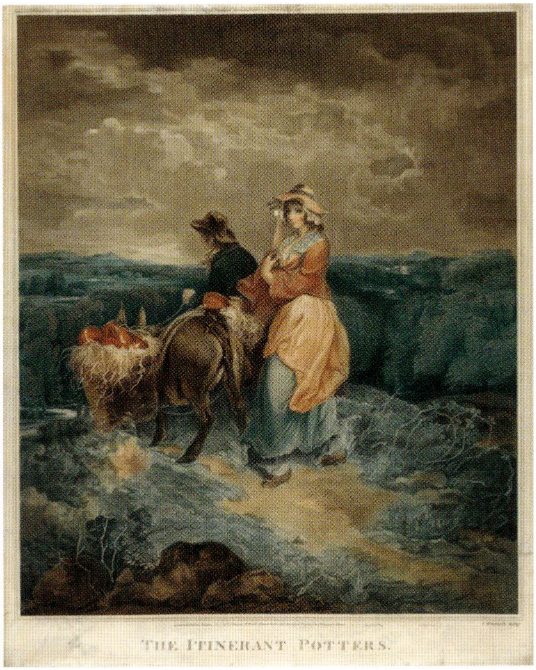

THE ITINERANT POTTERS

John Whessell (1797)

Until the 19th century it was usually very difficult for people living in the countryside to travel to towns and so itinerant traders and craftspeople would visit the various remote rural communities to bring them the wares that they could not otherwise access. It was a hard way to earn a living, but these potters at least can afford a mule to carry the heavy pots.

COTTONOPOLIS

Edward Goodall (1840)

Cotton had become so integral to Manchester's industry in the 1800s that the city was often referred to as Cottonopolis. Many authors explored the inequalities of life during this period, including Charles Dickens in Hard Times, *Elizabeth Gaskell in* North and South, *and George Eliot in* Felix Holt.

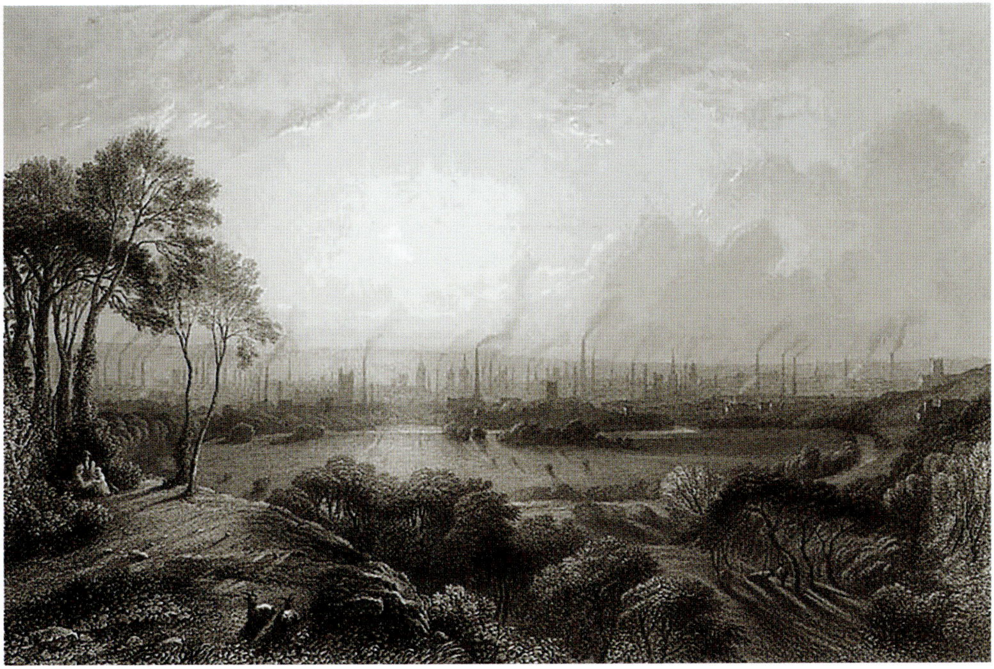

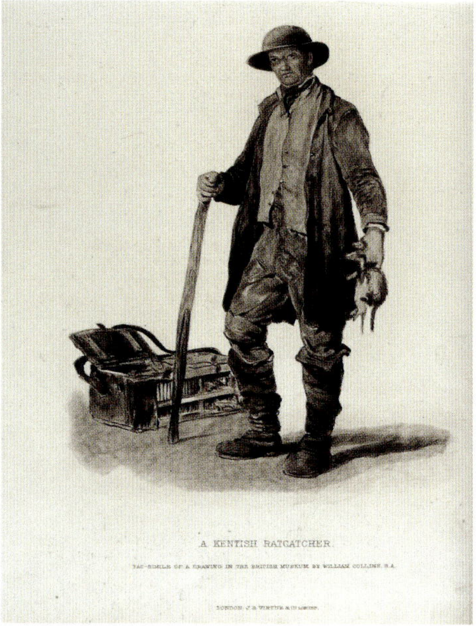

A KENTISH RAT CATCHER

W Collins (c.1788–1847)

Due to the loss of the commons, many peasants migrated to the cities, where the overcrowding led to rat infestations. Rat catchers became indispensable to city dwellers. In Henry Mayhew's "London Labour and the London Poor" he published detailed interviews with Jack Black, a celebrity rat catcher of the 1850s, whose card read, "Rat and mole destroyer to Her Majesty."

HUT AND CART

John Golden Short (c.1870)

Like many early photographs, the subject is mysterious to us now. Is this a gardener's hut where he ate his dinner and warmed himself on a cold day? A temporary dwelling built by an itinerant labourer in search of seasonal work? Or even a squatter's home, claiming a patch of waste or common land by erecting a dwelling and having a fire burning in the hearth in the course of one day?

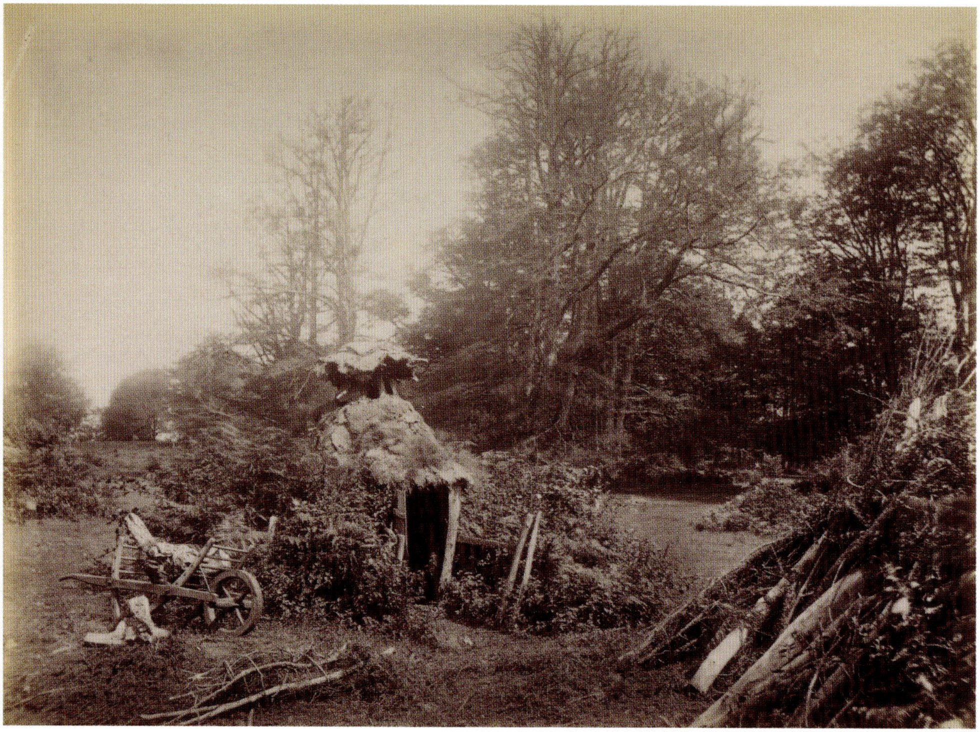

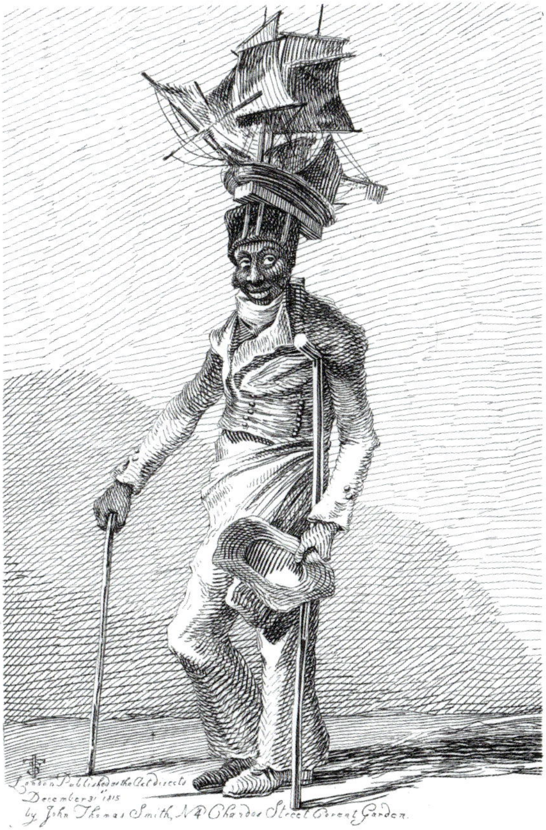

JOSEPH JOHNSON OF CHANDOS STREET, COVENT GARDEN

John Thomas Smith (1817)

This drawing of Joseph Johnson, published in Vagabondiana, *shows the street singer wearing a model of HMS* Victory *atop his hat, probably to communicate that he was injured while in the British Navy.*

THE POACHER – A HARE IN VIEW

Peter Henry Emerson (1888)

This photogravure was first published in Emerson's book Pictures of East Anglian Life *in 1888. There was a small scandal about this photograph, as while Emerson claimed that he never altered an image, the second time the image was published in a portfolio to accompany* Naturalistic Photography for Students of the Art, *it was noticed that the greyhound's tail had been edited out.*

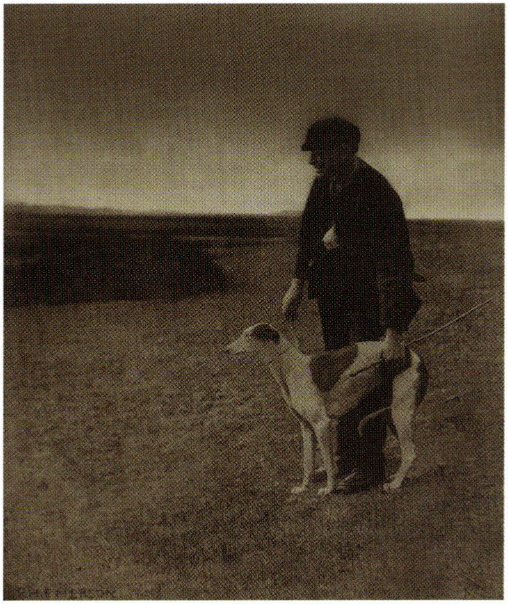

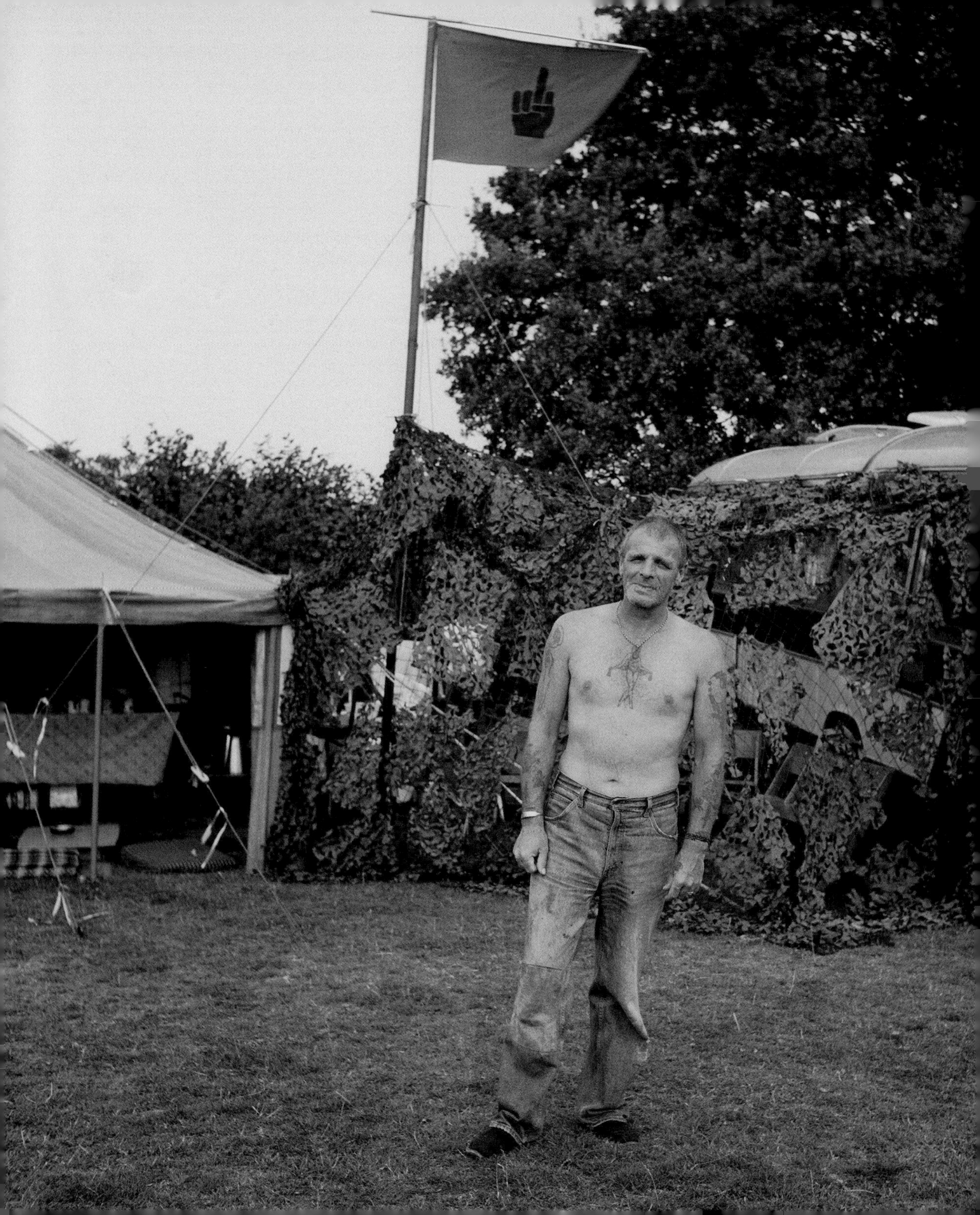

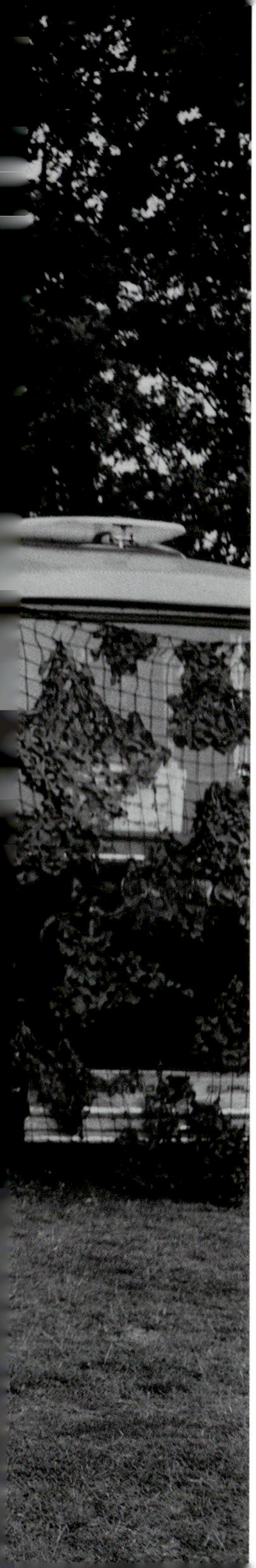

Vagabonds by Leah Gordon

The constructed images that follow are inspired, in part, by an 18th-century book of illustrations by John Thomas Smith, *Vagabondiana, or Anecdotes of Mendicant Wanderers through the Streets of London* (discussed in more detail in "Cosmology of the Rural", page 105). John Thomas Smith, a close colleague of the poet and artist William Blake, utilizes a documentary style of illustration to portray the reality for disenfranchised peasants who've had to move to the metropolis after the loss of the commons.

In the following pages, this idea is symbolized by the photographs, shot on large format analogue colour slide film, of isolated ruins of caravans in rural settings that portray life outside the narrow offerings of late capitalist Britain. This idea is also exemplified by the stage set for the renowned play *Jerusalem* by contemporary playwright Jez Butterworth, in which the character of Johnny "Rooster" Byron is a theatrical 21st-century vagabond hero. Today, *Jerusalem* is one of the most frequently performed plays by amateur dramatic societies in the UK. Portraits of amateur actors in their onstage costumes who have portrayed Rooster in local productions of Jerusalem are included here as symbols of resistance, dissent and radical withdrawal.

Similarly, images of New Age travellers and anti-road protesters from my extensive archive of analogue photographic portraits, taken in the 1990s, draw parallels between the outcomes of the enclosure acts and modes of collective resistance to Thatcher's Britain in techno-trance rave culture, which led to the repressive 1994 Criminal Justice and Public Order Act. They also depict contemporary actions and organizations to protect wildlife habitat from development, remaining common rights and public access to the land.

RAINBOW CIRCLE CAMP, FOREST OF DEAN, GLOUCESTERSHIRE (1990)

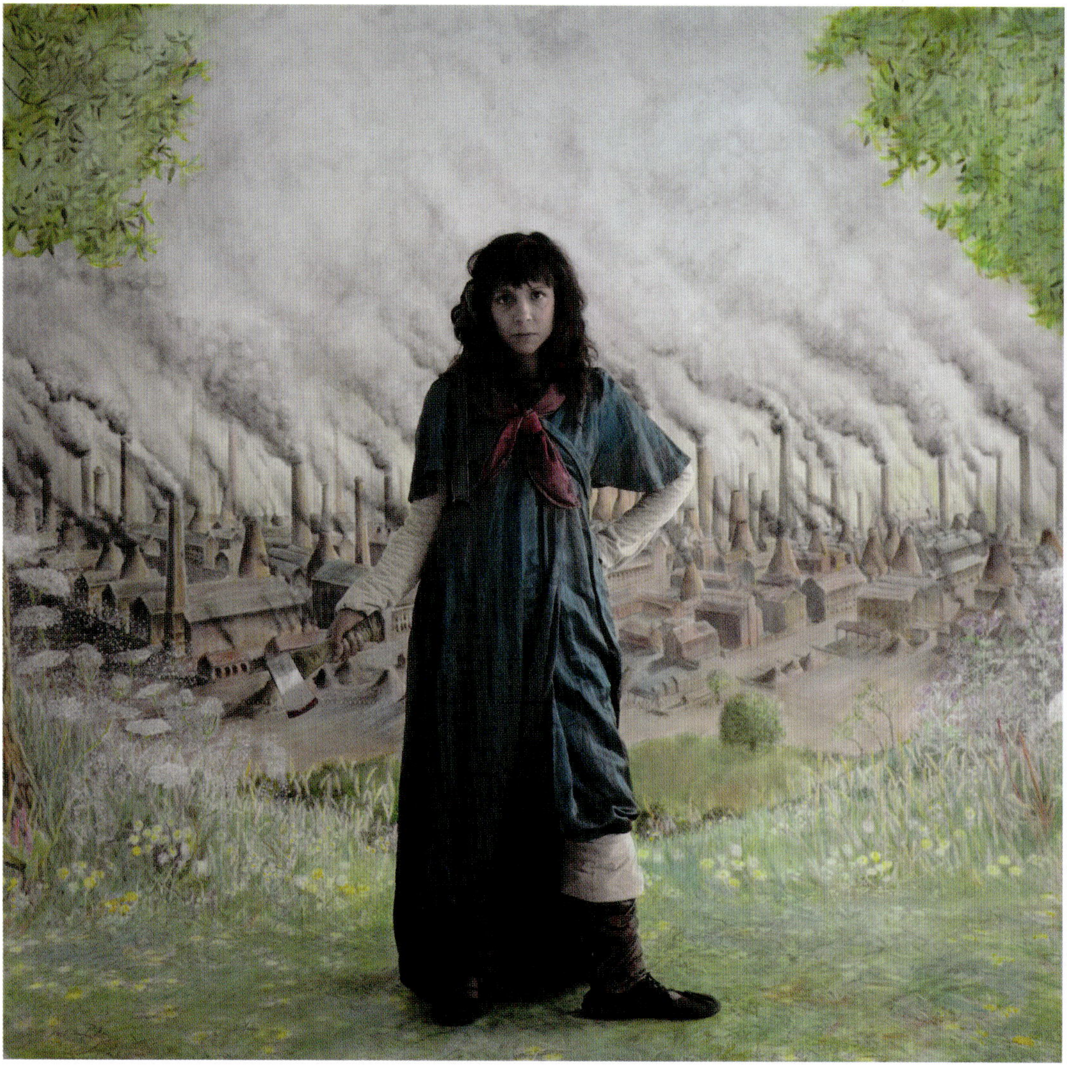

RURAL RIOTERS (2025) Hand-tinting by Marg Duston. A Meadow Arts commission

Many male rural activists, from the Swing Riots to the Rebecca Riots, dressed as women. This enabled them to travel unheeded to the riot locations, as women were less likely to be stopped and searched. It also enabled them to conceal their identities and, it has been suggested, added an edge of carnival and theatricality to the protests. But women also took part in machine-breaking, as the issues affected their livelihoods too. Many people think of the Luddites as anti-progress, but they weren't so much against modernization as the way in which factory owners were using machines to further exploit the workers.

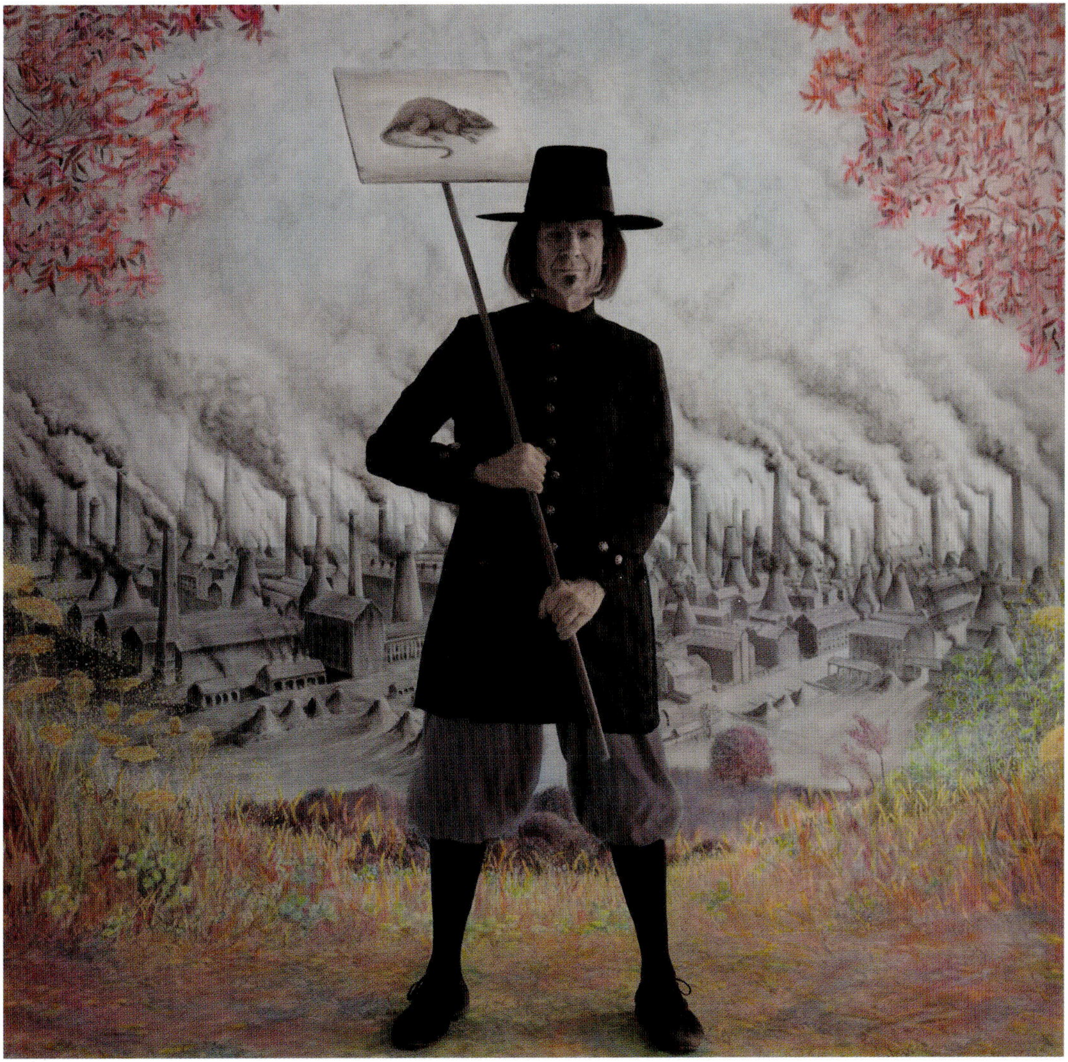

RAT CATCHER (2025) Hand-tinting by Marg Duston. A Meadow Arts commission

As life in the countryside became more difficult for the peasant classes, the migration to urban areas to find work and sustenance increased tenfold. This increase in population led to a massive rat infestation in the cities and therefore an increase in rat catchers. They employed many different methods to control the rats and were highly respected in the communities.

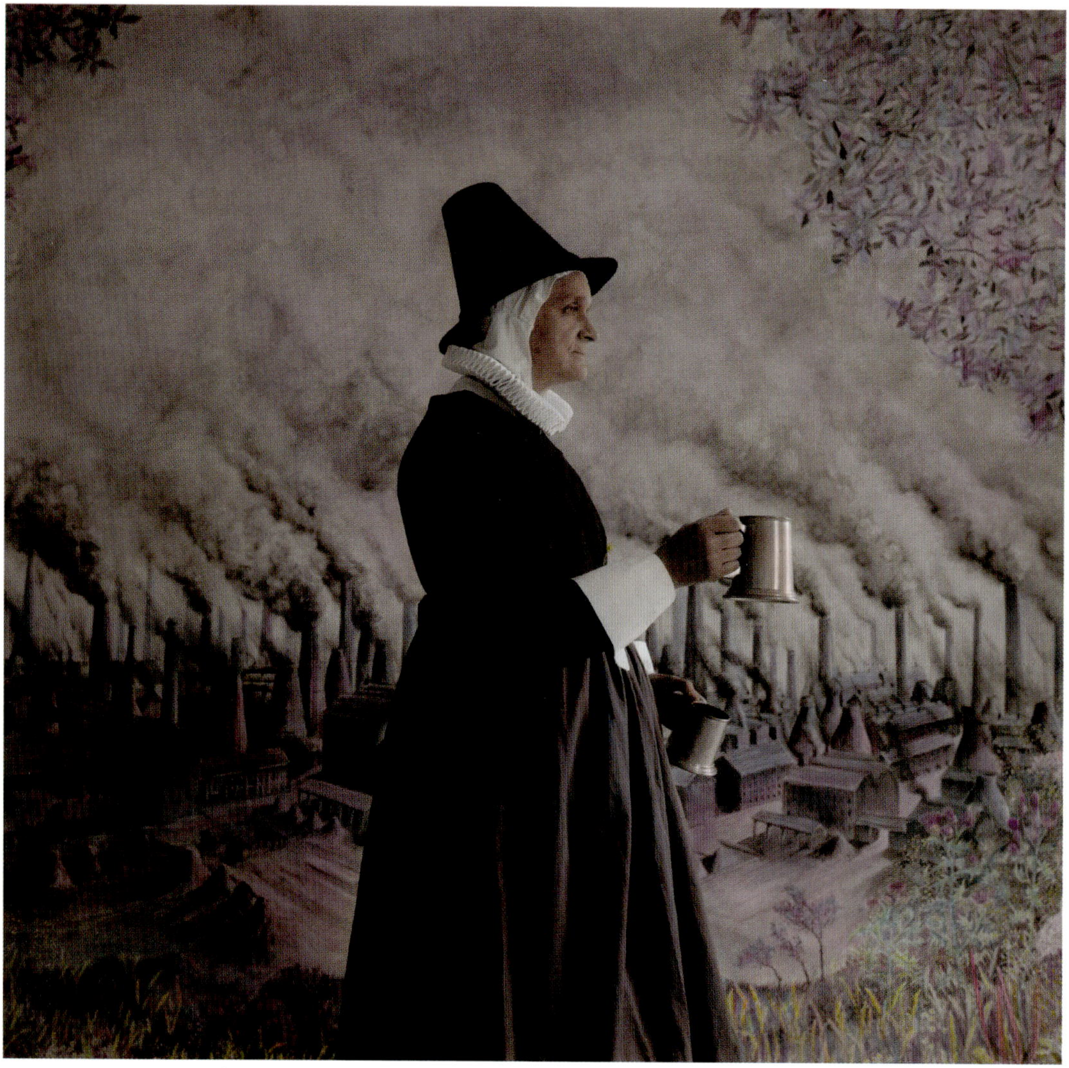

AN ALEWIFE (2025) Hand-tinting by Marg Duston. A Meadow Arts commission

The role and identity of the alewife became synonymous with the witch in the 16th and 17th centuries. Alewives had tall black hats in order to stand out in a crowded market square and often had broomsticks hanging over their doors as a symbol of their trade. These were often mature and independent women who, as Federici has posited in her book Caliban and the Witch, *became a threat to the progress of mercantile capitalism and were increasingly vilified during the enclosures.*

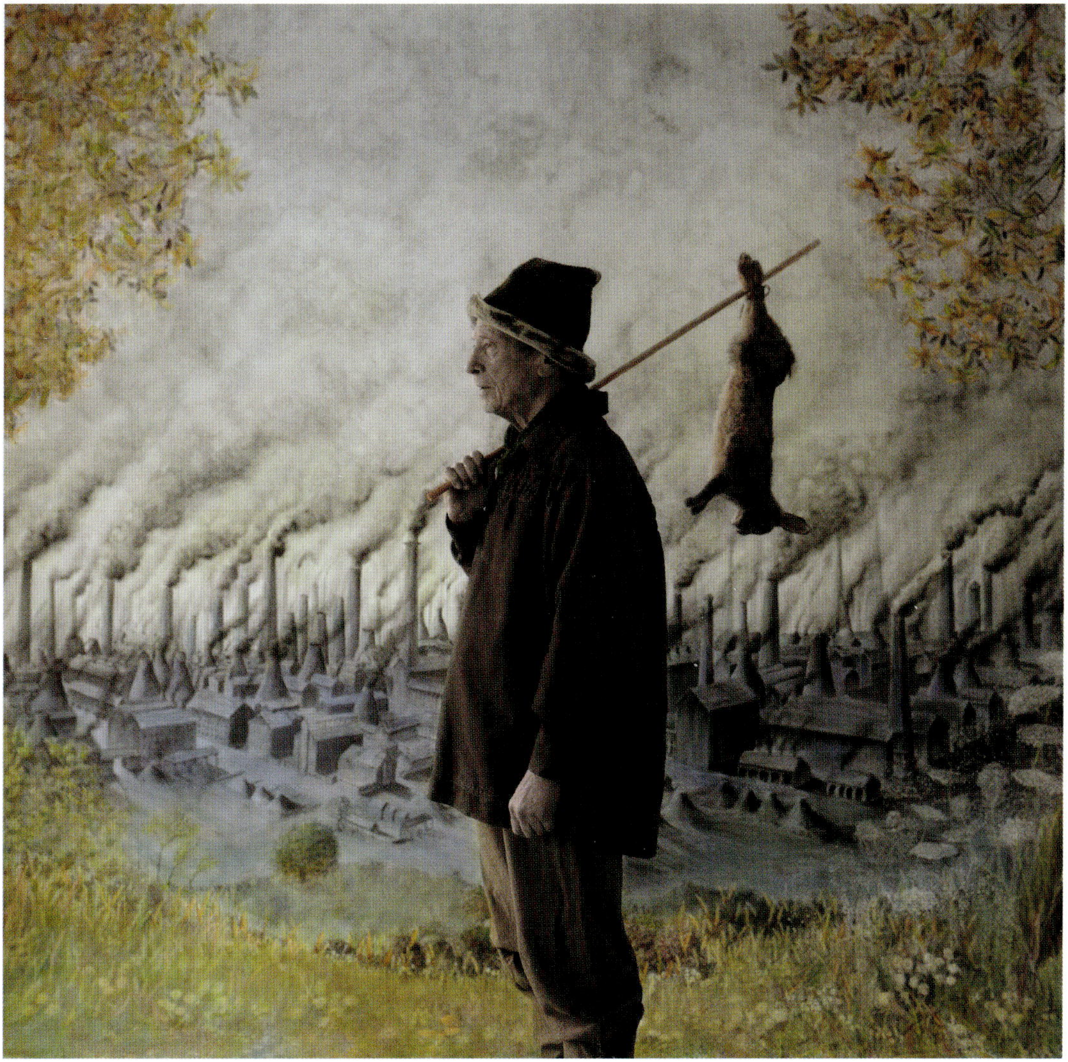

POACHER (2025) Hand-tinting by Marg Duston. A Meadow Arts commission

In addition to supplying the rural poor with much-needed protein, the poacher has long been a symbol of rural resistance and has been used to critique the criminalization of poverty. The Black Acts legalized the hanging and later the deportation of poachers. The last person hanged for poaching in England was Charles Smith, executed in 1822.

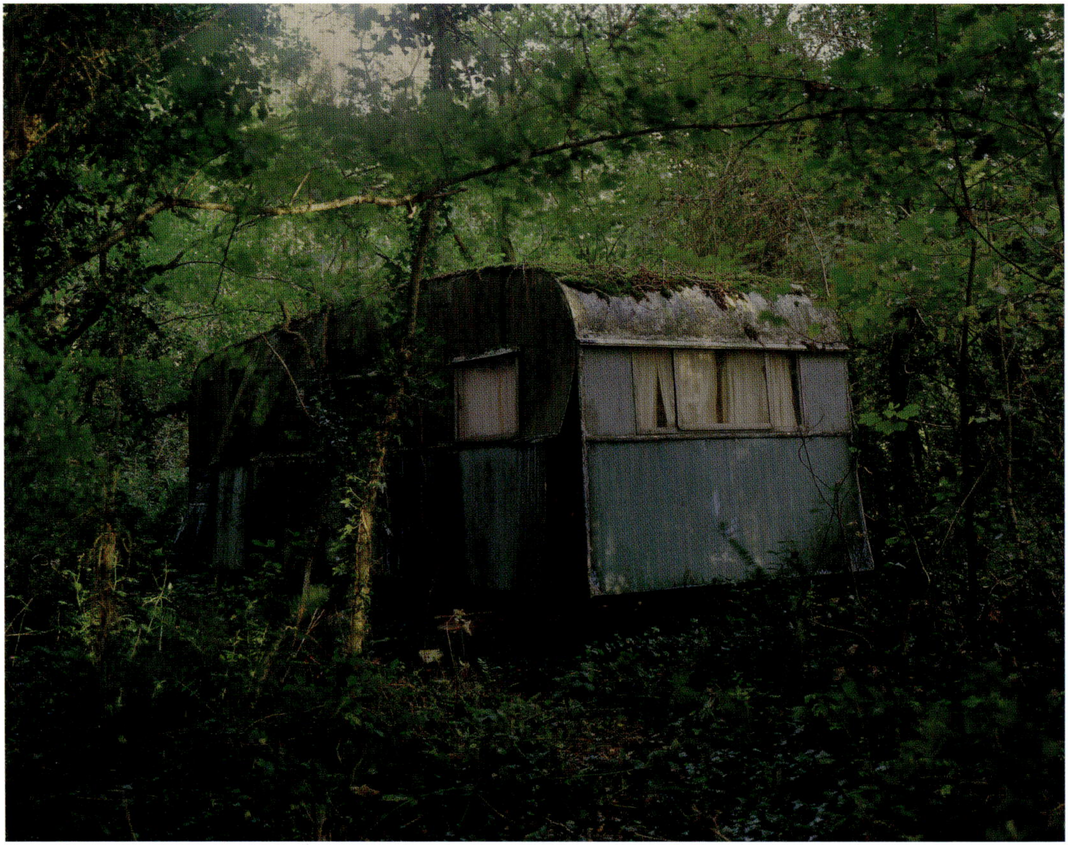

TY-RHOS, PENTRE EVAN WOOD, PEMBROKESHIRE (2023) A Meadow Arts commission

> *"I've seen a lot of strange things in this wood. I seen a plague of frogs. Of bees. Of bats. I seen a rainbow hit the earth and set fire to the ground. I seen the air go still and all sound stop and a golden stag clear this clearing. Fourteen-point antlers of solid gold."*[1]

JOHNNY BYRON aka ROOSTER in *Jerusalem*, Act III

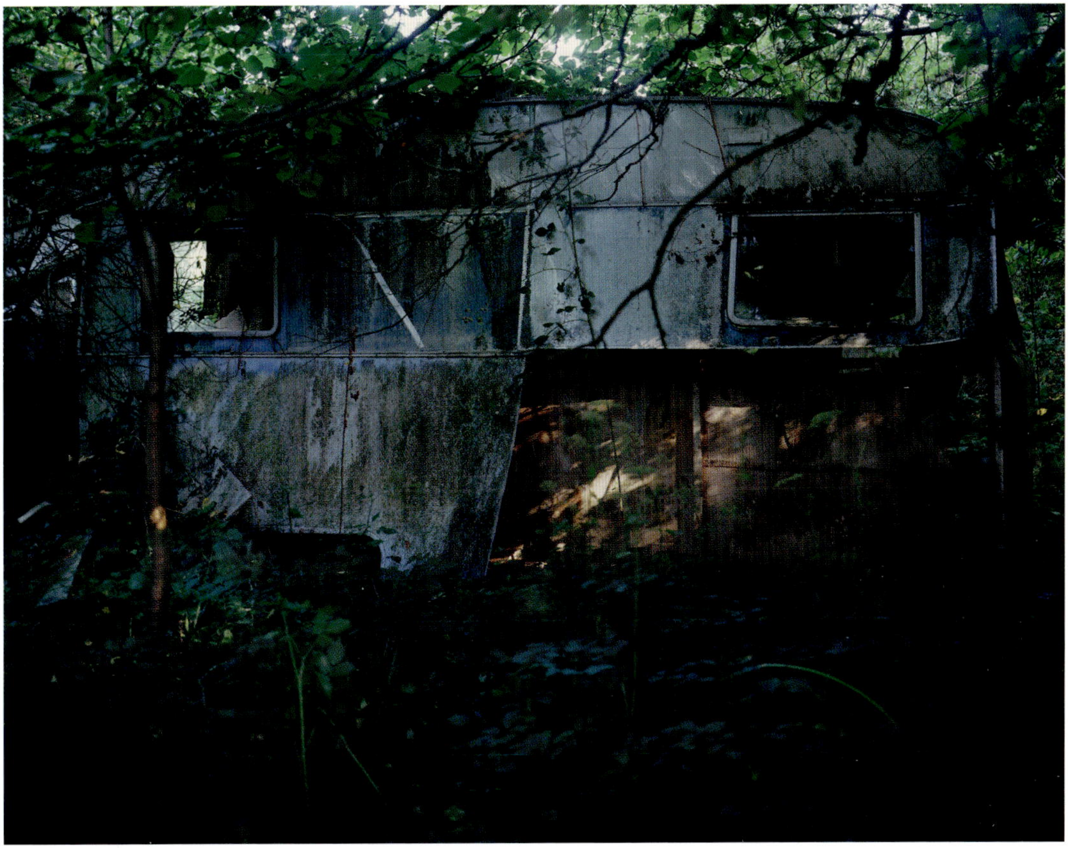

PONTRILAS, HEREFORD (2023) A Meadow Arts commission

"I heard an oak tree cry. I've heard beech sing hymns. I seen a man they buried in the churchyard Friday sitting under a beech eating an apple on Saturday morning."[2]

JOHNNY BYRON aka ROOSTER in *Jerusalem*, Act III

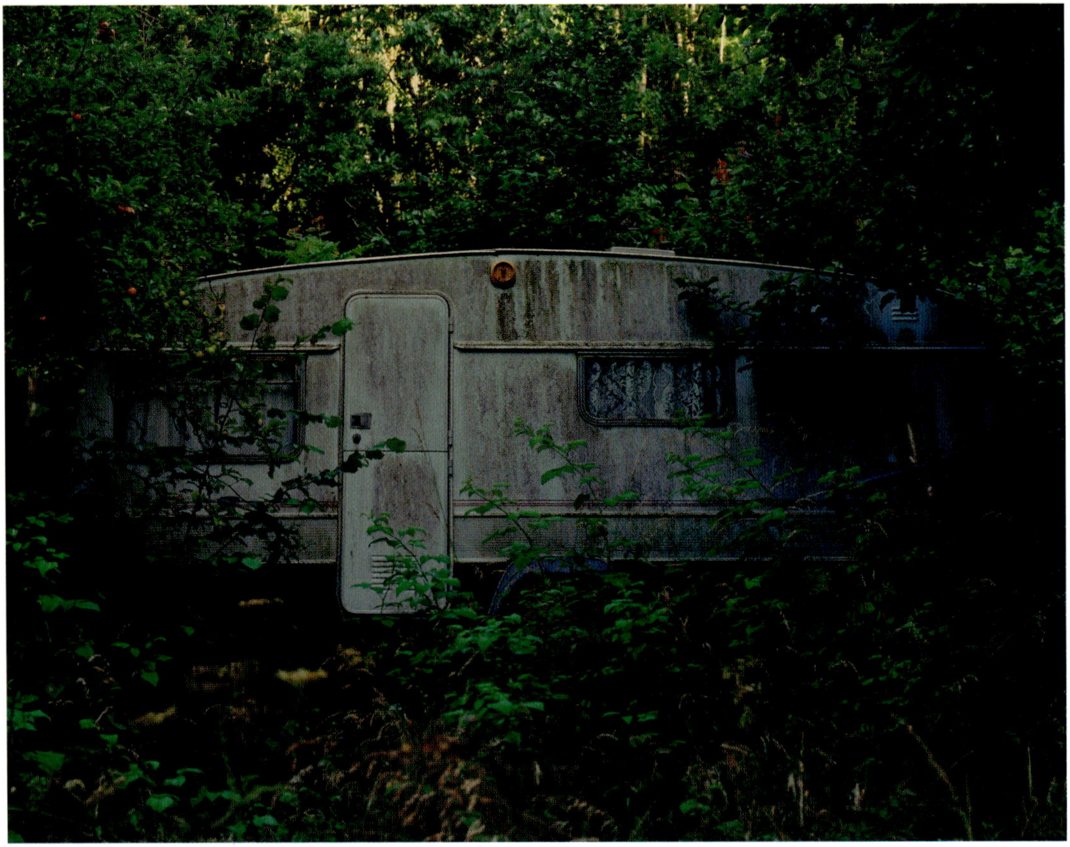

WILD ORCHARD, PONTRILAS, HEREFORD (2023) A Meadow Arts commission

> *"When the light goes, and I stare out into the trees, there's always pairs of eyes out there in the dark, watching. Foxes. Badgers. Ghosts. I seen lots of ghosts."*[3]
>
> JOHNNY BYRON aka ROOSTER in *Jerusalem*, Act III

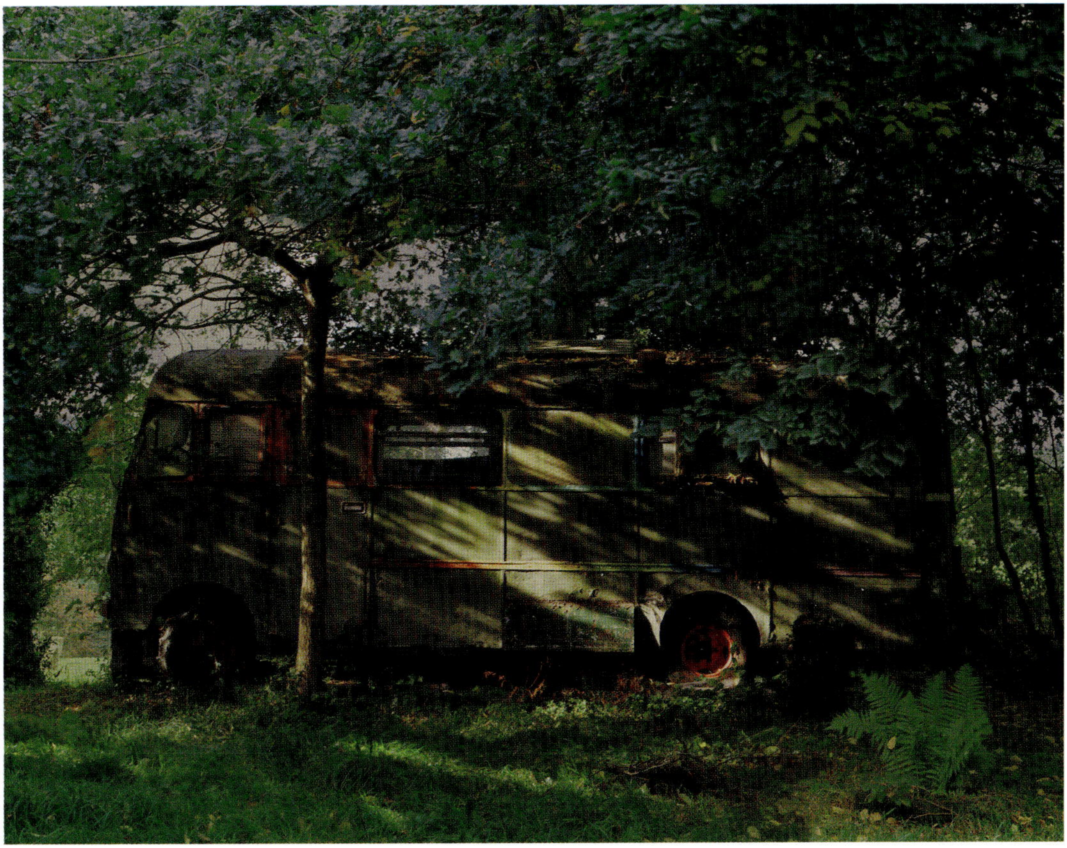

BATTLE OF THE BEANFIELD SURVIVOR, HATFIELD, LEOMINSTER (2023) A Meadow Arts commission

"I seen women burn love letters. Men dig holes in the dead of night. I seen a young girl walk down here in the cold dawn, take all her clothes off, wrap her arms round a broad beech tree and give birth to a baby boy. I seen first kisses. Last kisses. I seen all the world pass by and go."[4]

JOHNNY BYRON aka ROOSTER in *Jerusalem*, Act III

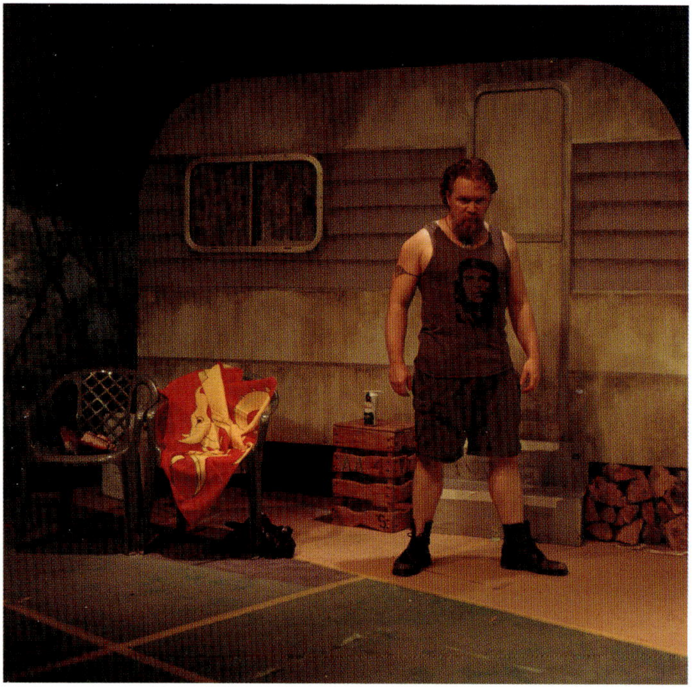

CHAZ DOYLE AS ROOSTER BYRON in the play *Jerusalem* at the South London Theatre, Norwood, directed by Charlotte Benstead (2024). A Meadow Arts commission

"Daredevil Johnny Byron is a combination of myths – some that he's created himself, and some that he believes in. These myths empower him but they also lock him in paralysis. So he's a tragic figure but also he's also heroic in his own way. He means a lot to the people around him and ultimately the community needs him for various reasons."

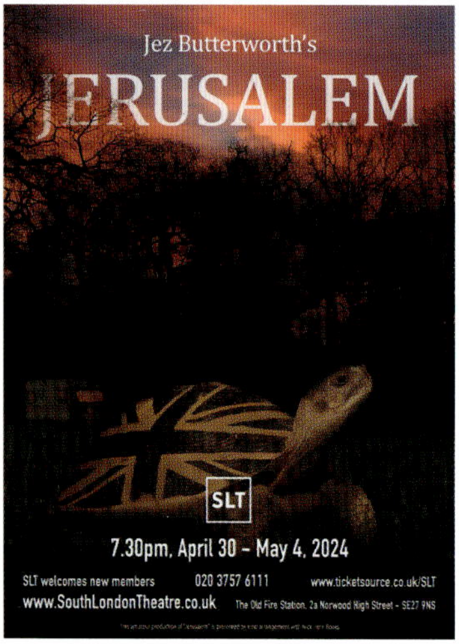

POSTER FOR *JERUSALEM* AT THE SOUTH LONDON THEATRE, NORWOOD

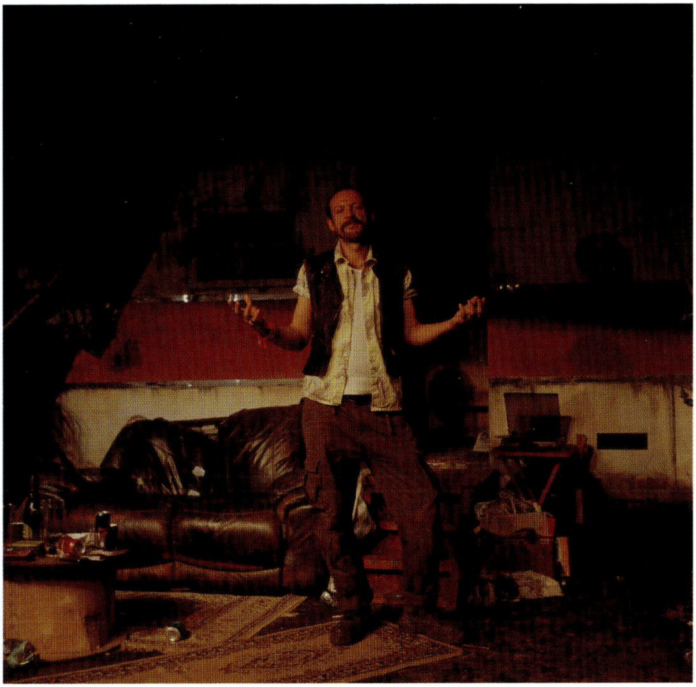

COLIN SMITH AS ROOSTER BYRON in the play *Jerusalem*, at The Old Court Theatre, Chelmsford, directed by Rebecca Skingley and Lauren Gladwin (2024). A Meadow Arts commission

Describing the play's lead character, Colin Smith notes, "I think he symbolizes freedom and the desire to live rather than be constrained by any kind of rules and regulations and governed by other people. As he says, the woodland is a free place and we should all be allowed to enjoy our pleasure without any kind of governance really."

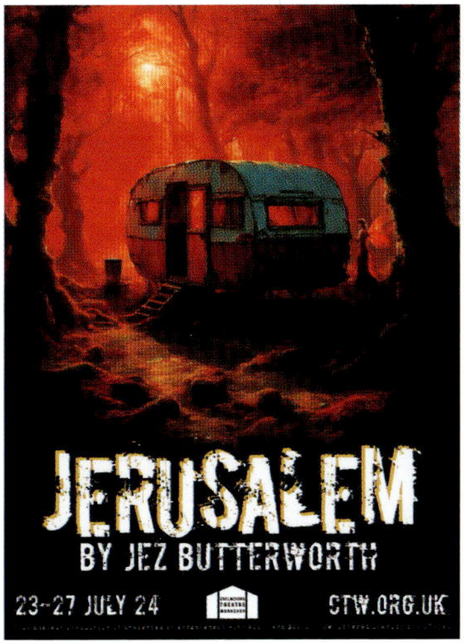

POSTER FOR *JERUSALEM* AT THE OLD COURT THEATRE, CHELMSFORD

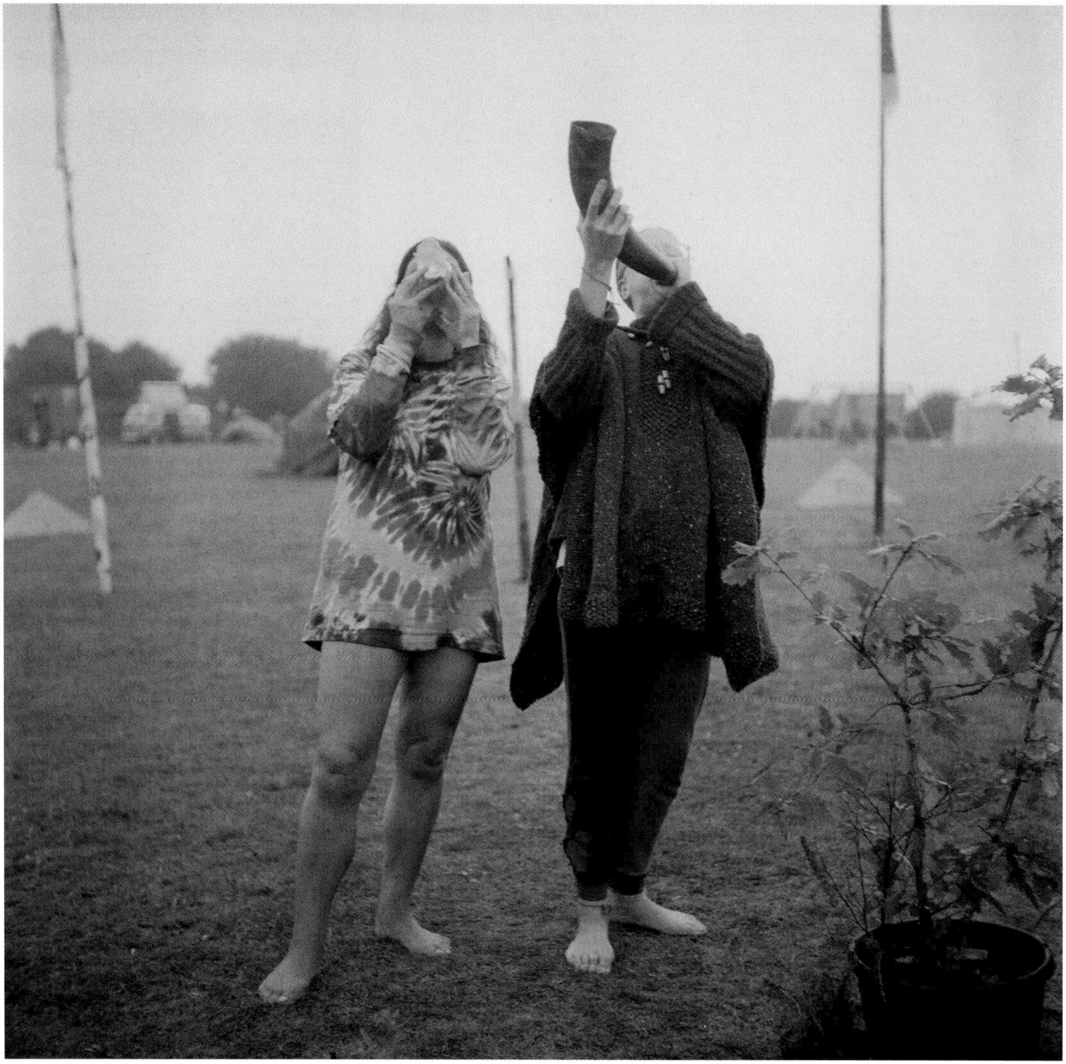

RAINBOW CIRCLE CAMP, FOREST OF DEAN, GLOUCESTERSHIRE (1990)

Rainbow Circle Camps developed out of the Glastonbury Green Gatherings. The first ones were held in the summer of 1988 and despite many evolutions and revolutions, they still take place. They had different themes such as Healing, Green Futures, Dance and Spirit, and the workshops on offer ranged from crystal meditation to nonviolent direct action.

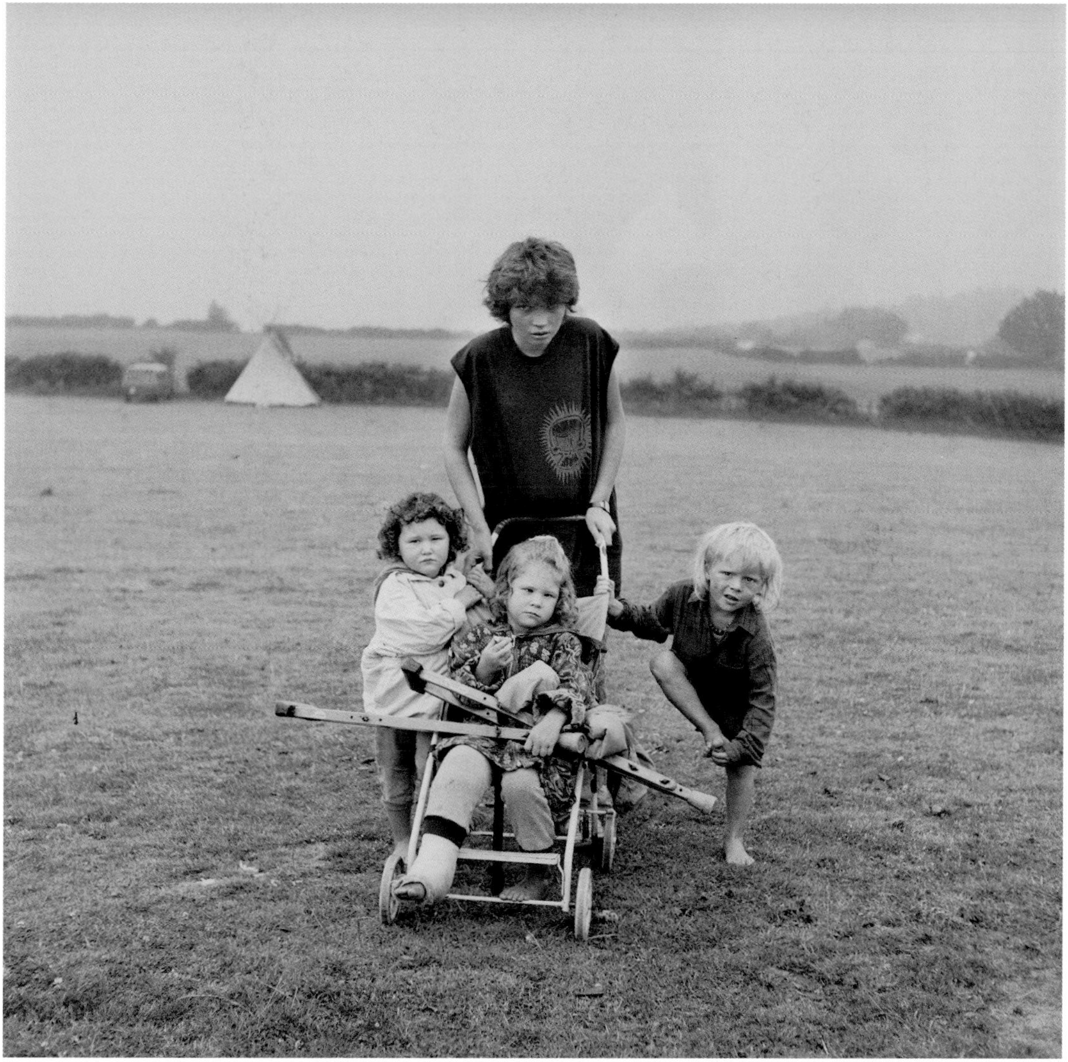

RAINBOW CIRCLE CAMP, FOREST OF DEAN, GLOUCESTERSHIRE (1990)

Children brought up in the restrictions of city and town life discovered a novel freedom and independence, and Traveller children had a chance to hang out with other kids. There was usually a "Kids' Area" where games and art activities took place. The Travellers' Skool Bus was often in attendance, an educational charity bus that toured Travellers' sites around Britain and provided educational support for Traveller children.

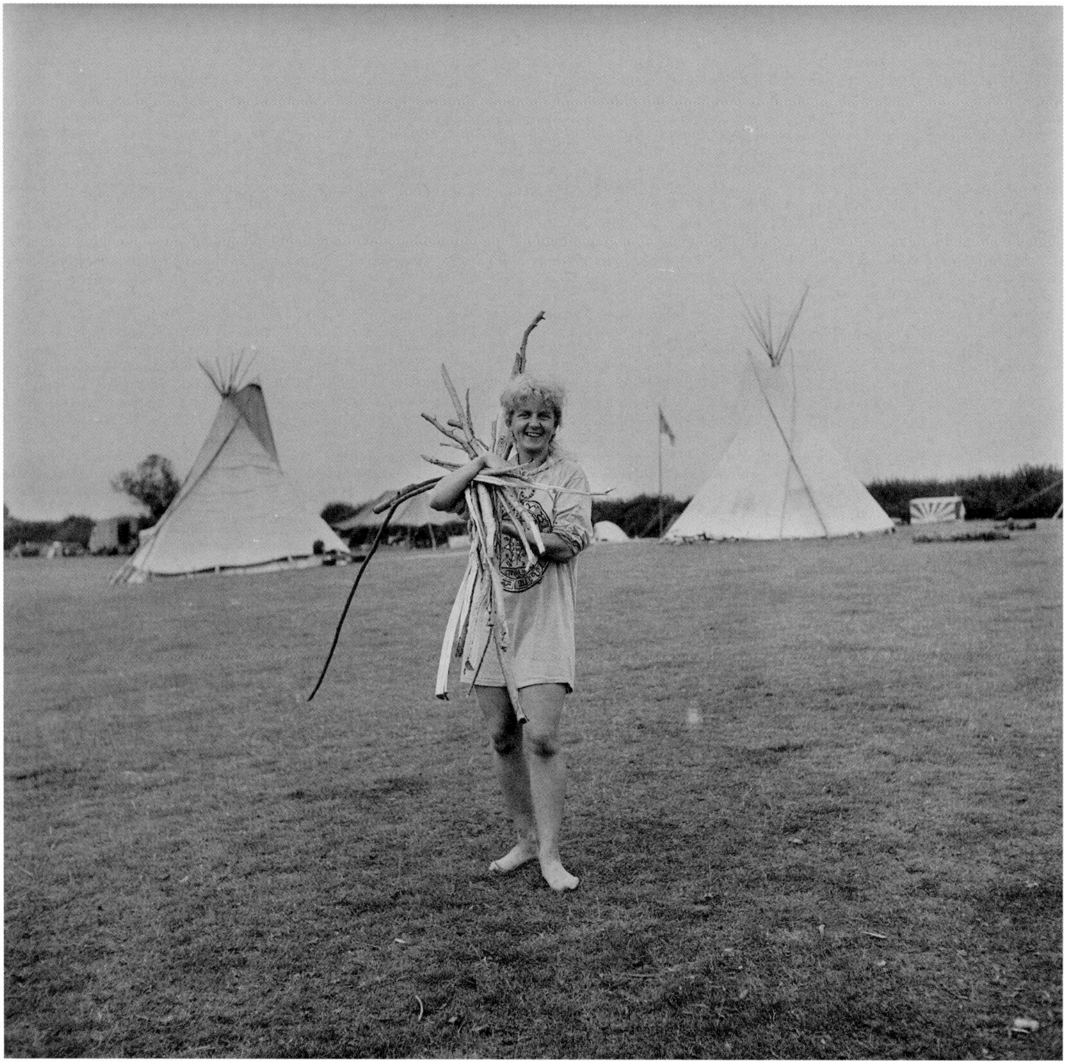

RAINBOW CIRCLE CAMP, FOREST OF DEAN, GLOUCESTERSHIRE (1990)

Constructed from a semi-circle of canvas and wooden poles, the tipi is a familiar sight at festivals and camps. It was the traditional dwelling of the semi-nomadic Indigenous people of the Great Plains. The smoke from the traditional open fire in the centre of a tipi was sucked out by the movement of air through the smoke flaps at the top. These need to be positioned facing away from the prevailing wind, a system possibly more suited to the prairies of North America. In a maritime climate like the UK, the wind direction is much more variable, meaning that the smoke flaps are usually pointing in the wrong direction and life in a tipi, though wonderfully close to Mother Earth, can be quite smoky.

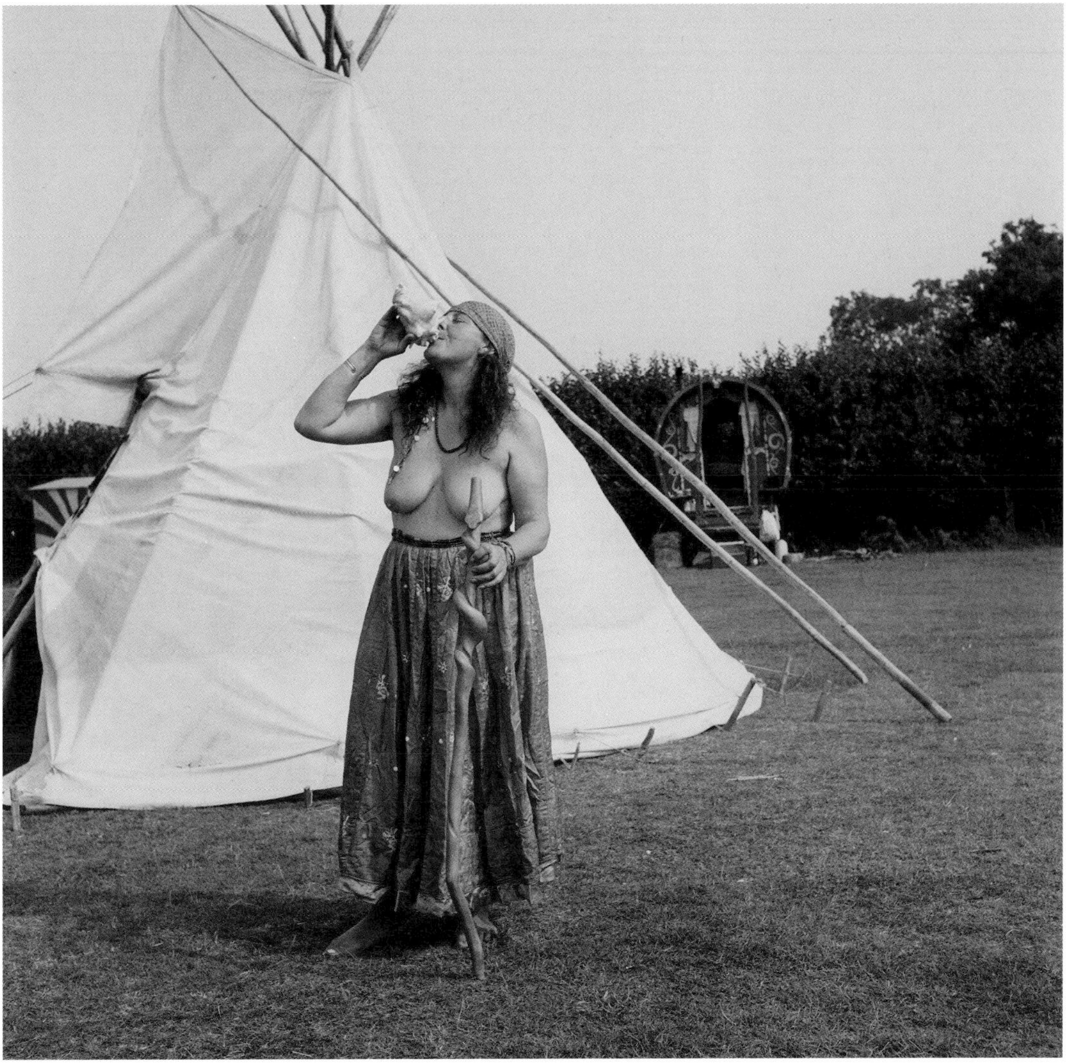

RAINBOW CIRCLE CAMP, FOREST OF DEAN, GLOUCESTERSHIRE (1990)

A conch was blown to signal the start of the open circle, the daily morning meeting. As well as an opportunity to tell people about the day's workshops, the circle was a chance to discuss issues on site, whether too many dogs running around in packs or problems with the earth privies. A talking stick was passed round (with only the person holding the stick being allowed to speak) and consensus was attempted. Nearly 40 years later, the camps still take place, as do the heated discussions, and the "experiment in living together cooperatively" continues.

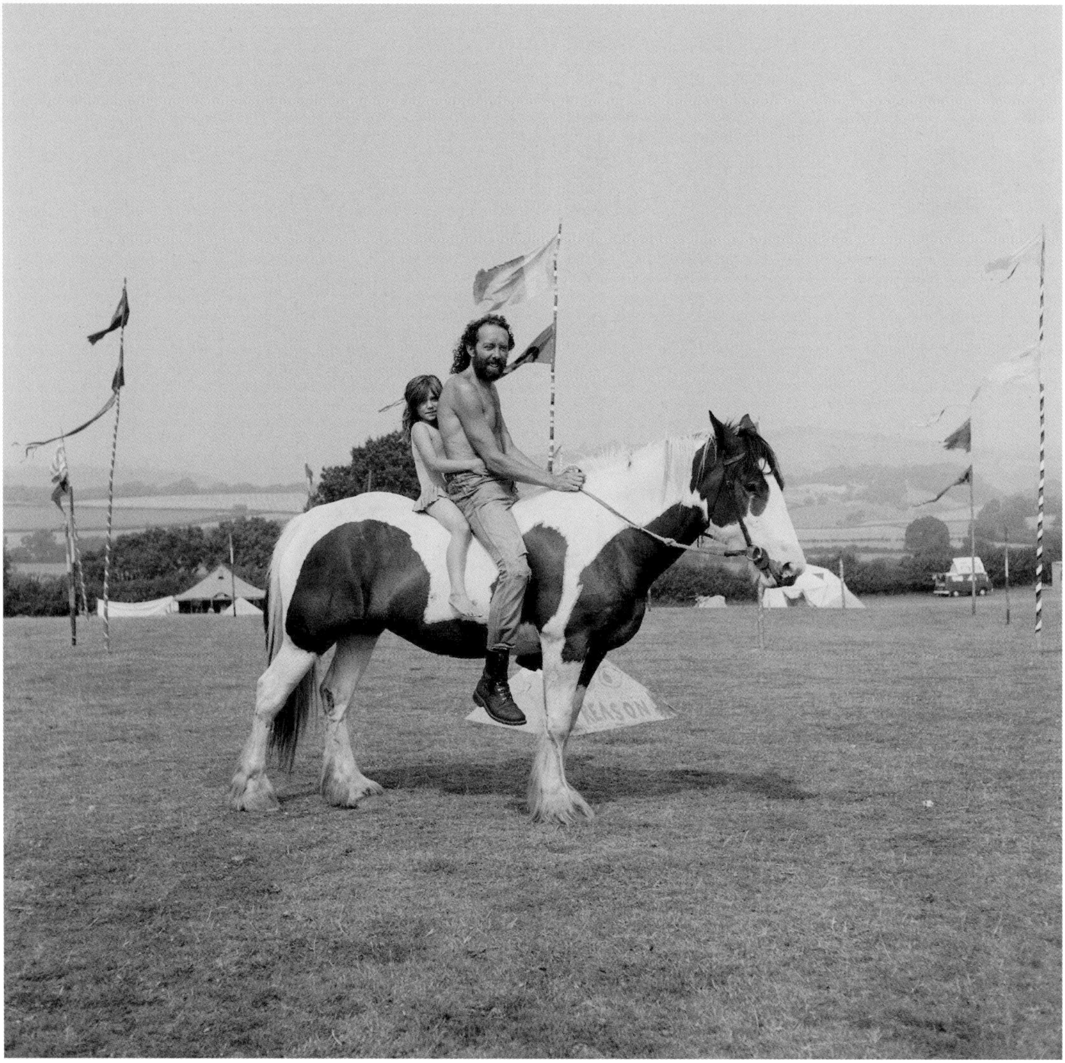

RAINBOW CIRCLE CAMP, FOREST OF DEAN, GLOUCESTERSHIRE (1990)

As well as an opportunity to spend a week or so camping in the countryside, participating in a communal way of life, in the early days at least, Rainbow Circle camps offered a safe place for New Age travellers, whether motorized or horse-drawn. They could enjoy a few weeks without fear of being made to move on unexpectedly.

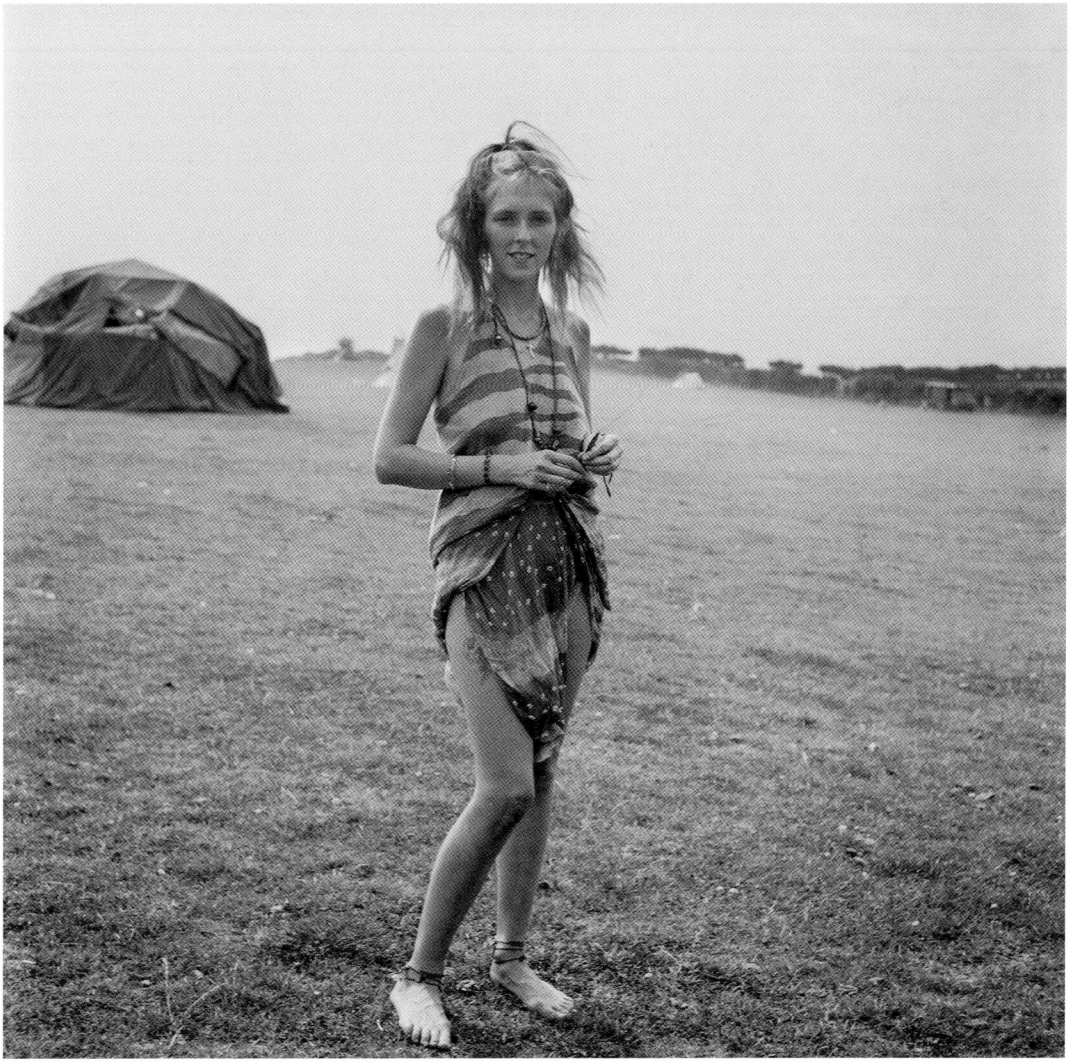

RAINBOW CIRCLE CAMP, FOREST OF DEAN, GLOUCESTERSHIRE (1990)

As temporary experiments in communal creative living, camps like Rainbow Circle demonstrated a way of life outside the strictures of capitalist, wage-driven society, with all its joys and pitfalls. After all, if people don't contribute what they can, whether money or effort, the infrastructure can't be paid for.

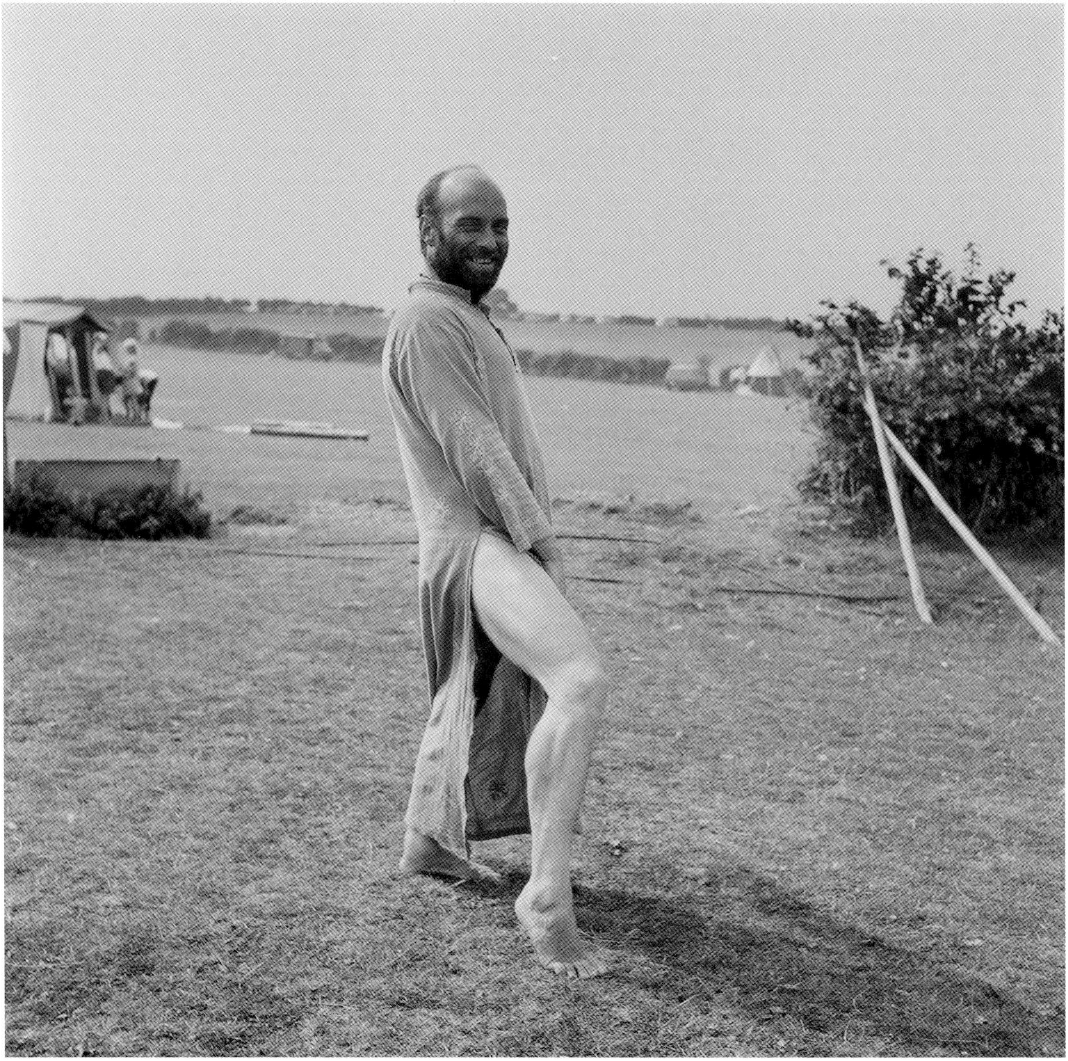

RAINBOW CIRCLE CAMP, FOREST OF DEAN, GLOUCESTERSHIRE (1990)

As one of the original organizers of the camps once said, "If fairs, festivals and camps have anything to offer at all, it's actually a way of healing the nation. Performance, art, culture – all these things cost nothing besides human effort, yet they can enrich the dignity of the human being. They can heal your soul and make you feel you're worth something – and you can do it with little impact on the planet."

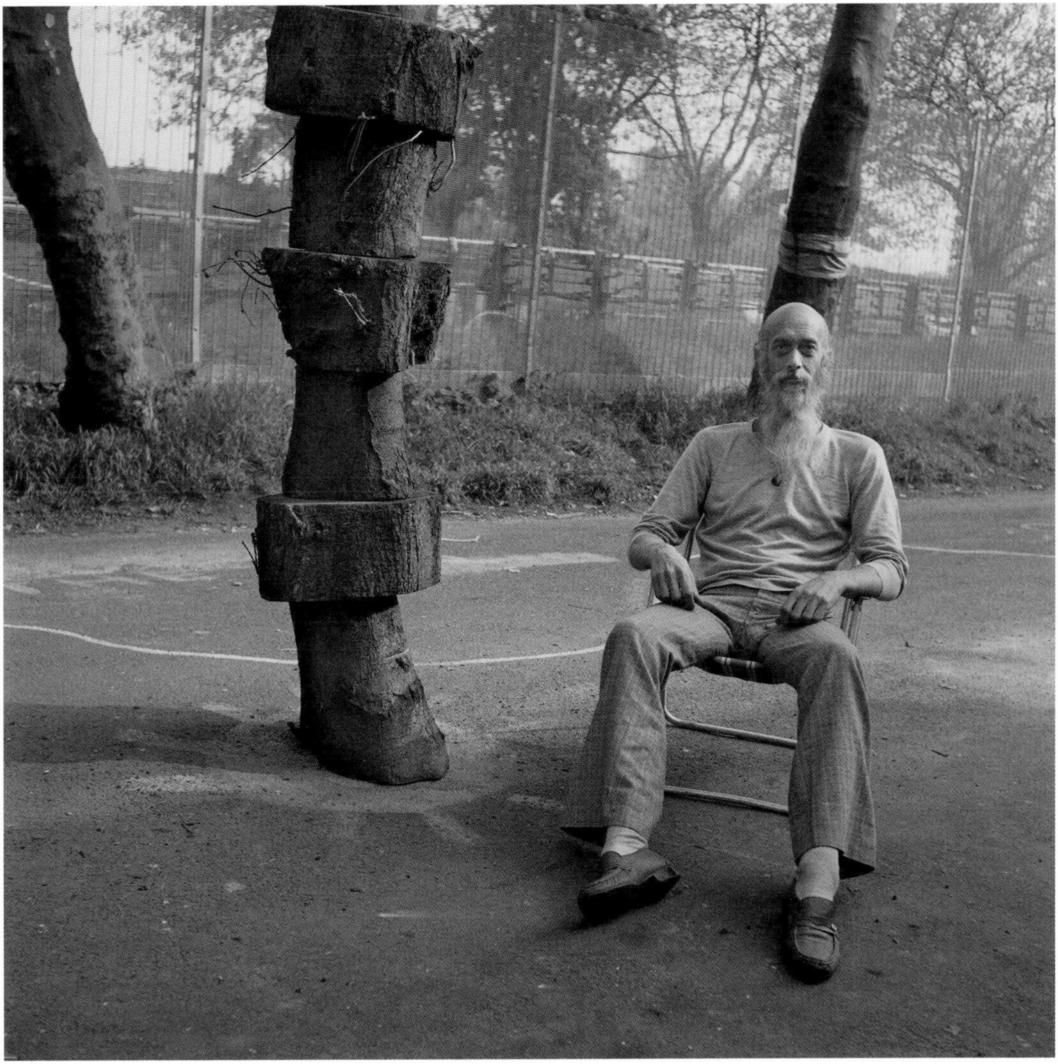

HENRY, OCCUPYING CLAREMONT ROAD AS PART OF THE M11 LINK ROAD PROTEST IN EAST LONDON (1994)

I (Leah) lived in Hackney in 1993 and, through friends in Wanstead and Leyton, became inspired by the activities of protesters around the tree on George Green, the houses due for demolition in Wanstonia and finally Claremont Street. I was inside one of the houses in Wanstead the night before the police came to evict everyone. The final barricades included huge boulders blocking the stairs to the big room on the first floor, where about 30 of us waited all night in a grim party atmosphere.

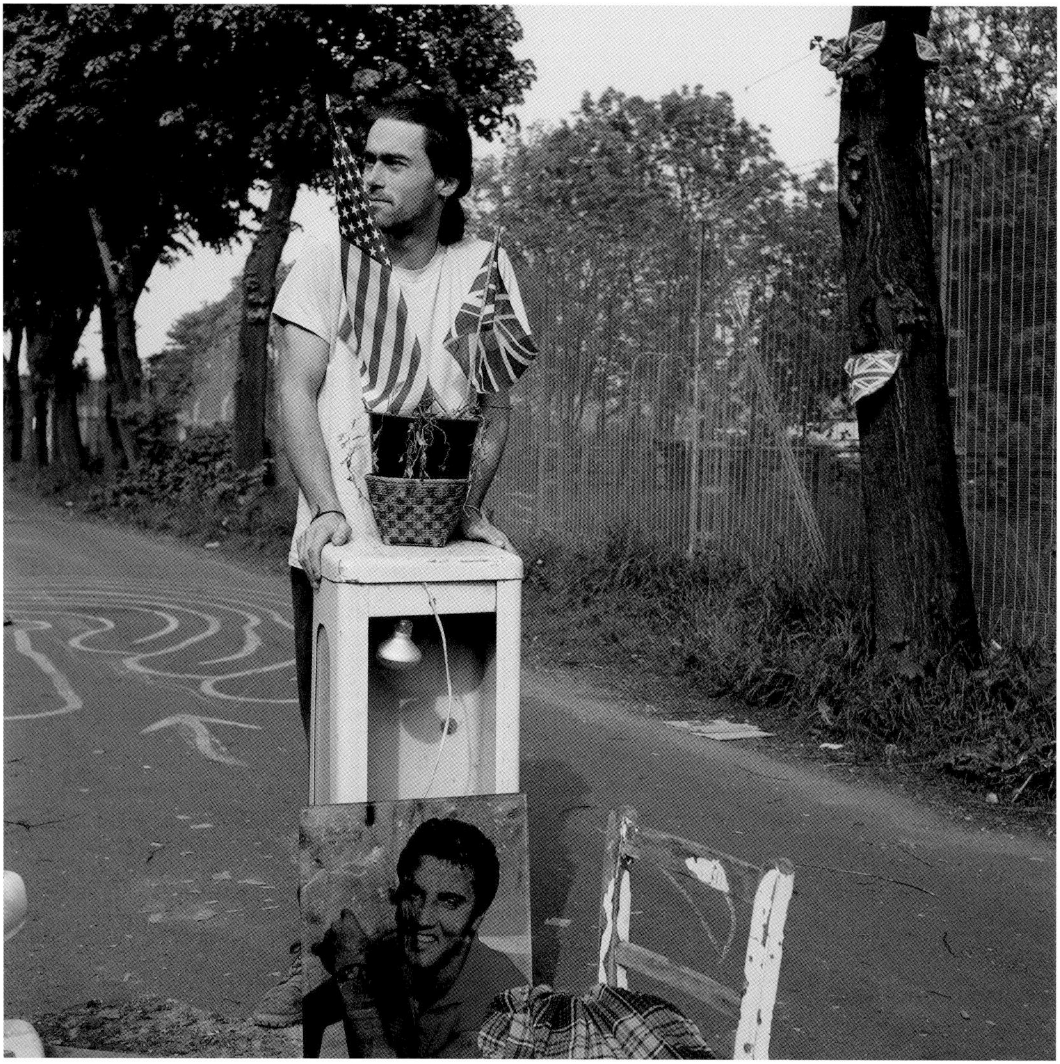

NEIL GOODWIN, OCCUPYING CLAREMONT ROAD AS PART OF THE M11 LINK ROAD PROTEST IN EAST LONDON (1994)

The first sign that something was happening was at dawn, when mysteriously the road went quiet – there was no longer any traffic in either direction. Then we understood the police had blocked the road at each end out of sight. After the carnival ambience of the night a more serious atmosphere settled on us. We waited with bated breath for what seemed like ages. I'm sure it was a police strategy to increase our stress levels.

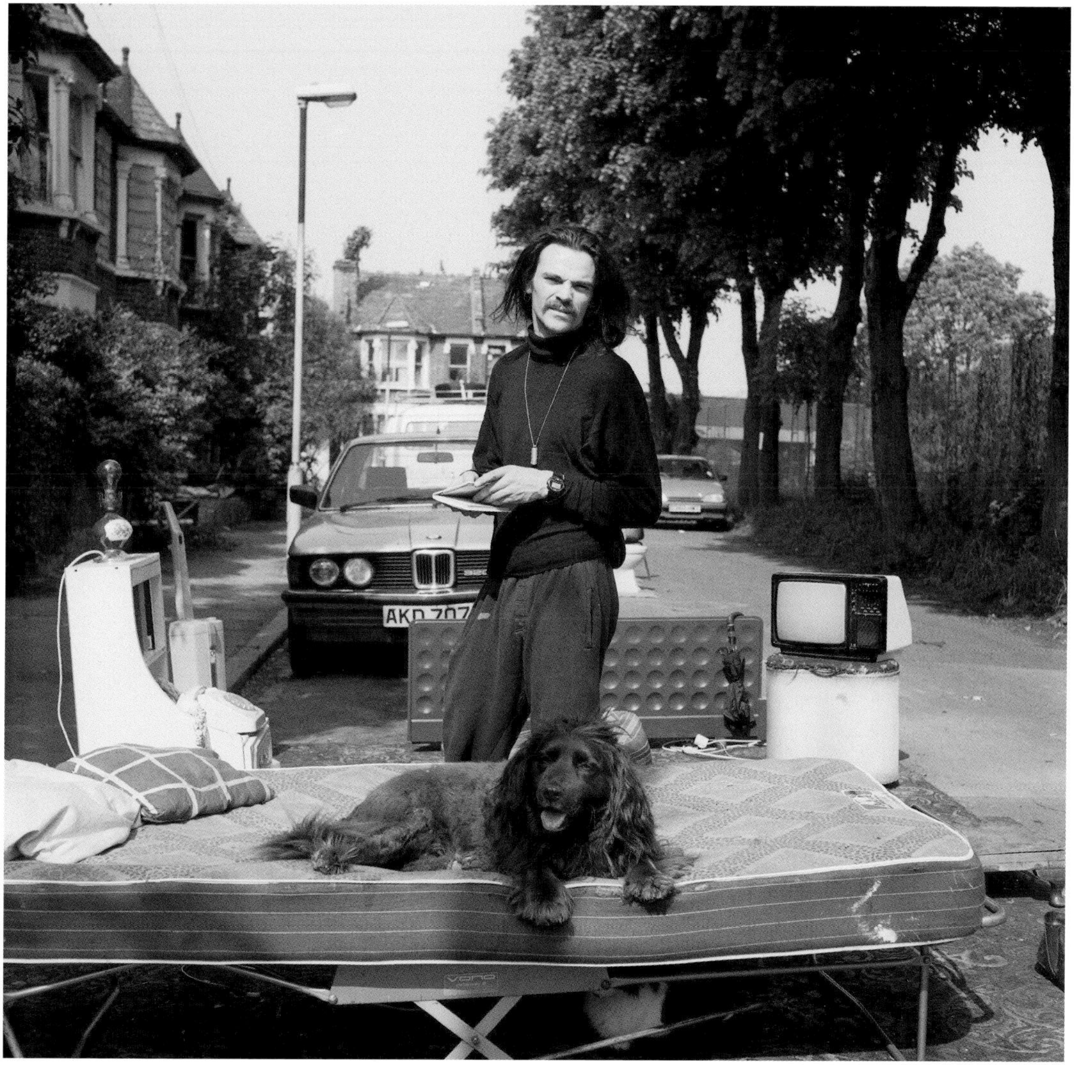

POOKIE, OCCUPYING CLAREMONT ROAD AS PART OF THE M11 LINK ROAD PROTEST IN EAST LONDON (1994)

After the long wait, the sight of the police vans arriving silently at dawn was almost a relief. It took them a couple of hours to clear the rubble blocking the staircase to our room. I had a small compact video camera and filmed them smashing their way through the reinforced door and forcibly removing people one by one. I was stationed by the front window and was able to throw my video cassette to a friend stationed in the garden below. He got it into the hands of a television reporter outside, who immediately broadcast it on the London news.

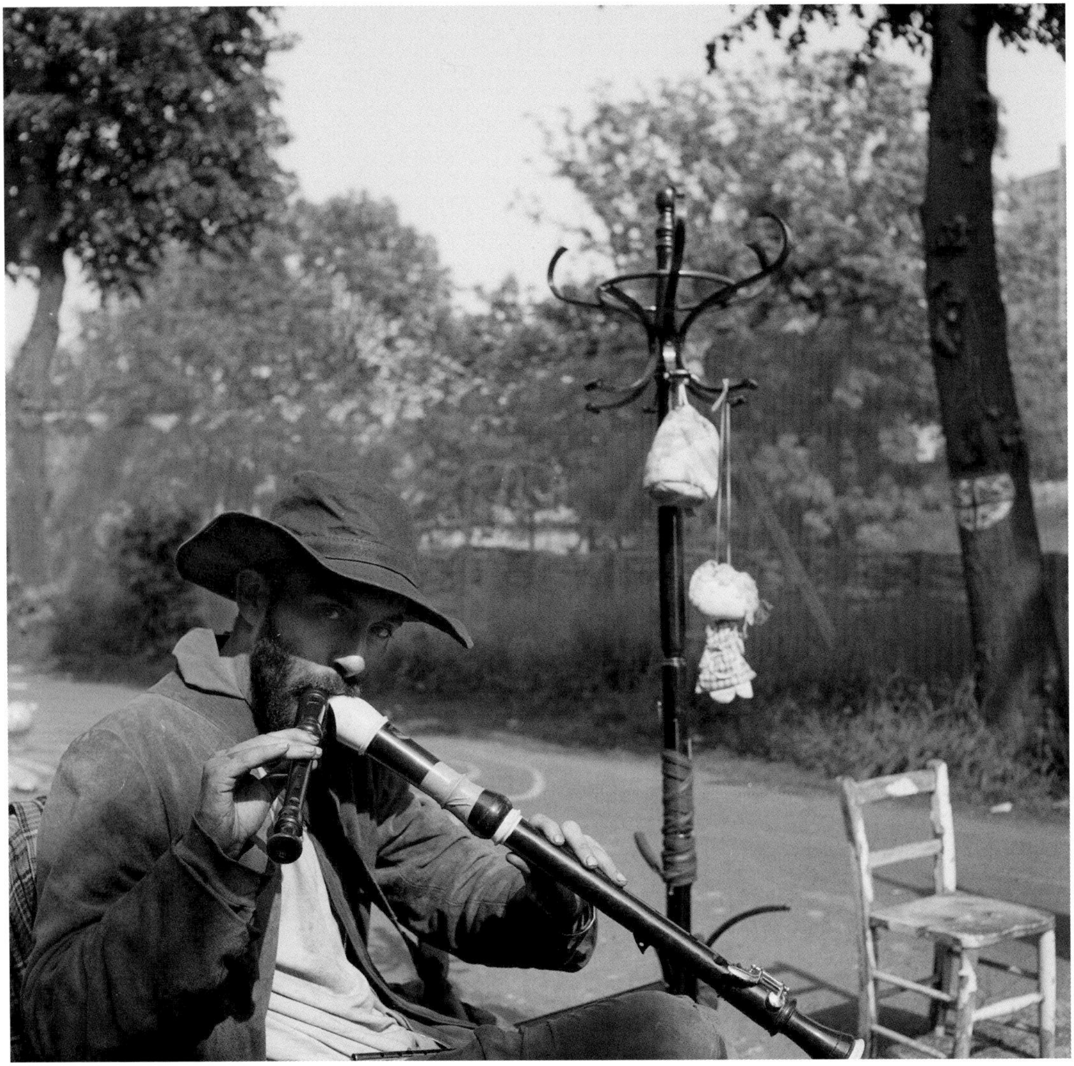

LEE TREE, OCCUPYING CLAREMONT ROAD AS PART OF THE M11 LINK ROAD PROTEST IN EAST LONDON (1994)

A friend and I became involved in the Claremont Road "micronation" occupation and started making a short film. Visits to Claremont Road were a mix of protest and play. There was a giant chessboard spanning the street with huge pieces fashioned from logs. Many of the houses had become art installations, with whole rooms painted in deep ochres or vibrant blues patterned with stars and magical symbols. Ephemera from the interior became sculptural objects in the exterior. Equally, nature and the street crept into the houses as art a real case of "the world turned upside down" in the 20th century. We interviewed Dolly Watson, who had lived in Claremont Road all her life, and many of the other protestors and activists. On the final evening, we found a perch on the roof close to the scaffolding tower, which was dedicated to Dolly, to film another day of destruction by the police. Again, this happened after a long night on the rooftops awaiting the sledgehammers of the law.

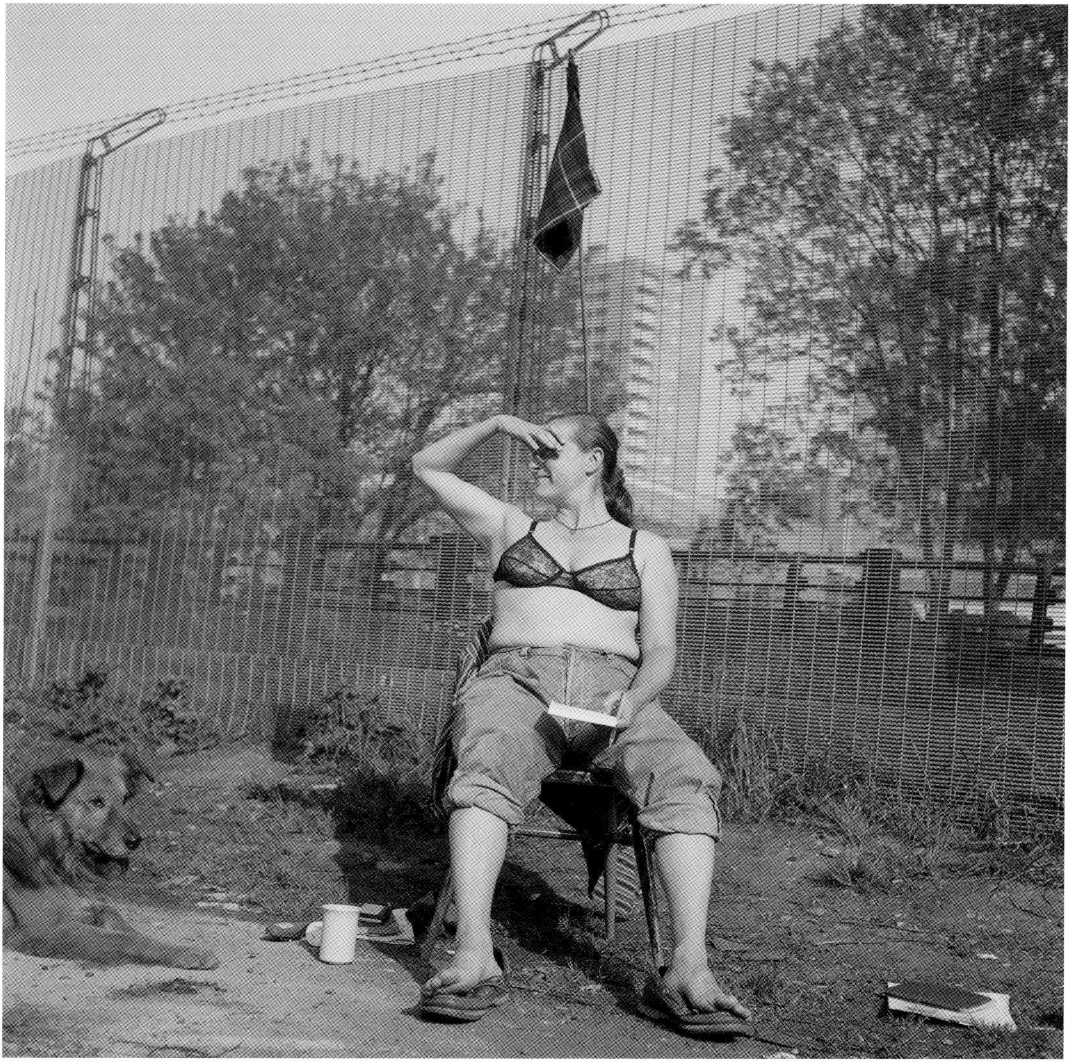

CHRISTINE BINNIE, OCCUPYING CLAREMONT ROAD AS PART OF THE M11 LINK ROAD PROTEST IN EAST LONDON (1994)

Christine already lived in the area when the protest began. She told me, "Living in Leytonstone in a house due to be demolished, life felt a bit meaningless. When a 'NO M11 LINK ROAD' march literally arrived on my doorstep, I spontaneously joined the protest. I met lovely people, I started getting up at 5am to stand by the road in rain, wind and car fumes, holding up my friends' paintings saying 'Babies' Lungs' and 'Let London Breathe'. I helped create the Art House. It was one of the best things I've ever done."

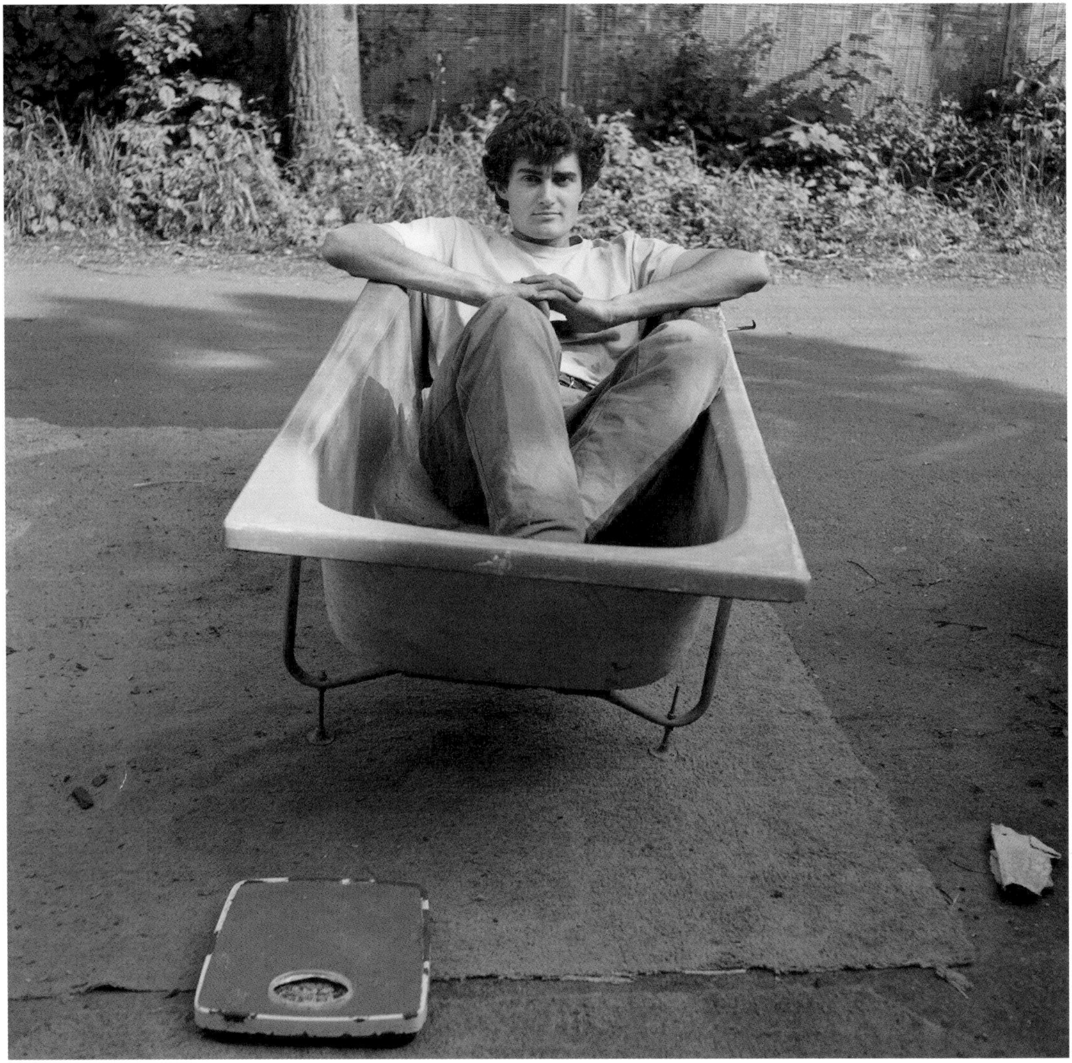

PAUL MOROZZO, OCCUPYING CLAREMONT ROAD AS PART OF THE M11 LINK ROAD PROTEST IN EAST LONDON (1994)

Paul was there from the beginning. As he said, "For me, it started off as a campaign about housing, trees and roads and ended up being about those things plus the small addition of the problem of capitalism and its relationship to work, people and nature. The road was built, but the campaign helped end the broader roads programme, led to the evolution of Reclaim the Streets, and strongly influenced later successful campaigns against coal and aviation expansion. I'll be forever grateful to the people I met and worked with on that campaign – from lifetime friends to the hundreds of people who came and gave time to the struggle."

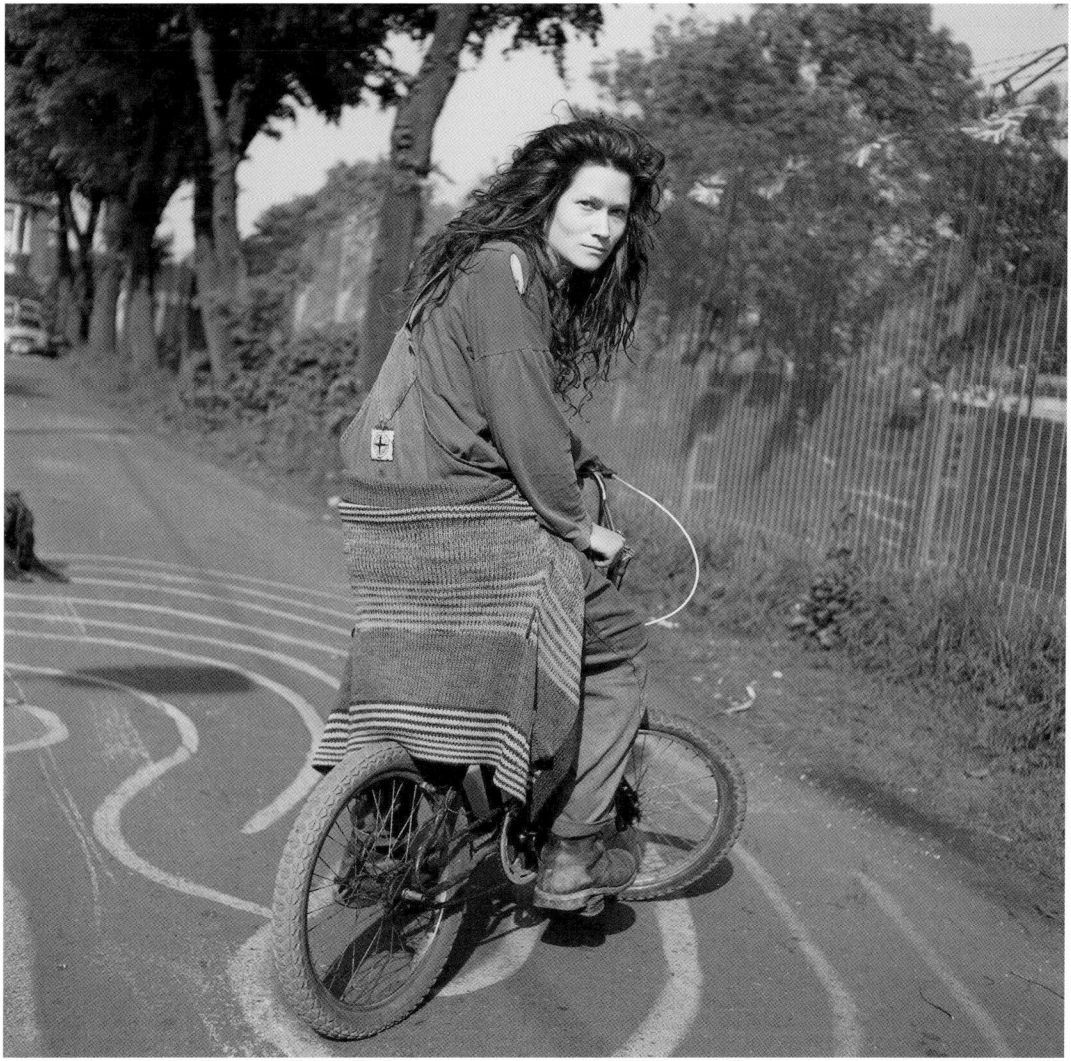

ALISON BUTLER, OCCUPYING CLAREMONT ROAD AS PART OF THE M11 LINK ROAD PROTEST IN EAST LONDON (1994)

After all these years, Alison's memories illuminate the multidimensional aspects of the campaign: "Claremont Road was the first place where I really felt like I belonged. The street became a haven for a bunch of misfits who suddenly found we could be part of something bigger than our individual struggles. That feeling was literally a lifesaver for some of us. Local rough sleepers, squatters, school children, environmentalists, ex-prisoners and pensioners – we worked, argued and played together to build barricades, tunnels, towers, treehouses, street art and community cafés. It was a tactical site of resistance, but also a messy, chaotic, loving home."

ARISE ALBION!

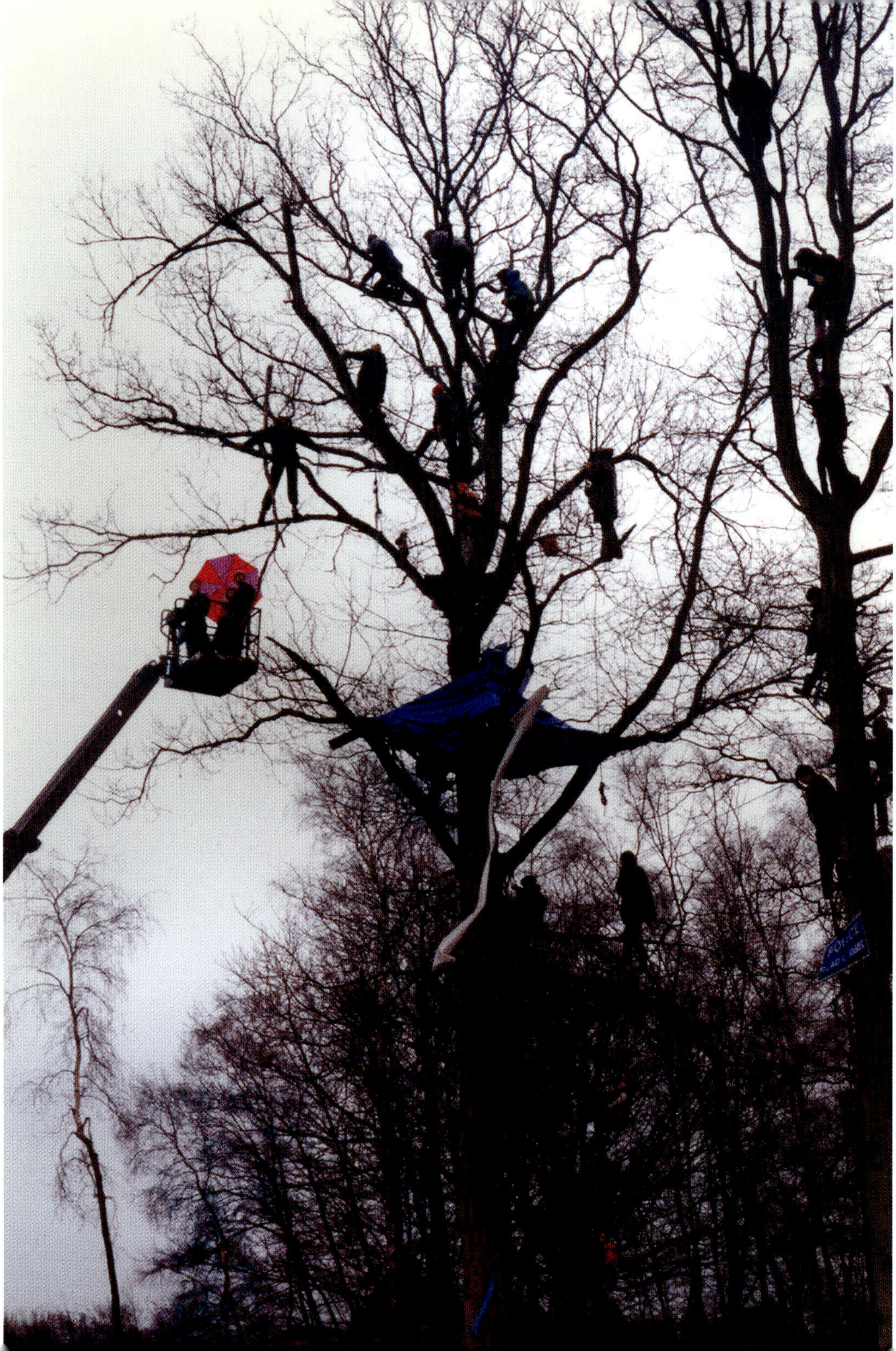

EVICTION AT TOT HILL, NEWBURY Nick Woolley (1996)

ARISE ALBION!

ANNABEL EDWARDS

"A play area for townies" was the headline-grabbing phrase that a local Plaid Cymru councillor used to describe plans for a new National Park in northeast Wales in 2024. Although his individual concerns about the proposal were valid, he framed them as if it were somehow outrageous that "townies" should claim the right to venture into the countryside for recreation. The long legacy of the rupture that took place after enclosure, when a large part of the rural population became an urban industrial population and land became concentrated in the ownership of a small minority, is still playing out across the UK. In England, currently approximately 58 million people live in urban areas and 10 million in rural, and the question of who owns the land and what rights the non-landowners have over the ground that makes up the country where they live is a perennial cause of friction. Ramblers, Gypsies, travellers, squatters, festival goers, ravers, allotment holders, nature lovers, antinuclear protestors, environmental protestors and wild swimmers have all protested their rights of access to the land and their desire to have a say in how it's used.

During the enclosures from the 17th to the 19th centuries, rural people moved to the industrial towns in search of work. To begin with, they maintained their connection with their former lives, keeping up fair and festival dates and returning to help with the harvest – but it didn't last. The poorer workers didn't have the time, the money or the opportunity for rural recreation. A survey of Manchester in 1832 described the population "crowded into one dense mass, in cottages separated by narrow, unpaved, and almost pestilential streets; in an atmosphere loaded with the smoke and exhalations of a large manufacturing city. The operatives are congregated in rooms and workshops during twelve hours in the day, in an enervating, heated atmosphere, which is frequently loaded with dust or filaments of cotton..."[1]

But throughout the 19th century, this new urban working class regrouped. The development of mutual societies and cooperatives and then unions enabled them to succeed in their demands for better working conditions through negotiation, strikes, marches and riots. By the latter part of the century, they had the time and energy to return to the countryside – this time in search of healthy recreation. Many of the northern industrial towns lie on the edge of great areas of moorland and the proximity of all this wild space, much of which was reserved for the grouse-shooting recreation of a few wealthy landowners, was an injustice too far. In 1896, when landowner and mill owner Colonel Richard Henry Ainsworth put a locked gate across the popular track that led up over his grouse moor on Winter Hill outside Bolton, he ignited what is probably the largest mass trespass ever. On the first weekend, 10,000 people marched up the hill, destroying the gate and ignoring the gamekeepers who'd been stationed there to stop them, and the following weekend 12,000 people did this again. This protest was estimated to include nearly 10 per cent of Bolton's population. Local poet and socialist Allen Clarke celebrated the event:

> Will yo' come o' Sunday mornin'
> For a walk o'er Winter Hill?
> Ten thousand went last Sunday
> But there's room for thousands still!
> Oh the moors are rare and bonny
> And the heather's sweet and fine
> And the roads across the hilltops –
> Are the people's – yours and mine![2]

The more famous Kinder Scout Mass Trespass took place in 1932 during the global Great Depression, the effects of which were particularly felt in the UK in the industrial north of England. Unemployment and poverty heightened the desire for access to the countryside for free, healthy exercise and immersion in nature. The trespass was organized by members of the British Workers' Sports Federation and the Young Communist League, and folk singer Ewan MacColl, who took part, summed it up in his famous song "The Manchester Rambler", which he wrote shortly afterwards and where he contrasts being a wage slave on a weekday to the freedom of spending Sunday up on the moors.

By the 1950s, the restless youths who wanted to break out of the cities took the form of mods and rockers descending on Brighton, Clacton and other coastal towns when searching for opportune space – in this case the beaches of England – on which to congregate and occasionally enact inter-tribal fights. They were expressing the perennial human need for communal celebration and ritual, the recognition of tribal identity, and the search for a common space on which to carry this out. Their successors, the hippies of the sixties and seventies, expanded this quest to a much greater degree with their free festivals and their political, philosophical and spiritual aspirations, not to mention a desire to get stoned and have a good time listening to music in a field.

The free festivals also had their roots squarely in the squatting and land reform movement. The Hyde Park Diggers, who directly referenced the 17th-century religious reformer Gerrard Winstanley's Diggers in their discussion of land reform and Winstanley's ideas of "the Earth as a Common Treasury for all", were part of the squatting movement that was developing in London and other cities at the time.[3,4] The squatting activists were ambitious and the first Windsor Free Festival took place in 1972, advertised as "Rent Strike: The People's Free Festival". The idea was to squat Windsor Park, the Queen's "back garden". The organizers pointed out that the young people who would be expected to die to defend their country should be able to share in more of its land, and it was an inspired location on which to proclaim peace and love and radical politics. About 700 people came to the first festival, which increased to about 8,000 at the 1973 festival. When even more people attended the third Windsor festival in 1974, the authorities decided enough was enough and about halfway through the festival's intended ten-day run, Thames Valley Police went in, truncheons swinging, to stop this "gigantic drug-inspired breach of the peace", as the chief constable described it. He also described all pop groups, without exception, as "a cancerous growth in society", so perhaps it was inevitable that under his leadership, the police violence, destruction of people's belongings and over 200 arrests that day caused widespread shock and prompted the Labour government to provide – for the first and only time in the history of free festivals – a venue for the following year's People's Free Festival at an old airfield at Watchfield in Oxfordshire.[5]

In the meantime, the first Stonehenge Free Festival had taken place, dreamed up by the charismatic Phil Russell, known as Wally Hope, who wanted to claim back Stonehenge, which he "regarded as sacred to the people and stolen by the government and make it a site for free festivals, free music, free space, free mind".[6] After the festival, which a few hundred people attended, Phil and a small group, who called themselves collectively the Wallies, remained camping next to Stonehenge for a couple of months until they were evicted. They said they worshipped the sun and wanted to stay next to Stonehenge to see what they could learn from proximity to such a sacred place: "Our generation is the best mass movement in history, experimenting with anything in our search for love and peace. Knowledge, kicks, religion, life, truth... Our temple is sound. We fight our battles with music... We have guitars instead of tommy guns."[7] After the disaster of the Windsor festival, where Russell had been beaten up while trying to persuade rampaging policemen to choose peace and love by dancing among them, a less urban, more spiritual festival was planned for; hence the giant druid on the poster advertising the 1975 festival. Phil Russell never attended it as he had been arrested and sent to a psychiatric hospital in May. He was released days after the festival was over, a broken man, destroyed by the sledgehammer of antipsychotic drugs. He died shortly afterwards. As this was understandably seen to be a deliberate action of the state, he became an early martyr of the burgeoning festival and alternative movement.

The summer solstice Stonehenge festivals grew into month-long encampments, and the idea of the stones as a place of New Age pilgrimage gradually developed, so that it became matter of fact for passing hippies to explain that "people have been coming here for thousands of years to have a festival. They can't stop us. It's our sacred place."[8]

In *The Dawn of Everything*, anthropologist David Graeber and archaeologist David Wengrow describe 2,500-year-old Stonehenge, whose stones frame the midsummer sunrise and the midwinter sunset, as "the last in a long sequence of ceremonial structures", which for centuries were built and rebuilt out of both wood and stone by people who converged on the locality from remote corners of Britain at significant times

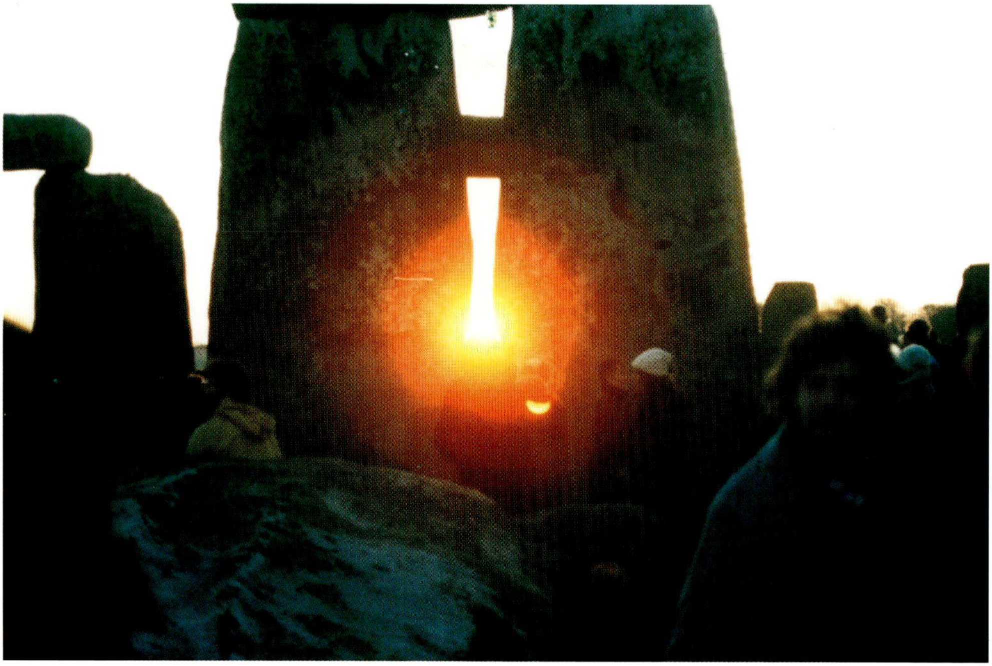

SUNRISE BETWEEN THE STONES AT STONEHENGE ON THE WINTER SOLSTICE Mark Grant (1985)

of the year. They explain that what the seasonal pattern of these "alternating phases of dispersal and monumental construction" suggests is "that from the very beginning, or at least as far back as we can trace such things, human beings were self-consciously experimenting with different social possibilities."[9]

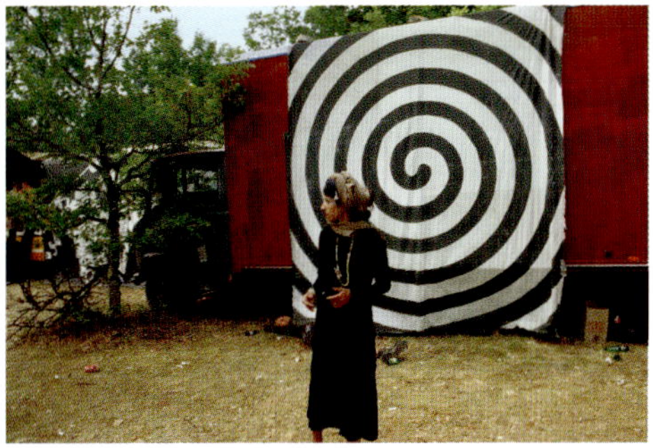

SPIRAL TRIBE BUS from the "Le Crowbar" series, Tom Hunter (1995)

Somehow, partially by intent and partially by good luck, a bunch of hippies, squatters and dopeheads had tapped into the ancient story of Stonehenge and its power as a symbol of social and political change. As mentioned earlier, Jez Butterworth's play *Jerusalem* tells the story of the attempted eviction and destruction of Johnny "Rooster" Byron, a Dionysian figure living in a bus in the woods and acting as an anarchic Lord of Misrule for generations of young people who need a space to party or just to get away from their everyday lives. Butterworth engages with the mythic element of the British landscape; the drum that Rooster beats at the end of the play as the enemy forces close in on him is the drum that the giant who claimed to have built Stonehenge gave him: "This is for you. If you ever get into any bother, or need a hand, just bang this drum and us, the giants, we'll hear it, and we'll come."[10]

Festivals were happening nearly every weekend throughout the summer and people began living in vehicles and travelling between festivals. By the second half of the 1970s, people started to follow this way of life throughout the year, with a collection of old buses, vans, trucks and ambulances travelling from site to site; and the New Age traveller or Peace Convoy grew out of the festival scene in this way. Unemployment and homelessness were high and living in a vehicle as part of a developing community was an attractive alternative for some people. However, a nomadic lifestyle isn't easy in a small, heavily developed and intensively farmed country such as England. Finding somewhere to park was difficult, so once the travellers had found somewhere, they tended to stay there until they were evicted.

This prejudice against the nomadic way of life runs deep. As humanity settled into farming, there must have been irritation and envy at the apparent carefree life of the nomad, not tied to one place by a cycle of crops and the accompanying administrative burden of daily life in a developing sedentary society, with all its rules, regulations and inequalities. The Convoy understood what the Roma Gypsies had known for centuries: that an enclosed landscape isn't a welcoming one, even if their settled antagonists subconsciously envy their freedom.

In *Against the Grain*, the political scientist and anthropologist James C Scott describes the age of the "barbarians", when the first states were being created (and lost and created again) and there existed "hordes" of people who still lived a hunter-gatherer nomadic existence on the outside of settled states.[11] These peoples had a symbiotic relationship with the early states but from the states' point of view, "They are uncaptured at the very least, and at worst, represent a nuisance and threat that must be exterminated."[12] According to Scott, the ancient tension between the settled, domesticated subjects of the early states and the "undomesticated" non-state people on the periphery still plays out today.

The Stonehenge festival continued until 1985, when the presence of a growing number of people travelling around, trying to find places to park, squatting fields to hold festivals, taking and selling drugs with relative impunity, and generally living outside of mainstream society was found sufficiently alarming by the Conservative government for them to decide to deal with the issue conclusively.

At a time when violent confrontation with the miners at Orgreave in South Yorkshire had set the tone for government reaction to a perceived internal threat, an ambush was planned to make sure that the Convoy couldn't continue. As the vehicles were making their way to Stonehenge for the summer solstice, police roadblocks forced them to stop. Seeing riot police making their way down the line of vehicles and smashing windscreens as they went, then dragging the occupants out, those in the vehicles further back broke through into a field beside the road to escape. When they found themselves trapped in the field, the standoff eventually degenerated into mad scenes of vehicles frantically driving around the field to avoid the police, who, appearing to be affected by some kind of violent frenzy, forced each vehicle to stop and then smashed their way into the buses, dragging men and women out by their hair and hitting them with truncheons. Despite the presence of children and babies, even pregnant women were witnessed being hit. It became known as the Battle of the Beanfield, but it was probably rather more one-sided than the word "battle" suggests.[13]

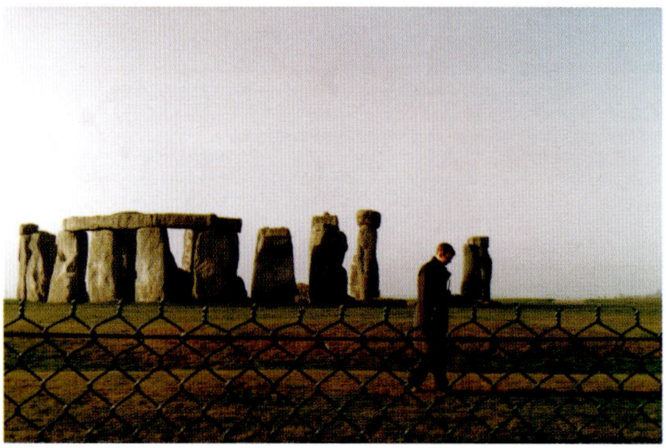

STONEHENGE FENCED OFF AND POLICE PROTECTED
Annabel Edwards (1992)

Around the same time, the government began to introduce legislation to restrict assemblies and trespass in the 1986 Public

Order Act, which imposed new conditions on public assemblies, including protests, in order "to prevent serious public disorder, serious criminal damage or serious disruption to the life of the community". The new conditions included various limitations on the number of people who could gather in one place, and the length and location of the protest. The police were given increased powers to arrest people who didn't comply. Section 39 gave police new powers to clamp down on Gypsy, Roma and Traveller communities. If two or more people were trespassing on land with the intent to reside, and had already been asked to leave by the landowner, the police could evict them if they were perceived to have caused damage to the land, or if there were 12 or more vehicles. Any resistance would empower the police to make arrests and impound vehicles, even if the vehicle was someone's home.

The Peace Convoy had gained its name through its links with Greenham Common and Molesworth peace camps, which were both set up in 1981 after the announcement that the United States Air Force would be basing its mobile nuclear cruise missiles at the two RAF bases. The peace camps were set up on squatted land adjacent to the air bases, and in a sense, the protestors were challenging the state's use of the land for nuclear armaments and also claiming their right to use land for protest. The name Greenham Common is a reminder that unenclosed common land is particularly vulnerable to being taken over in this way as it is perceived to be accessible and expendable land that isn't being used for agriculture. Part of Greenham Common had been requisitioned in 1941 for use as an air base. The women's camps at Greenham were evicted on numerous occasions throughout the 1980s, and hundreds of people were arrested for trespass. As they cut the wire of the fence, the women proclaimed, "We need to come in there, it's common land..."

The peace camp at Molesworth RAF base in Cambridgeshire had been started by various Christian peace groups. In August 1984, the Green Collective, who had organized the successful first Green Field at the 1984 Glastonbury Festival, were looking for a new site for their annual summer Green Gathering festival.[14] They decided to hold it on land within the perimeter of the base at Molesworth. The Peace Convoy had limped their way to Molesworth after having been attacked by the police at Nostell Priory free festival in Yorkshire, where many of their vehicles and belongings had been destroyed. After the Green Gathering ended, some of the green activists and convoy members stayed on and their encampment became known as Rainbow Fields Village. This grew into an ad hoc community of over one hundred adults, living in tents and vans with children and animals. As a demonstration of the "Bread not Bombs" ideology, they ploughed up some of the 600-acre site and planted wheat, which they harvested and sent to famine-stricken Eritrea, more of a symbolic gesture than actual aid. In February 1985, over

3,000 military and police personnel were used to evict the village and erect two three-metre-high fences around the seven-mile perimeter of the base overnight. This extraordinary peace-time troop deployment cost over £6m, and gave Michael Heseltine, Margaret Thatcher's defence minister, the excuse to pose around the Molesworth site in a camouflage jacket. Many of the travellers evicted from the camp were caught up in the Battle of the Beanfield later that year.[15]

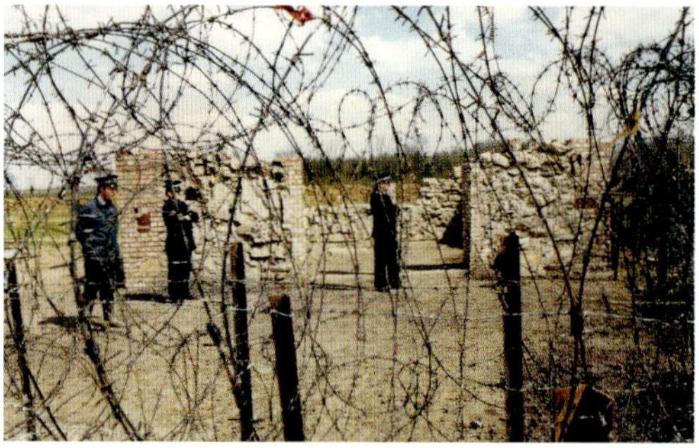

POLICE IN FRONT OF RUINS OF PEACE CHAPEL AT RAF MOLESWORTH Tony Grist (1980s)

Although the events of 1985 saw the dispersal of the Peace Convoy and the end of the Stonehenge Free Festival, many groups of travellers carried on, identifying forgotten corners of the countryside to park in and holding festivals. Meanwhile, in the cities, youth were taking over unused urban spaces for parties; often, these were warehouses that had been left empty as industry declined. The raves then moved out into the M25 periphery but were also becoming more commercial – whether through young Thatcherite entrepreneurs holding legal raves, or large illegal ones where criminal drug gangs were increasingly becoming involved. The free party scene wanted to resist this commercialization and evolved out of the extensive squatting communities throughout London and cities such as Nottingham.

As Mark Angelo Harrison of the free party sound system Spiral Tribe has described, squatting created a community and also freed people from the need to earn their rent, so it gave them more time to be creative.[16] Collectives such as Spiral Tribe, Bedlam and DiY wanted to maintain the idealism of free music and free creativity. In the early nineties, they realized that by teaming up with the travellers and their free festivals, they could move out of the city and its environs and find free space in the countryside, creating a nomadic techno shamanism, where various youth cultures could achieve

HARRY ON TOUR WITH VOX POPULI SOUND SYSTEM from the "Le Crowbar" Series, Tom Hunter (1995)

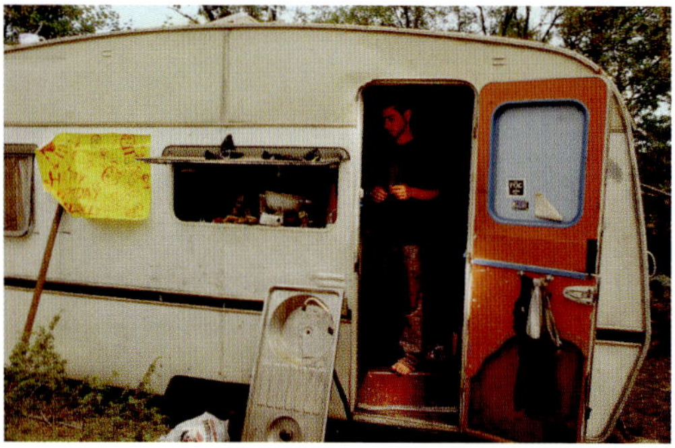

collective euphoria, fuelled by the recently introduced drug ecstasy. The collectives rejected hierarchy and commercialism, and Spiral Tribe once, in tribute to one of their political heroes, Gerrard Winstanley, held a rave in an abandoned mansion on St George's Hill in Surrey, where the original Diggers set up their commune, now an exclusive gated community for the very wealthy.

There were definitely tensions between some of the travellers and the ravers. The more hippy festival goers weren't impressed by the loud driving beats, but the more hard-core travellers welcomed them and the new energy they brought. Spiral Tribe like to claim that it is folk music – very loud folk music – as the musical expression of the actual folk.[17]

The final straw for the authorities was the week-long gathering at Castlemorton Common near Malvern in Worcestershire, when the Avon and Somerset police decided to stop a convoy of vehicles travelling to Avon Free Festival, which had been held in the Bristol area for a number of years; they took the view that if the festival goers were out of the county, the problem was someone else's. The police in Worcestershire then started funnelling people towards Castlemorton Common as a convenient piece of open land. Word spread via a recorded phone message and thanks to a combination of it being a Bank Holiday weekend with great weather, suddenly over 30,000 people gathered there for the week. The moral panic caused by Castlemorton, including references to "medieval brigands", resulted in the repressive Criminal Justice and Public Order Act of 1994. It targeted all kinds of collective trespass, criminalizing previously civil offences, repealed the duty of councils to provide Gypsy and Traveller sites, and included the notorious clause banning gatherings of 20 or more people where the music was characterized "by the emission of a succession of repetitive beats".[18]

The same year, another front opened in the pushback against the rural status quo. Inspired by the peace camps, particularly Greenham, a group of young activists set up camp outside Winchester to protest against the M3 extension, which was planned to cut a vast swathe out of beautiful chalk downland containing two SSSIs (Sites of Special Scientific Interest) and an important archaeological site. After the conventional procedures had been followed and failed to stop the project, a group calling themselves the Dongas Tribe (after the deep trackways across the land) started a campaign of

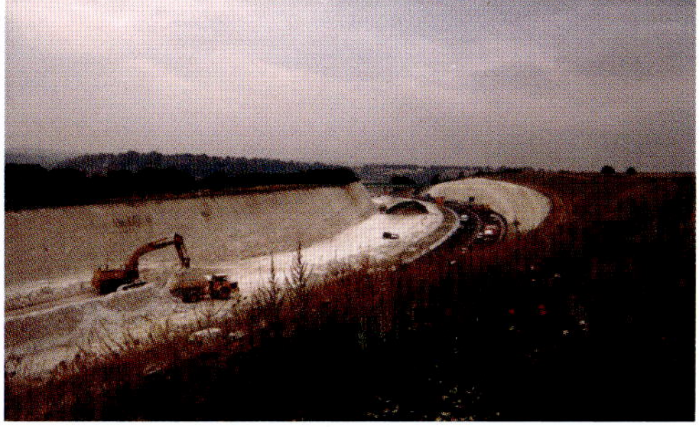

TWYFORD DOWN CUTTING Chris Woodford (1994)

nonviolent direct action. They relentlessly tried to slow down or stop the road building, supergluing keyholes on machinery and gates, digging out the dam in the Twyford navigation canal, attaching themselves to bulldozers with bicycle D-locks or lying down in their path, known as "digger diving". The final showdown came in December 1992, memorialized as Yellow Wednesday, when security guards in fluorescent yellow dealt ruthlessly with the protestors. By the end of the week, the path of the road had been cleared, with "three thousand years of history, destroyed in just three hours", as one of the Dongas Tribe described it.[19]

The Conservative government had an extensive road-building plan, and the resistance of the Dongas in protecting the landscape, while also trying to live as a community connected with the land, inspired many other road protests across the country. In 1993, the campaign against the M11 link road in east London saw an influx of protesters, who moved into the threatened streets, often occupying the houses that were empty after the local residents had been relocated or evicted. They employed tactics such as declaring part of Wanstead to be the micronation of Wanstonia, and arranging for mail to be delivered to a tree, which enabled it to be classified as a legal dwelling. Whereas Twyford Down had been about the destruction of the rural landscape, the M11 campaign was more politicized, as it wasn't only about the destruction of urban green space but of entire communities, as their houses were demolished and a busy highway cut their neighbourhood in two.

The last major stronghold in the path of the link road was Claremont Road. As elsewhere along the route, there were a number of local residents who refused to move and who joined forces with the hippies, travellers and activists. In Claremont Road, one of these was Dolly Watson, who had lived there nearly all her life and stalwartly refused to move until she became ill just before her 93rd birthday. She became something of a legend, stating her support unequivocally: "They're not dirty hippy squatters, they're the grandchildren I never had."[20] During the summer of 1994, the street became a traffic-free protest zone, as the protestors prepared for the inevitable eviction by police and security guards. Nets were strung between the roofs of the houses and the trees along the railway, houses were barricaded, and a tunnel was constructed to bring in resources and people in the event of a siege. In addition, the road became a community and art space with music, parties, two cafes and furniture brought out from the abandoned houses, reclaiming the tarmac as a communal space, and with scrap sculptures that often doubled as road barriers.[21]

Many of the tactics employed by road protestors involved a great deal of personal danger – a neck rarely feels as vulnerable as when D-locked to a giant piece of machinery that an irate workman is trying to start. Some Claremont Road protestors lay on the

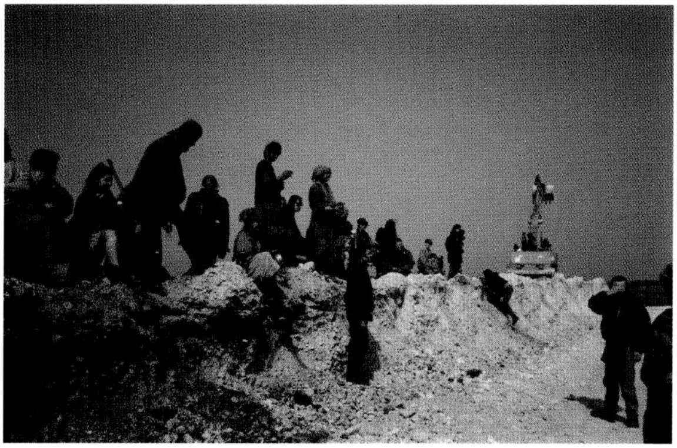

TWYFORD DOWN DIGGER Annabel Edwards (1993)

tarmac with their arms locked into holes in the ground, leaving their heads in disconcerting proximity to the boots of the 700-strong eviction force.

In 1996, at the A30 road protest, a young man known as Swampy became a folk hero for living in a tunnel for over a week. That same year, the Newbury bypass, which involved the felling of nearly 10,000 trees, saw the protestors living in treehouses and moving from tree to tree by means of simple walkways consisting of one rope for your feet and a second slightly higher rope to hold on to, 60 feet above the ground. The violence of the fightback against the protestors was shocking. Hundreds of private security guards were brought in and the under-sheriff of Berkshire commented that in other countries they would have used machine guns.

Although none of these protests actually succeeded in stopping the building of those particular roads, the escalation of costs and the increase in public awareness of the environmental damage being caused resulted in most of the proposals being shelved and a change of policy, recognizing that ever more road building and ever more dependence on the car was unsustainable.

Although the change in policy brought about by many of these protests is now widely recognized as being beneficial to society, the Public Order Act, 2023, brought in by the Conservative government, would make all these actions impossible. It is now an offence to even carry some glue or a bicycle D-lock if a police officer suspects you might be thinking of merely *helping* someone to "lock on", and tunnelling and preventing construction works are also included in the legislation. The Serious Disruption Prevention Orders (SDPOs) give the right to track and ban individuals from protesting or associating with other protestors, essentially taking away a person's right to protest. The definition of "serious disruption" is vague to the degree that it could conceivably extend to any disruption at all and means that any minor protest activity could be criminalized.[22] Concern about the all-encompassing effects of the law has been so great that the UN Human Rights Council urged the UK to reverse the "deeply troubling" legislation that is "incompatible with the UK's international human rights obligations regarding people's rights to freedom of expression, peaceful assembly and association".[23]

If the Criminal Justice and Public Order Act of 1994 (CJA) appeared repressive and authoritarian, this new legislation, 20 years later, appears to be even more so. The laws passed after Castlemorton brought an end to the heyday of the free festivals and raves springing up round the country; many of the free sound systems left the UK at that time and continued on mainland Europe. However, it's worth noting that free parties haven't gone away completely; they are just more secretive. During lockdown, the youthful desire to find a space to gather and party defied the social suppression, and outdoor raves and warehouse parties took place throughout the country.

In her book *Dancing in the Streets*, the writer and political activist Barbara Ehrenreich argues that this desire to express joy collectively is "encoded into us". She talks about the joy of solidarity in the face of overwhelming state and corporate power, and goes on to describe the contemporary "carnivalization" of protest demonstrations, which refers directly back to historical folk customs such as "rough music" or charivari. This was when a crowd would gather to mock, in various creative and colourful (and occasionally cruel) ways, those who transgressed that community's norms, whether medieval adulterers, 17th-century enclosers, 19th-century wife beaters or early 20th-century industrial strike-breakers. The action would be accompanied by the "rough music" of chants and songs, and a cacophony of noisy instruments – from pots and pans to drums and horns.[24,25] In fact, the word "protestival" was coined around the time of the Claremont Road protest; while the use that the women of Greenham and the road protestors made of this tradition carries on today in the performative protests of contemporary climate and Right to Roam activists.

In addition to a knowledge of the history of enclosure and land ownership which informed the demands for access to the countryside throughout the 20th century, contemporary research and focus on the interplay of colonization and enclosure motivates the current land activists. There is an increasing awareness that enclosure was exported around the world by the colonizers, and that slave plantation money fuelled some of the enclosure of land in the 18th and 19th centuries. And enclosure continues, both internationally and in the UK, as public assets become private ones, whether that is in the form of the privatization of the water supply or new developments in London that appear to all extents and purposes to be public spaces, until private security guards exercise their power to stop you taking photographs, let alone protesting.

The resurgence of interest in folk traditions and even morris dancing is part of the awareness that the common people are more effective in their resistance to the relentless global corporatization of everyday life when they have a strong sense of their own identity. The protests over rights of access and wild camping on Dartmoor in the 2020s may seem

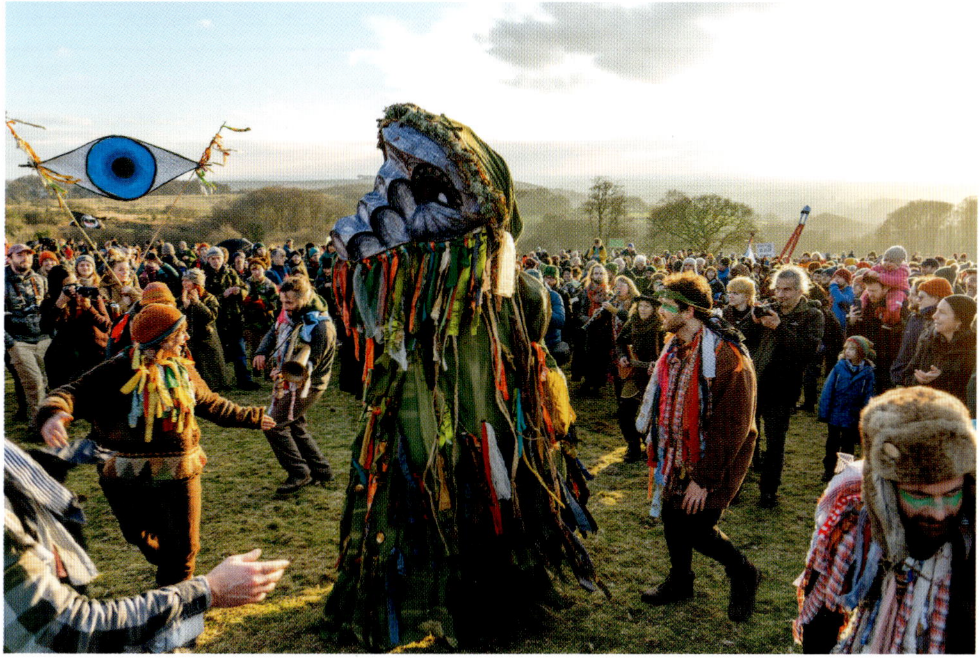

RIGHT TO ROAM GATHERING TO RAISE OLD CROCKERN AND DEFEND WILD CAMPING
David Pearson (2023)

to suggest that nothing much has changed in the English countryside, when the barrister representing the landowner Alexander Darwall can argue in the High Court that there is only a right to walk or ride across Dartmoor, and thus wild camping, or even stopping for a picnic, would be trespass. However, as storyteller Lisa Schneidau, who is one of the Dartmoor activists and a member of the radical Beltane Border Morris group, has pointed out, Darwall has "basically reinvigorated the access movement in this country... there are thousands of people who are now activists off the back of this... So in some ways we have to thank Mr Darwall for radicalizing people."[26]

ALLOTMENTS

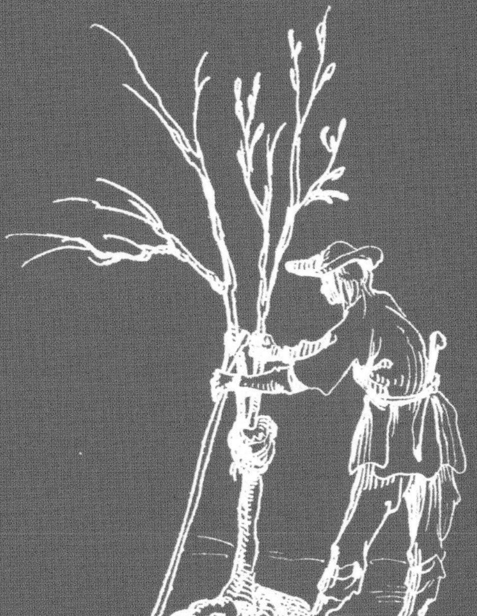

Introduction to Allotments

The short-lived Digger settlements of St George's Hill, Weybridge, Surrey, where members of the dissident group the Diggers planted beans and vegetables from 1649 to 1650, could be considered the first examples of allotments in England and a radical attempt at reversing the abject losses of the commons. In the 19th century, the land available to the poor was greatly diminished, especially after the General Enclosure Act of 1845, which made the process of enclosure easier and faster to authorize. However, at the same time there was a promise of the provision of "small field gardens" for the landless within this act. This promise was further formalized and sanctioned in the 1908 Small Holdings and Allotment Act, which required local authorities to provide allotment gardens for their communities.

ALLOTMENT WITH SUNFLOWER

Vincent Van Gogh (1887)

As more and more people lost access to land to support themselves, the cost of Poor Relief increased. In 1806 the first enclosure bill was passed that actually set aside land for allotments. Opinions differed among the ruling class as to whether this would protect the poor from starving when wages were low and employment sporadic, or discourage them from working because they'd be too busy on their plot or become too independent and not reliant on wages. To prevent this, strict rules concerning plot size and selling surplus produce were developed.

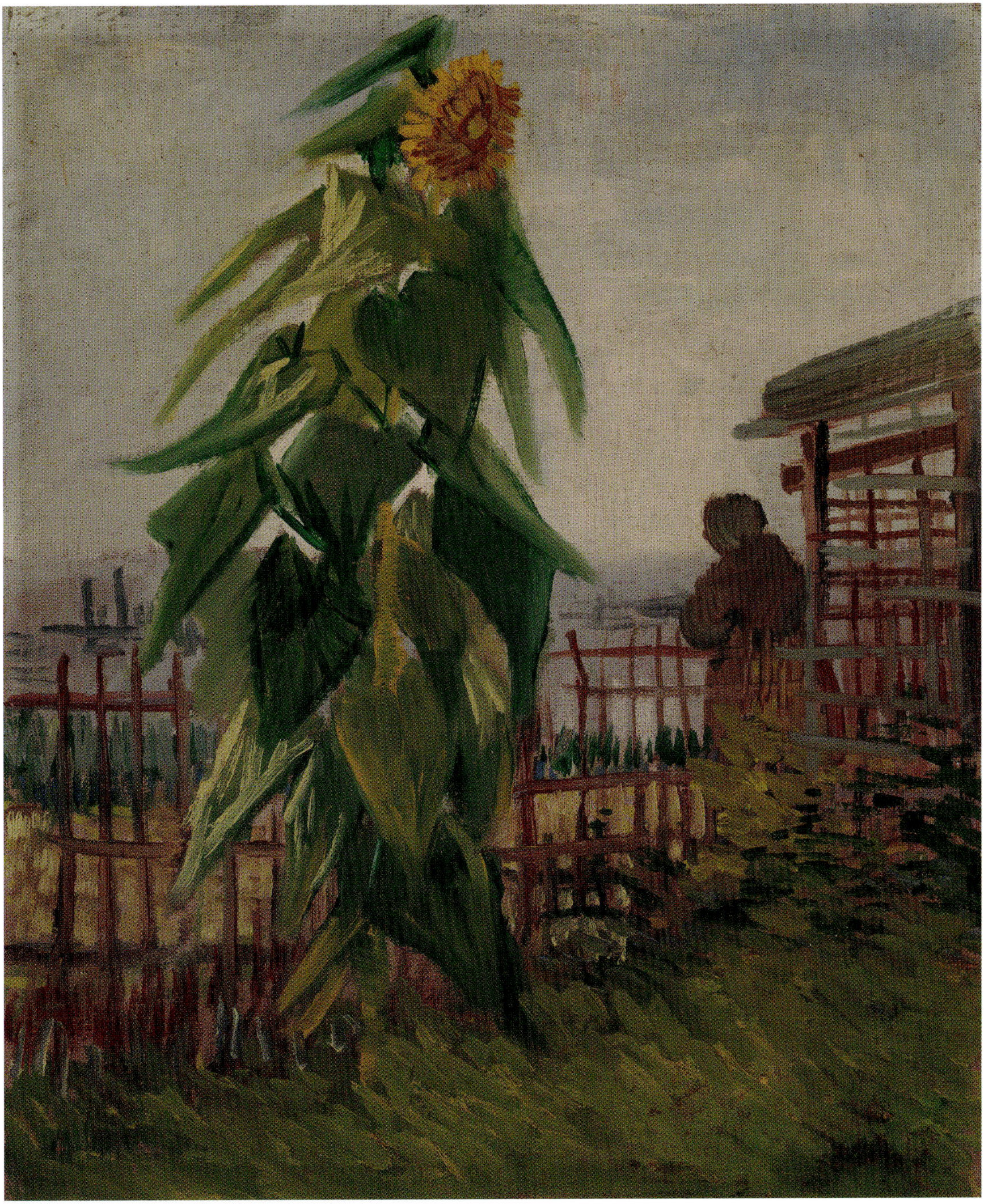

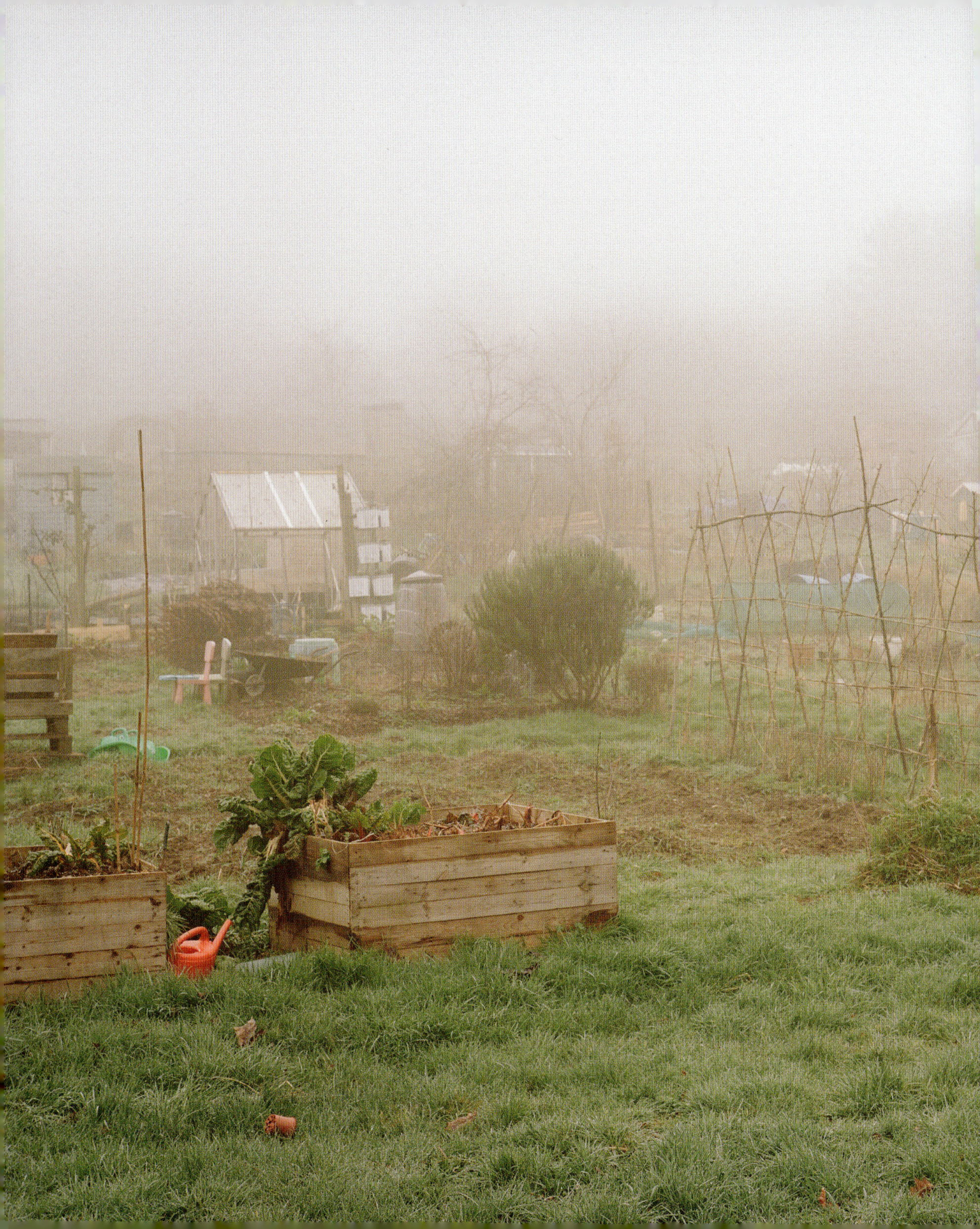

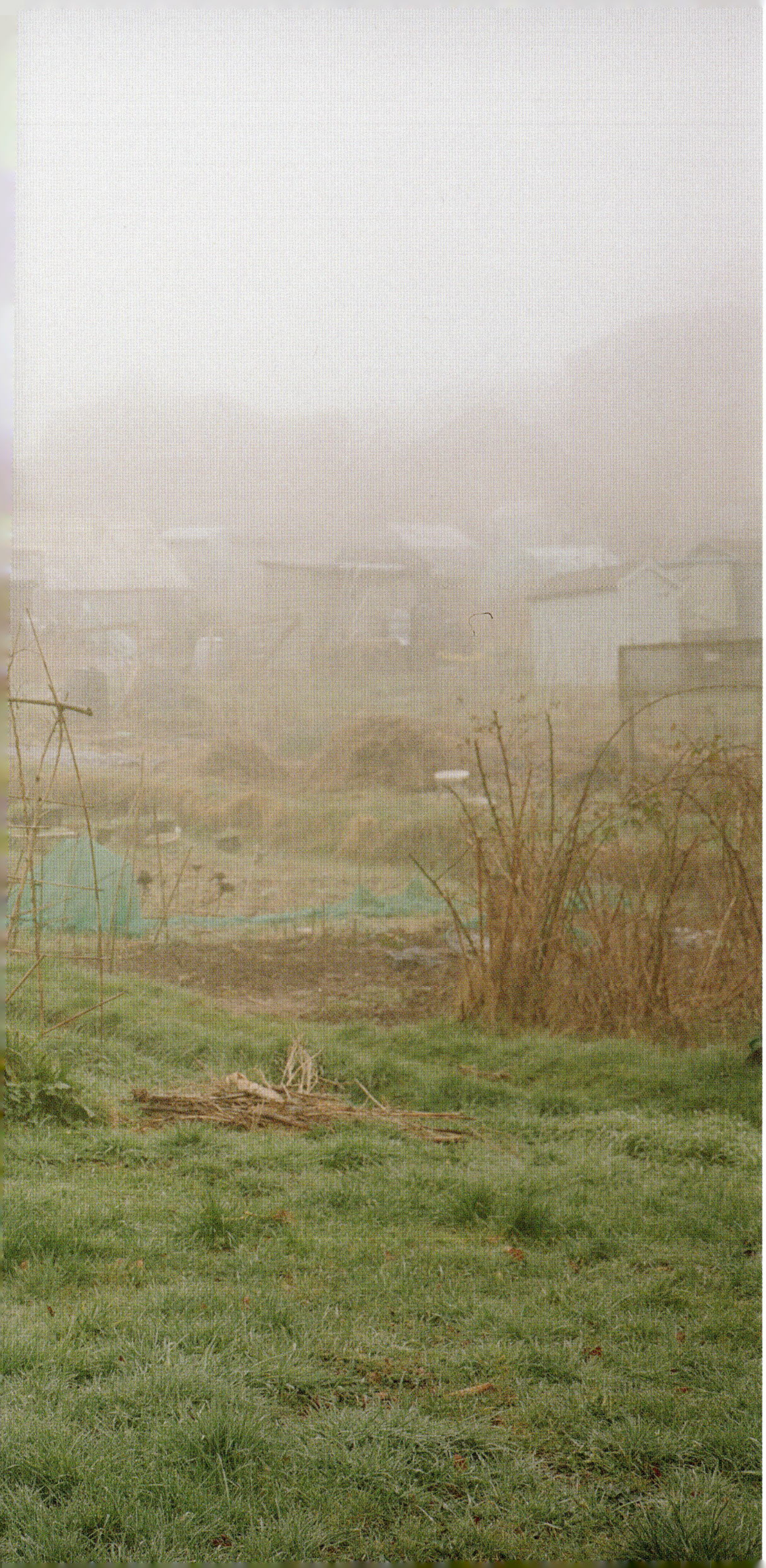

THE ALLOTMENT, DORKING

Martin Salter (2024)

One of the early advocates of allotments was Joseph Arch. From a family of farm labourers, he started work at the age of nine as a crow-scarer, working 12 hours a day, and later he became a hedge cutter. His experiences made him recognize the importance of collective organization for agricultural workers, and alongside others he formed the National Agricultural Labourers' Union in 1872. In 1885 he became a Liberal MP, after the vote was given to non-property owners. It was known as the "Three Acres and a Cow" election after the Liberal Party's radical land reform policies, which included the compulsory purchase of land to create smallholdings.

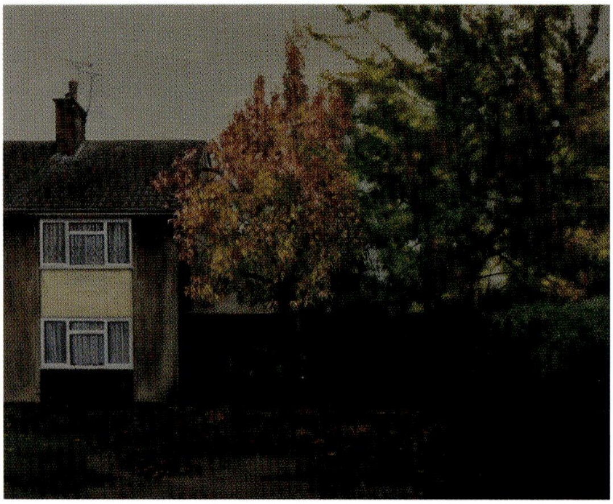

THE LAST AUTUMN George Shaw (2007-2008)

The recurring subject of George Shaw's paintings is the suburban council estate, Tile Hill, in Coventry, where he grew up. Like many parts of England, Coventry was badly bombed during World War II, and the estates built to replace the destroyed housing were part of the post-war vision of providing more spacious dwellings with gardens for everyone.

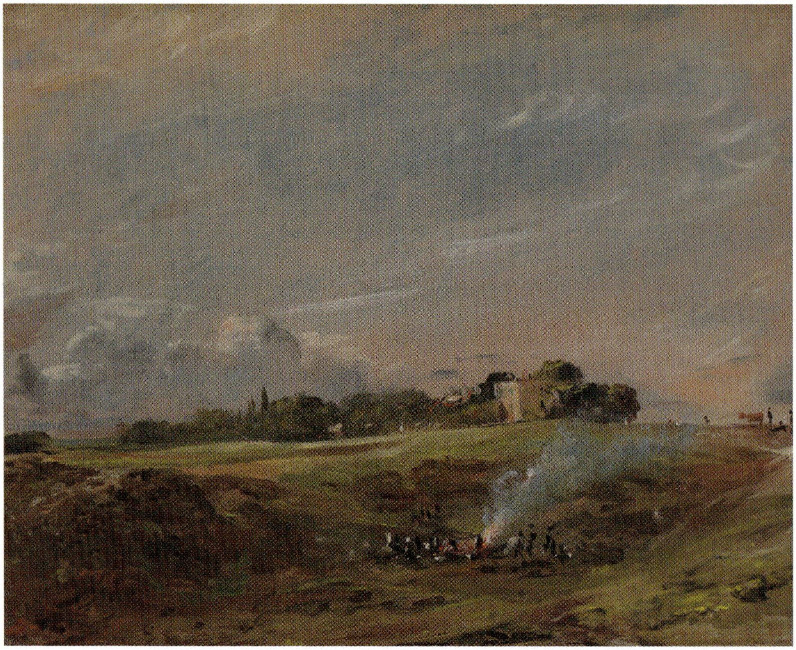

HAMPSTEAD HEATH, WITH A BONFIRE John Constable (c.1822)

London's Hampstead Heath is one of the green spaces in the city that have been preserved for the benefit of the urban population. The Open Spaces Society was founded in 1865 as the Commons Preservation Society in response to threats to London commons. Throughout the 19th century, Londoners gathered in their hundreds, and sometimes their thousands, to destroy enclosure fences in places such as Wandsworth and Tooting Commons, One Tree Hill, and Epping Forest – known as the People's Forest after the 1878 Epping Forest Act preserved it "as an open space for the recreation and enjoyment of the public".

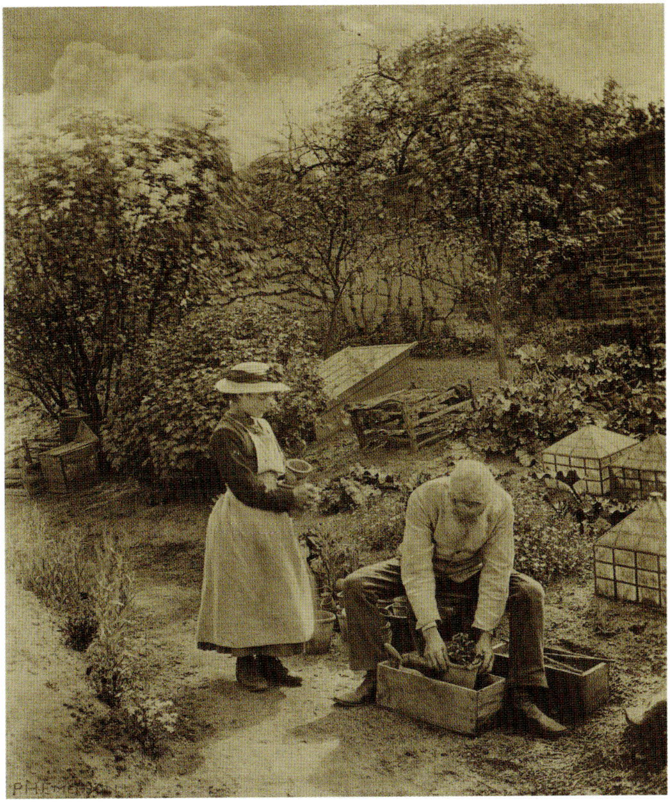

A GARDEN END. SUFFOLK

Peter Henry Emerson (1888)

Peter Henry Emerson, born 1856, photographed rural life in both Norfolk and Suffolk. His large format platinum prints recorded a way of life on the East Anglian fenlands that was already in a state of flux and decline.

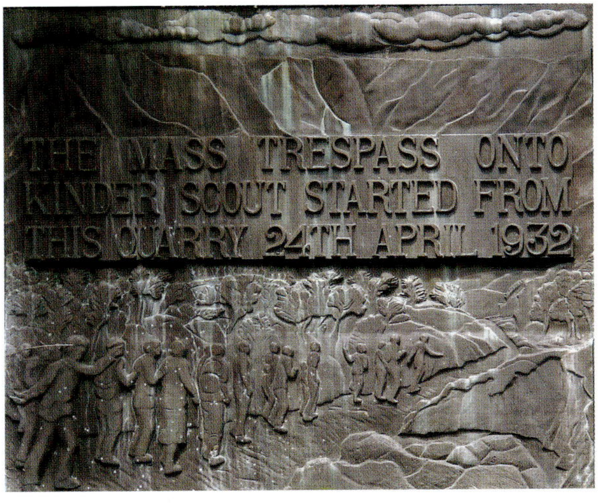

BOWDEN BRIDGE MASS TRESPASS PLAQUE

Marcin Floryan (2007)

Kinder Scout Mass Trespass was the most famous of the continual trespasses into countryside that took place during the 19th and 20th centuries. As well as having to face belligerent gamekeepers, the ramblers had to face the Derbyshire police who were keen to stop the "trespassers". Their over-enthusiasm to stop innocent ramblers continued into the 21st century when during the Covid lockdown they were accused of overreach when they employed drones to track walkers and dyed a beauty-spot blue lagoon black to deter visitors.

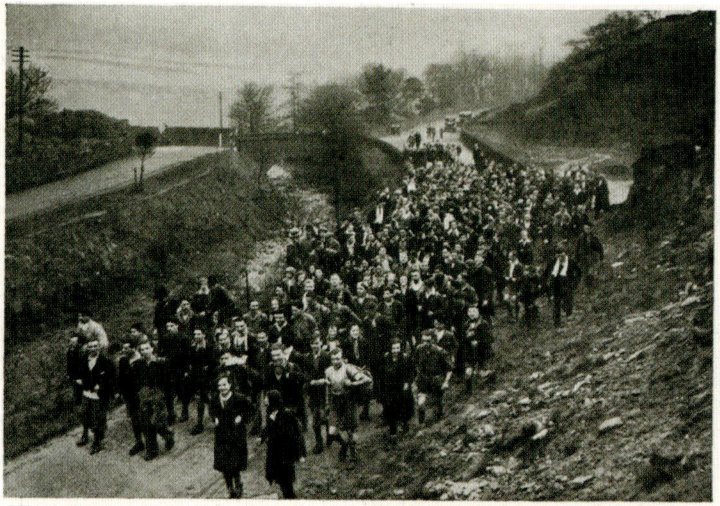

PEAK DISTRICT RAMBLERS IN TROUBLE: WALKING TOWARDS KINDER SCOUT ON THE OCCASION OF THEIR BATTLE WITH THE GAMEKEEPERS.

MASS TRESPASS OF KINDER SCOUT Chronicle (1932)

All the actions by ramblers to gain access to the countryside were part of the movement that recognized the health value of time spent in the fresh air in a green space, whether a wild moor, city park or allotment. Working on an allotment is beneficial for health in many ways – an increased sense of community, regular physical exercise and the less tangible magic of being surrounded by plants.

THE ARTIST'S GARDEN AT DURBINS, GUILDFORD

Roger Fry (ca.1915)

Roger Fry, born 1866, was a member of the Bloomsbury Group. Gardens were a significant aspect of the artistic practice of the Bloomsbury artists as their exterior lives matched their interior imaginaries. Ottoline Morrell, Virginia Woolf, Vanessa Bell and Vita Sackville- West all created compelling green spaces that challenged contemporary orthodoxies of horticultural design. Roger Fry and his wife moved to their house, Durbins, overlooking the Surrey Hills, as they hoped that closeness to nature would help his wife, Helen's, mental health.

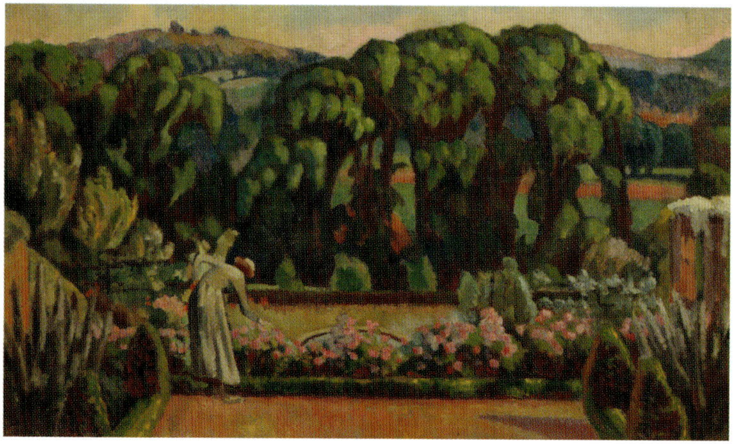

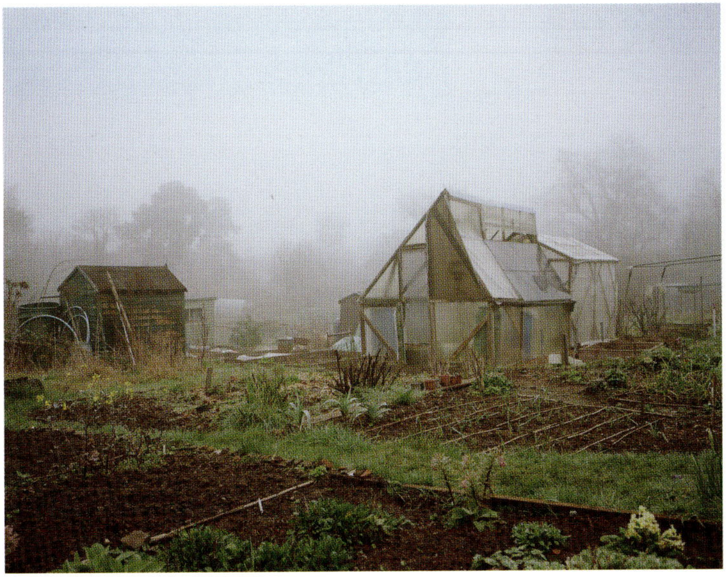

THE ALLOTMENT, DORKING

Martin Salter (2024)

In many cities migrant populations took on allotments not only for the sense of community but in order to grow vegetables not easily available in the shops, such as callaloo, commonly used in Afro-Caribbean cooking, or mulukhiyah, a spinach-like vegetable used in North Africa and the Middle East.

ANIMATED IMPLEMENTS

Charles Williams (1811)

Charles Williams was a British caricaturist, etcher and illustrator who died in 1830. This illustration was dedicated to the Carpenters and Gardeners of Great Britain.

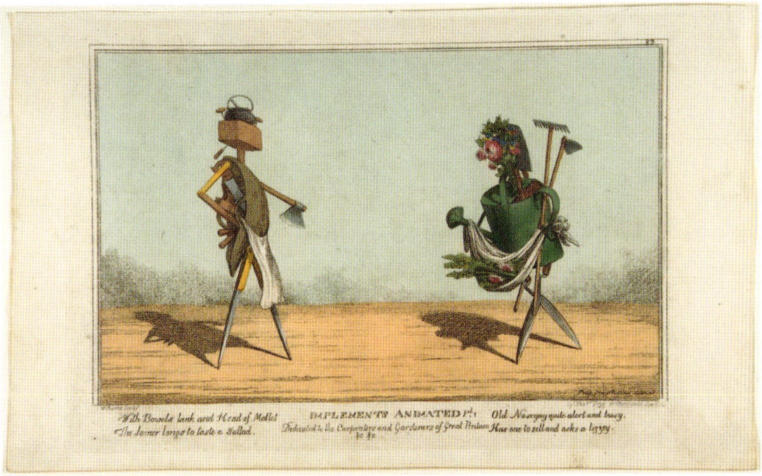

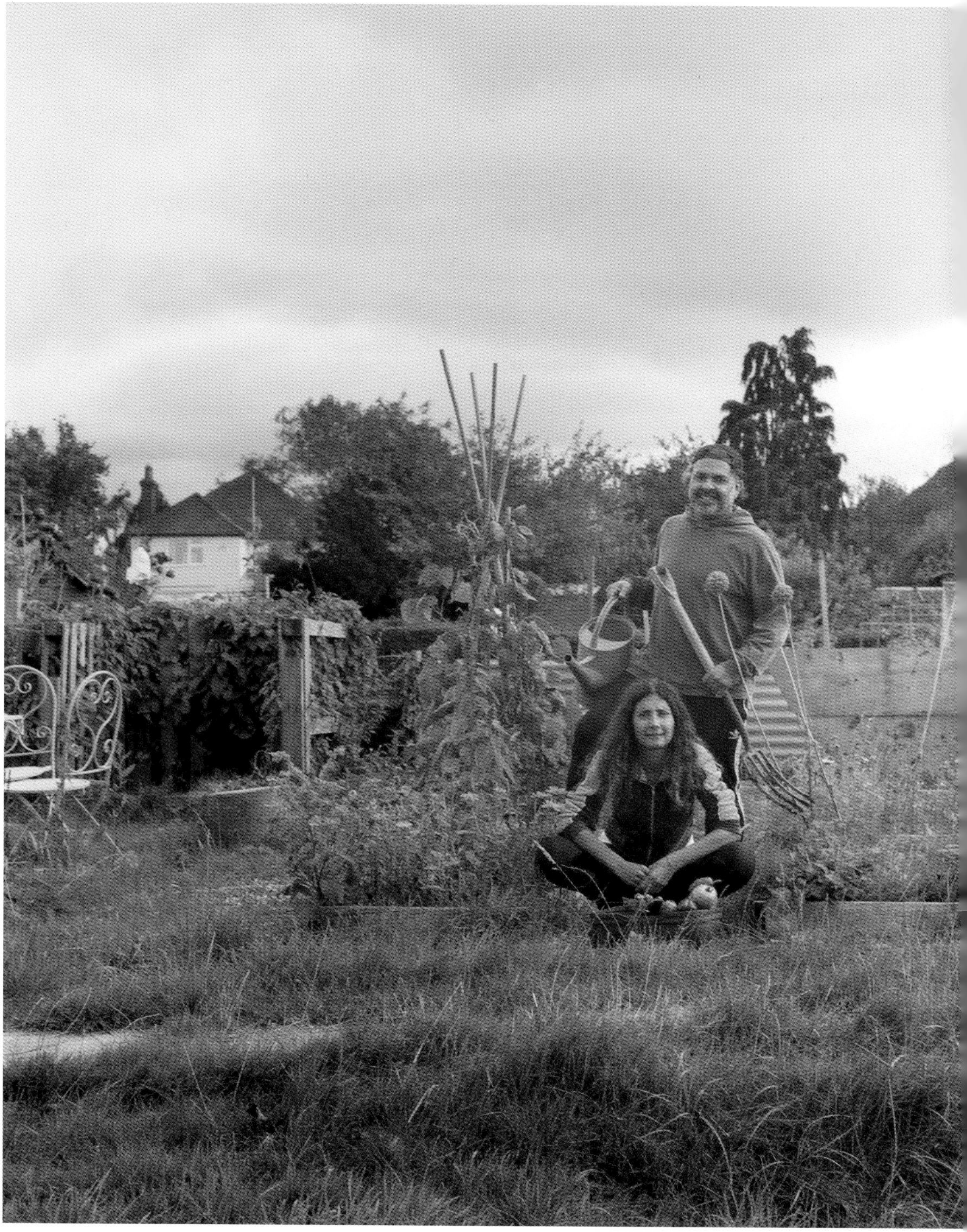

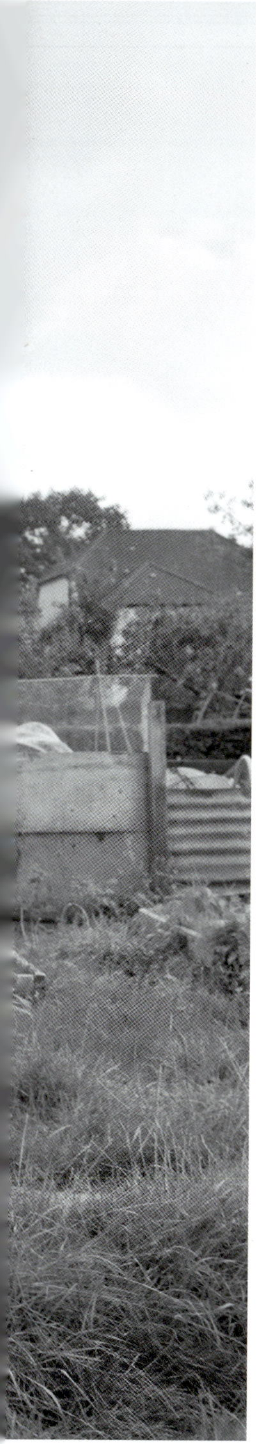

Allotments by Leah Gordon

The allotments in Coventry are an example of positive strategies to reunite people of all races with the commons. The Coventry Labourers' and Artisans' Co-operative Society was set up in 1843 by the ribbon manufacturers James Cash and Charles Bray to provide allotments for their workers. Coventry still has many of them and these portraits of current allotment holders, or allotmenteers, in the city attempt to show how allotments represent the urban classes' attempt to reverse enclosure and restore small plots of land to the landless. These are some of the few contemporary successors of common land rights, although in recent years there have been increasing threats upon the survival of some allotments due to incursions by landowners and property developers.

I have photographed the allotmenteers from Earlsdon and Beechwood allotments in their plots alongside colour slide film images of their produce. Their short comments in the captions can help us understand the vital importance of access to the land for both physical and mental health.

MANJIT AND DALJIT DUNNETT, allotment holders in Earlsdon allotments, Coventry (2024). A Meadow Arts commission

"We started the allotment about four years ago," Manjit and Daljit explain. "We're learning by trial and error. It's one thing knowing when to sow and transplant seedlings, another to know when to harvest them! Then there are the birds, rabbits, mice and even a badger that like to try to get a share of the goodies. Regardless of the outcome, it's lovely to connect with the earth and give reverence to the intricacy and perfection of nature. It's a lot of hard work but very rewarding when you have a basket of home-grown organic vegetables to take home."

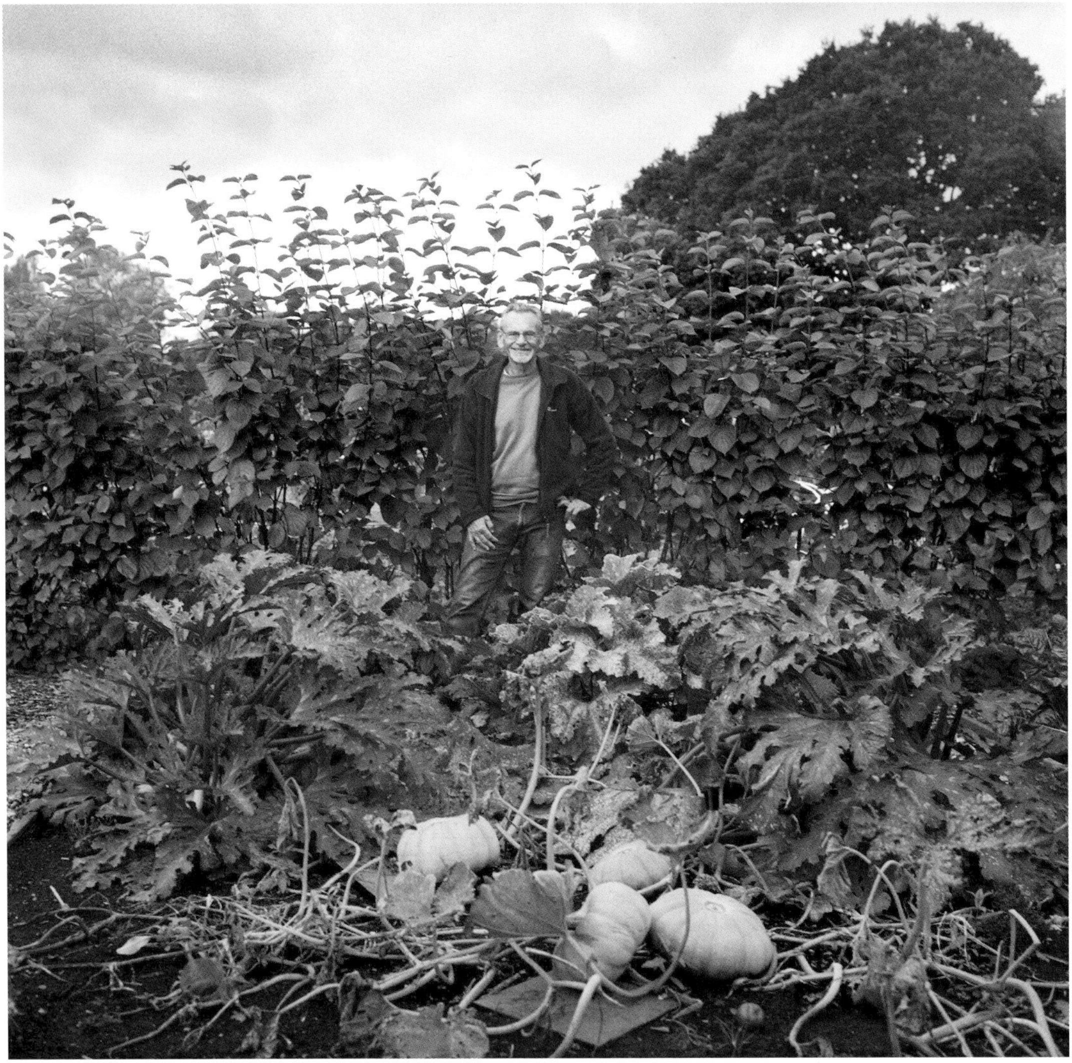

PETER SHIPTON, allotment holder in Earlsdon allotments, Coventry (2024) A Meadow Arts commission

Peter Shipton explains, "The allotment gives me a peaceful time with nature in an urban environment. It's good for both my physical and mental health and rewards me with organically grown fruit and vegetables throughout the year. The allotment is my happy place."

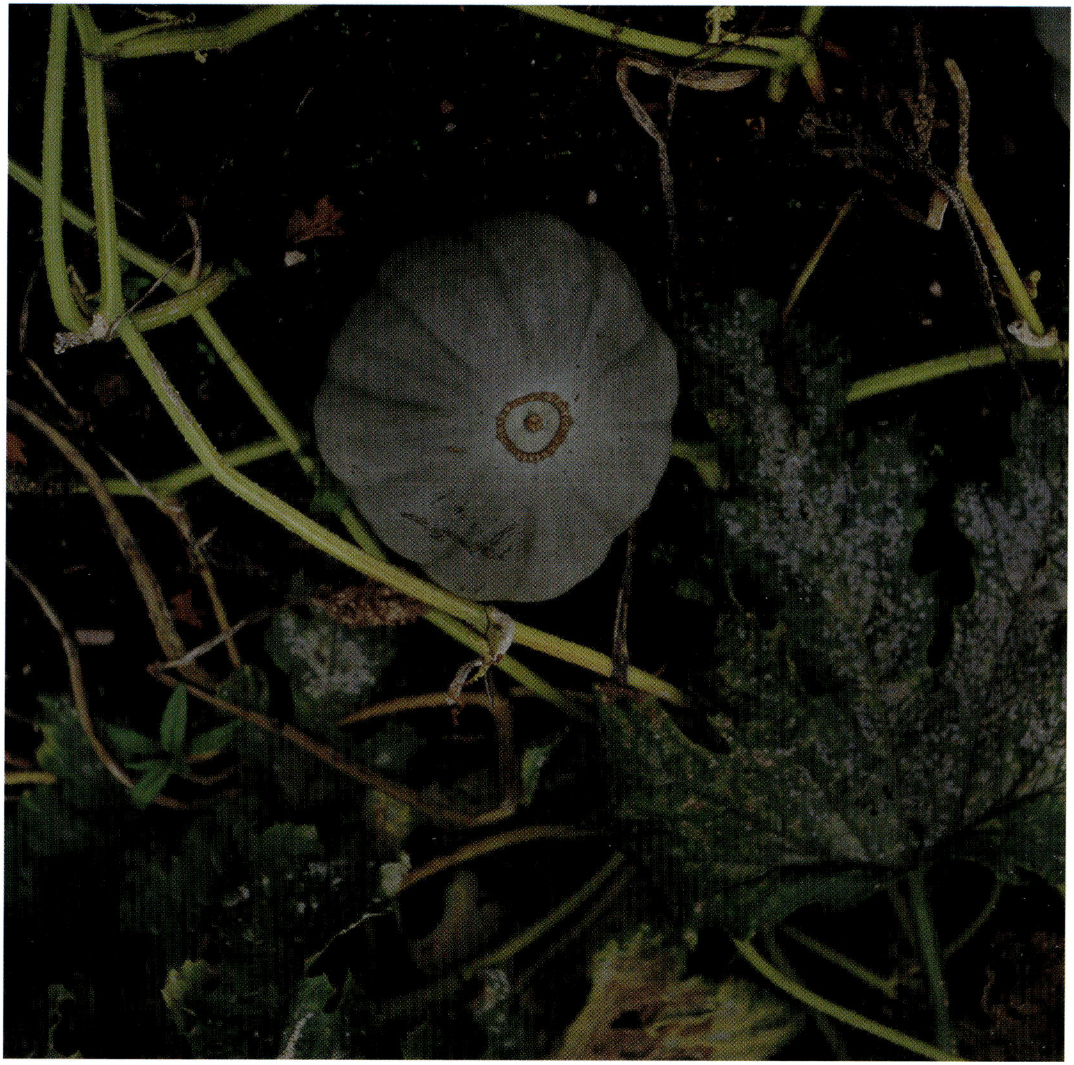

A "CROWN PRINCE" PUMPKIN A Meadow Arts commission

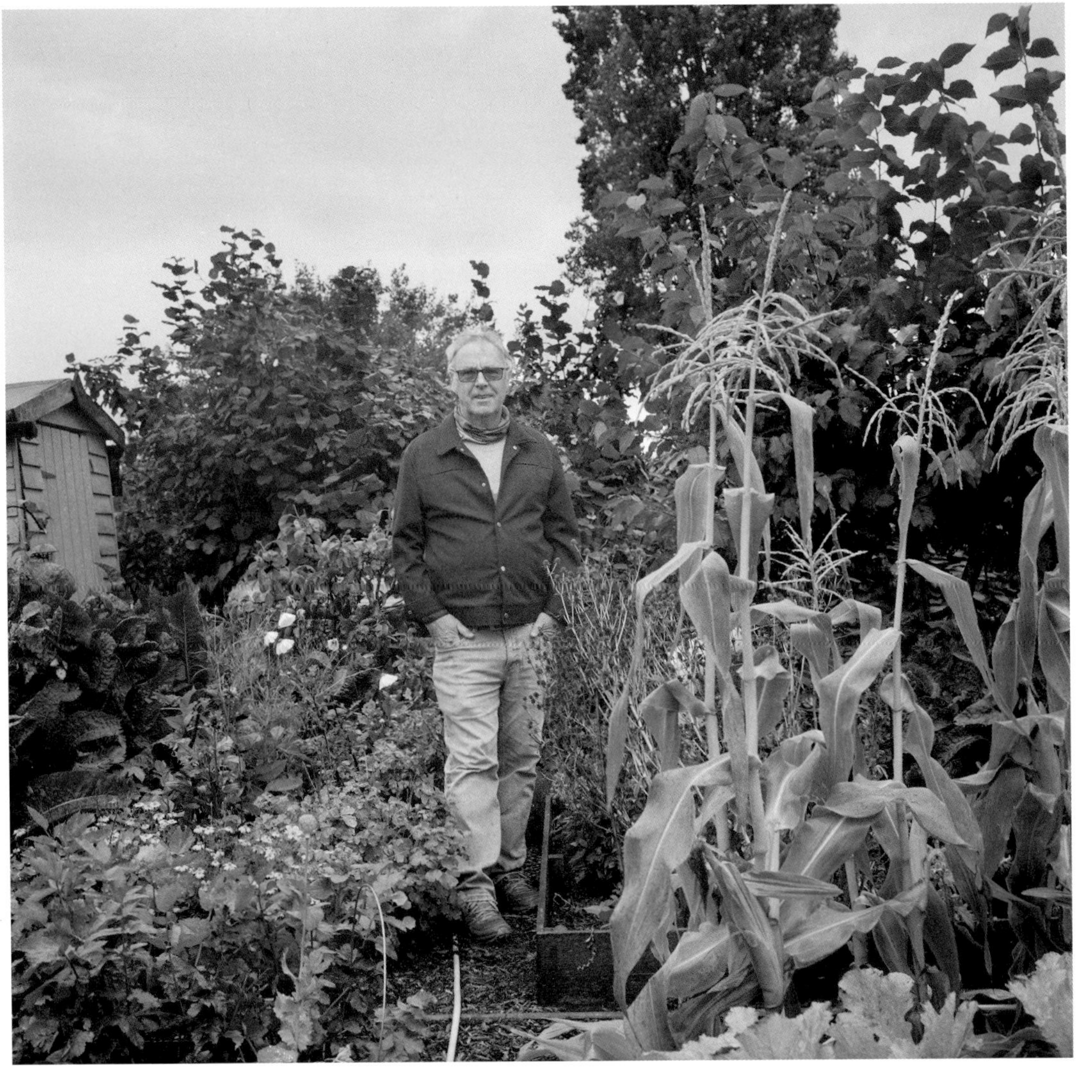

GRAHAM HILL, retired schoolteacher and allotment holder at Earlsdon allotments, Coventry (2024). A Meadow Arts commission

"I think the stereotype of the old man on his allotment is gone," Graham says. "Today, lots of younger people use their allotments as spaces where their children can play outside, and the kids learn where their food comes from. People from diverse backgrounds grow different vegetables using different techniques, which is good because then we all get to learn new ideas and improve what we can achieve."

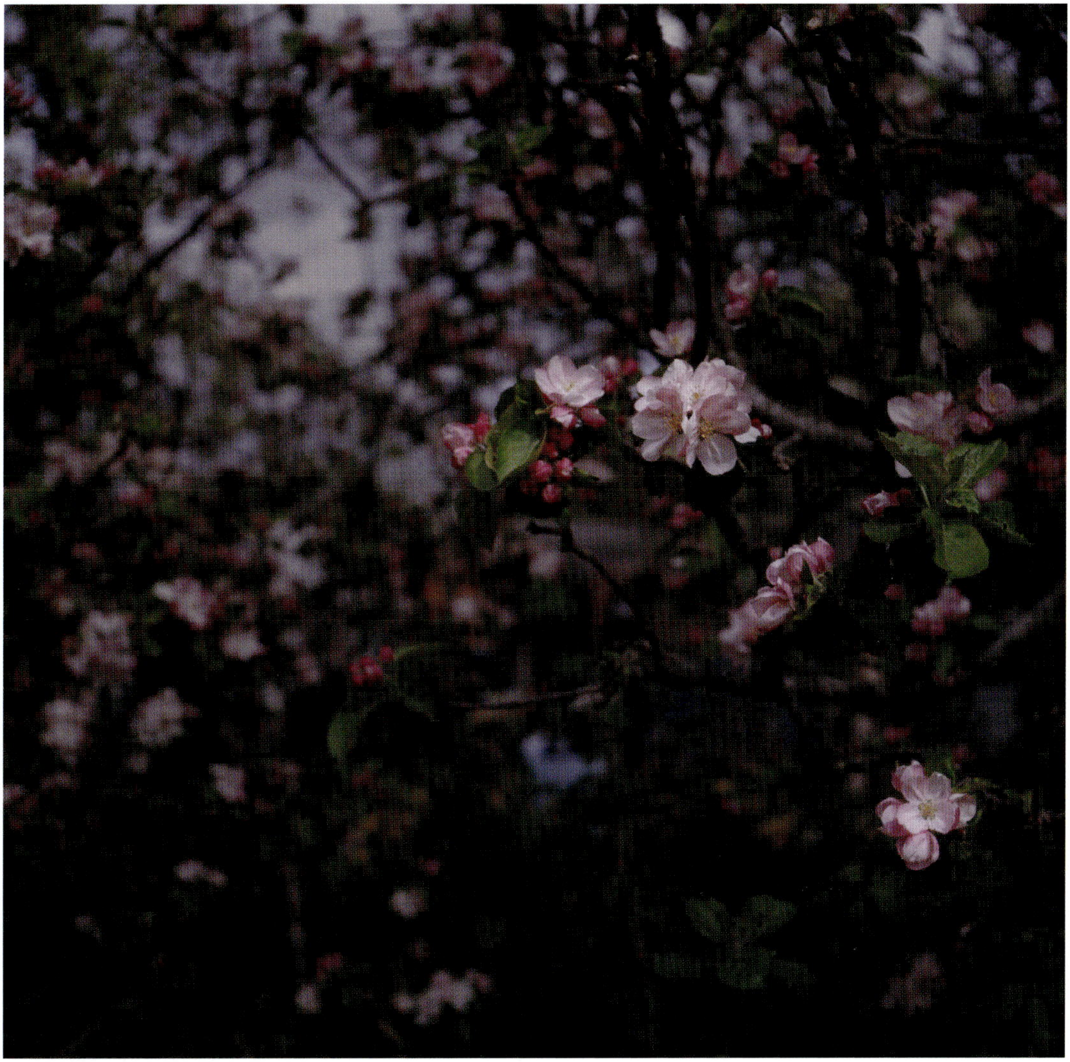

SPRING BLOSSOM ON GRAHAM HILL'S APPLE TREES A Meadow Arts commission

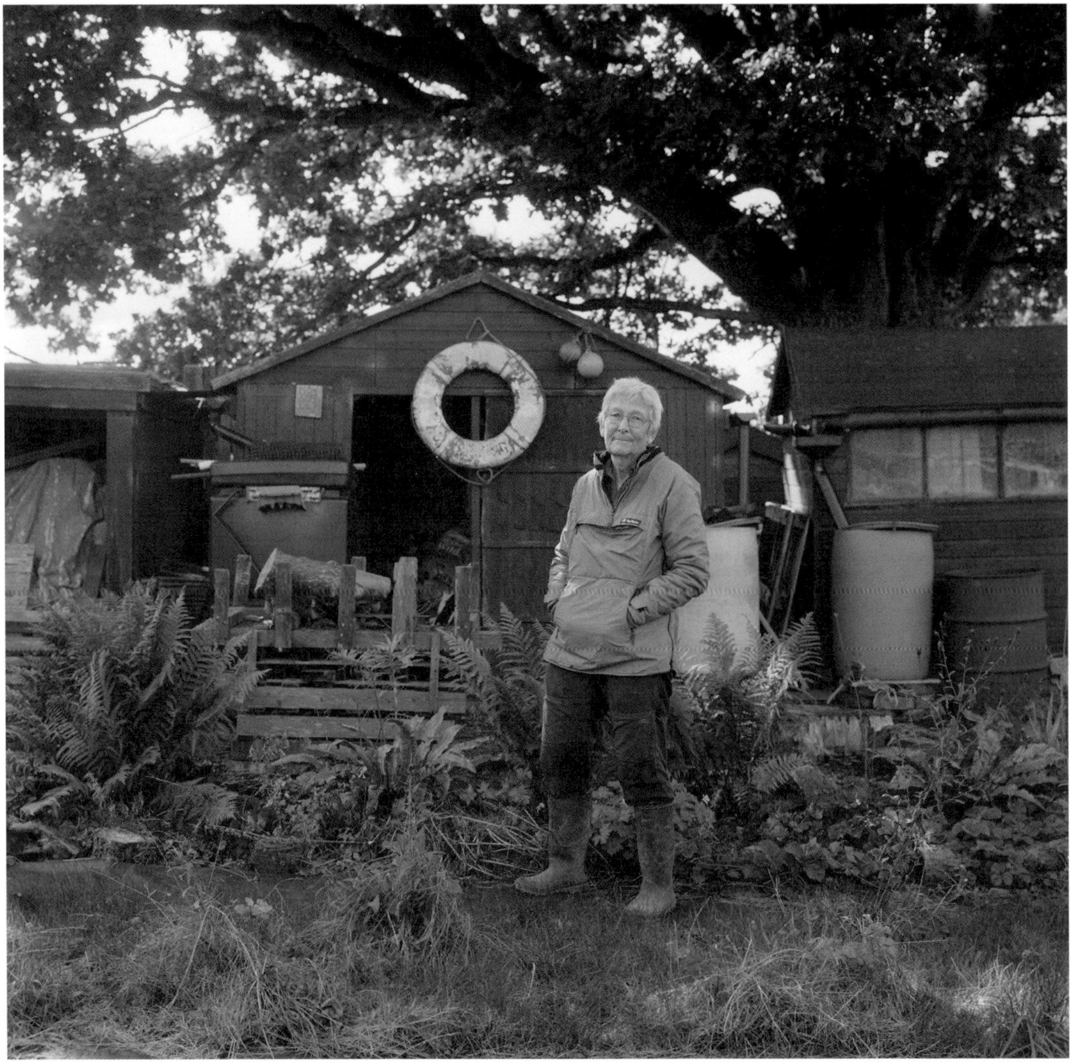

HELEN ANSELL, allotment holder in Earlsdon allotments, Coventry (2024). A Meadow Arts commission

Helen says, "On the allotment I am tuned in to a different world, the wind and the sun on my face, the song of the birds, the changing seasons, the texture of the soil, the steady development of the crops from seed to harvest. And there is huge joy in picking food I've grown myself: in digging up the buried treasure of early potatoes with children and grandchildren, or biting into a sweet home-grown tomato."

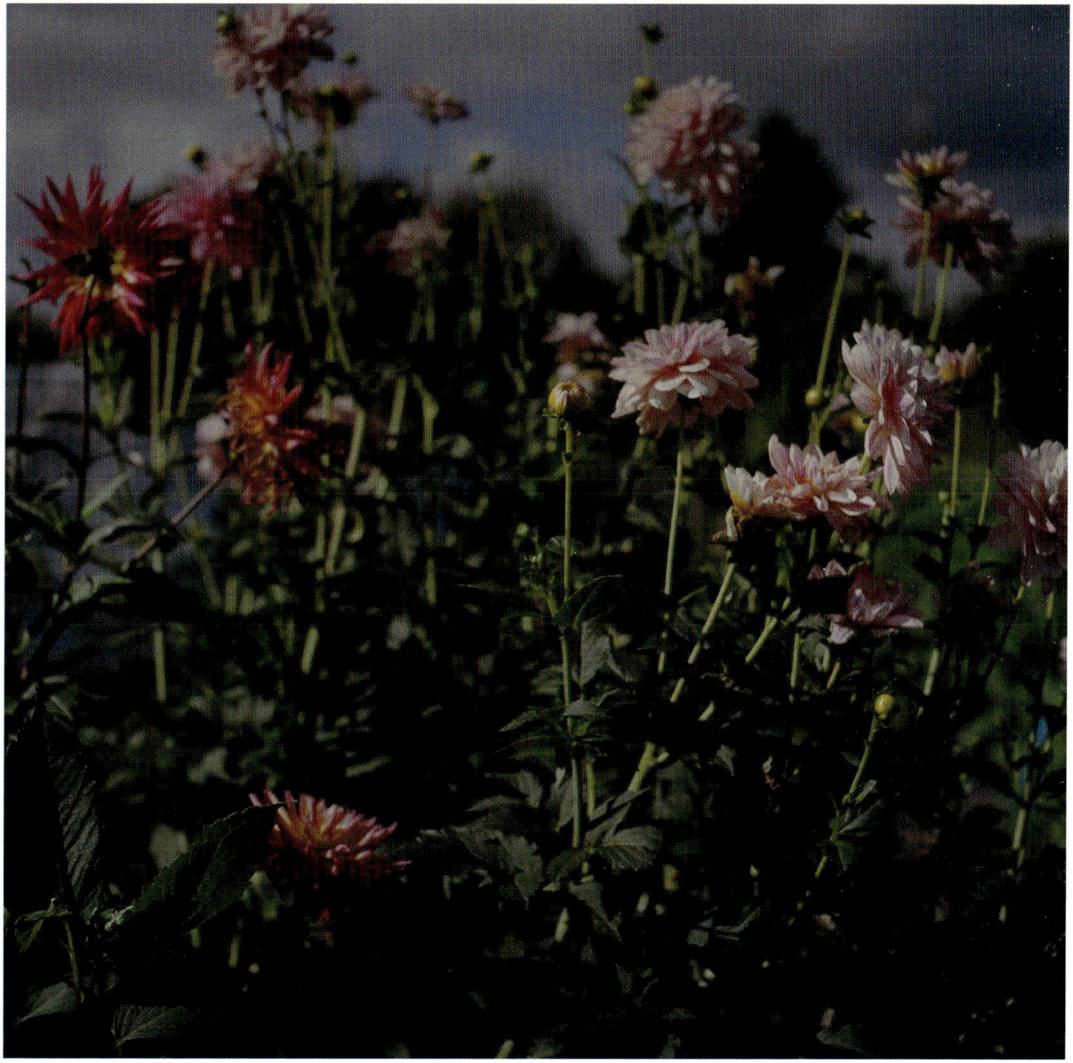

SOME OF HELEN'S DAHLIAS A Meadow Arts commission

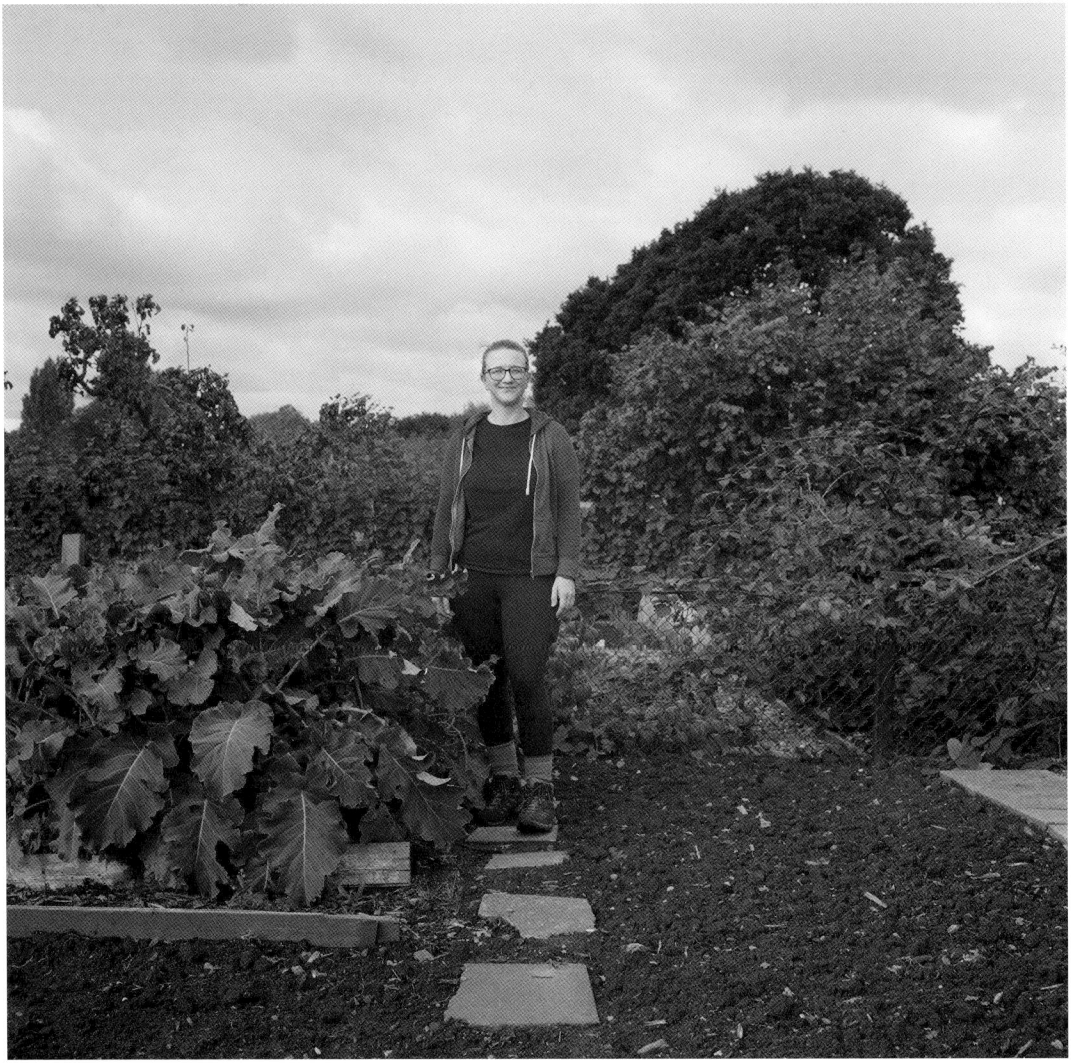

FELICITY HAINES, volunteer for Carriers of Hope community allotment, Earlsdon allotments, Coventry (2024). A Meadow Arts commission

The Carriers of Hope allotment "provides a safe and supportive environment for refugees and asylum seekers to improve their wellbeing while growing food for our World Foods Food Hub" (from the project website).

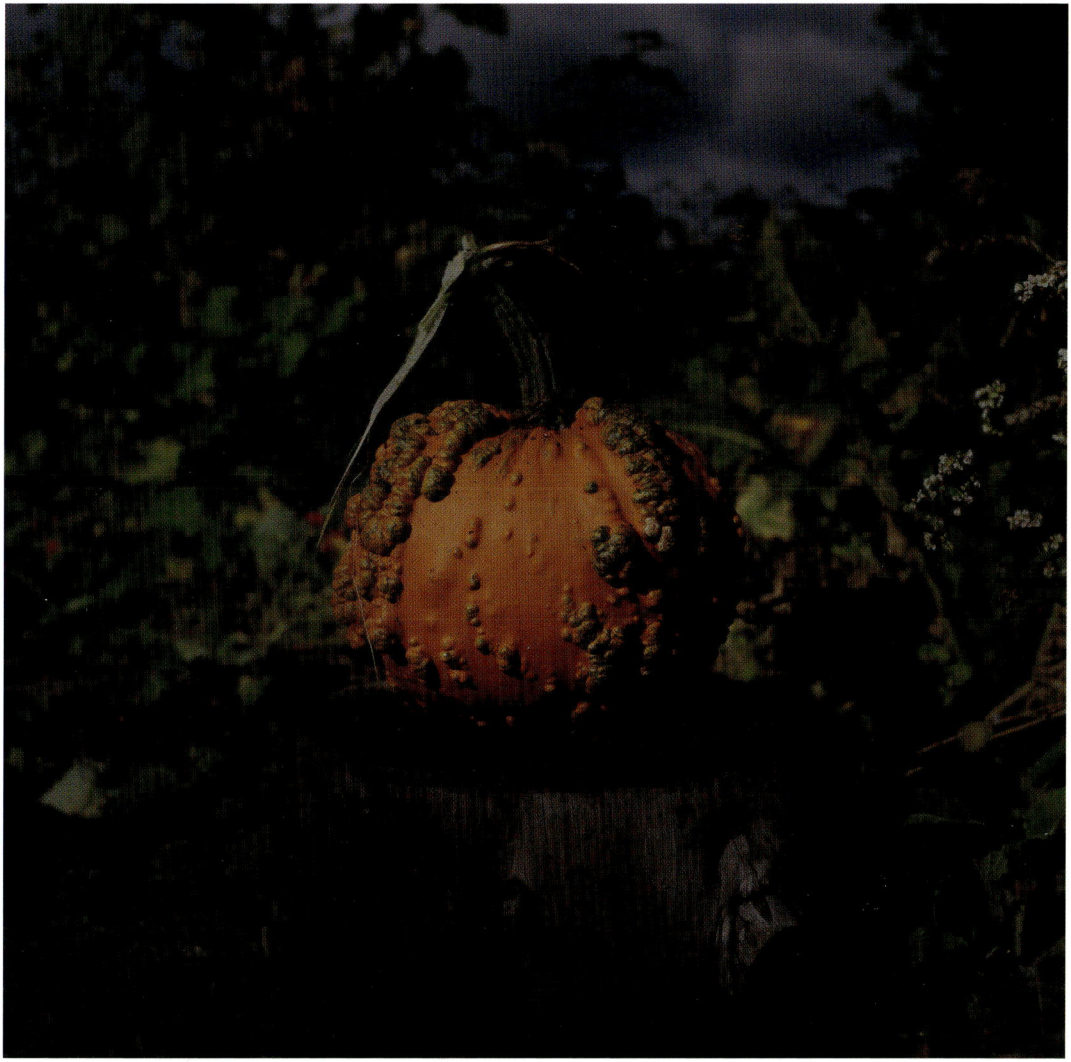

A HARVESTED PUMPKIN A Meadow Arts commission

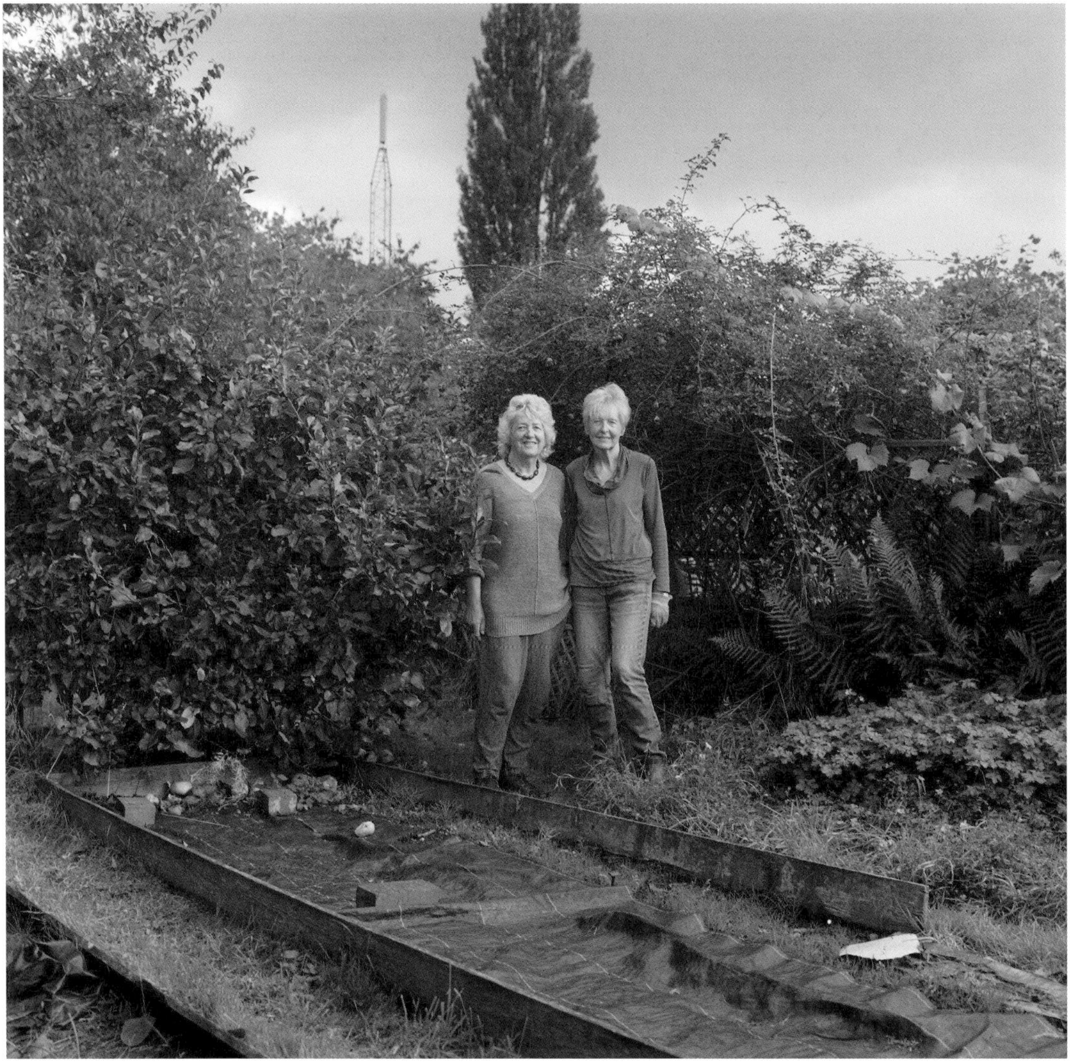

HELEN AND CHRISTINA CZUDEJ, sisters and allotment holders at Earlsdon allotments, Coventry (2024). A Meadow Arts commission

"We treasure our allotment as a peaceful meadow retreat where we can watch the seasons change," the sisters agree. "We especially love observing the new shoots emerging in the spring, hearing bees humming over the herb garden, watching foxes basking in the sunlight and listening out for the cries of sparrowhawks circling above the trees. However, the best bit is trudging home with a basket full of fruit and vegetables to eat at a family barbeque, accompanied by a large glass of wine."

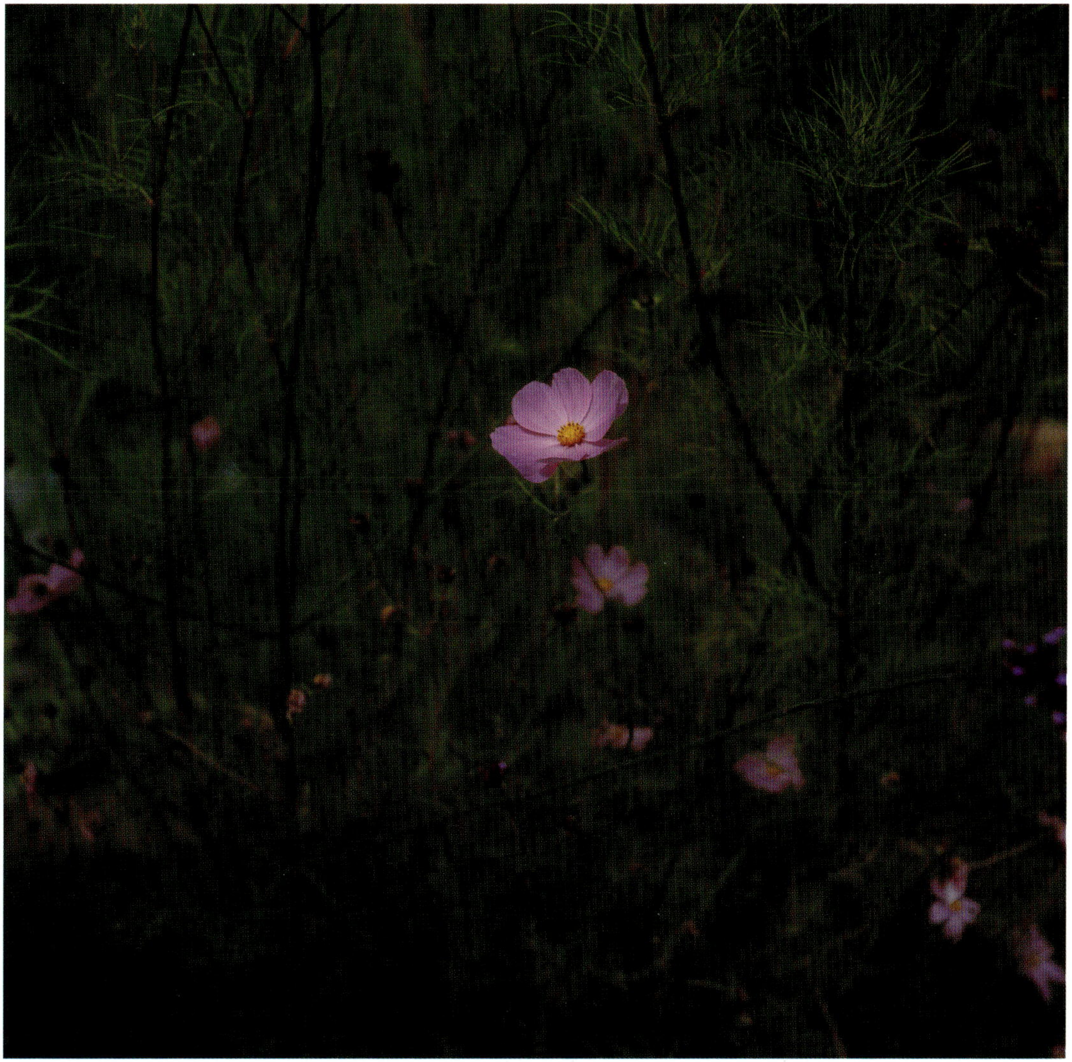

COSMOS, A PLANT THAT ATTRACTS POLLINATORS A Meadow Arts commission

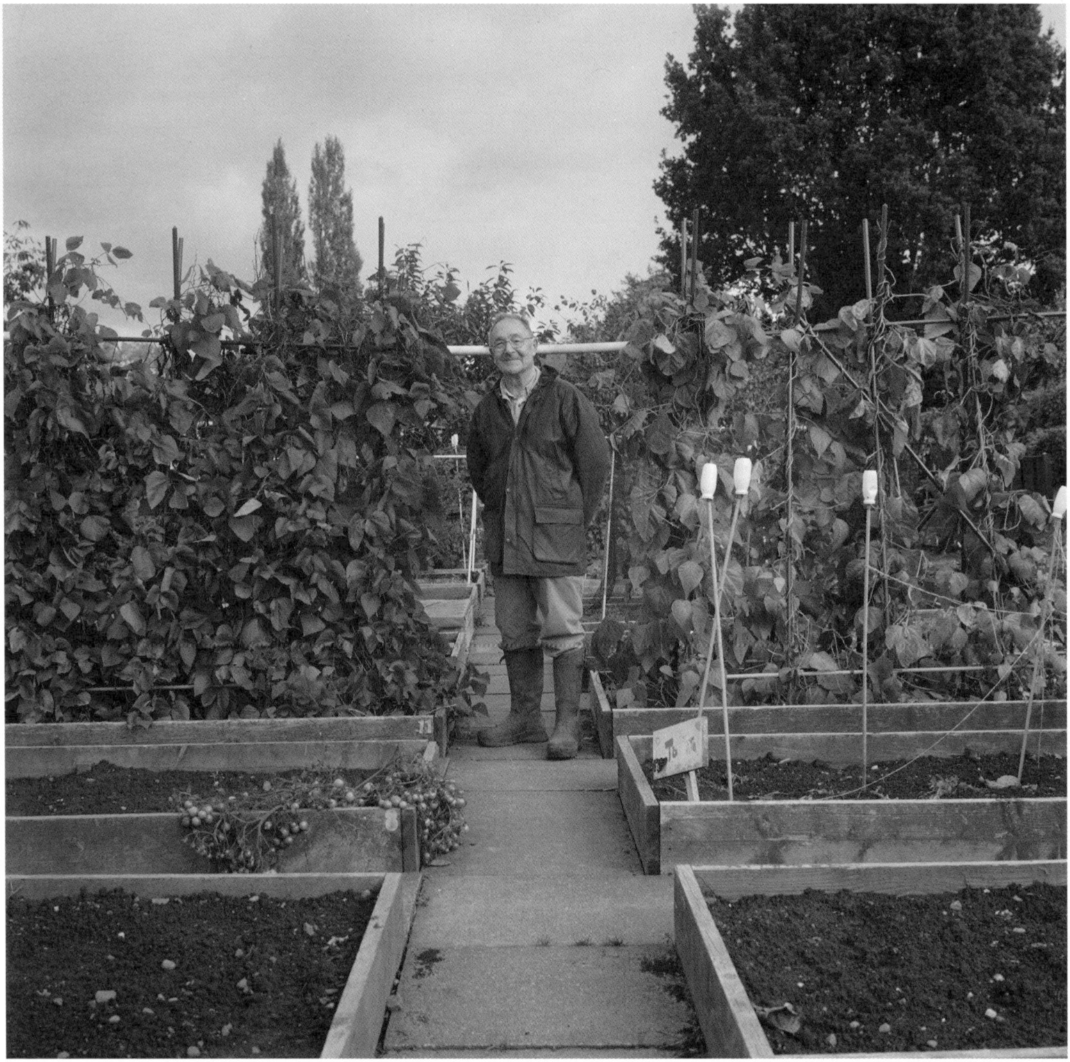

WILLIAM PAUL ANSELL, allotment holder at Earlsdon allotments, who also runs the Primary Allotments project for local primary school children, Coventry (2024). A Meadow Arts commission

William says, "The allotment is a special place where time goes slower and I can relax. I find the process of planting, cultivating and harvesting fruit and vegetables for the table very rewarding and it helps me keep active. I feel being part of the allotment community is essential for my wellbeing."

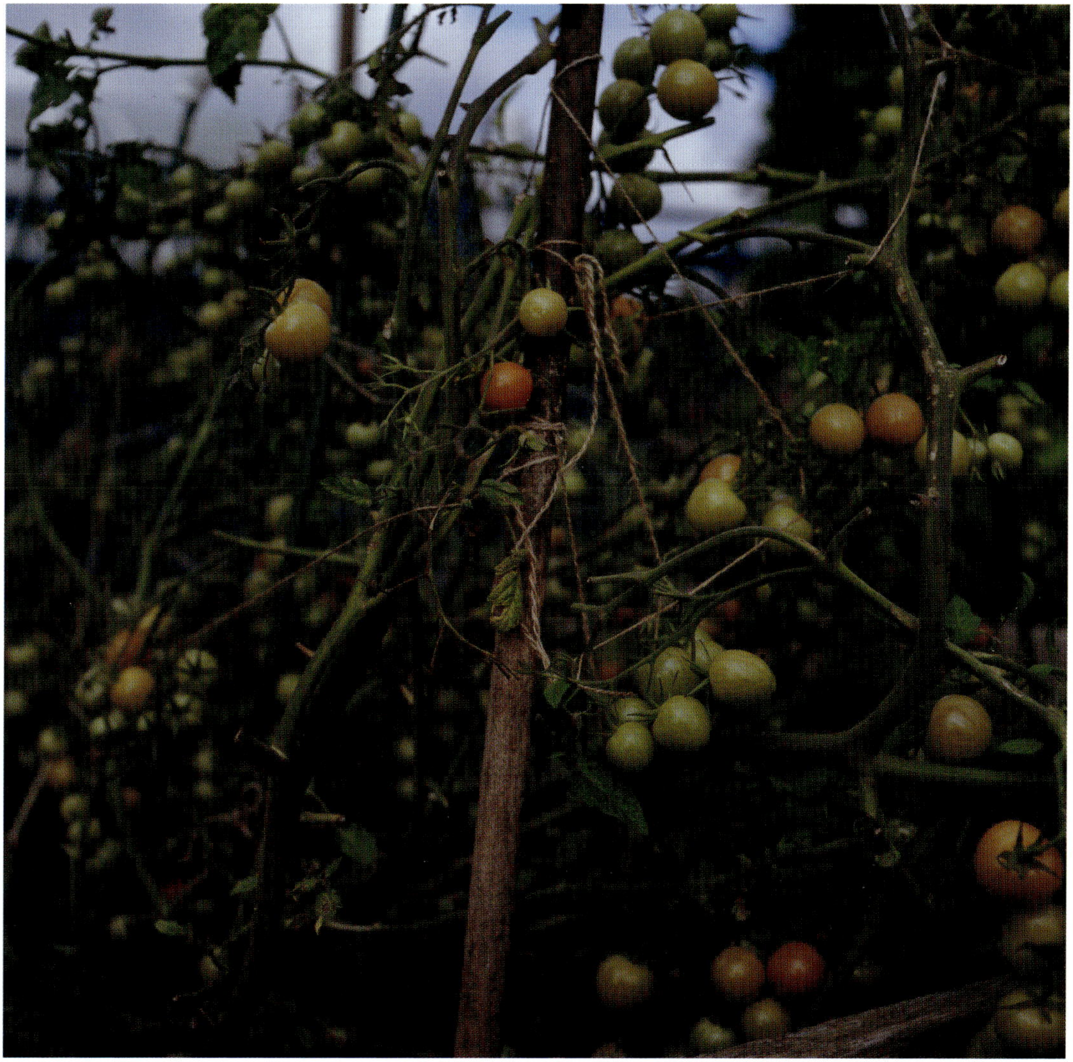

THE "PRIMABELLA" variety of tomato grown by William (although he worries they don't look their best). A Meadow Arts commission

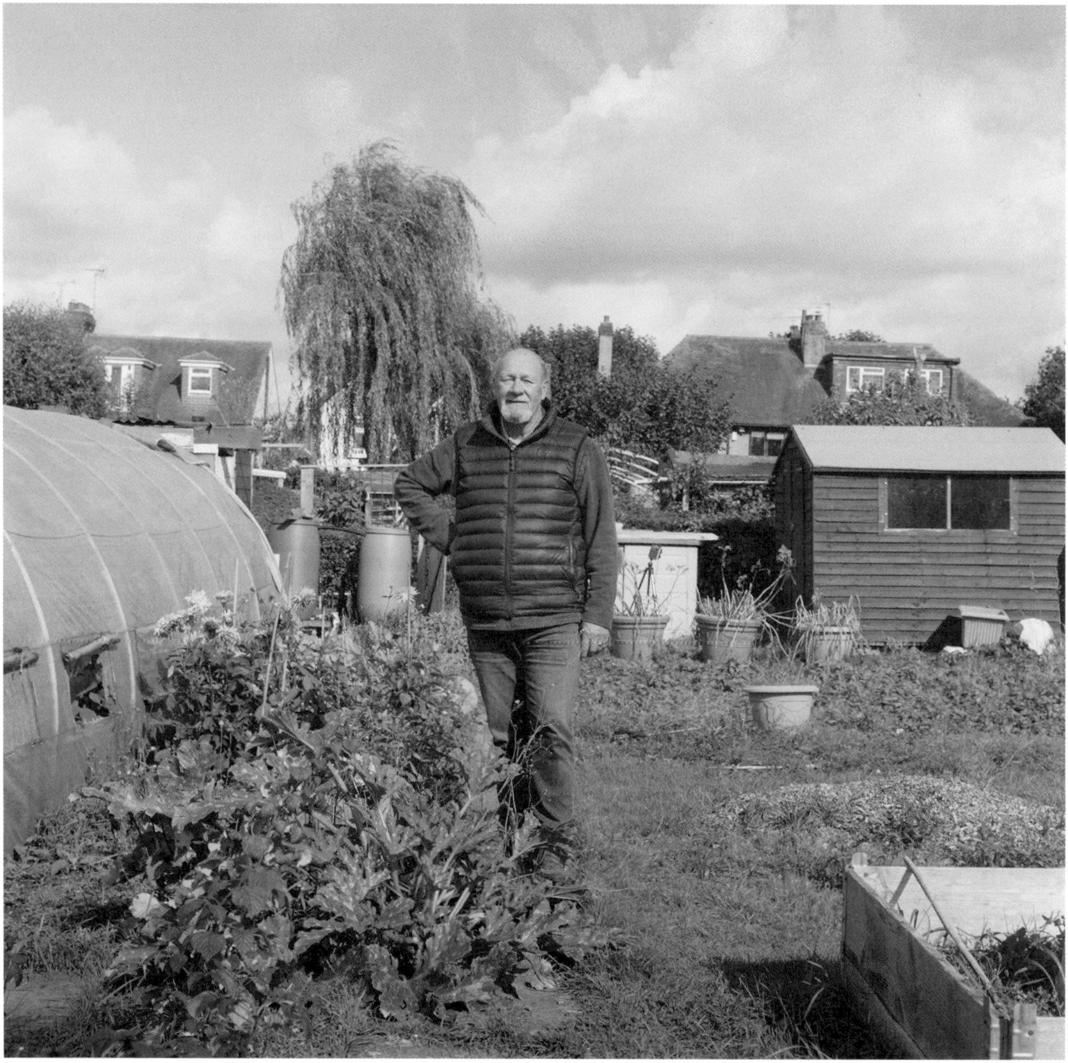

ROBERT JOHNSON, committee member and allotment holder at Earlsdon allotments, Coventry (2024). A Meadow Arts commission

"Running an allotment is both rewarding and mentally stimulating, and helps develop positive emotional skills," Robert says. "It's also good for your health. It brings the community together, as we share notes and pass on any tips we've learned over the years. Our community is now attracting a younger generation to become gardeners."

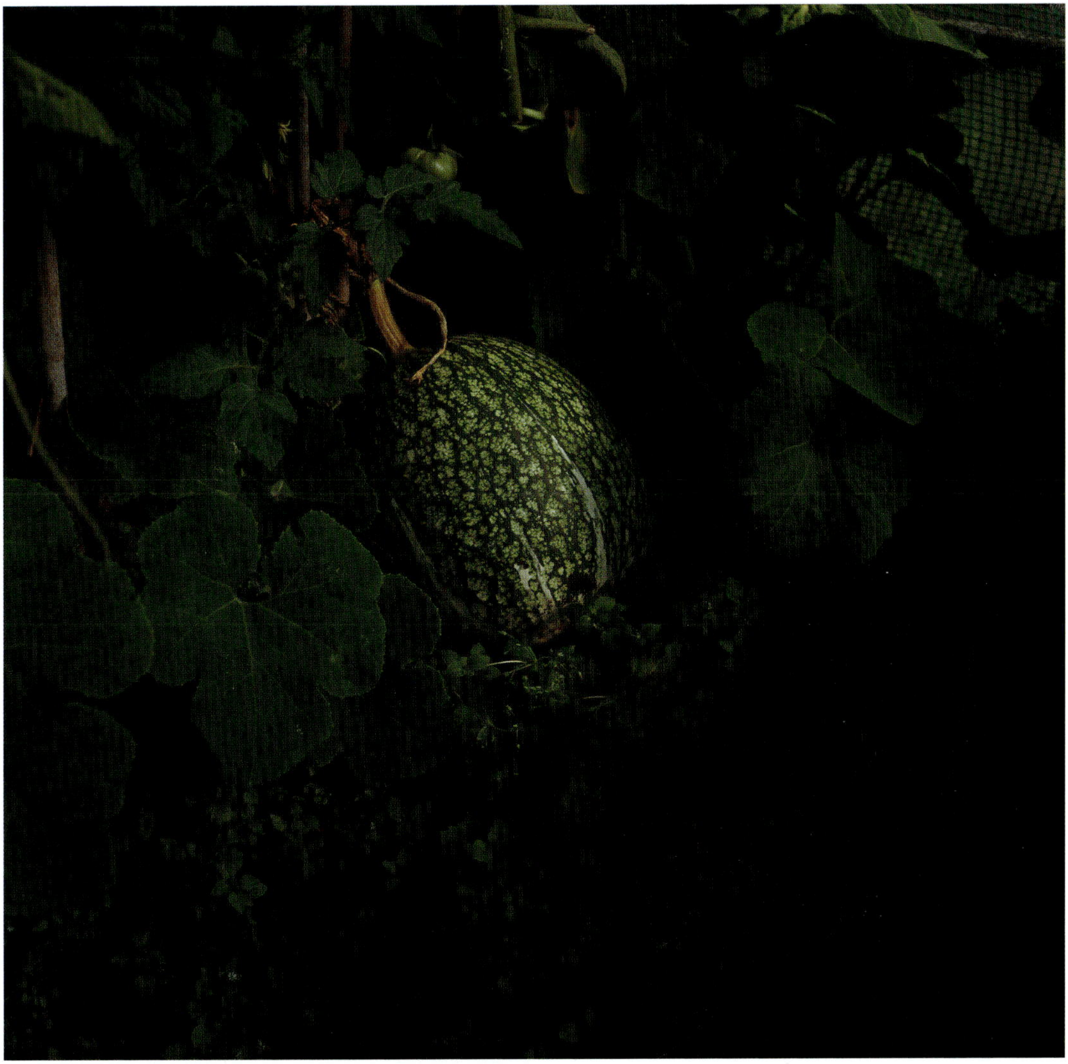

A CROP OF SHARK FIN MELONS GROWN BY ROBERT JOHNSON A Meadow Arts commission

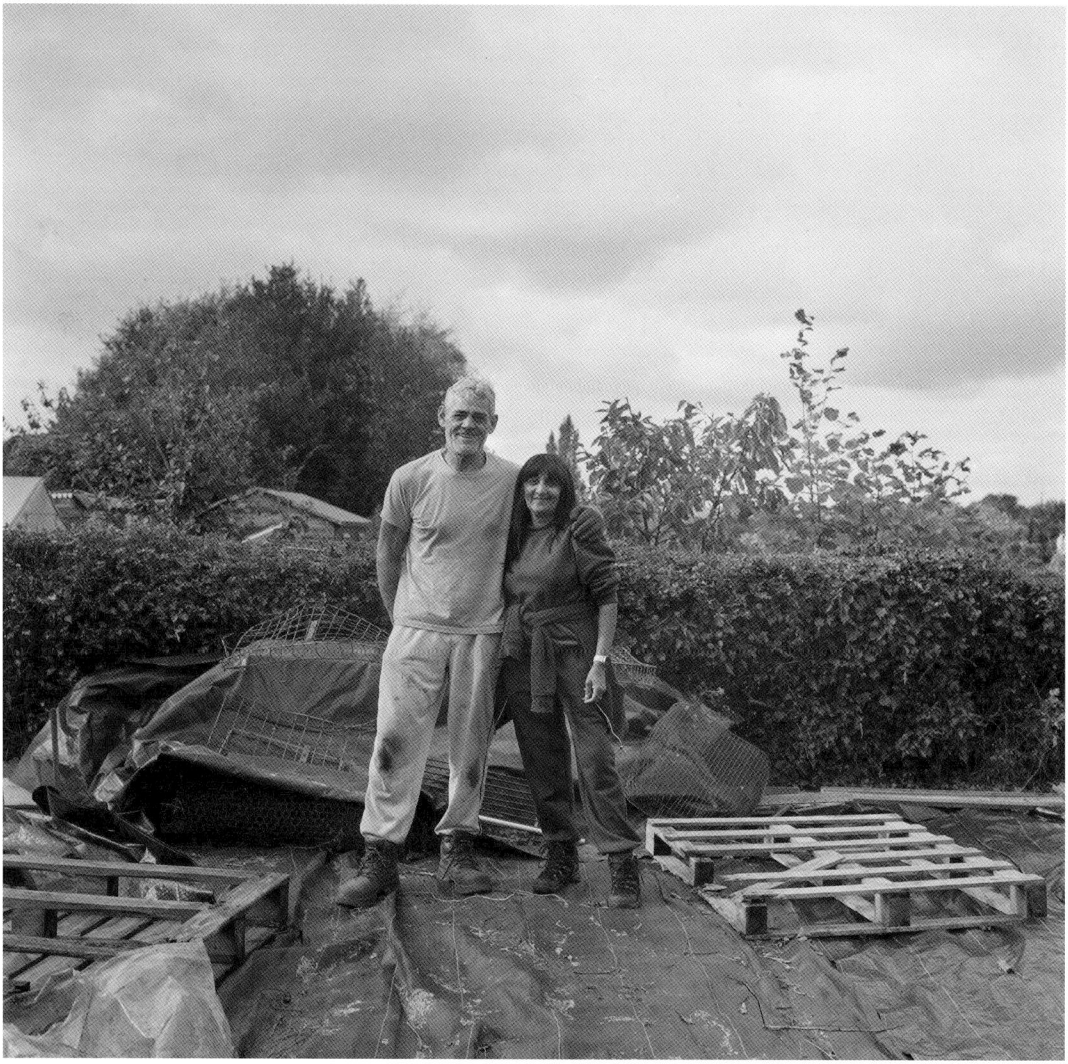

HEMLATA AND DEAN SMITH, new allotment holders at Beechwood allotments, Coventry (2024). A Meadow Arts commission

"When you walk through the gates of an allotment, you forget about all your worries and the hustle and bustle of daily life," Hemlata and Dean explain. "And growing your own organic food is very satisfying, knowing no chemicals have been used, and it actually tastes so much better. Some of the older plot holders have a wealth of knowledge and we learn so much just from being around them. On the allotment, almost everything is recycled. We've just acquired an old greenhouse that we'll rebuild and make good."

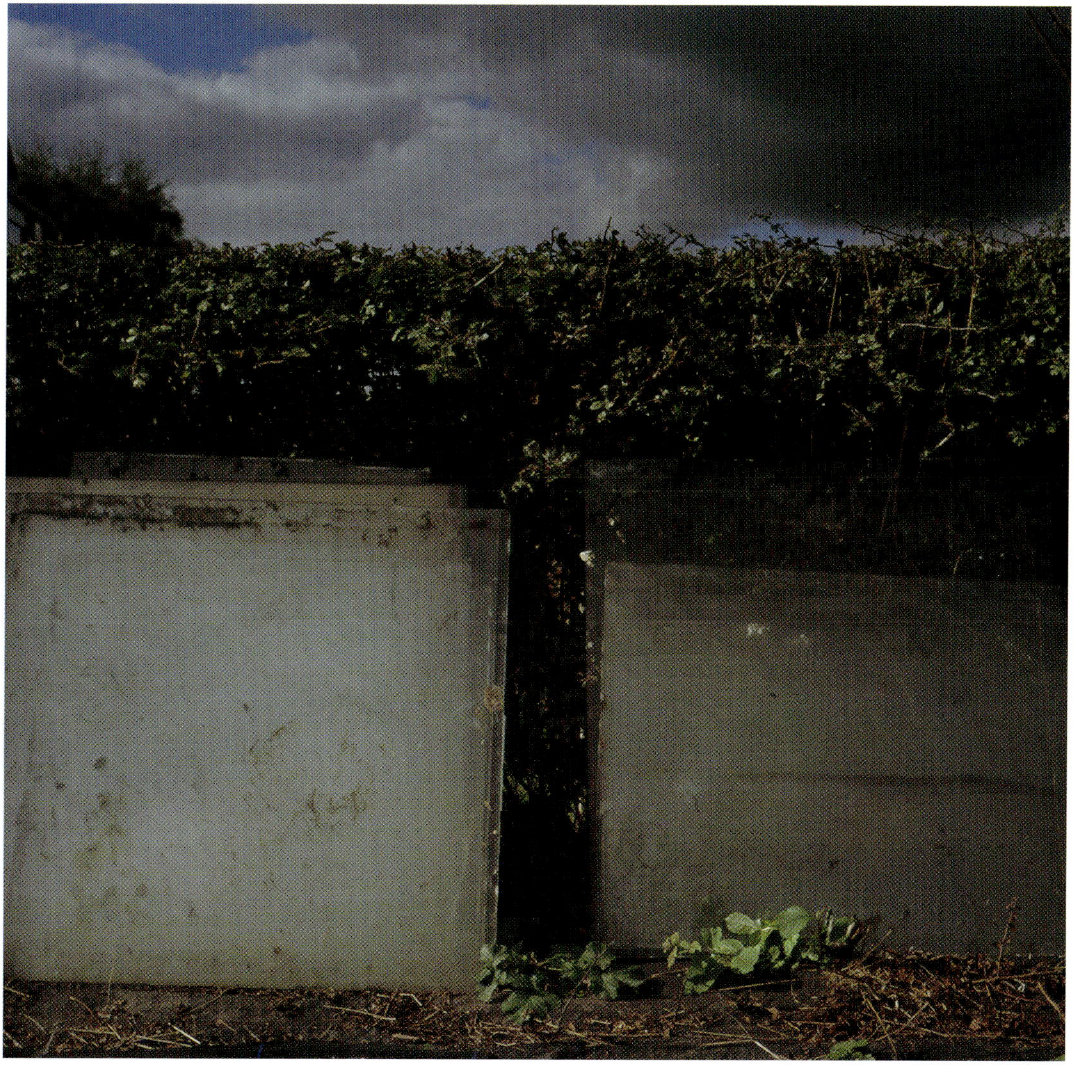

SHEETS OF GLASS FOR THE SMITHS' SOON-TO-BE-UPCYCLED GREENHOUSE A Meadow Arts commission

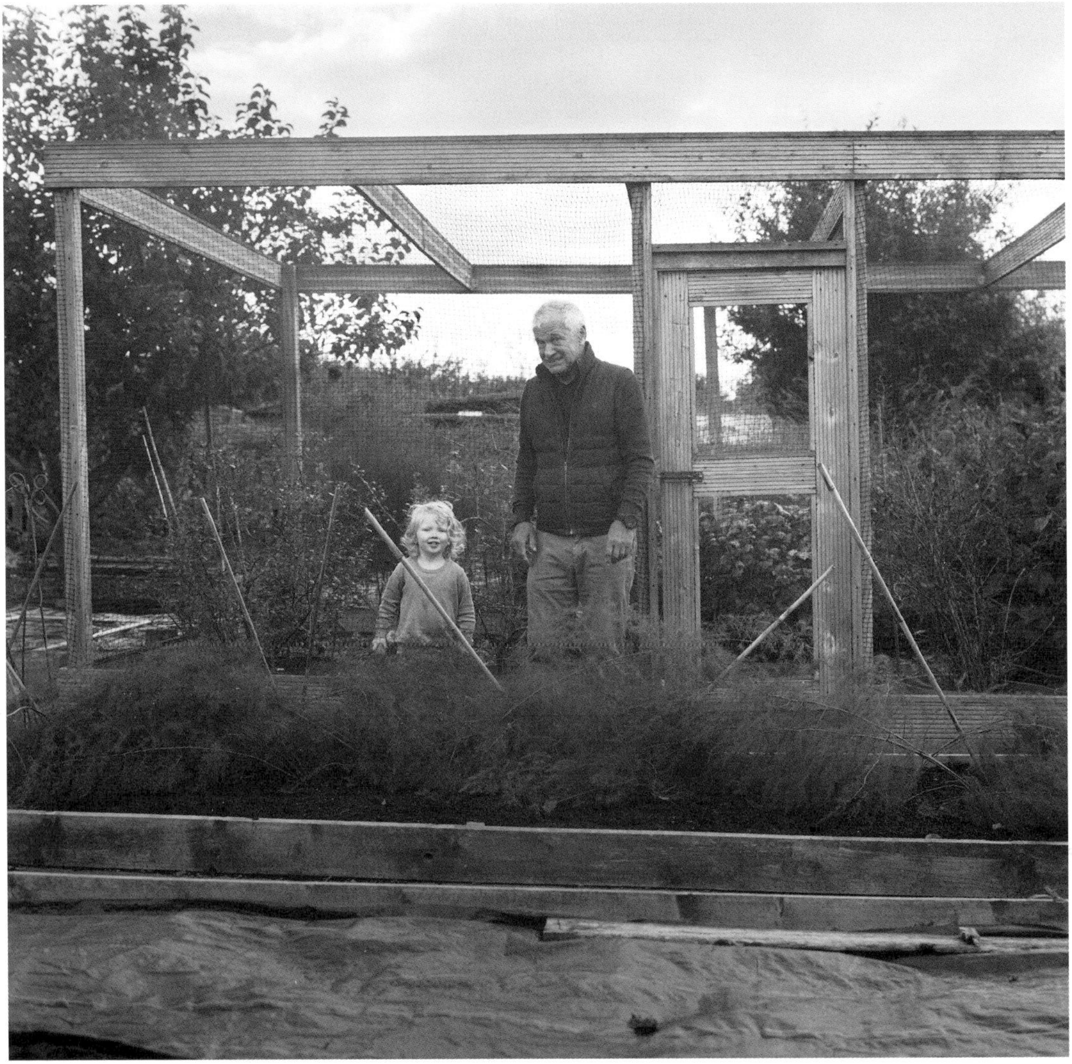

BILL HEDGES, allotment holder at Earlsdon allotments, Coventry (2024) A Meadow Arts commission

According to Bill, his allotment is "a place of relaxation, calm and tranquillity".

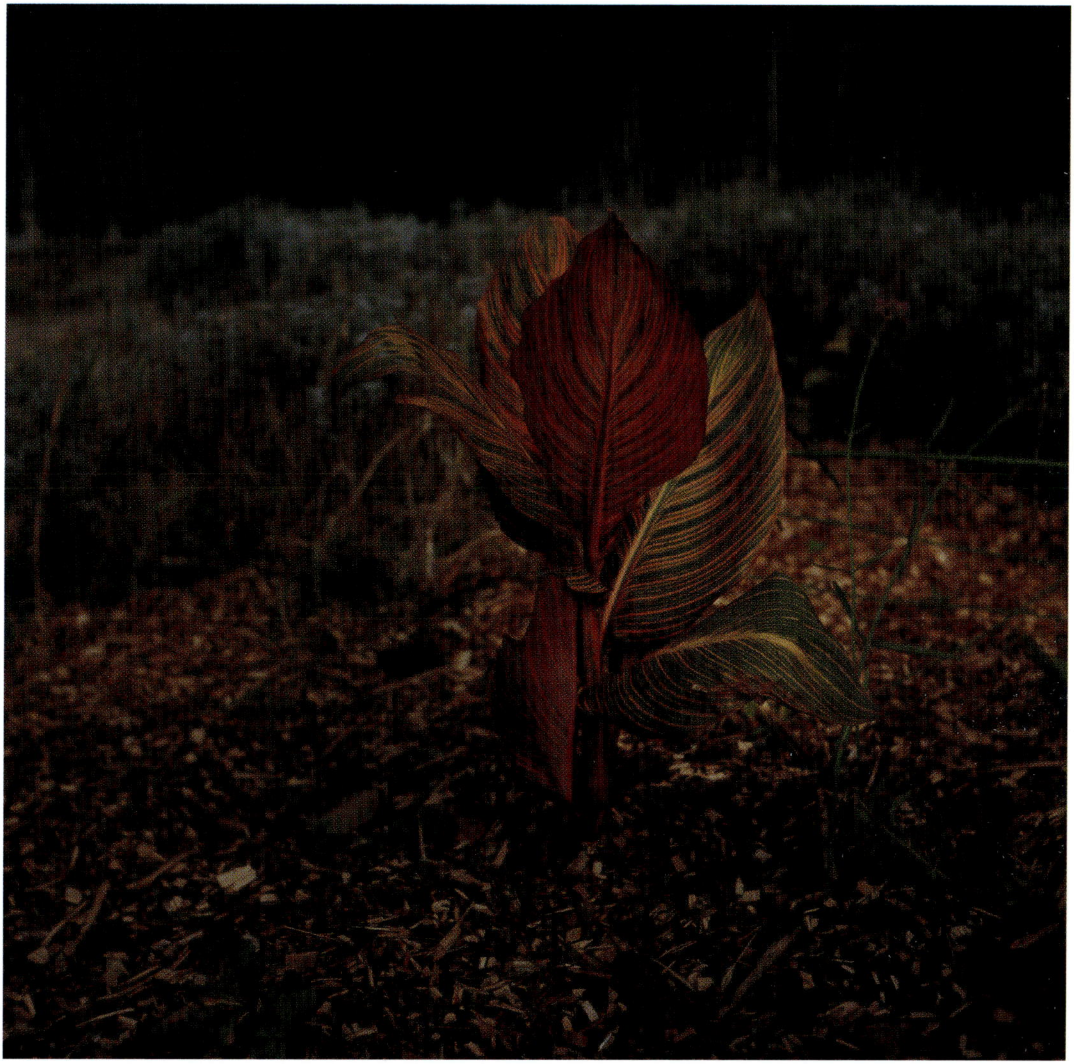

ONE OF BILL'S CANNA LILIES, WHICH GROW TALL WITH DRAMATIC FOLIAGE AND EXOTIC ORANGE FLOWERS
A Meadow Arts commission

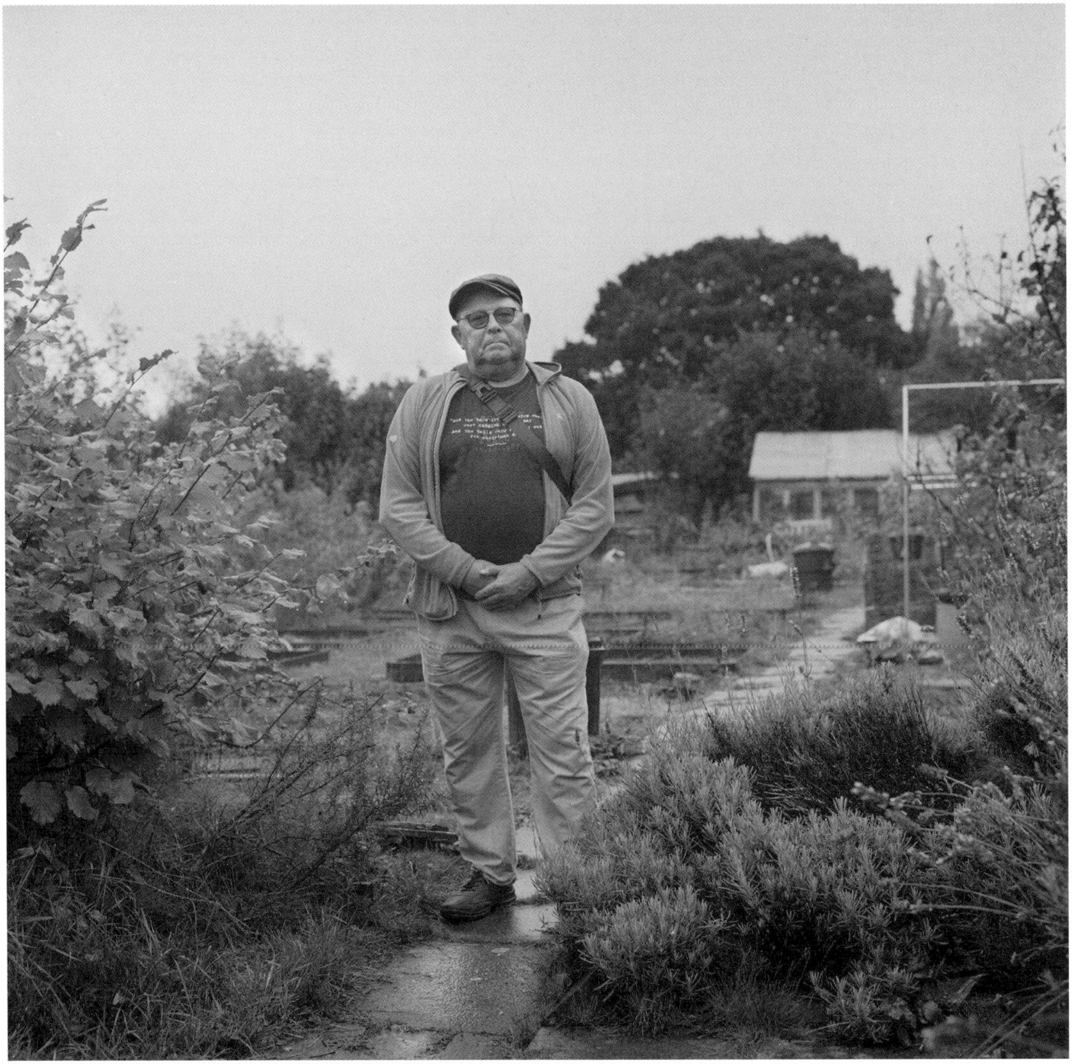

GRAHAM PAINE, retired schoolteacher and allotment holder at Earlsdon allotments, Coventry (2024). A Meadow Arts commission

Graham Paine explains, "This allotment is a really good way of getting out of the house and an opportunity to meet up with my friend Graham Hill. It's great to have young people down here with families as it teaches them the value of growing your own food."

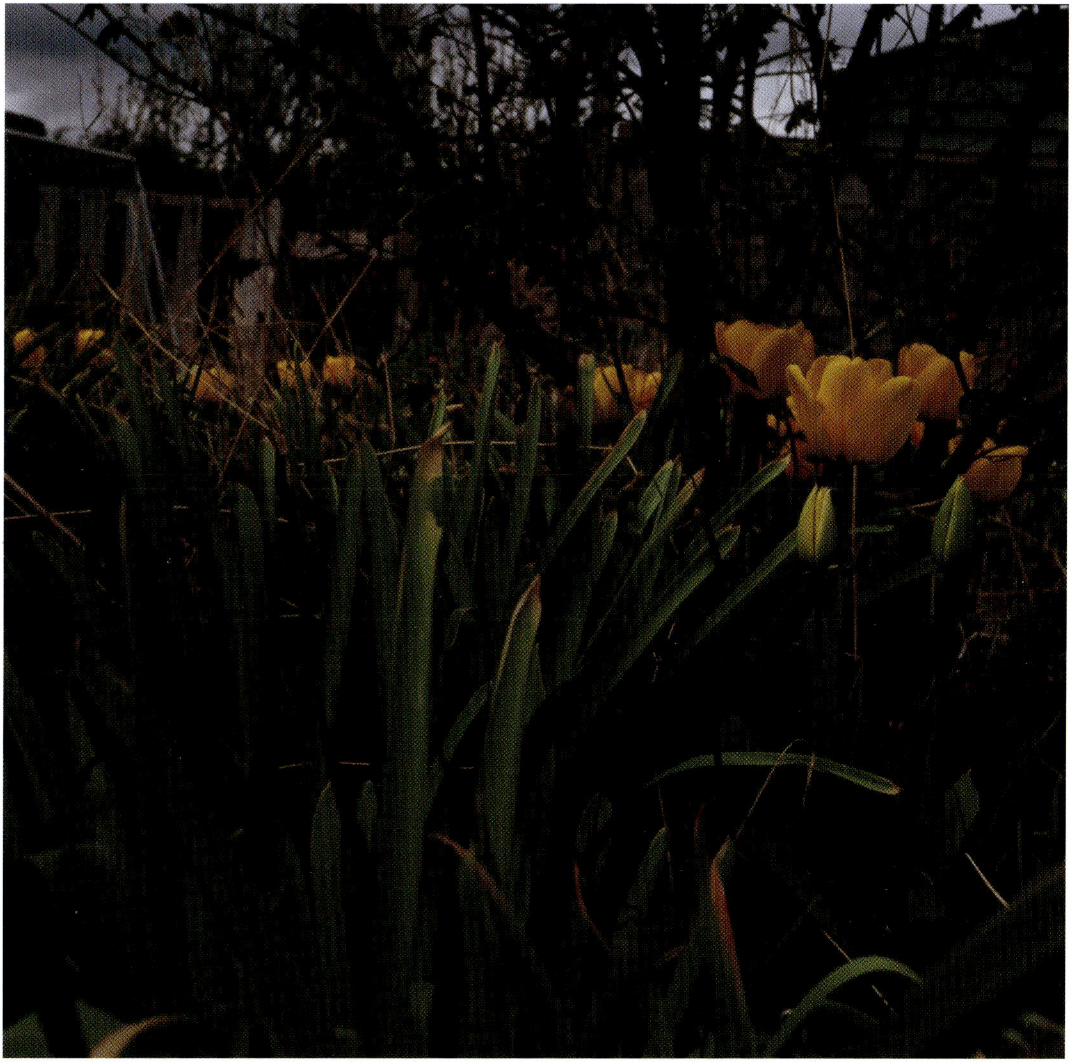

SPRING TULIPS A Meadow Arts commission

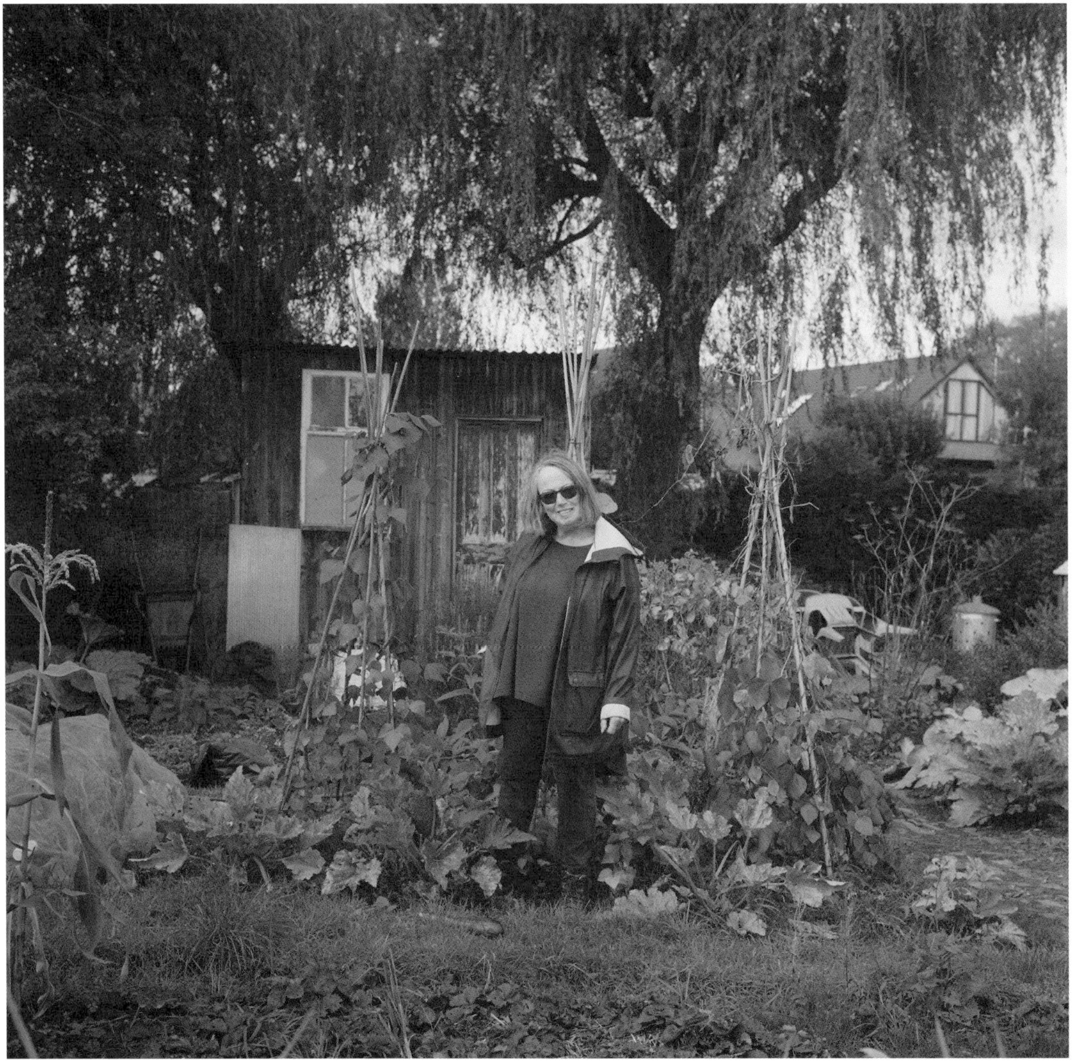

ANN THOMSON, allotment holder at Earlsdon allotments and volunteer for Carriers of Hope community allotment, Coventry (2024). A Meadow Arts commission

Ann volunteers for Carriers of Hope, which supports refugees, asylum seekers and other migrants in Coventry. She also has her own allotment, where she grows fruit and vegetables.

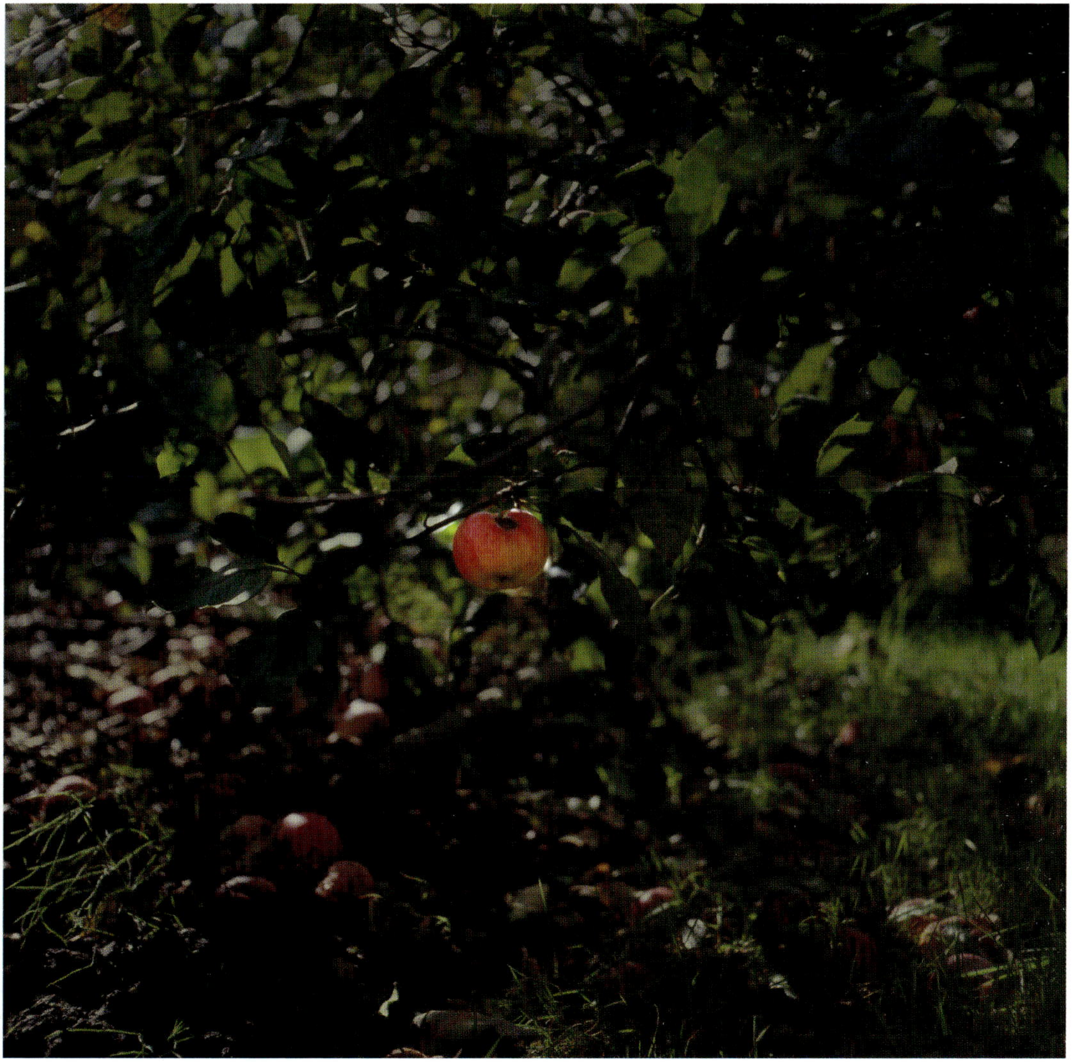

APPLES GROWN ON ANN'S ALLOTMENT A Meadow Arts commission

SELECTED BIBLIOGRAPHY

Angus, Ian, *The War Against the Commons: Dispossession and Resistance in the Making of Capitalism*, Monthly Review Press, 2023

Barrell, John, *The Dark Side of the Landscape: The rural poor in English painting 1730–1840*, Cambridge University Press, 1980

Beynon, Helen with Gillham, Chris, *Twyford Rising: Land and Resistance*, Sarsen Press, 2020

Boyce, James, *Imperial Mud: The Fight for the Fens*, Icon Books, 2020

Butterworth, Jez, *Jerusalem*, Nick Hern Books, 2014

Charlesworth, Andrew, ed., *An Atlas of Rural Protest in Britain, 1548–1900*, Routledge, 2018

Christophers, Brett, *The New Enclosure: The Appropriation of Public Land in Neoliberal Britain*, Verso, 2018

Clare, John, *Major Works*, Oxford University Press, 2004

Cooper, Quentin and Sullivan, Paul, *Maypoles, Martyrs & Mayhem: 366 days of British myths, customs & eccentricities*, Bloomsbury, 1994

Crouch, David and Ward, Colin, *The Allotment: Its Landscape and Culture*, Little Toller Books, 2023

Empson, Martin, *Kill all the Gentlemen: Class struggle and change in the English countryside*, Bookmarks Publications, 2018

Engels, Friedrich, *The Condition of the Working Class in England*, Oxford University Press, 1993

Ehrenreich, Barbara, *Dancing in the Streets: A History of Collective Joy*, Holt, 2006

Federici, Silvia, *Caliban and the Witch: Women, the Body and Primitive Accumulation*, Autonomedia, 2004

Fowler, Corinne, *Green Unpleasant Land: Creative Responses to Rural England's Colonial Connections*, Peepal Tree Press, 2020

Graeber, David, and Wengrow, David, *The Dawn of Everything: A New History of Humanity*, Allen Lane, 2021

Griffin, Carl, *Protest, Politics and Work in Rural England, 1700–1850*, Palgrave Macmillan, 2014

Hammond, J L and Hammond, Barbara, *The Village Labourer*, Longmans, Green and Co, 1911

Harrison, Harry, *Dreaming in Yellow: The Story of the DiY Sound System*, Velocity Press, 2022

Harrison, Mark Angelo, *A Darker Electricity: The Origins of the Spiral Tribe Sound System*, Velocity Press, 2023

Hayes, Nick, *The Book of Trespass: Crossing the Lines that Divide Us*, Bloomsbury, 2020

Hill, Christopher, *The World Turned Upside Down: Radical Ideas During the English Revolution*, Maurice Temple Smith, 1992

Hobsbawm, Eric and Rudé, George, *Captain Swing*, Phoenix Press, 2001

Hopkins, Harry, *The Long Affray: The Poaching Wars in Britain*, Faber and Faber, 2008

Hutton, Ronald, *The Stations of the Sun: A History of the Ritual Year in Britain*, Oxford University Press, 1996

Jensen, Oskar, *Vagabonds: Life on the Streets of Nineteenth-Century London*, Duckworth, 2023

Linebaugh, Peter, *Stop, Thief: The Commons, Enclosures and Resistance*, PM Press, 2014

Linebaugh, Peter and Rediker, Marcus, *The Many-Headed Hydra: The Hidden History of the Revolutionary Atlantic*, Verso, 2000

Linklater, Andro, *Owning the Earth: The Transforming History of Land Ownership*, Bloomsbury, 2015

Marx, Karl, *Capital: A Critical Analysis of Capital Production*, Wordsworth Editions, 2013

Mayhew, Henry, *London Labour and the London Poor*, Penguin Books, 1985

McKay, George, *Senseless Acts of Beauty: Cultures of Resistance since the Sixties*, Verso, 1996

Navickas, Katrina, *Protest and the Politics of Space and Place 1789–1848*, Manchester University Press, 2016

Neeson, J M, *Commoners: Common Right, Enclosure and Social Change in England, 1700–1820*, Cambridge University Press, 1993

Palmer, Roy, *A Ballad History of*

England, from 1588 to the present day, Batsford, 1979
Perelman, Michael, *The Invention of Capitalism, Classical Political Economy and the Secret History of Primitive Accumulation*, Duke University Press, 2000
Pleij, Herman, *Dreaming of Cockaigne: Medieval Fantasies of the Perfect Life*, Columbia University Press, 2001
Rimbaud, Penny, *The Last of the Hippies: An Hysterical Romance*, Active Distribution, 2009
Scott, James C, *Against the Grain: A Deep History of the Earliest States*, Yale University Press, 2017
Sharp, Buchanan, *In Contempt of All Authority: Rural Artisans and Riot in the West of England, 1586–1660*, University of California Press, 1980
Shoard, Marion, *This Land is our Land: The Struggle for Britain's Countryside*, Gaia Books, 1997
Shrubsole, Guy, *Who Owns England: How We Lost Our Green & Pleasant Land & How to Take It Back*, William Collins, 2019
Standing, Guy, *Plunder of the Commons: A Manifesto for Sharing Public Wealth*, Penguin Books, 2019
Smith, John Thomas, *Vagabondiana: Or Anecdotes of Mendicant Wanderers Through the Streets of London*, Chatto and Windus, 1874
Thompson, E P, *Customs in Common*, Merlin Press, 1991
Thompson, E P, *The Making of the English Working Class*, Penguin Books, 1991
Thompson, E P, *Whigs & Hunters: The Origin of the Black Act*, Breviary Stuff Publications, 2013
Waites, Ian, *Common Land in English Painting 1700–1850*, Boydell Press, 2012
Way, Twigs, *Allotments*, Shire Publications, 2008
Winchester, Simon, *Land: How the Hunger for Ownership Shaped the Modern World*, William Collins, 2021
Winstanley, Gerrard, *A Common Treasury*, edited and selected by Andrew Hopton, Verso, 2011
Wood, Andy, *Riot, Rebellion and Popular Politics in Early Modern England*, Palgrave, 2002

END NOTES

ENCLOSED LAND AND VANQUISHED PEASANTS

1. Francis Pryor, *Britain BC, Life in Britain and Ireland before the Romans* (Harper Collins, 2003), pp.79–90. (Perhaps an echo of this reverence remains as the Abbots Bromley Horn Dancers perform their annual folk ritual with antlers attached to their heads.)
2. Frederick Turner, ed., *The Portable North American Indian Reader* (Penguin, 1977), p.246.
3. Holy See Press Office, *Joint Statement of the Dicasteries for Culture and Education and for Promoting Integral Human Development on the "Doctrine of Discovery"* (Vatican, 30 March 2023).
4. Robert J Miller, "The Doctrine of Discovery", *The Indigenous Peoples' Journal of Law, Culture, & Resistance*, 2019, vol. 5, pp.38–9.
5. Andro Linklater, *Owning the Earth* (Bloomsbury, 2014), p.5.
6. Ibid.
7. John Chapman, "The Extent and Nature of Parliamentary Enclosure", *The Agricultural History Review*, 1987, vol. 35, no. 1, pp.28–32.
8. Christopher Dyer, *Making a Living in the Middle Ages* (Yale University Press, 2002), pp.272–93.
9. Jean Froissart, *Chronicles*, transl. Thomas Johnes and ed. Henry Dunster, (J. M. Dent, 1906), p.207-8.
10. Thomas Walsingham, *Historia Anglicana,* trans. and quoted in R B Dobson, The Peasants' Revolt of 1381 (Macmillan, 1970), p.272.
11. Ibid., pp.310–11.
12. Christopher Dyer, *Making a Living in the Middle Ages*, pp.291–3.
13. Joan Thirsk, *The Agrarian History of England and Wales* (Cambridge University Press, 1967), p.219.
14. Thomas More, *Utopia*, ed. William Dallam Armes, (Macmillan, 1912), p.38.
15. Ronald Hutton, *The Witch* (Yale University Press, 2017), pp.180–1.
16. Quoted in Barrett L Beer, *Rebellion and Riot* (Kent State University Press, 1982), pp.105–6.
17. Ibid., passim.
18. Norfolk Record Office, Norwich, C.S3/12A quoted in John Walter, "A 'Rising of the People'? The Oxfordshire Rising of 1596", *Past & Present*, no. 107, 1985, p.92.
19. Steve Hindle, "Imagining Insurrection in 17th-Century England:Representations of the Midland Rising 1607", *History Workshop Journal*, no. 66, Autumn 2008.
20. Privy Council Order on Leicester Forest, 31 May 1628 in *Acts of the Privy Council of England*, 1627–8, pp. 475–7, quoted in Buchanan Sharp, *In Contempt of All Authority* (University of California Press, 1980), p.90.
21. Public Record Office, S.P. 16/188/20, copy of affidavit by Robert Bridges submitted to the Court of Exchequer, 5 April 1631, quoted in Sharp, *In Contempt of All Authority*, p.97.
22. Sharp, *In Contempt of All Authority*, passim.
23. Christopher Hill, *The World Turned Upside Down* (Penguin, 2019), pp.2–3.
24. Ibid., pp.84–6.
25. Gerrard Winstanley, *A Declaration from the Poor Oppressed People of England* (1649) in G H Sabine, ed., *The Works of Gerrard Winstanley* (Cornell University Press, 1941), p.270.
26. Gerrard Winstanley, *A Watch-word to the City of London and the Armie* (1649), ibid., p.315.
27. Gerrard Winstanley, *The New Law of Righteousnes* (1649), ibid., p.194.
28. Gerrard Winstanley, *The True Levellers Standard Advanced* (1649), ibid., p.257.
29. John Gurney, *Gerrard Winstanley, The Digger's Life and Legacy* (Pluto Press, 2013).
30. Silvia Federici, *Caliban and the*

Witch (Penguin, 2004), p.184.

31. Sharp, *In Contempt of All Authority*, pp.252–5.
32. Quoted in "The City of Coventry: The Common Lands" in *A History of the County of Warwick: Volume 8, the City of Coventry and Borough of Warwick*, ed. W B Stephens (Victoria County History, 1969), British History Online website. Available at: www.british-history.ac.uk/vch/warks/vol8/pp199-207 [accessed 17 Mar 2025].
33. "The City of Coventry: The Common Lands", ibid.
34. "A Relation of a Short Survey of the Western Counties: Made by a Lieutenant of the Military Company in Norwich" in 1635, quoted in Jeremy Purseglove, *Taming the Flood* (William Collins, 2015), p.54.
35. Jim Snee Heritage, "Lincolnshire's Last Hunter-Gatherers", blog, Heritage Lincolnshire website. Available at: www.heritagelincolnshire.org/blogs/lincolnshires-last-hunter-gatherers-by-jim-snee [accessed 31 Mar 2025].
36. Quoted in Joan Thirsk, English *Peasant Farming: The Agrarian History of Lincolnshire from Tudor to Recent Times* (Routledge and Kegan Paul, 1957), pp.29–30.
37. Ibid.
38. Michael Perelman, *The Invention of Capitalism* (Duke University Press, 2000), p.14.
39. J L and B Hammond, *The Village Labourer 1760–1832* (Allan Sutton, 1987), p.43.
40. Ibid., p.54.
41. Letter to Lord Carlisle, *Carlisle Papers,* Historical Mss. Commission, p.301, quoted in Hammond, *The Village Labourer 1760–1832*, p.66.
42. Ibid., pp.65–70.
43. Ibid., passim.
44. John Clare, "Remembrances", *Selected Poems and Prose of John Clare* (Oxford University Press, 1966), p.196.
45. Jonathan Bate, *John Clare, A Biography* (Picador, 2003), p.48.
46. Clare, "The Mores", *Selected Poems and Prose of John Clare*, p.189.
47. Bate, John Clare, passim.
48. John Billingsley, "Uselessness of Commons to the Poor", Annals of Agriculture, 1798.
49. *An Inquiry into the Connection between the Present Price of Provision and the Size of Farms*, (1773) p 81.
50. "Report on Shropshire", *Annals of Agriculture*, 1794.
51. Letter from C Landor to the Marquis of Anglesey, dated 26 April 1824, quoted in J M Neeson, *Commoners: Common Right, Enclosure and Social Change in England*, 1700–1820 (Cambridge University Press, 1993), pp.326–7.
52. Arthur Young, *An Inquiry into the Propriety of Applying Wastes to the Better Maintenance and Support of the Poor* (1801), pp.42–3.
53. J M Neeson, *Commoners*, pp.190–7.
54. Corinne Fowler, *Green Unpleasant Land* (Peepal Tree, 2020), passim.
55. E P Thompson, *Whigs and Hunters* (Penguin Books, 1977), passim.
56. Harry Hopkins, *The Long Affray, The Poaching Wars in Britain* (Macmillan, 1986), p.58.
57. W H Hudson, *A Shepherd's Life* (Methuen, 1910), p.98.
58. Quoted in Hammond, *The Village Labourer 1760–1832*, p.279.
59. Letter from the governor of Van Diemen's Land to Lord Goderich, March 1834, quoted in Hammond, *The Village Labourer 1760–1832*, p.324.
60. Geoffrey Sharman, "Swing Rioters under the Southern Cross", Tasmanian Family History Society website, Available at: www.hobart.tasfhs.org/swing-rioters/riots_introduction.php [accessed 31 Mar 2025].
61. William Cobbett, *Rural Rides* (Penguin, 2001), passim.
62. Quoted in Eric Hobsbawm and George Rudé, *Captain Swing* (Phoenix Press, 2001), p.246.
63. William Cobbett, *Cobbett's*

Weekly Political Register, vol. 71, no. 4, 22 January 1831.

64. Sidney Pollard in Peter Mathias, M M Postan, eds., *The Cambridge Economic History of Europe*, vol. 7 (Cambridge University Press, 1978), p.116.
65. Joan Thirsk, *The Agrarian History of England and Wales*, p.255.

COSMOLOGY ENDNOTES FOR PAGES 105–113

1. Ian Waites, *Common Land in English Painting* 1700–1850 (Boyden Press, 2012), p.51.
2. See: https://camdenartcentre.org/whats-on/jesse-darling-2
3. See: https://www.pilarcorrias.com/exhibitions/296-rachel-rose-enclosure/

VAGABONDS ENDNOTES FOR PAGES 140–173

1. Jez Butterworth, *Jerusalem* (Nick Hern Books, 2014), p.102.
2. Jez Butterworth, *Jerusalem* (Nick Hern Books, 2009), p.102.
3. Jez Butterworth, *Jerusalem* (Nick Hern Books, 2009), p.102.
4. Jez Butterworth, *Jerusalem* (Nick Hern Books, 2009), p.102.

ARISE ALBION! ENDNOTES FOR PAGES 174-189

1. James Phillips Kay, MD, *The Moral and Physical Condition of the Working Classes Employed in the Cotton Manufacture in Manchester* (Ridgway, 1832), p.10.
2. Paul Salveson, "Remembering Winter Hill, Britain's Biggest Mass Trespass", *Tribune*, 2021. Available at: https://tribunemag.co.uk/2021/09/remembering-winter-hill-britains-biggest-mass-trespass
3. Gerrard Winstanley, *The True Levellers Standard Advanced: Or, The State of Community opened, and Presented to the Sons of Men* (London, 1649); reproduced in Tony Benn, ed., Gerrard Winstanley, *A Common Treasury* (Verso, 2011), p.8.
4. Tony Benn, *Gerrard Winstanley*, p.8.
5. "Ex-police Chief Dies", *Oxford Mail*, 28 September 1978.
6. Andy Worthington, "It's 25 years since the last Stonehenge Free Festival", website, 2009. Available at: www.andyworthington.co.uk/2009/06/20/its-25-years-since-the-last-stonehenge-free-festival/
7. Phil Russell, aka Wally Hope, 1974, quoted in *The Last of the Hippies – An Hysterical Romance* by Penny Rimbaud (Active Distribution, 2009), p.33.
8. Observation made to the author, Stonehenge, summer solstice, 1992.
9. David Graeber and David Wengrow, *The Dawn of Everything, A New History of Humanity* (Penguin Books, 2022), p.105.
10. Jez Butterworth, *Jerusalem* (Nick Hern Books, 2009), p58.
11. James C Scott, *Against the Grain, A Deep History of the Earliest States* (Yale University Press, 2017), pp.219–56.
12. Ibid., p.221.
13. Sheila Craig, ed., *Stonehenge '85 – Souvenir Issue* (Unique Publications, 1986).
14. Bruce Garrard, ed., *The Green Collective, the Best from the Mailing, 1984* (Unique Publications, 1986), p.6.
15. Bruce Garrard, *Rainbow Fields is Home, The Story of Rainbow Village at Molesworth August 1984–1985* (Unique Publications, 1992).
16. Mark Angelo Harrison, in interview with Stephen Coates, *Bureau of Lost Culture* podcast, episode 121, 28 July 2024.
17. Mark Angelo Harrison quoted in Richard Lowe and William Shaw, *Travellers* (Fourth Estate, 1993), p.168.
18. Mark Angelo Harrison, *A Darker Electricity, The Origins of the Spiral Tribe Sound System* (Velocity Press, 2023), passim
19. Quoted in Helen Beynon with Chris Gillham, *Twyford Rising, Land and Resistance* (Helen Baczkowska, 2020), p.89.
20. Ed Swan, "The M11 Link Road: 20

years on", *Waltham Forest Echo*, 4 November 2014.

21. "Towers of Strength, Inside Europe's longest eviction", *Squall Magazine*, no. 5, 1995.
22. Clare Evans, "The Public Order Act 2023: Has our Right to Protest been Restricted?", Human Rights Dept, Saunders Law, 18 July 2023. Available at: www.saunders.co.uk/news/the-public-order-act-2023-has-our-right-to-protest-been-restricted/
23. "UN Human Rights Chief urges UK to reverse 'deeply troubling' Public Order Bill", 27 April 2023. Available at: www.ohchr.org/en/press-releases/2023/04/un-human-rights-chief-urges-uk-reverse-deeply-troubling-public-order-bill
24. Barbara Ehrenreich, *Dancing in the Streets*, A History of Collective Joy (Henry Holt, 2006), pp.248–60.
25. E P Thompson, "Rough Music Reconsidered", *Folklore*, 1992, vol. 103, no. 1, pp.3–26.
26. Interview with Leah Gordon, 10 Sept 2024.

PICTURE CREDITS

Key

a above
b below
c centre
l left
r right

P7 *German Peasants' War 1524 - 1526, concept for a column commemorating the defeat of the peasants, 1525 by Albrecht Dürer. Courtesy of INTERFOTO / Alamy Stock Photo.*

P8 *The Doonicans*, 1987 © Leah Gordon.

P9 *The Doonicans EP*, 1987. Cover linocut and design by Matthew Weir.

P11 *Grandad Jesse Walker and Son Jesse Walker* © Leah Gordon.

P13 *Dorothy and Jesse Walker in Ellesmere Port*, 1982 © Leah Gordon.

P14 *German Peasants' War 1524 - 1526, concept for a column commemorating the defeat of the peasants, 1525 by Albrecht Dürer. Courtesy of INTERFOTO / Alamy Stock Photo.*

P15 *Travellers' Library*, photographed by Leah Gordon from a 1928 Jonathan Cape edition of William by E H Young.

P27 *A boy sitting on a fence, scaring away crows with a pair of clappers,* 19th century by William Bromley © Wellcome Collection.

P28-29 *Gathering Twigs*, c. 1550 by Simon Bening courtesy of Getty Museum, LA.

P30a *Gleaners in the Wheat Field*, 1847 by John Martin courtesy of National Gallery of Art, Washington DC.

P30b *Leech Finders*, 1814 by George Walker courtesy of Science Museum, London

P31 *A Man Knocking Acorns from a Tree; Zodiacal Sign of Sagittarius*, Workshop of Willem Vrelant (1454–1481) courtesy of Getty Museum, LA.

P32a *Cottage on Fire at Night*, between 1785 and 1793 by Joseph Wright of Derby, courtesy of the Yale Center for British Art, Paul Mellon Collection.

P32b *The Shepherd*, from *Songs of Innocence*, ca. 1795 by William Blake, courtesy of the YaleCenter for British Art, Paul Mellon Fund.

P33a *Adam and Eve (Labour: When Adam Delved and Eve Span, Who Was Then the Gentleman?)*, 1895 or later, after Sir Edward Burne-Jones, artist Carl Hentschel courtesy of the Metropolitan Museum of Art. Rogers Fund, 1921.

P33b *A Shepherd and his Flock under the Moon and Stars*, ca. 1827 by Samuel Palmer, courtesy of the Yale Center for British Art, Paul

Mellon Collection.

P34 A GRAIN Projects commission © Leah Gordon.

P36 A GRAIN Projects commission © Leah Gordon.

P37 A GRAIN Projects commission © Leah Gordon.

P38 A GRAIN Projects commission © Leah Gordon.

P39 A GRAIN Projects and Meadow Arts commission © Leah Gordon.

P40 A GRAIN Projects commission © Leah Gordon.

P41 A Meadow Arts commission © Leah Gordon.

P42 A GRAIN Projects commission © Leah Gordon.

P43 A GRAIN Projects and Meadow Arts commission © Leah Gordon.

P44 A Meadow Arts commission © Leah Gordon.

P45 A Meadow Arts commission © Leah Gordon.

P46 A Meadow Arts commission © Leah Gordon.

P47 A GRAIN Projects and Meadow Arts commission © Leah Gordon.

P48 A Meadow Arts commission © Leah Gordon.

P49 A Meadow Arts commission © Leah Gordon.

P50 *A Study for the Pilkington Crest, a Mower with a Scythe*, Francis Place, courtesy of the Yale Center for British Art, Paul Mellon Collection.

P55 *Mr. Henry as Jack Straw by Anon, 1848, publisher John Fairburn. Courtesy of the Metropolitan Museum of Art.*

P58 *Ox Turned Butcher* by John Ashton, originally published in *The Humour, Wit and Satire of the Seventeenth Century*, 1882 courtesy of the collection of the University of Toronto Library.

P60 *The History of Witches and Wizards*, 1720, courtesy of the Wellcome Collection.

P64 *The Poacher* by Thomas Rowlandson, courtesy of The Metropolitan Museum of Art, The Elisha Whittelsey Collection, The Elisha Whittelsey Fund, 1959.

P65 *Crowd by a Gibbet*, Thomas Rowlandson, courtesy of the Yale Center for British Art, Paul Mellon Collection.

P67 *Labourers at Rest*, Thomas Rowlandson, courtesy of the Yale Center for British Art, Paul Mellon Collection.

P68 *Haymaking*, 1815 by David Cox, courtesy of the Yale Center for British Art, Paul Mellon Collection.

P71 *The World turned upside down: or, No news, and strange news. by James Kendrew, printer, 1820 courtesy of the Miniature Book Collection (Library of Congress)*

P73 *An original portrait of Captain Swing*, 1830 by Anon courtesy of the British Museum

P74-75 *Herne's Oak from The Merry Wives of Windsor*, ca. 1857, George Cruikshank, courtesy of the Yale Center for British Art, Paul Mellon Fund.

P76a *May Day*, 1817 by John Thomas Smith, from Vagabondiana. Scan from original book.

P76b *The Leader of the Luddites*, 1812 by Anon. Hand-coloured etching, courtesy of Niday Picture Library / Alamy Stock Photo.

P77a *The Workers' Map Pole*, 1894 by Walter Crane courtesy of the William Morris Gallery.

P77b *Fools; or Jesters*, 1813, by John Augustus Atkinson, courtesy of the Yale Center for British Art, Paul Mellon Collection.

P78a *Overton Mummers*, c.1930, by George Long, courtesy of the Museum of English Rural Life, University of Reading.

P78b *The Fool Plough* from *The Costume of Yorkshire*, 1813 - 1814 by George Walker, engraved by R. & D. Havell, courtesy of The New York Public Library, Rare Book Division.

P79a *Swing Riots in Kent mob burning a farm*, 1830, by Anon. Historical Images Archive / Alamy Stock Photo.

P79b *May Day*, 1824 by an unknown artist, after Henry William Bunbury, courtesy of the Yale Center for British Art, Paul Mellon Collection.

P80 A Meadow Arts commission © Leah Gordon.

P82 © Leah Gordon.

P83 A Meadow Arts commission © Leah Gordon.

P84 © Leah Gordon.

P85 © Leah Gordon.

P86 A Meadow Arts commission © Leah Gordon.

P87 A Meadow Arts commission © Leah Gordon.

P88 A Meadow Arts commission © Leah Gordon.

P89 A Meadow Arts commission © Leah Gordon.

P90 © Leah Gordon.

P91 A Meadow Arts commission © Leah Gordon.

P92 © Leah Gordon.

P93 © Leah Gordon.

P94 A Meadow Arts commission © Leah Gordon.

P95 A Meadow Arts commission © Leah Gordon.

P96 A Meadow Arts commission © Leah Gordon.

P97 © Leah Gordon.

P98 A Meadow Arts commission © Leah Gordon.

P99 A Meadow Arts commission © Leah Gordon.

P100 A Meadow Arts commission © Leah Gordon.

P101 A Meadow Arts commission © Leah Gordon.

P104 *Three Peasants in Conversation*, ca. 1497 by Albrecht Dürer, courtesy of the Metropolitan Museum of Art, Fletcher Fund, 1919.

P107 *The Netherlandish Proverbs (The Blue Coak)*, Pieter Bruegel the Elder courtesy of Gemäldegalerie, Berlin

P109 *Reapers*, 1795 by George Stubbs. Courtesy of the Yale Center for British Art. Paul Mellon Collection

P110 *Beer Street*, William Hogarth, courtesy of the Metropolitan Museum of Art, Gift of Sarah Lazarus, 1891.

P111 *An itinerant vendor selling pipes is surrounded by a crowd of children, dogs and passer-by*, 1816 by J T Smith, scan from original book.

P112 *HOARDING, ENCLOSURES* by Jesse Darling at Camden Arts Centre, 2022, photography by Eva Herzog © Jesse Darling.

P115 *The Ploughed Field*,1923 by John Sell Cotman. Courtesy of The Print Collector / Alamy Stock Photo.

P117 *Trellis*, 1864 by William Morris and Philip Webb, courtesy of the Metropolitan Museum of Art. Purchase, Edward C. Moore Jr. Gift, 1923.

P118 *This Island Earth*, by Abigail Lane, 2022 © Abigail Lane. All Rights Reserved, DACS/Artimage, photography by John Spinks.

P121 *Blue Bunker, Greenham Common Nature Reserve*, 2021 by Alison McKenna courtesy of John Marchant Gallery.

P124al *Echoes of the Land I*, 2024 by Poppy Lennox. Plaster, liquid rust, copper powder, crystallised salt and pure silk thread on wood, 21 x 16 cm, © Poppy Lennox, Image © Demelza Lightfoot.

P124ar *Echoes of the Land V*, 2024 by Poppy Lennox. Plaster, liquid rust, copper powder, crystallised salt and pure silk thread on wood, 21 x 16 cm, © Poppy Lennox, Image © Demelza Lightfoot.

P124bl *Echoes of the Land IX*, 2024 by Poppy Lennox. Plaster, liquid rust, copper powder, crystallised salt and pure silk thread on wood, 21 x 16 cm, © Poppy Lennox, Image © Demelza Lightfoot.

P124br *Echoes of the Land XII*, 2024 by Poppy Lennox. Plaster, liquid rust, copper powder, crystallised salt and pure silk thread on wood, 21 x 16 cm, © Poppy Lennox, Image © Demelza Lightfoot.

P125a *The Fragile Shell of The Present Collapses*, 2025 by Hugo Winder-Lind. Oil on Canvas. © Hugo Winder-Lind, 2025. Photograph by Jess Hall © Jess Hall, 2025.

P125b *New Season*, 2021 by Abigail Lane. © Abigail Lane. All Rights Reserved, DACS/Artimage, photography Doug Atfield.

P126 *Green Man*, 1972, Barbara Hepworth. Tate, presented by Rose and Chris Prater through the Institute of Contemporary Prints 1975. Barbara Hepworth © Bowness. Photo: Tate.

P127a *Healer – Portrait of Lizzie*, 2024 by Cathy de Monchaux, © Cathy de Monchaux, photography by Lizzie Buchanan.

P127b *The Dark Glow*, 2024 by Laura Olohan. 46 x 36 cm, Oil on Canvas.

P128a *FutuRoma*, 2018 by Delaine Le Bas, © Delaine Le Bas.

P128bl *News from Gypsyland Love is Anarchy*, 2019 by Delaine Le Bas, installation view at Delainia: 17071965, *Unfolding* at Tranway Glasgow, 2024. Photograph by Alexander Christie. © Delaine Le Bas.

P128br *Roma Helter Skelter (Self Portrait)* 2005 - 2018 by Delaine Le Bas, courtesy of the artist, Yamamoto Keiko Rochaix, London. Photograph by Alexander Christie. © Delaine Le Bas.

P129a View During the Performance for a Video Work, *Incipit Vita Nova*, 2023, Delaine Le Bas & Hera Santos at Wysing Costume Design & Props Delaine Le Bas Styling Delaine Le Bas & Hera Santos. Photograph by Lincoln Cato. © Delaine Le Bas.

P129b *There's an Old Woman Dwells upon Tappington Moor*, 1911 by Arthur Rackham, courtesy New York Public Library.

P130 *Meet Your Neighbours - (Engrained) Woven Into The Fabric Of Our Society*, 2005 by Delaine Le Bas, courtesy of the artist, Yamamoto Keiko Rochaix, London. Photograph by Alexander Christie.

P130al *Curse English Heritage (Xerox)*, 1990 by Jamie Reid. Courtesy of John Marchant Gallery.

P131ar *Curse English Heritage Bag*, 1990 by Jamie Reid. Courtesy of John Marchant Gallery.

P131b *Access to Stones*, 1990 by Jamie Reid. Courtesy of John Marchant Gallery.

P132a *Cottage in a Field*, 1979 by Ken Kiff. © Ken Kiff. All rights reserved, DACS 2025. Photo by Angelo Plantamura.

P132b *Sun and Singing Bird*, 1985 by Ken Kiff. © Ken Kiff. All rights reserved, DACS 2025. Photo by Angelo Plantamura.

P133a *Landscape* by Paul Nash. Courtesy of the Yale Center for British Art, Bequest of Elizabeth S. Tower.

P133b *The Wilmington Giant*, 1939 by Eric Ravilious. Courtesy of steeve-x-art / Alamy Stock Photo.

P134a *Avebury Series No.2*, 1973 by Derek Jarman. In the collection of Derby Museums. Courtesy of Keith Collins Will Trust.

P134b *The Passing Wind*, 2023-2024 by George Shaw. Humbrol enamel on board, 43x53cm. Courtesy of Anthony Wilkinson Gallery, London. © George Shaw. Photo: Matthew Hollow.

P135a *Car Boot Sale, Sayers Common, Sussex*, 2025 by Jeff Pitcher © Jeff Pitcher.

P135bl *Jack in the Green, Hastings*, 2024 by Jeff Pitcher © Jeff Pitcher.

P135br *The Horns of Ock Street*, 2017 by Ben Edge. Artwork © Ben Edge. Painting Photography by Sylvie Tata.

P136al *The Lesson of the May Pole*, 2019 by Kahn and Selesnick © Kahn and Selesnick

P136ar *The Augury of the Compass*, 2019 by Kahn and Selesnick © Kahn and Selesnick

P136bl *Deadly Nightshade*, 2021 by Mathew Weir. Blood on Paper, 24x18.5cm

P136br *Man with Death Upon His Back*, 2021 by Mathew Weir. Blood on Paper, 24x18.5cm

P137al *Songs of Experience: The Clod & the Pebble*, from *Songs of Innocence and Experience*, ca. 1825 by William Blake. Courtesy of the Metropolitan Museum of Art, Rogers Fund, 1917.

P137ar *The Sleeping Shepherd*, 1830 by Samuel Palmer. Courtesy of the Yale Center for British Art, Paul Mellon Collection.

P137bl *Songs of Experience: The Garden of Love*, from *Songs of Innocence and Experience*, ca. 1825 by William Blake. Courtesy of the Metropolitan Museum of Art, Rogers Fund, 1917.

P137br *The Timber Wain*, 1833 - 1834 by Samuel Palmer. Courtesy of the

Yale Center for British Art, Paul Mellon Collection.

P139 *An historic early woodcut engraving showing a vagrant traveller holding his staff and a brace of poached rabbits in the 17th century*. Courtesy of Colin Waters / Alamy Stock Photo.

P141 *Rabbits*, 1816 by Thomas Lord Busby, from Costume of the Lower Orders of the Metropolis. Scan from original book.

P142-143 *Poachers Surprised*, c.1800 by Henry Thomas Alken. Courtesy of the Yale Center for British Art, Paul Mellon Collection.

P144a *The Gipsies* (also known as *Wooded Landscape with Gipsies round a Camp Fire*), 1764 by Thomas Gainsborough (etching), Joseph Wood (engraving). Published by John Boydell. Courtesy of the Yale Center for British Art, Paul Mellon Collection.

P144b *The Friar and the Boy*, reproduced in *Chap-books of the Eighteenth Century* by John Ashton, courtesy of the New York Public Library

P145a *The Itinerant Potters*, 1797 by John Whessell after Francis Wheatley. Courtesy of the Yale Center for British Art, Paul Mellon Collection.

P145b *Cottonopolis*, 1840 by Edward Goodall. Public Domain Image sourced from Wikimedia Commons: https://commons.wikimedia.org/wiki/File:Cottonopolis1.jpg

P146a *A Kentish rat-catcher* by W. Collins. Courtesy of the Wellcome Collection.

P146b *Hut and Cart*, 1870s by John Golden Short. Courtesy of the Yale Center for British Art, Gift of Charles Isaacs and Carol Nigro.

P147a *Joseph Johnson of Chandos Street, Covent Garden*, 1817 by John Thomas Smith, from Vagabondiana. Scan from original book.

P147b *The Poacher - A Hare in View* by Peter Henry Emerson, 1885-88, courtesy of the George Eastman Museum.

P148 © Leah Gordon.

P150 A Meadow Arts commission © Leah Gordon.

P151 A Meadow Arts commission © Leah Gordon.

P152 A Meadow Arts commission © Leah Gordon.

P153 A Meadow Arts commission © Leah Gordon.

P154 A Meadow Arts commission © Leah Gordon.

P155 A Meadow Arts commission © Leah Gordon.

P156 A Meadow Arts commission © Leah Gordon.

P157 A Meadow Arts commission © Leah Gordon.

P158a A Meadow Arts commission © Leah Gordon.

P158b Poster by Bryon Fear for South London Theatre, Norwood.

P159a A Meadow Arts commission © Leah Gordon.

P159b Poster by Lauren Gladwell for Old Court Theatre, Chelmsford.

P160 © Leah Gordon.

P161 © Leah Gordon.

P162 © Leah Gordon.

P163 © Leah Gordon.

P164 © Leah Gordon

P165 © Leah Gordon.

P166 © Leah Gordon.

P167 © Leah Gordon.

P168 © Leah Gordon.

P169 © Leah Gordon.

P170 © Leah Gordon.

P171 © Leah Gordon.

P172 © Leah Gordon.

P173 © Leah Gordon.

P176 *Eviction at Tot Hill*, Newbury, 1996. Photograph by Nick Woolley. Sourced from Wikimedia Commons Under Creative Commons CC BY-SA 2.5: https://commons.wikimedia.org/wiki/File:Tot_Hill_eviction.jpg

P180 *Sunrise between the stones at Stonehenge on the Winter Solstice*, 1985. Photograph by Mark Grant. Sourced from Wikimedia Commons Under Creative Commons Attribution 2.5 Generic: https://commons.wikimedia.org/wiki/File:StonehengeSunrise1980s.jpg

P181 *Spiral Tribe Bus* from the 'Le

Crowbar' series, 1995. Photograph by Tom Hunter.

P182 *Stonehenge Fenced off and Police Protected*, 1992. Photograph by Annabel Edwards

P184a *RAF Molesworth, Police in front of ruins of Peace Chapel*. Photograph by Tony Grist. Sourced from Wikimedia Commons Under Creative Commons CC0 1.0 Universal Public Domain Dedication: https://en.m.wikipedia.org/wiki/File:RAF_Molesworth_early_80s_2.jpg

P184b *Harry on Tour with Vox Populi Sound System* from the 'Le Crowbar' series, 1995. Photograph by Tom Hunter.

P185 *The M3 cutting at Twyford Down*, 1994. Photograph by Chris Woodford. Sourced from Wikimedia Commons Under Creative Commons Attribution-ShareAlike 2.5 Generic: https://commons.wikimedia.org/wiki/File:Twyford_down.jpg

P187 *Twyford Down Digger*, 1993. Photograph by Annabel Edwards.

P189 *Right to Roam gathering to raise Old Crockern and defend wild camping on Dartmoor National Park England UK*, 2003. Courtesy of David Pearson / Alamy Stock Photo.

P191 *Gardener Pruning a Tree*, 1628 by Jacques Callot, courtesy of the National Gallery of Art, Washington, Rosenwald Collection.

P193 *Allotment with Sunflower*, 1887 by Vincent van Gogh. Van Gogh Museum, Amsterdam (Vincent van Gogh Foundation).

P194-195 *The Allotment, Dorking*, 2024. Photograph by Martin Salter

P196a *The Last Autumn*, 2007-2008 by George Shaw. Humbrol enamel on board, 43x53cm. Courtesy of Anthony Wilkinson Gallery, London. © George Shaw. Photo: Matthew Hollow.

P196b *Hampstead Heath, with a Bonfire* by John Constable. Courtesy of Yale Center for British Art, Paul Mellon Collection.

P197a *A Garden End. [Suffolk.]* by Peter Henry Emerson, 1888 courtesy of the Getty Museum.

197b *Bowden Bridge Mass Trespass Plaque*, 2007. Photograph by Marcin Floryan. Sourced from Wikimedia Commons under Creative Commons Attribution-Share Alike 3.0 Unported CC BY-SA 3.0: https://commons.wikimedia.org/wiki/File:Bowden_Bridge_mass_trespass_plaque_2007.jpg

198a *Mass Trespass of Kinder Scout*, 1932. Courtesy of Chronicle / Alamy Stock Photo.

198b *The Artist's Garden at Durbins, Guildford* by Roger Fry, ca. 1915, courtesy of Yale Center for British Art, Paul Mellon Fund.

P199a *The Allotment, Dorking*, 2024. Photograph by Martin Salter.

P199b *Implements Animated, Pl. 1, Dedicated to the Carpenters and Gardeners of Great Britain* by Charles Williams. Courtesy of The Metropolitan Museum of Art, The Elisha Whittelsey Collection, The Elisha Whittelsey Fund, 1978.

P200 A Meadow Arts commission © Leah Gordon.

P202 A Meadow Arts commission © Leah Gordon.

P203 A Meadow Arts commission © Leah Gordon.

P204 A Meadow Arts commission © Leah Gordon.

P205 A Meadow Arts commission © Leah Gordon.

P206 A Meadow Arts commission © Leah Gordon.

P207 A Meadow Arts commission © Leah Gordon.

P208 A Meadow Arts commission © Leah Gordon.

P209 A Meadow Arts commission © Leah Gordon.

P210 A Meadow Arts commission © Leah Gordon.

P211 A Meadow Arts commission © Leah Gordon.

P212 A Meadow Arts commission © Leah Gordon.

P213 A Meadow Arts commission © Leah Gordon.

P214 A Meadow Arts commission © Leah Gordon.

P215 A Meadow Arts commission © Leah Gordon.
P216 A Meadow Arts commission © Leah Gordon.
P217 A Meadow Arts commission © Leah Gordon.
P218 A Meadow Arts commission © Leah Gordon.
P219 A Meadow Arts commission © Leah Gordon.
P220 A Meadow Arts commission © Leah Gordon.
P221 A Meadow Arts commission © Leah Gordon.
P222 A Meadow Arts commission © Leah Gordon.
P223 A Meadow Arts commission © Leah Gordon.

INDEX

Index of artists and artworks

SUBJECT INDEX